Urban Life and Culture in Southeastern Europe

Anthropological and Historical Perspectives

Edited by

Klaus Roth and Ulf Brunnbauer

Ethnologia Balkanica

Journal for Southeast European Anthropology
Zeitschrift für die Anthropologie Südosteuropas
Journal d'anthropologie du sud-est européen

Volume 10/2006

LIT

ISSN 1111-0411

The journal is published by the International Association for Southeast European Anthropology (InASEA). It publishes articles by members of InASEA as well as by non-members. All articles are anonymously reviewed.
Languages of publication: English, French, German
Contributions must be supplied with a short abstract in English.

Cover photograph: City centre of Tirana, 1940 © Gentiana Kera.

Subscription: Subscription price (one volume per year):
Students: 10 €, Individuals: 16 €, Institutions: 20 €
Individuals and institutions in Southeast Europe: 10 €.

Bibliographic information published by the Deutsche Nationalbibliothek
The Deutsche Nationalbibliothek lists this publication in the Deutsche Nationalbibliografie; detailed bibliographic data are available in the Internet at http://dnb.d-nb.de.

ISBN 978-3-8258-9903-5

A catalogue record for this book is available from the British Library

Chausseestr. 128 – 129
D-10115 Berlin

Auslieferung/Distribution:

LIT Verlag Fresnostr. 2, D-48159 Münster
Tel. +49 (0) 2 51/620 32 - 22, Fax +49 (0) 2 51/922 60 99, e-Mail: lit@lit-verlag.de

Distributed in the UK by: Global Book Marketing, 99B Wallis Rd, London, E9 5LN
Phone: +44 (0) 20 8533 5800 – Fax: +44 (0) 1600 775 663
http://www.centralbooks.co.uk/acatalog/search.html
Distributed in North America by:

Transaction Publishers
New Brunswick (U.S.A.) and London (U.K.)

Transaction Publishers
Rutgers University
35 Berrue Circle
Piscataway, NJ 08854

Phone: +1 (732) 445 - 2280
Fax: + 1 (732) 445 - 3138
for orders (U. S. only):
toll free (888) 999 - 6778
e-mail:
orders@transactionspub.com

Contents

Editorial

This volume of Ethnologia Balkanica, the journal of the International Association for Southeast European Anthropology (InASEA), consists of papers which were presented at the third InASEA conference on "Urban Life and Culture in Southeastern Europe", that took place in Belgrade, 26–29 May 2005.[1] It thus continues the topic of volume 9, which already included papers from the conference, and gives further evidence of the growing interest in urban anthropology in Southeastern Europe, a long neglected field of study.

Cities, their cultures and patterns of everyday life, as well as their social and economic trajectories have traditionally received only little interest by ethnographers, anthropologists and historians in Southeastern Europe. This fact is all the more striking as cities and towns are, today, not only the places of residence of the majority of the population in every Balkan country but, from a historical as well as contemporary perspective, are highly illustrative of the cultural and social dynamics of the region. Even a superficial look at urban architecture reveals the many cultural influences shaping Southeastern Europe which, on the one hand, make the societies of the region so heterogeneous and, on the other, link the cultures of Southeast Europe to other parts of Europe and the Near East. Towns and cities have also been arenas of vital social and cultural processes that have transformed Southeast Europe in the last two centuries, with an increasing dynamic during the last decades, not to forget the role of cities as centres of political power projected on the whole state.

As both volumes of Ethnologia Balkanica demonstrate, an increasing amount of scholarship by ethnologists and scholars from neighbouring disciplines is devoted to cities in past and present to uncover the manifold, and often highly dramatic, cultural and social processes which, though acted out in the urban setting, more often than not affected the entire society. Recent research looks into questions of urban identity, and the role ethnicity plays in cities and towns, especially with an eye on the inter-ethnic contact which is so typical of cities in South-

[1] The conference was made possible by the generous funding and support of: Wenner-Gren Foundation for Anthropological Research (USA), Stability Pact for Southeastern Europe (sponsored by the German Ministry of Foreign Affairs), Ministry of Science and Environmental Protection of the Republic of Serbia, Südosteuropa-Gesellschaft (Germany), School of Philosophy (Belgrade), City of Belgrade, Municipality of Vračar (Belgrade), Embassy of the Republic of Austria in Belgrade, Ethnographic Museum (Belgrade), National Museum (Belgrade), Fresh & Co (Subotica, Serbia).

eastern Europe. Cities have also been explored as sites of marginality, where groups on the margins of society carve out an often fragile existence, exploiting the relative anonymity of the urban space or occupying special niches in its complex social fabric. Sometimes it is these seemingly marginal groups that pave the way for innovation. Generally, innovation and modernity are often associated with the urban realm, although the relation between modernity and the city is more complex and often ambiguous, as other research indicates. In Southeastern Europe, we find a real, and perceived, chasm between "modernised" city life and "traditional" rural life, although both phenomena were results of the same process, i. e., ambivalent modernisation and the uneven distribution of its benefits. Historical research also discusses the attention political elites in the Balkans have paid to the development of their cities, which were supposed to become showcases of their nation-building efforts. Despite these developments, though, cities and towns in Southeastern Europe have often remained closely linked to the countryside, or even underwent a process of "ruralization" or "rurbanization".

The papers of this volume revolve around these major topics, presenting case-studies based on original research. Several papers analyse the social, spatial and material topography of cities. One focus of these articles are issues of town planning and the material reconstruction of cities over the last two centuries. Articles also highlight how urban populations made sense of their habitat, and how they changed it by their social practices. Another topic, explored by several papers and highly significant for Southeast European cities, are urban-rural relations. These are evident on the level of social practices (such as town-bound mobility) and of ideological programmes as well: political groups have often shared visions of the urban and the rural, pinning their utopias either on the city or the village. Cities and towns, as other papers reveal, are also central arenas for the negotiation of ethnic relations, and in some places the urban matrix was even determined by ethnic or religious affiliation.

Many papers of the volume discuss different aspects of social and cultural change emerging in cities. Actually, in many respects, cities kick-started changes that were to affect the whole society, and cities have also been particularly prone to the adoption, and modification, of external cultural influences. One such field are gender relations, where women in cities have explored new freedoms. Particular urban social institutions, such as the corso, are discussed in detail in an attempt to decipher what urbanity and urban culture really mean and how they are, symbolically as well as practically, manifested. Finally, issues of popular culture in cities are explored, which again points to the frequent avant-garde role of cities in cultural development. But, as some papers argue, urban life, especially in times of general crisis, also includes conflicts, political or others, that are often related to the struggle for public space, an important though scarce commodity in cities.

This issues brings the results of the Belgrade conference to an end, but at the same time it marks a new beginning: from volume 10 on, Ethnologia Balkanica will be published by LIT-Verlag, a renowned German publishing house. With its fast growing anthropological section and its interest in Southeast European studies, this publishing house was an obvious choice for the Executive Committee of InASEA.

The next two volumes of *Ethnologia Balkanica* will publish papers presented at the 4th InASEA conference on issues of regionalism, regional cultures and regional identities in Southeast Europe, which will take place in Timişoara in May 2007.

Ulf Brunnbauer Berlin, November 2006

Dieser Band von *Ethnologia Balkanica,* der Zeitschrift der Internationalen Vereinigung für die Anthropologie Südosteuropas (InASEA), vereint Artikel, die bei der dritten Konferenz der InASEA über „Städtisches Leben und Stadtkultur" in Belgrad am 26.–29. Mai 2005 präsentiert wurden und setzt somit den thematischen Schwerpunkt von Band 9 fort.[2] Diese zwei Bände von *Ethnologia Balkanica* bezeugen das wachsende Interesse für urbane Anthropologie in Südosteuropa - ein bislang vernachlässigtes Forschungsfeld.

Die Kultur und das Alltagsleben von Städten in Südosteuropa, ihre sozialen und ökonomischen Entwicklungstendenzen haben lange Zeit relativ geringes Interesse bei Ethnologen und Historikern genossen. Diese Tatsache ist um so erstaunlicher, wenn man sich vor Augen hält, dass heute in jedem Land Südosteuropas die Mehrheit der Bevölkerung in Städten lebt. Darüber hinaus können Städte in vielerlei Hinsicht beispielhaft für die kulturellen und sozialen Dynamiken der Region stehen. Selbst ein oberflächlicher, nur auf das materielle Antlitz der südosteuropäischen Städte gerichteter Blick verdeutlicht die Vielzahl an kulturellen Einflüssen, welche die Gesellschaften Südosteuropas einerseits so heterogen machen und andererseits mit anderen Kulturräumen in Europa und dem Nahen Osten verbinden. Städte waren auch zentrale Schauplätze der sozialen und kulturellen Prozesse, die Südosteuropa während der letzten beiden Jahrhunderte nach-

---

[2] Diese Tagung wurde ermöglicht durch die finanzielle und organisatorische Unterstützung der folgenden Institutionen: Wenner-Gren Foundation for Anthropological Research (USA), Stabilitätspakt für Südosteuropa (finanziert aus Mitteln des Auswärtigen Amtes der BRD), Ministerium für Wissenschaft und Umweltschutz der Republik Serbien, Südosteuropa-Gesellschaft (BRD), Philosophische Fakultät der Universität Belgrad, Stadt Belgrad, Gemeinde Vračar (Belgrad), Botschaft der Republik Österreich in Belgrad, Ethnografisches Museum (Belgrad), Nationalmuseum (Belgrad), Fresh & Co (Subotica, Serbien).

haltig transformierten, mit einer sich beschleunigenden Dynamik während der letzten Jahrzehnte. Nicht zuletzt spielten Städte als Zentrum der politischen Macht eine entscheidende Rolle für die Entwicklung der Region.

Wie aber diese beiden Bände der *Ethnologia Balkanica* zeigen, gibt es eine wachsende Beschäftigung mit dem Phänomen Stadt in Südosteuropa sowohl bei Ethnologen als auch bei Forschern aus Nachbardisziplinen. Sie beschäftigen sich mit den vielfältigen kulturellen und sozialen Prozessen in Vergangenheit und Gegenwart, die nicht nur die Städte, sondern vielfach die gesamte Gesellschaft verändern. Aktuelle Forschung betrachtet beispielsweise die Frage der urbanen Identität und die Rolle von Ethnizität im städtischen Leben, wobei die Multiethnizität vieler Städte Südosteuropas besondere Aufmerksamkeit erfährt. Städte werden auch als Orte erforscht, in denen marginale Gruppen versuchen, einen Platz zu finden, oftmals die relative Anonymität der Stadt ausnutzend und besondere Nischen besetzend. Nicht selten sind es gerade solche marginalen Gruppen, die den Weg für gesellschaftlichen Wandel weisen. Generell werden Städte in Südosteuropa oftmals mit Innovation und Modernität assoziiert, obwohl die Beziehung zwischen der Moderne und der Stadt komplexer und widersprüchlicher ist, als der erste Blick vermuten lässt. Für Südosteuropa war lange Zeit die Kluft zwischen „modernisiertem" städtischem und „traditionellem" ländlichem Leben typisch, wobei aber beide Pole Aspekte ein und desselben Prozesses, nämlich einer ambivalenten Modernisierung waren. Modernisierungserfolge waren zwischen Stadt und Land häufig ungleich verteilt, was gegenseitige Ressentiments verursachte. Historische Forschung zeigt auch die Strategien von politischen Eliten auf, ihre (Haupt-)Städte zu Schaufenstern des Erfolges der Nationsbildung, die sich auch als Modernisierung verstand, zu machen. Aber trotz dieser Entwicklungen blieben Stadt und Land vielfach miteinander verbunden, was sich auch im Begriff der „Ruralisierung" oder auch „Rurbanisierung" zur Beschreibung der Urbanisierung in Südosteuropa widerspiegelt.

Die Artikel dieses Bandes kreisen um diese zentralen Themen. Sie beruhen auf neuer Forschung zu relevanten Fallstudien. Eine Reihe von Artikeln analysiert die soziale, räumliche und materielle Topografie von Städten als Basis für die Aneignungs- und Sinngebungs-, aber auch transformierenden Praktiken ihrer Bewohner. Ein Fokus dieser Beiträge ist Stadtplanung und Stadtrekonstruktion während der letzten beiden Jahrhunderte. Ein anderes Thema, dem sich einige Artikel widmen und das für Südosteuropa von herausragender Bedeutung ist, sind die Beziehungen zwischen Stadt und Land. Diese sind nicht nur auf der Ebene der sozialen Praktiken evident (z. B. in Form der Landflucht), sondern auch auf der ideologischen Ebene: Politische Gruppierungen äußeren immer wieder sehr klare Vorstellungen über Stadt bzw. Dorf und verbinden mit einem der beiden ihre Gesellschaftsutopien. Eine besondere Form der sozialen Topografie von Städten ist schließlich ihre ethnische Struktur, weisen doch viele Städte der Balkanhalbinsel historisch (und teilweise auch heute noch) eine mehr oder minder deutliche ethnische bzw. konfessionelle Segmentierung auf.

Einen weiteren Schwerpunkt der Beiträge dieses Bandes bilden verschiedene Aspekte des sozialen und kulturellen Wandels, der Städte in Südosteuropa kennzeichnet. Städte haben ja vielfach Wandlungsprozesse angestoßen, die dann nach und nach die gesamte Gesellschaft ergriffen haben. Städte waren auch besonders offen für die Annahme - und Modifikation - von außen kommender kultureller Einflüsse. Ein solches Feld des Wandels waren etwa Geschlechterbeziehungen, da sich Frauen in Städten neue Freiheit erkämpften und erprobten. Einige Artikel analysieren spezifische soziale Institutionen der Stadt, um zu zeigen, was urbane Identität und Kultur für die betroffenen Menschen tatsächlich bedeuten und wie sich diese symbolisch sowie praktisch manifestieren. Schließlich werden Phänomene der Popularkultur in Städten diskutiert, waren Städte doch vielfach der soziale Ort, wo neue kulturelle Praktiken entwickelt wurden. Aber dabei darf - wie aus einigen Beiträgen deutlich wird - nicht vergessen werden, dass Städte auch Orte des Konflikts sind, z. B. zwischen bestimmten sozialen Gruppen in ihrem Kampf um die Besetzung des öffentlichen Raumes.

Mit der Publikation der letzten Konferenzbeiträge aus Belgrad markiert dieser Band aber nicht nur ein Ende, sondern auch einen Anfang: Er ist das erste Ergebnis der neuen Partnerschaft zwischen InASEA und dem renommierten LIT-Verlag. Der Wechsel zu LIT mit dessen wachsender Zahl von Publikationen im Bereich der Anthropologie und der Ost- und Südosteuropaforschung war für den Vorstand der InASEA ein naheliegender Schritt.

Die folgenden zwei Bände der *Ethnologia Balkanica* werden der nächsten InASEA-Konferenz, die im Mai 2007 in Timişoara zum Thema „Regionalismus, regionale Identitäten und Kulturen in Südosteuropa" stattfinden wird, gewidmet sein.

Ulf Brunnbauer Berlin, November 2006

La présente livraison d'*Ethnologia Balkanica,* revue de l'International Association for Southeast European Anthropology (InASEA), rassemble les contributions présentées lors de la troisième Conférence de l'InASEA, tenue à Belgrade du 26 au 29 mai 2005[3] et consacrée à «La vie et la culture urbaines en Europe du Sud-

---

[3] La conférence a bénéficié du généreux soutien de la Wenner-Gren Foundation for Anthropological Research (USA), du Pacte de Stabilité pour l'Europe du Sud-est (à travers le Ministère allemand des Affaires étrangères), du Ministère de la Science et de la Protection de l'environ-

est». Ce volume prolonge le numéro 9 consacré à cette même conférence et montre ainsi l'intérêt croissant que représente un sujet de recherche jusque là négligé.

Il est vrai que la culture et la vie quotidienne des les villes, ainsi d'ailleurs que leurs trajectoires sociales et économiques, n'ont pas retenu l'attention qu'elles méritaient de la part des ethnographes, des anthropologues et des historiens du Sud-est de l'Europe. Cela est d'autant plus étonnant que la majorité des populations des pays balkaniques réside dans des villes. Les villes illustrent fort bien par ailleurs et à plusieurs égards les dynamiques culturelles et sociales de cette région. Un simple regard superficiel porté sur l'aspect matériel de l'architecture urbaine révèle les nombreuses influences culturelles à l'œuvre dans l'Europe du Sud-est, ce qui illustre d'un côté l'hétérogénéité des sociétés qui y habitent et d'autre part montre les liens que les cultures du Sud-est entretiennent avec les autres parties de l'Europe et le Proche-Orient. Les villes ont également été les creusets de processus sociaux et culturels importants qui ont transformé le Sud-est de l'Europe au cours des deux derniers siècles, et plus encore durant les dernières décennies. On ne saurait oublier le rôle des villes en tant que centres du pouvoir politique dans le développement de la région.

Les deux volumes d'*Ethnologia Balkanica* montrent qu'un nombre croissant d'ethnologues et de chercheurs des disciplines voisines consacrent désormais leurs recherches aux questions urbaines. Ces études couvrent une gamme de processus culturels et sociaux passés et présents qui, loin de n'affecter que les villes, transforment à plus d'un titre l'ensemble de la société. Les recherches les plus récentes s'appliquent par exemple à l'identité urbaine et au rôle que l'ethnicité joue dans la vie urbaine, et particulièrement à la composition multi-ethnique de nombreuses villes. Les villes sont aussi étudiées en tant que lieux de la marginalité pour les groupes sociaux qui y mènent une existence précaire à l'abri d'un relatif anonymat et dans des «niches» qu'ils s'y ménagent. Il arrive parfois que ces groupes marginaux soient les vecteurs de l'innovation. De manière générale, l'innovation et la modernité sont souvent associées à l'urbanité bien que la relation entre modernité et ville soit plus complexe et souvent ambiguë, comme le montrent d'autres recherches. Ainsi, en Europe du Sud-est, on a longtemps opposé la vie «moderne» à la ville à la vie «traditionnelle» à la campagne, alors que ces deux pôles représentent deux aspects du même processus, à savoir une modernisation ambivalente et une distribution inégale des bénéfices qui en découlent, laquelle a créé un ressentiment réciproque. Les recherches en histoire font voir aussi les stratégies des élites

---

nement de la République de Serbie, de la Südosteuropa-Gesellschaft (Allemagne), de la Faculté de philosophie (Belgrade), de la Ville de Belgrade, de la Municipalité de Vračar (Belgrade), de l'ambassade de l'Autriche à Belgrade, du Musée ethnographique et du Musée national (Belgrade) et de Fresh & Co (Subotica, Serbie).

politiques pour faire de leur ville (capitale) l'illustration de la réussite de la construction nationale, entendue également comme modernisation. Cependant malgré ces développements, la ville et la campagne demeurent à plusieurs égards liées, ce qui s'exprime aussi bien dans les termes de «ruralisation» que de «rurbanisation», utilisés pour décrire l'urbanisation dans le Sud-est.

Les articles contenus dans ce volume tournent autour de ces thèmes centraux. Ils s'appuient sur des recherches récentes de cas pertinents. Une série d'articles analyse la topographie sociale, spatiale et matérielle des villes du point de vue des pratiques d'appropriation, de signification mais également de transformation de leurs habitants. La planification urbaine et la reconstruction des villes au cours des deux derniers siècles en représentent le point focal. La relation ville-campagne, fondamentale pour la région, est aussi traitée dans certains articles. Non seulement du point de vue évident de l'exode rural, mais aussi d'un point de vue idéologique: les groupes politiques tiennent toujours des discours très clair sur la ville et le village et tendent à lier leurs utopies sociales à l'un des deux. Finalement si la structure ethnique des villes constitue aussi une des formes de la topographie sociale des villes, il se trouve que, historiquement mais aussi en partie actuellement, de nombreuses villes de la péninsule balkanique présentent une segmentation plus ou moins évidente en fonction de l'ethnie ou de la confession.

D'autres articles contenus dans ce volume traitent des divers aspects du changement socio-culturel caractéristique des villes. Les villes ont été en effet à la source de nombreux changements qui se sont propagés progressivement dans la société tout entière. Les villes ont toujours été promptes à accepter – et à modifier – les influences venant de l'extérieur. C'est le cas notamment pour ce qui concerne les relations de genre, du fait que dans les villes, les femmes acquirent et exercèrent de nouvelles libertés. Certains articles analysent des institutions sociales spécifiques de la ville de manière à montrer en quoi l'identité et la culture urbaine affecte en réalité les habitants et comment celles-ci de manifestent pratiquement et symboliquement. Enfin les phénomènes liés à la culture populaire sont étudiés, dans la mesure où les villes ont été à plus d'un titre le lieu social où de nouvelles pratiques ont pu se développer. Mais il ne faudrait pas oublier non plus – ainsi que le signalent certains articles – que les villes sont également le lieu de conflits, par exemple entre certains groupes sociaux dans leur lutte pour occuper l'espace public.

Cette publication marque la fin des contributions présentées à la Conférence de Belgrade mais elle inaugure en même temps une nouvelle collaboration de l'InASEA avec la maison d'édition allemande bien connue, LIT-Verlag. Ce changement s'imposa comme évident pour le Comité directeur de l'InASEA, étant donné le nombre croissant de publications assurées par cette maison dans le domaine de l'anthropologie et de la recherche dans le Sud-est européen.

Les deux prochains volumes d'*Ethnologia Balkanica* seront consacrés à la prochaine conférence de l'InASEA, qui aura lieu à Timisoara sur le thème «Régionalisme, identités et cultures régionales».

Ulf Brunnbauer

Berlin en novembre 2006

Negotiating Tradition and Ambition: A Comparative Perspective on the "De-Ottomanisation" of Balkan Cityscapes

Maximilian Hartmuth, Istanbul

Introduction

Despite a number of excellent contributions in the last two decades,[1] critical scholarly literature on urban and architectural transformations in Southeast Europe in the 19th and 20th centuries remains very limited. Not only have certain clichés (to be discussed in the course of this paper) proved to be long-lived in the more generalist literature, but very similar if not identical contemporaneous developments across the borders of the modern nation states remain largely unobserved.[2] Moreover, in this age of nationalisms, when the "Ottoman town" in the Balkans was to be transformed into a "modern European city", many advances were not as unique as is sometimes held to be, but were really regional developments that also included some towns that remained Ottoman. This has been concealed by a literature largely concerned with case studies. The lack of regional, comparative approaches to this topic apparently coincides with the split into different areas of specialisations and national historiographies.

---

[1] Of these studies of the history of urban form and "urban process", Çelik (1986) is recommended for Istanbul, Bastéa (2000) for Athens, and Yerolympos (1996) for Thessaloniki. Popescu (2004) and Pantelić (1997) deal specifically with the impact of nationalism on architecture, at the same time addressing general developments in Romanian and Serbian cities respectively. Many other Balkan cities still await comprehensive and critical studies. Despite appearing narrowly themed on the work of Austro-Hungarian architects in Bulgaria, Doytchinov and Gantchev's book (2001) can serve as a sufficient introduction to the Bulgarian case. Sarajevo's urban transformation under Austro-Hungarian rule has been addressed by many studies, most directly by Donia (2002), largely relying on classic works by Yugoslav authors. In the interesting case of Sarajevo, analogous developments in a regional, post-Ottoman, or even colonial context are usually completely ignored. I have tried to address this shortcoming in the article "K. (u.) K. colonial? Contextualizing and Interpreting Architecture and Urbanism in Bosnia-Herzegovina 1878–1918" in a forthcoming (2007) volume entitled "WechselWirkungen. The political, social and cultural impact of the Austro-Hungarian occupation of Bosnia-Herzegovina (1878–1918)", eds. Clemens Ruthner, Raymond Detrez et al.

[2] In this respect, the work of Yerolympos (1996) has a pioneering role. Although her research is centred on Thessaloniki, concise surveys on contemporary developments in other Balkan countries (excluding Bosnia and Albania) and cities are provided, as suggested in the title. An urban planner, she is more concerned with technical aspects, yet arrives at a similar conclusion: "Little is known about the tremendous changes that took place in the Balkan cities in the hundred years between 1820 and 1920 [as] the historians of the Balkans simply note the cities' break with their Oriental past and their swift progress towards Westernisation" (1996: 9).

Signifying the regionality of these phenomena, I will argue that it was really the "Balkan City" that did not discontinue its existence as a regional type after the end of the Ottoman rule.[3] We cannot speak certainly of a normative urban type, but likewise cannot overlook common characteristics not found outside of the region, the rationale being that similar paths for emancipation from Ottoman models were chosen for Serbian, Greek, Bulgarian, Bosnian, and Romanian cities, with consequently similar results. As architecture is never an innocent bystander, the focus of this study – architecture and urban planning – should not be misread as a singular detail, but be understood as a materialisation, and thus an integral part of the cultural policy of de-Ottomanisation, which – as nearly all decisive cultural change – proved most evident in urban centres. Rather than reiterating what is already well documented in numerous urban histories, I will seek to shed light on the concepts and ideas that shaped these transformations.

Maria Todorova, who was among the first to use the term,[4] viewed de-Ottomanisation as a process which aimed to achieve the coveted ideal of the polar opposite of being Ottoman (or Oriental), namely a steady Europeanisation, Westernisation or modernisation of society. It was supposed to bring in a new set of relations both in the family and in society as a whole, based on individuality and rationality, an entirely different position for women, a revised role for children and child rearing, and a new work ethos (Todorova 1995: 60).

Pointing out the difficulty or even impossibility of differentiating between Ottoman and traditional local cultures, she remarks that "de-Ottomanisation", "de-Orientalisation", and "de-Balkanisation" are often treated as synonyms (ibid., 55). Following Todorova's line of reasoning it would in fact be even somewhat misleading to speak of an "Ottoman legacy in the Balkans", as the Balkans *are* the

---

[3] While indeed sharing a common historical development with their Southeast European counterparts until the 20th century, it makes sense to exclude the cities of modern Turkey from this concept, for we there find a different urban/architectural typology as the post-Ottoman legacy. Instead of extensive social housing complexes from the socialist period we stumble on mushrooming (post-)shantytown settlements *(gecekondu)* which at their height housed half of the inhabitants of Turkey's major cities. A massive population pressure on urban centres in the second half of the 20th century has also resulted in the substitution of much of the (often dilapidated) 19th century fabric, which still characterises the city centres of most Balkan capitals and also Istanbul, but few other towns in Anatolia. In principle, the cities of Muslim Turkey have also preserved their often acclaimed silhouettes dominated by slender minarets piercing the sky, while this feature has long been sacrificed in most Balkan cities. On the other hand, even Turkish authors like Akın (2001: 226) have noted that – somewhat ironically – architectural ensembles from the Ottoman period have often been better conserved in the (first de-Ottomanizing, then socialist) Balkans than in Turkish Anatolia. On urban and architectural transformation in post-Ottoman Turkey, reference should be made to the outstanding study by Bozdoğan (2001).

[4] For earlier uses of the term cf. Lory 1985, Roth 1989.

Ottoman legacy. European ideals thus came to be accepted as markers of cultural emancipation. This project, demonstrating not only a break with, but a total rejection of the Ottoman past, was most visible in the architecture of the new capitals.[5]

The making and breaking of cities

With the exception of the already large Bucharest, other cities were routinely mocked as being mere villages when first designated as capitals. They were not nominated for their cultural significance but in the main for the benefits gained from their geographical location (Belgrade, Sofia, Tirana), or for a legendary if distant legacy (Athens).[6] Other key towns such as Plovdiv, Novi Sad (the "Serbian Athens"), Thessaloniki, Prizren, or Bitola were by 1878 not only often far from the ideal of ethnic homogeneity but still lay outside the territory of the new Balkan states. Once included in the territory of "their" national states, the previous significance of these towns was forfeited at the expense of the new capitals, whereby important "latecomers" like Thessaloniki and Novi Sad accordingly came to uphold a regional identity within the modern nation state which continues until present.

By the beginning of the Balkan Wars (1912–1913), the Balkan capitals had not only acquired a European façade but had also finally consolidated their positions as such, often against initial reservations from within. With the prominent exception of the earlier case of Athens (after 1830), the last third of the 19th century witnessed the most crucial urban interventions – manifestations to the enthusiasm for a "liberation" from the Ottoman "yoke" and, theoretically, its legacy. A noticeable European influence in architecture, even if only nominal, however, had already penetrated many Balkan towns while they were still under Ottoman sovereignty, not least through the Western influence mediated via Istanbul. Occidentalist tendencies in the architecture of the imperial capital's court society can be observed already in the early 18th century, but in the Balkan provinces it is

---

5 On capital city formation in Southeast Europe see also Heppner's twin volumes (1994 and 1998), a first attempt to bring together a series of urban histories from different countries under one umbrella. The foci of the contributions by different authors, however, strongly vary. Given the generosity of the geographical dimensioning – in addition to the classic Balkan countries, cities not only in Slovenia, Croatia, and Transylvania but also in the Ukraine, Slovenia, and Hungary were included – the approach is different from the one followed in this essay: culture (and contemporarity) as context for synthesis, not geography.

6 We should also keep in mind that the first capitals of Bulgaria, Greece, Montenegro, and Albania, were not yet Sofia, Podgorica, Athens, and Tirana but Tărnovo (1878–79), Cetinje (until 1918), Nafplion (1830–34), and Durrës (1913–20) respectively. During Miloš Obrenović' rule over the autonomous Serbian principality, Kragujevac, not Belgrade, served as capital between 1818 and 1839.

the late 18th to mid-19th century merchant house that is most often associated with an instant Western influence.

While we first encounter several stages of a gradual Europeanisation of an Ottoman folk idiom, the period between 1878 and World War One saw a much more aggressive Europeanisation in both architecture and overall redesign of the post-Ottoman town. The model of the compact European city of the turn of the century took over: laid out on a grid plan, dominated by wide streets lined with multi-storey mixed usage buildings with continuous façade elaboration. European historicisms and eclecticisms began to dominate the architectural scene and soon replaced previous housing forms. The strict separation between *çarşı* (commercial district) and *mahalle* (residential district), typical for the Ottoman town, was ultimately abolished. By the outbreak of World War One the old mazes of narrow semi-private alleys had largely disappeared from the town centres at the expense of wide boulevards and avenues intersecting at right angles and squares. To fill the gap left by the absence of a local body of architects trained in designing buildings and cities in the contemporary "European taste", foreign architects and planners were invited to become active between the Save river, the Carpathian mountains, and the Bosphorus. In due course they were succeeded by the first generation of local architects trained most often in Austria-Hungary, Germany or, in the Romanian case, France, before the first architectural schools were eventually established in the region in the late 19th or early 20th century.

The changes resulting from the rejection of the Ottoman past in its political, cultural, and economic dimensions and its replacement with a European perspective also imported a novel architectural typology that had no real tradition in Ottoman practice: buildings for national assemblies, public libraries, opera houses and theatres, museums, universities, train stations, apartment buildings, monumental churches, and banks. The absolute abandonment of Ottoman architectural forms, hence, was less due to a change in the taste of the masses than to developments irrevocably triggered by the new realities. The urban transformations essentially went hand in hand with the success of institution-building, a more abrupt or more gradual process in different regions. While these reforms along European models were immediately launched in Greece by the Bavarian Regency in the 1830s, in Serbia only a decade later, upon change of rule from the Obrenovići to the Karađorđevići dynasties, the foundation for a Western-type state apparatus was laid. Despite the efforts for an immediate break, Bulgarian institutions were not consolidated until the end of the 19th century. In the peculiar case of Romania, the drive for Europeanisation even preceded the political break with the empire (Todorova 1995: 57). In her outstanding study of Athens, Eleni Bastéa claims that the new buildings and streets, as visible markers of progress and success, were in fact often the only bright spots on the horizon:

> "The internal instability of the new state was concealed under this expensive, monumental architecture, which bestowed a stamp of grandeur and permanence to the city and its institutions ... Was the elaborate late-nineteenth-century architecture a reflection of domestic well-being and refined culture? In the case of Greece neither the economic nor the political reality can afford us any direct correlations between the built environment and the actual conditions of the nation. In fact, the finely articulated mansions on Stadium or Athenas Street, privately financed with diaspora money, stood in sharp contrast to the kingdom's finances ... [Greece] was forced to declare bankruptcy in 1893. Social problems ran even deeper" (Bastéa 2000: 43, 146, 194).

The architecture of nationalism

Falling into an age of national emancipation, these processes coincided with the trend of pronouncing a society's particularities through architecture, giving birth to so-called "national styles". The safeguarding of national identity was seen as an artistic programme that should also be articulated by architecture through the formulation of a style expressive of the nation's traditions. While Greece had chosen its glorified antiquity, and accordingly Neo-Classicism as the historical reference for the urbanistic and architectural reinvention of Athens, Serbs and Bulgarians sought their national styles in the Byzantine-inspired church architecture of their medieval state formations. After the unification of Aegean Macedonia, Epirus, and Western Thrace with the modern Greek state, a few "Neo-Byzantine" buildings also appeared in northern Greece in the 1920s, but evidently never came close to the prominence that Neo-Classicism enjoyed as *the* Neo-Hellenic national style, though it was an international style at the same time. In Romania, on the other hand, the ecclesiastical architecture of the Middle Ages was only one factor in the hybrid "Neo-Romanian" style, which actually was more of an umbrella label for combinations drawn from a presumably local vocabulary than it was a coherent style.

Sarajevo witnessed the introduction of an idiom often wrongly portrayed as exclusively invented for Bosnia by Austro-Hungarian architects. Orientalist architecture, often improperly simplified as the "Moorish" or "pseudo-Moorish", sometimes also "neo-Islamic", was an eclectic integration of citations from the Muslim architectures of Spain and North Africa, almost totally disregarding the Ottoman architectural heritage of the province as a source of inspiration at the expense of an imagined local. A misunderstood metaphor for continuity of "oriental architecture" in Bosnia, this style was promoted by the Habsburg officials as a compromise (reconciliation?) between Orient and Occident. It was a foreign-sponsored "national style" for a multi-confessional Bosnian nation that did not yet (and never really came to) exist. In the case of Albania, the absence of such efforts might be explained by its comparatively late independence from the Ottoman Empire (gained in 1913),[7] a generally lower level of development, and a multi-confessional population divided into Muslim, Orthodox, and Catholic communities. In Albania, religion, and consequently the preference for the monumental architecture of one community or period, did not play the vital rule in the nation-building process that it had played in all other Balkan countries.

Paradoxically, these "national" styles rather became *regional* styles, as Byzantinising and orientalising architecture appeared under different guises in various parts of the Balkans. Of course, such designs appeared in the West as well, albeit to a lesser degree, but in Southeastern Europe their application signalled a different agenda, one of political nature. Aesthetic or functional considerations were of secondary interest to "nationalist architects", as Pantelić (1997: 16) maintains, while the actual aim was to define a style that would be particular to the nation and that would convey abstract concepts such as national spirit or national character through architecture. Architecture, in its unavoidable visuality, must have been considered quite an attractive medium to communicate nationalist ideals in an age where illiteracy was still widespread.

An initial problem in the formulation of "national styles", however, was the lack of familiarity with the particular distant cultural heritage and the deficiency in education needed to study it. The Greeks were fortunate, as this task had been undertaken by the Philhellenes decades earlier. Concluding a Neo-Classical redesign in the 1820s, Edinburgh, for example, presented itself as a "modern Athens" (see Lowrey 2001) only a year before modern Greece became independent. Organised research into the other Balkan nations' medieval architectural monuments, however, only started after the 1860s. As the decision to employ Neo-Classicism as the national style for a resurrected Greek state had been essentially made in Western Europe, Serbian, Bulgarian, and Romanian medievalist revivalisms also depended for a long time on the classes on Byzantine (that is, Constantinopolitan or Venetian Byzantine) architecture taught at Western universities rather than on the actual church architecture of the medieval Balkan states which, while clearly inspired by Byzantine models, did exhibit certain regional peculiarities.[8] Only over

[7] Tirana, however, became the capital of Albania only in 1920. As a consequence of the Balkan Wars (1912–1913), two towns often considered as "capital" of Albania in the late Ottoman period, Prizren and Ioannina, found themselves outside the borders of the modern Albanian national state, whose first capital was Durrës.

[8] Whether the medieval church architecture of Serbia and Bulgaria, as well as that of the Armenians, Georgians, and even Russians, shall be included in surveys of "Byzantine" architecture has been a recurrent topic of debate (see Mango 1991). The label "Neo-Byzantine" for the medievalist revivals of our period, while less contradictory in the Greek

time did these revivalisms become archaeologically more correct in their "national" aspirations and move from an international Neo-Byzantine style to more local ones. The model chosen for Belgrade's monstrous Saint Sava cathedral, construction of which started in 1935 and was stopped under Tito only to be resumed after his death, was, however, again not a Serbian one, but – in a delicate allegory – the "mother church" of all Orthodox Christianity, the Hagia Sophia in Constantinople, built well before the still pagan Serbs established themselves in the Balkans. In its central-domed design, dimension, appearance, and regional context, one could argue that the cathedral of Saint Sava in Belgrade, deemed to be a "national monument", actually has more in common with classical Ottoman mosques (save for the minarets) than it has with Serbian medieval architecture.[9]

"Islamic" city and "Turkish" house

As Southeast European nationalisms were constructed primarily around religious and/or linguistic identities, the crucial division between Islam and Christianity led to the import of ideas almost exclusively from the Christian West and Russia. Balkan nationalism irrevocably destroyed the imagined community of Orthodox Christianity, yet ironically managed to preserve a "frozen, unchangeable and stultifyingly uniform image of the Muslim community, and consistently dealt with it in *millet* terms" (Todorova 1995: 58–9). As a consequence, notions of religious determinism in regard to urban form (the "Islamic" or "Muslim" city), as well as ethnically exclusive attributions of architectural forms (the "Turkish house"), became firmly established.

Much of the bias against the Ottoman town model was certainly rooted in the Western orientalist concept of the "Islamic city", which sought to explain the decline of Near Eastern cities in the 19th century through its disaggregated cellular structure and consequent lack of true civic spirit, as opposed to a more integrated

---

case than in that of the Serb and Bulgarian "national styles", has thus been avoided in this essay. The "national styles" were locally understood as such as sui generis ("Serbo-Byzantine" or "style of the old monuments") and not as a reference to the actual Byzantine Empire and its architecture. Ćurčić (1979), however, suggested treating monuments such as the famed medieval Serbian church of Gračanica (near Prishtina) within the context of late Byzantine architecture. He refers not only to style but also to Serbia's overall orientation towards the Byzantine spiritual world and civilisation during the reign of King Milutin (1282–1321). A diametrically opposite approach can be found in the works of Bulgarian scholars, who repeatedly portrayed the really typically Byzantine 14th century churches of Mesembria (Nesebăr) on the Black See as "the swan song of mediaeval Bulgarian architecture" (Kiel 1985: 23).

9 This, of course, is due to the substantial impact Byzantine architecture (and particularly the overwhelming Hagia Sophia) had on Ottoman architecture in its classical period, coinciding with the empire's expansion into the Balkans and Central Europe.

and autonomous "Occidental city".[10] Western spectators pitied the "Muslim" town, distinguished by labyrinths of streets often ending in cul-de-sacs, as a "degenerate heir of a glorious [Greco-Roman] past" (Raymond 1994: 11), which colonialist urbanism sought to restore. Ludá Klusákova, however, maintains that the stereotypical image of the Ottoman town dates back already to the sixteenth century, developing simultaneously with the general image of Ottoman society:

> "To the eyes of Western visitors, the Turks did not care about comfort or elegance. They were scarcely even repairing the roofs to provide dry stables for their horses. Turkish dignitaries were fond of gardens and roomy houses, but ... their accommodation lacked grandeur ... Especially in the case of Buda, the neglect of the old palaces of Hungarian nobility as well as other buildings was taken to be a typically Turkish attitude" (Klusákova 2001: 358, 364).

The self-colonisation of the Balkans through the process of Europeanisation equally identified the "Turkish town" – routinely characterised by narrow, crooked streets and lack of order, open space, symmetry and hygiene – as an obstacle to the region's European perspective, wherein modern nations were thought to be best represented by well-ordered cities. In this context, the efforts of the Ottoman Empire to modernise its cities along European principles fell into oblivion. The principle of orthogonal grid plans with regular, wide streets with continuous façade elaboration and neo-Classical architecture reached Istanbul and the "liberated" Athens at roughly the same time. It is equally ironic that Sarajevo, of all present Balkan capitals the only one actually ruled by a European empire in the crucial period of 1878–1918, best preserved its Ottoman/non-European character. Instead of razing the Ottoman town, a new, typically Central European city was developed just where the other ended. In contrast to other Balkan capitals, where the Ottoman fabric was either demolished or successively eaten up by the European town, in Sarajevo it is still possible to survey in one and the same city the difference between European and Ottoman concepts of urban "centre". The *çarşı* – the heart of the Ottoman city – is horizontally oriented and, except for the monumental public buildings (mosque, medrese, hamam, etc.), almost exclusively commercial. The residential quarters *(mahalle),* composed of usually detached single-family houses, were typically located on nearby hill slopes to command an enjoyable view.[11] The

[10] More recent scholarship has been devoted to the deconstruction of the notion that any phenomenon in the civilisation of a Muslim country was totally conditioned by Islam, (including the physical structure of the city), as a myth, and has insisted on the singularity of each Ottoman city. See Eldem et al. 1999, Raymond 1994.

[11] What is sometimes presented as "old town" is thus not really the urban core of the Ottoman-period settlement, from which a modern town would have developed, but only one preserved *mahalle*.

"European" centre of Sarajevo, on the other hand, is composed of street corridors aligned with multi-storey mixed usage buildings, a pattern only infrequently interrupted by squares in front of churches, parks, or promenades. This difference in spatial organisation has often been commented on by Western observers,[12] who considered the *mahalle* "suburbs" or "villages" only loosely connected with the town "centre", which eventually resulted in the recurrent evaluation of Ottoman cities, even the capital Istanbul, as merely large villages.

Recent scholarship has also reassessed the supposed "Turkishness" of the Ottoman-period vernacular style in the Balkans. To understand the reaction against it, it is imperative to first identify the fundamental features of what has come to be known as "Turkish house" (alternatively "Balkan house", "Ottoman house", or – probably most correct – "Southeast European/West Anatolian town house of the Ottoman period"). As for de-Ottomanisation, the discussion of ground plans – a prominent subject of many if not most studies on the Ottoman-period house – or of interiors bore no immanent relevance, the architectural identity of the stereotypical "Turkish house" may here be simply characterised by its visual "otherness" vis-à-vis contemporary European models: whitewashed, asymmetrical in plan, widely overhanging roofs, and – for the Western observer by far the most distinguishing feature – a first floor, room, or bay window projecting from the ground floor on the upper levels.[13] For many Turkish scholars this feature is so self-evident that whole books written about the "Turkish house" habitually fail to mention or explain it. The fact that the literature, if at all, employs an inconsistent terminology by using a dozen different terms[14] for what the untrained eye of an outsider, who is used to continuous façade elaboration, might identify as the singular principle of towering elements above the ground floor, only supports this void.

While the most obvious explanation for this distinctive characteristic may be the desire to gain usable space above the ground floor, projections of the wall often accommodate social areas that enable desired seating in higher positions and boast a three directional view through the continuous fenestration around the projection. Visually challenging gravity, in addition to being able to afford con-

[12] For the observations of European travellers on Ottoman Balkan cities see Jezernik 1998, Mazower 2002, and Klusákova 2001. While the latter is concerned with accounts from before the 19th century, Mazower focuses on 19th century Thessaloniki and deals more generally with Europeans' confrontations with a multitude of local realities in a fairly comprehensive manner. Even if perhaps too exclusively relying on information provided by his travellers, Jezernik's study stands out for portraying the developments in selected cities throughout the 19th century as witnessed by different visitors at different times.

[13] This is, however, also not really an element totally unheard of in Europe, if we compare it with urban dwellings from the Middle Ages (e. g. the English "Tudor House").

[14] *Cumba, çıkma, şahnisin,* bow and bay window, projection, projecting alcove, oriel, protruding rooms, jettied, jutted or cantilevered upper floor, overhangs, etc.

struction of two- or three-storeyed buildings, may well have underlined social status. The significance of this feature, however, is that it long managed to subjugate diverse, consciously pronounced foreign tendencies, as seen in the transitional period between Ottoman and European architectural mainstreams in the Balkans, with the *konaks* of Plovdiv and Belgrade as the best known examples. Widely considered a trademark of the "Bulgarian National Revival", some of the most prominent "Plovdiv symmetrical houses" were in fact built by a Greek master from Constantinople for Greek merchants. The relationship of the "Bulgarian National Revival" architecture to very similar contemporaneous buildings, albeit on a smaller scale, in Greece and Western Anatolia has not yet been satisfactorily established. While Bulgarian authors (see Doytchinov and Gantchev 2001: 49–54) have concluded that the migrating masons and decorators must have been reasonably acquainted with contemporary trends in the West, with certain elements of Bulgarian merchant houses chiefly linked to Viennese Baroque, Cerasi (1998: 137–138) sees their source of inspiration in the buildings of much closer Istanbul.

While the construction of projections above the ground floor, so much identified with the Ottoman, was even banned in the de-Ottomanizing 19th century Balkans (in Bucharest as early as 1804; see Popescu 2004: 33), in Istanbul it was eventually formally accepted as a long standing tradition when rationally defined and limited by the building regulations of 1864 (Enlil 2000: 308–9), yet not as a "national" but as a local tradition. Muslims, Christians, Jews, even the Western European foreigners living in the city had their houses built with a *cumba* or *çıkma*. Moreover, there was often no genuine difference in style between the Muslim or Christian houses of Istanbul except for the building material, as the Muslim majority *intra muros* continued to prefer wooden constructions. Even though perishable and prone to fire, wood long remained the preferred building material in the Balkans as well. The shape and architecture of Ottoman towns and houses that we have therefore come to know best is that of the late 18th and 19th centuries. Showing an astounding unity over a vast, ethnically and geographically variegated region, Cerasi (1998: 149) explains the "not very significant" differences registered within this core area of the empire – the Balkans and Western Anatolia – as due to epoch and social class rather than to region, climate, or ethnic group. It is therefore not a surprise that the traditional "Turkish house" museum in Sarajevo *(Svrzina kuća)* is in fact the preserved home of an affluent Bosnian Serb, not a Muslim.[15]

---

[15] The audience's reactions to slides shown during my presentation at the conference "Urban Culture and Life in Southeast Europe" confirmed these suppositions. Unable to access my photographs from Southeast Europe, I had decided to simply use those taken more recently in Turkey. While no one would object to displaying the Greek-built town of Şirince in Western Anatolia as an example for a typical Balkan townscape of the Ottoman period, when showing

An exclusive "ethnic authorship" of this architecture, as implied in the category "Turkish house", has to remain a speculation. Did the typical "Turkish-Ottoman" house of the core area, with its sharply defined characteristics not found in other cultures, exist as a distinct type before the 17th century and then impose itself on the non-Turkish Balkan communities when they began to prosper? Was it a syncretist product of a multiethnic society, typologically consolidated from the 17th century onwards? (Cerasi 1998: 116) Or, as sometimes suggested by authors from the Balkans, was it simply based on an "orientalisation" of primitive pre-Ottoman models? Maintaining that "the assumption that the origin of the type was exclusively Turkish will not stand up to scrutiny", Cerasi (1998: 138) also challenges the popular theory that the organisation of the "Turkish house" was rooted in Turkic nomadic tent culture. Cerasi asserts that, while admitting that nomadic traditions might have strengthened the taste for some spatial conceptions such as the centred symmetrical room, they "could not have imposed the overall form when the Ottoman-Turkish house was being constituted" (ibid.).

Interestingly, Carel Bertram noted that images of the typical Balkan-Ottoman house and townscape, found so noteworthy by Western travellers, did not figure in Ottoman novels, poetry, or folk songs from the 18th and 19th centuries, nor are they the background of urban histories or drawings (Bertram 1998: 2–5). References to architecture are often limited to major monuments. Bertram moreover holds that the Ottoman house, as a "national" trademark, had in fact only entered consciousness and imagination when its ability to be an appropriate site for "modern" lifestyles was becoming questioned. Starting in the late Ottoman period, the house was the site of the modernisation process, and new objects entered everyday life, not for the sake of being "Western" but because people began to live and work differently. The traditional house with its multi-functional rooms – as opposed to the mono-functional room organisation of the European house – was eventually rendered outdated.

From rejection to rehabilitation, and from the Balkans to Europe and back

After mentioning similar processes in the Balkans, it must be stressed that the early Turkish Republican era equally identified the Ottoman house as representing a dark age that was to be succeeded by the modern European cubic house, marking the end of history. Only in the 1950s did the "Ottoman" or "Turkish" house

a slide of 17th century houses in the Ankara citadel one conference participant thought to have recognised the (Vlach) houses of Kruševo that he knew as "traditional Macedonian houses". Another participant believed to have seen a fairly recently constructed "neo-traditional" apartment building in Selçuk (Western Anatolia), or at least a very similar building in his native Bulgaria.

become to be seen as a symbol of cultural survival. By the 1960s, once the nation was secure with its Turkish identity and comfortable and proud of its Ottoman past as well, the late Ottoman period and its houses could safely become a symbol of a "traditional time" (Bertram 1998: 4 f.). However, in an ironic twist of history, the rehabilitation of architectural elements original to the Ottoman-period "vernacular" had started earlier in the Balkans, albeit in a different guise. In the "Romanian National Style", which sought to eclectically merge various forms of vernacular and monumental architecture on Walachian and, to a lesser extent, Moldavian soil into a style representative for one Romanian nation with different cultural traditions, a conscious reinvention of the *çıkma* (in Romanian *cicma*), hitherto prohibited by decree, reappeared as early as in the late 19th century. In Sarajevo, the very architects who had come to Austro-Hungarian Bosnia in their late twenties to accelerate the architectural transformation of the provincial capital into a typically Central European city, in their later lives became the proponents of a reorientation towards the vernacular style of construction. Shortly before World War One, they developed what they called the "Bosnian Style" *(Bosanski slog)* as a reinterpretation of traditional Bosnian Ottoman-period house forms filtered through a European aesthetic, at the age when the Art Nouveau movement was at its peak. In 1911 some Austro-Hungarian architects, maybe driven by a guilty conscience for their previous efforts in "modernizing" the traditional Bosnian townscape, even pleaded in the Bosnian parliament for the preservation and documentation of the Ottoman architectural heritage of the province.

Also in neighbouring Serbia, opposition emerged against both the Serbo-Byzantine "national style" and the "German" architecture of the kingdom's capital, headed by intellectuals promoting a reorientation to the Ottoman-period vernacular instead of an "imported" and "foreign" artistic vocabulary. In a 1907 essay the painter and decorator Dragutin Inkiostri objected to the belief that "our own architectural style can only be created under the influence of the Byzantine-Romanesque architecture of our old churches. But the Byzantine-Romanesque style is not a Serbian style, neither is it appropriate to the character of the people nor the spirit of our workers, since it were not Serbs who had designed these churches but very weak masters from the West. We have to start searching for our style in the works of our peasants and shepherds, from the hands of which these works emerged like the national songs from their throats" (Inkiostri 1907/1972: 42).

Inkiostri's strategy for a nostrification of the "Turkish house" was to emphasise that these buildings were in fact built by "old-Serbian and Macedonian" masons (Inkiostri 1907/1972: 41). Branislav Kojić, as one of the main protagonists of the style occasionally labelled "Folklorism", put Inkiostri's ideas into practice in the interwar years, although he evidently did not take peasants' dwellings but wealthier houses of the Ottoman period in Serbia as models. Again we find parallels in neighbouring Romania where, when the – at that time rather un-Romanian –

seaside was suddenly discovered by the wealthier Bucharest society, architects turned to the typically Ottoman townscapes and houses of the Dobrudja region as inspiration for the architectural identity of their seaside villas. This phenomenon was most visible in Balcic (today's Balčik in Bulgaria). A few years later the famed architect Sedad Hakkı Eldem eventually began to rediscover the forms of the old houses as a source for the new Turkish Republican architectural style.

In another ironic twist, the same socialist-Yugoslav Bosnia, that intended to level the old Ottoman bazaar quarter of Sarajevo in order to wipe away the traces of a backward, "feudal" past (see Alić, Gusheh 1999), witnessed the implementation of Juraj Neidhardt's projects, who had rediscovered the "Muslim house" as a local resource for his designs of workers' settlements in central Bosnia. Having worked for Le Corbusier in the interwar years, his enthusiasm for the cubism and simplicity of Ottoman-period houses in Bosnia was shared by many Western, or Western trained modernists who thought to have rediscovered in the Mediterranean vernacular the "unwritten principles" of modern architecture: human scale, unobstructed views, lots of light, geometry, flexible spaces, spatial links to nature, use of local materials, and traditional building techniques (Alić 1999).

Efforts like those of Neidhardt, however, were not limited to Bosnia-Herzegovina, where a large Muslim population had remained. Dragiša Brašovan's workers' settlement for the cable factory at Jagodina (1952) is an example from neighbouring Serbia. It should be noted that both Brašovan and Neidhardt were in fact born in what were at that time still Austro-Hungarian provinces, united with the previously Ottoman territories under a Yugoslav banner only after World War One. Trained in Budapest and Vienna respectively, they came to reinterpret the heritage of an entirely different architectural tradition in an approach not dissimilar to that of Western architects discovering the "other" in the Muslim (Arab) world, but in this case within the borders of their own "national state". In one instance Yugoslav architects were perhaps even more radical in reviving Ottoman-period models than their Turkish counterparts led by Eldem. Chiefly in Central and Northern Bosnia we find whole compact commercial districts for smaller and middle-sized towns unmistakably designed after the Ottoman-period *çarşı*. And, more recently, even the parish house of the Saint Sava cathedral in Belgrade, the Serbian nationalistic architectural project par excellence, employs – just like Turkish architecture ritualistically does since the works of Eldem – projections and an overhanging roof as a reference to tradition. Whether this alludes to national, local, regional, or foreign traditions is in the eye of the beholder.

As I hope to have demonstrated throughout this essay, a regional contextualisation of urban and architectural transitions in the Balkan countries in the 19th and 20th centuries not only reveals striking parallels, as similar circumstances caused similar responses, but also inconsistencies in these processes. The conflict arising from the imagineering of national identities, including the obscurity of presumed sources of local traditions, was duly reflected in the architecture of the region.

References

Akın, Nur 2001: Balkanlarda Osmanlı dönemi konutları [Houses from the Ottoman period in the Balkans]. İstanbul: Literatür yayıncılık.

Alić, Dijana 1999: From Ottoman House to Bosnian Style: Neidhardt's Design for Workers Housing in Bosnia and Herzegovina (1939 to 1942). In: InSite, Faculty of the Built Environment, Sydney, 1: 1–6.

Alić, Dijana, Maryam Gusheh 1999: Reconciling Competing National Narratives in Socialist Bosnia and Herzegovina: The Baščaršija Project (1948–53). In: Journal of the Society of Architectural Historians 58, 1: 6–25.

Bastéa, Eleni 2000: The Creation of Modern Athens. Planning the Myth. Cambridge: Cambridge UP.

Betram, Carel 1998: After the Ottomans are Gone: Imagining the Turkish Ottoman House. In: Stanley Ireland, William Bechhoefer (eds.), The Ottoman House. Papers from the Amasya Symposium, 24–27 September 1996. Ankara: British Institute for Archaeology, 2–8.

Bozdoğan, Sibel 2001: Modernism and Nation Building: Turkish Architectural Culture in the Early Republic. Seattle: University of Washington Press.

Çelik, Zeynep 1986: The Remaking of Istanbul. Portrait of an Ottoman City in the Nineteenth Century. Seattle: University of Washington Press.

Cerasi, Maurice 1998: The Formation of Ottoman House Types. A Comparative Study in Interaction with Neighboring Cultures. In: Gülru Necipoglu (ed.), Muqarnas XV. An Annual on the Visual Culture of the Islamic World. Leiden: E. J. Brill, 116–156.

Ćurčić, Slobodan 1979: Gračanica. King Milutin's Church and Its Place in Late Byzantine Architecture. University Park: Pennsylvania State UP.

Donia, Robert J. 2002: Fin-de-Siècle Sarajevo: The Habsburg Transformation of an Ottoman Town. In: Austrian History Yearbook 33: 43–76.

Doytchinov, Grigor, Christo Gantchev 2001: Österreichische Architekten in Bulgarien 1878–1918. Vienna, Weimar, Cologne: Böhlau.

Eldem, Edhem, Daniel Goffman, Bruce Masters 1999: The Ottoman City between East and West. Aleppo, Izmir, and Istanbul. Cambridge: Cambridge UP.

Enlil, Zeynep Merey 2000: Residential Building Traditions and the Urban Culture of Istanbul in the 19th century. In: Nur Akın, Afife Batur, Selçuk Batur (eds.), Seven Centuries of Ottoman Architecture. A Supra-National Heritage. Istanbul: YEM, 306–315.

Heppner, Harald (ed.) 1994: Hauptstädte in Südosteuropa. Vienna, Weimar, Cologne: Böhlau.

Heppner, Harald (ed.) 1998: Hauptstädte zwischen Save, Bosporus und Dnjepr. Geschichte - Funktion - Nationale Symbolkraft. Vienna, Weimar: Böhlau.

Inkiostri, Dragutin 1907: Naša arhitektura [Our architecture]. Reprinted 1972 in: Srpska Arhitektura 1900–1970 [Serbian architecture, 1900–1970]. Belgrade: Muzej Savremene Umetnosti, 41–44.

Jezernik, Božidar 1998: Western Perceptions of Turkish Towns in the Balkans. In: Urban History 25, 2: 211–30.

Kiel, Machiel 1985: Art and Society of Bulgaria in the Turkish Period. A Sketch of the Economic, Juridical, and Artistic Preconditions of Bulgarian Post-Byzantine Art and Its Place in the Development of the Art of the Christian Balkans, 1360/70–1700. A New Interpretation. Assen: Van Gorcum.

Klusákova, Ludá 2001: Between Reality and Stereotype: Town Views of the Balkans. In: Urban History 28, 3: 358–377.

Lory, Bernard 1985: Le sort de l'héritage ottoman en Bulgarie. L'exemple des villes bulgares 1878–1900. Istanbul.

Lowrey, John 2001: From Caesarea to Athens: Greek Revival Edinburgh and the Question of Scottish Identity within the Unionist State. In: Journal of the Society of Architectural Historians 60, 2: 136–157.

Mango, Cyril 1991: Approaches to Byzantine Architecture. In: Oleg Grabar (ed.), Muqarnas VIII: An Annual on Islamic Art and Architecture. Leiden: Brill, 40–44.

Mazower, Mark 2002: Travellers and the Oriental City, c. 1840–1920. In: Transactions of the Royal Historical Society 6, 12: 59–111.

Pantelić, Bratislav 1997: Nationalism and architecture: The creation of a national style in Serbian architecture and its political importance. In: Journal of the Society of Architectural Historians 56, 1: 16–41.

Popescu, Carmen 2004: Le style national roumain. Construire une nation à travers l'architecture. Rennes: Presses Universitaires de Rennes.

Raymond, Andre 1994: Islamic City, Arab City: Orientalist Myths and Recent Views. In: British Journal of Middle Eastern Studies 21, 1: 3–18.

Roth, Klaus 1989: Osmanische Spuren in der Alltagskultur Südosteuropas. In: Hans G. Majer (ed.), Die Staaten Südosteuropas und die Osmanen. Munich, 319–332.

Todorova, Maria 1995: The Ottoman Legacy in the Balkans. In: Günay Göksu Özdoğan, Kemâli Saybaşılı (eds.), Balkans. A Mirror of the New International Order. Istanbul: Eren, 55–74.

Yerolympos, Alexandra 1996: Urban Transformation in the Balkans (1820–1920): Aspects of Balkan Town Planning and the Remaking of Thessaloniki. Thessaloniki: University Studio Press.

"National" architecture in Sofia and Belgrade, and a contemporary building in Istanbul

Reinterpretations of the Balkan/Ottoman/Turkish vernacular in Bucharest, Belgrade, and Selçuk (Turkey)

Orientalist/Neo-Islamic/"Moorish" Architecture in Ottoman Istanbul and Austro-Hungarian Sarajevo

Ottoman-period houses in Bucharest (“Une rue de Bucharest. D’après M. Doussault”, 1841, detail) and a “Bosnian Style” building in Austro-Hungarian Sarajevo

“Oriental” features in Romanian “national” architecture and a contemporary building in Istanbul

Peripheral Zones of Serbian Towns: Spatial Development and Way of Life

Marija Maksin-Mićić, Belgrade

1. Introduction

In the countries of Northern and Western Europe, where the urbanisation process has almost reached its final stage, more than three quarters of the inhabitants live in urban settlements. Moreover, the traditional division into urban and rural settlements practically does not exist any more because the essential differences in the quality of life and spatial arrangement have diminished to a considerable extent. In Serbia, the share of the urban population has increased over the last half century from 22.5% in 1953 to 46.6% in 1981, to 54.0% in 1991 and to 56.4% in 2002.[1]

Like in some other European countries, Serbia is faced with a polarisation between regions: on the one hand, an increasing concentration of population and on the other, depopulation. The first category includes most urban areas. In urban areas in European countries in general, two opposite trends are simultaneously recorded: a relative decrease in the number of inhabitants and population density in central town districts and growth in population and population density in the suburbs and peripheral zones,[2] manifested by the large territorial expansion of urban sprawl (e.g. in France, Portugal, Spain and Italy). The highest population growth in most European countries, therefore, is recorded in suburbs and periurban zones surrounding urban centres and conurbations (especially in Paris, Lisbon, Porto, Madrid, Athens and Thessalonika). In Serbia, like in Italy for example, this phenomenon is evident not only around large cities, but also around the majority of medium-sized and small towns (such as Kragujevac, Niš, Užice, Smederevo, Valjevo, Knjaževac, etc.).

---

[1] The numbers for Serbia proper, i.e. without the Autonomous Provinces of Vojvodina and Kosovo, are: 21.2 percent (1953), 47.8 percent (1981), 54.1 percent (1991), and 56,4 percent (2002).

[2] The definitions used in these paper are: *Suburb* – a residential community lying on the outskirts, or in the vicinity of a town; it is inhabited by urban population, or population with an urban life style; it is functionally and spatially integrated with the town. *Peripheral zone* – a zone (or a wide belt) encompassing a town, in which planned or unplanned urban sprawl takes place; it is inhabited by people from the town or its surroundings, with urban or rural life styles; it includes open spaces, suburbs and certain rural settlements. *Periurban zone* – a contact zone between the town and villages in its surroundings; it includes the peripheral zone and rural area.

Serbia is faced with the following problems due to the uneven distribution of its population, resulting from different living conditions (cf. Perišić 1985: 14–6, 255–257):

- Increased regional disparities caused by demographic change;
- tendencies towards excessive urban sprawl and the shift of the population from central town districts and rural areas to suburbs and peripheral zones, which causes great social and territorial imbalances;
- the population shift to urban centres located in large river valleys and along main transport corridors, as well as the process of suburbanisation, exert pressure for new building construction on open spaces, often in regions with best-quality agricultural land, natural values and vulnerable ecosystems. Hence, problems of maintaining a balance between the protection and development of these areas arise;
- retarded development of most rural areas due to depopulation and the ageing of the population still living there.

In other words, the problems are similar or identical to those faced by most European countries (cf. European Commission 1994).

For more than four decades, the urban areas in Serbia have been undergoing major changes in their function, physical structure and organisation. Such changes have had both positive and negative consequences, whereby the latter include irrational urban sprawl, i. e., spatial squandering which resulted in a sharp rise in the prices for municipal infrastructure and services. Unplanned and unregulated construction, especially during the past twenty years, resulted in the formation of rings and agglomerations around the towns and cities in Serbia. However, neither solutions nor adequate experience so as to ensure spatial rehabilitation and, at least to some degree, spatial arrangement and the improvement of the quality of life in such agglomerations, are in place (Maksin-Mićić, Perišić 2005: 302).

2. Peripheral zones of Serbian towns

a) Origin and growth

Until World War II, the network of settlements in Serbia mainly consisted of very small towns and many villages. Urban settlements had no peripheral zones. Instead, towns and cities were surrounded by rural settlements.

After World War II, migratory movements from rural to urban areas were encouraged for ideological reasons, due to the lack of confidence in the peasantry and with a view to achieving working class supremacy. Migrations were encouraged by artificial and non-economically based industrialisation, which led to the creation of new jobs and employment opportunities for unskilled and semiskilled workers in towns – by pursuing urban-centric housing policies and organisation of public services, by the system of selective social security (only for employees of socially-owned enterprises), as well as by the dis-investment of public funds in rural settlements (Petovar 2003: 12). Like other Balkan countries under the socialist system, Serbia had no real economic potential for industrialisation (through which the process of forming the working class was conducted); however, the rural population and agricultural farms were marginalised, and rural areas lacked government support for their economic and social development.

The government proved unable to direct urban development and to ensure the spatial, social and cultural integration of the rural migrants who had left their villages. Therefore, the accelerated population growth in urban areas was not accompanied by qualitative changes in urban development, and neither by the formation of peripheral town zones. Industrialisation turned out to be the main reason for the rapid growth of peripheral town zones, where many rural migrants settled.

Serbia's abrupt urbanisation and industrialisation were experienced as a great surprise. Insofar as the regulations and control of spatial arrangement and construction were concerned, the relevant government and planning bodies were absolutely unprepared for the events taking place during the past fifty or so years (the so-called "ostrich urbanism") and especially during the past three decades, when large settlements were formed in peripheral town zones.[3] For a very long time, the greatest attention was devoted to the arrangement and construction of central town districts, while peripheral zones were neglected from a social, economic as well as legal viewpoint. These are the main reasons why such zones in Serbian towns have been constructed without any planning, regulation or control. Since government and government-owned enterprises were unable to solve the housing problem of all the incoming population in urban areas, either in central districts or in new settlements with high-rise buildings, these people built their houses by themselves in large peripheral town zones, with little financial assistance from their enterprises and credits, but mostly working alone and with the help of their relatives (Živković 1972, Saveljić 1988, Stojanović 1990, Petovar 2003).

It is estimated that more than half of the migrating rural population has so far settled in peripheral town zones. This estimate is based on the fact that in almost every period between the censuses, some parts of those zones were incorporated into towns (administratively and statistically), while the zones themselves continued to grow and import new population. The problem of definition in such surveys arises from the use of different criteria in setting up the boundaries of the city/town and its peripheral zone: formal criteria (statistical, administrative, building

[3] One of the largest settlements in Belgrade's peripheral zone, Kaluđerica, corresponds to a medium-sized town in Serbia according to its number of inhabitants (over 75 000).

land boundaries, boundaries of the master plan of the town and its peripheral zone) and/or factual and functional ones.[4]

Since population mobility is closely related to the age of the migrants, it causes spatial segregation with respect to the age distribution of the population: the younger population settles in and around urban centres, while the older population remains in, or begins to return to rural areas. Since 1980, the younger generation has been showing a marked tendency towards settling in peripheral zones rather than in central town districts. These processes change the age distribution of the population, resulting in imbalanced natural growth in the districts and zones that export and import population. Therefore, the population in central town districts is ageing, while rejuvenation is recorded almost exclusively in the settlements of their peripheral zones (e. g. in Belgrade, Niš, Valjevo, Smederevo, Pirot, Knjaževac, etc.).

b) The example of Valjevo and its peripheral zone[5]

In the period between the first and last censuses conducted in Serbia after World War II (1948 and 2002), the number of inhabitants in the Municipality of Valjevo increased by little more than one-third (from 70459 to 96761). After 1981, population growth began to lose pace and in the period 1991–2002, a decrease in the number of inhabitants was recorded for the first time. The territory of the Municipality of Valjevo comprises 78 settlements, which are functionally classified into urban (two), suburban (one), and rural (65 settlements). There are very great differences in total population dynamics and population potential between these functionally different settlements (see Table 1). In the period 1948–2002, such as in the whole territory of the Republic of Serbia, the number of inhabitants in the municipal centre and its suburban settlements increased enormously, as opposed to rural settlements where the population was almost halved. According to the relevant statistical data, the increase in the number of inhabitants in the town is considerably higher (by almost four times) than in the suburban settlements (40%). However, this is not the actual state of the population because between the censuses, parts of three of the settlements in the peripheral zone of Valjevo were merged with the town.

---

4 According to all formal criteria, Kaluđerica does not belong to Belgrade but, functionally, it forms its constituent part.

5 Valjevo is the seat of a municipality and regional centre in the north-western part of Central Serbia. It is located at the interface between two regions – the Kulubara river valley and the Valjevo mountains. Its best functional and transport links are those with Belgrade, then those with the towns at the border between Serbia and the Republika Srpska in Bosnia-Herzegovina and, finally, with the urban and industrial centres of its surroundings (Mionica, Šabac, etc.).

Table 1. Change in the number of inhabitants of the Municipality of Valjevo by type of settlement (1948–2002)

type of settlement	number of inhabitants according to census data						
	1948	1953	1961	1971	1981	1991	2002
total	70459	76104	81173	88267	95449	98226	96761
urban	15869	21208	28519	39850	50286	59146	61270
suburban	6912	6935	7387	8251	10304	9467	9822
rural	47678	47961	45267	40166	34859	29613	25669

type of settlement	index of change						
	1953/48	1961/53	1971/61	1981/71	1991/81	2002/91	2002/48
total	108.0	106.7	108.7	108.1	102.9	98.5	137.3
urban	133.6	134.5	139.7	126.2	117.6	103.6	386.1
suburban	100.3	106.5	111.7	124.9	91.9	103.7	142.1
rural	100.6	94.4	88.7	86.8	85.0	86.7	53.8

According to the 2002 census, about 48% of the total population in the municipality accounted for rural immigrants, hence the ratio of the autochthonous population to immigrants is almost fifty-fifty. More immigrants had come from the same municipality (59.5%) than from other municipalities (27.9%). Conversely, regional emigration in Valjevo took precedence over the local one (45.3% vs. 35.8%).

3. Patterns of urban sprawl and lifestyle in peripheral town zones

a) General remarks

The second half of the 20th century was characterised by significant urban sprawl along access roads. Instead of wide and continuous peripheral zones, a pattern of radial spreading emerged. The radial system of settlement and construction along access roads enables the inhabitants to have good and direct transportation links with their workplaces in town and their farms in the rural areas. In other words, access roads to towns in Serbia are a prerequisite for urban sprawl in peripheral zones. Migrants usually settled along the roads by which they had arrived in the town from their village, i.e., along the roads connecting hilly and mountain regions with urban centres. One of the basic features of the peripheral zones of Serbian towns is that they are populated by migrants, many of whom are related to each other, from the same or neighbouring villages located in the dominantly hilly and mountainous regions of Serbia. For this reason, settlements along certain roads are characterised by social homogeneity and solidarity among their inhabitants with respect to their subsistence and house building.

The open spaces of peripheral town zones with less expensive (agricultural and forest) land offer a number of locations with larger and cheaper plots for the construction of residential, commercial and industrial buildings than in central urban districts. In most cases, one-storey houses are built, which is not very rational in terms of population density and the provision of utility and social infrastructure. It also contributes to urban suffocation and the loss of urban identity in urban-rural, i.e., peripheral zones. Due to unplanned and irrational construction, the peripheral zones occupy a larger area than other town districts. During the past forty years, in most towns, the signposts indicating the town boundary/name were moved several times towards the periphery, evidence of the municipal government's formal conviction that peripheral zones, as well as some villages in the suburbs, became part of the town.

The tendency to move micro, small and medium-sized enterprises engaged in secondary and tertiary activities from town centres to these zones, or to develop them there, brought about a change in land use, from residential, to mixed residential-business, and exclusively business purposes. This is especially evident along the main roads into a town or major urban centre, where markets develop around them.

These tendencies, coupled with the intensification of commuting, also exert an influence on the social and economic transformation of the population in peripheral zones. Insofar as the occupational structure of the population is concerned, the share of employees in the secondary and tertiary sectors, as well as of households with non-agricultural and mixed sources of income, has noticeably increased in these zones. It is estimated that the share of households with mixed sources of income is the highest, and considerably higher than given by official statistics, because many households are still engaged in agriculture, mostly in the rural areas they came from. Most of these inhabitants maintain certain social and economic relations with their kin in the village, most frequently with their parents. They also go to their villages from time to time, or lease agricultural land in the peripheral town zone and engage in agriculture as a secondary job. By that, their once core activity (farming) becomes a secondary source of income after settling in a peripheral town zone.

The crucial point here is that most immigrants in peripheral town zones manage to organize micro, small or medium-sized businesses quite easily. In contrast to the period of intensive industrialisation and settlement in these zones during the 1970s and 1980s, most people could not have made a living during the transition period by working only in the industrial sector. On the other hand, they have access to cheaper construction land in the peripheral town zone, which is conveniently located in relation to the major market and well suited for the development of small businesses.

b) Examples of urban sprawl from Valjevo and Knjaževac

Post-World War II development brought about a considerable quantitative growth of Valjevo, while at the same time intensifying its central functions. During the past decade, though, some of its municipal functions (e.g. the industrial sector) were weakened, thus diminishing the influence of the urban centre. At the same time, there was a tendency towards the shifting of the secondary and tertiary sectors from the town centre to the peripheral zone. The most intensive development of the industrial and service sectors is recorded in suburban settlements along the road to Belgrade, i.e., the major market (see figure 1).

In 2004, the built-up areas in the municipality of Valjevo accounted for about 4.5% of its entire territory (4069 hectares), whereby 3.8% of the total area was covered by settlements and 0.7% by roads.[6] There is a very high disproportion in the level of building occupancy between urban, suburban and rural settlements. Urban settlements occupy about 1149 hectares (28.2% of the total built-up area), suburban settlements 548 hectares (13.5%) and rural settlements 2372 hectares (58.3%). Considering the mentioned tendency towards the periodic incorporation of built-up areas in the peripheral zone into the town, it is estimated that the real share of the peripheral zone in the total built-up area is considerably higher (about 20%) or, in other words, that it is equal to the share of the town districts.

People settling along the access roads to Valjevo mostly came from the hilly and mountain regions of the Valjevo Municipality. For example, the settlement of Sedlari, which is located along the south-west road to Bajina Bašta, is populated by households from the municipality's hilly and mountain regions gravitating towards that road (from the villages of Vujinovača, Brezovice, Jovanja, etc.), as well as from the neighbouring municipalities (Bajina Bašta, etc.). Settlement was especially intensive during the 1970s.

According to official statistical data, more than 80% of households in Valjevo have non-agricultural sources of income; ten percent have mixed sources, while agricultural households account for only six percent. However, the survey conducted in 2005 shows that more than 50% of households engage in agriculture as a secondary job on the farms they have come from.[7] Almost the whole second generation of immigrants, who arrived during the 1970s, is now employed in

---

6 See the document by the Institut za arhitekturu i urbanizam Srbije [Institute of Architecture and Regional & Urban Planning of Serbia]: Analitičko-dokumentaciona osnova Prostornog plana opštine Valjevo [Analytical-documentary Foundation of the Spatial Plan of the Valjevo Commune] (2004).

7 The Survey was conducted by the Institute of Architecture and Regional & Urban Planning of Serbia, entitled "Razvoj i uređenje rubne zone Valjeva [Development and Rehabilitation of the Peripheral Zone of Valjevo]". This was part of the Technological Development Research Programme by the Ministry of Science and Environmental Protection of the Republic of Serbia.

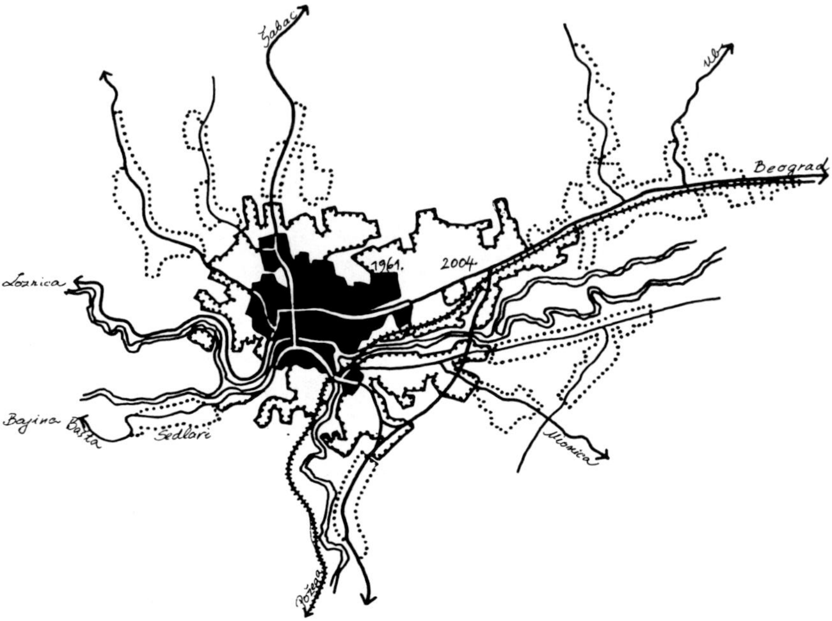

Figure 1. Valjevo Sprawl Pattern

small-sized and micro enterprises, specializing in the foodstuffs industry or in the service sector (in particular car and agricultural machinery repair services). All of these businesses are located along the access road to Valjevo. The proximity of the market and access to information and innovations resulted in the diversification of, and specialisation in production by agricultural households. Agricultural products are often provided by households from the villages on the regional road to whom farming is a secondary job, while many a purely agricultural households specialises in cattle raising. The former are located closer to the regional road, while the latter are distant, but have relatively good access to the regional road too. In general, there is a clear spatial and functional differentiation of the settlements between zones with a rudimentary urban and zones with a rural life style.

In the second example, Knjaževac, the signpost indicating the town was moved three times during the past twenty years. The major feature of the peripheral zone of Knjaževac is that immigrants settling there came from the same mountain regions within the municipality, along the main access roads to the town. The population of Kalna and the surrounding villages in the south-eastern mountain region of the municipality settled along the road from Knjaževac to the border with Bulgaria, in the south-eastern part of the peripheral zone, forming a 2.5 kilo-

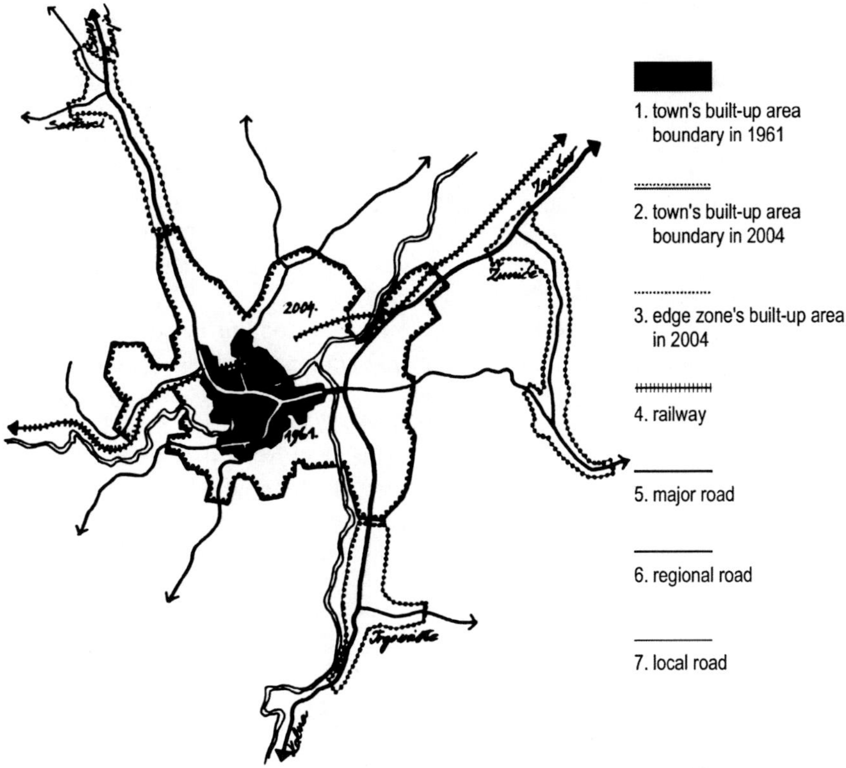

Figure 2. Knjaževac sprawl pattern

metre-long street. Almost all those living in this street are related to each other, since all of them emigrated from several neighbouring villages. They have preserved a semi-urban, semi-rural way of life. The typical pattern was that the whole family from the mountain village would join one household member who had already taken up work in Knjaževac, bought a plot and built a house there. As for their social life, they have preserved the relations they had maintained in their mountain villages, so that they show solidarity with each other, as well as a very pronounced common concern for the neighbours' well-being. In other words, there is a distinct collectivism in these communities as contrasted to individualism prevailing in the central town districts and among "old town" families. The same occurs along the regional road to Soko Banja, in the northwest part of the peripheral zone of Knjaževac (see figure 2).

4. Quality of life and spatial organisation in peripheral zones

a) The quality of life

The term "quality of life" has a very broad meaning, which has not yet been precisely defined. The normative way of defining quality of life is most frequently confined to an attempt to determine the marginal values of its comparative advantages. In essence, quality of life is assessed relative to an individual, i.e., the conditions under which he/she realises him/herself as a member of a specified group, society or region. Therefore, the quality of life is mostly frequently investigated through specified target groups of inhabitants of a town, a peripheral zone and/or a rural settlement (Pušić 1997: 395–401).

In general, the living conditions and the quality of life in peripheral town zones, especially with respect to their material equipment and the availability of utilities and social infrastructure, are much better than in economically undeveloped rural settlements with poor infrastructure in the hilly and mountain areas from which the population has emigrated. On the other hand, they are less favourable than in central town districts. The quality of life in peripheral town zones, thus, can be assessed with respect to the following indicators:

- Accessibility to the central town district (distance, public transport and travel time);
- quality of material conditions, transport and utility infrastructure, communal services supply (water, sewerage, electric power, telephone, heating, solid waste removal) and, generally, connection to the municipal infrastructure;
- availability of social infrastructure, as well as public and other services (proximity, organisation of delivery);
- existence of basic urban elements in the arrangement of streets, parks, squares etc.;
- access to funds for the improvement of living conditions and of spatial arrangements as well as possibilities for organising development;
- size and quality of buildings, patterns of housing plot arrangement.

The accessibility of the central town district is satisfactory in all medium and small-sized towns, since their peripheral zones are located on the daily (i.e., 30-minute) isochrone of the town centre. Since the peripheral zone develops along the main roads, its inhabitants have good transport links and easy access to suburban public transport. Most frequently, though, the dispersed municipal functions (commerce, elementary education, workplaces, etc.) are not available at walking distance, which especially affects the most vulnerable target groups – small children and the elderly.

The transport infrastructure in the peripheral zone includes access roads, which have been constructed according to plan and in conformity with specified technical documentation, as well as streets in the settlements which have been spontaneously built, unplanned like the settlements themselves. In other words, one cannot speak about an actual street network. Spatial conditions for setting up an adequate network of hierarchically arranged streets are frequently lacking. The existing streets are not in conformity with technical specifications. As a rule, they have no pavement, parking space, green strips, etc.

Peripheral town zones have local water supply and are connected to the municipal water system only exceptionally, mostly when part of such a zone is transformed into a town district. If there is any sewage disposal system, it is also local and not connected to the municipal one, nor are waste waters treated before their release into streams. Septic tanks are dominant, but there are also cesspits. Local water supply and sewerage have been constructed with private funds, frequently without valid technical documentation and supervision during construction and, in particular, they lack adequate maintenance during operation. In other words, the construction and operation of hydraulic systems in peripheral town zones is fraught with problems. Thus, it cannot be said that these settlements are supplied with safe and high-quality drinking water, nor that the collection, conveyance and treatment of waste waters from households, farms and manufacturing facilities are safe.

The supply of these zones with electric power and telephone lines is mostly satisfactory and close to the urban standards. Less satisfactory is the availability of other utilities. Peripheral town zones are not connected to the district heating system, and municipal utility services organise the collection of solid waste only once a week and only for those parts of the zones which are located on the daily isochrone of the town. The question of the graveyards in these zones is also problematic, as they are not part of the municipal system.

The greatest problem is probably the accessibility of social infrastructure, as well as public and other services, and the provision of adequate facilities. In contrast to the planned development of the urban area, where housing construction was accompanied by the construction of the facilities required for public services and services which meet the daily needs of the population, peripheral town zones do not have such facilities and have been neglected by municipal authorities. The provision of child-care services and adequate facilities – kindergartens and primary schools – has also been neglected, so that the most vulnerable age groups – preschool children and children attending the first four grades of primary school – have to commute to the appropriate institutions in the town. Thus, they are not in the same position as children of the same age living in the town, whose schools are located at walking distance from home.[8] The situation is similar with respect to the provision of primary health care. Even if health stations or surgeries are available, medical services are only periodically provided, so that the inhabitants

---

[8] The case of Kaluđerica is just the opposite: due to a great number of children, its eight-year primary school organises classes in three daily shifts!

are referred to health institutions in the town. One related problem results from the fact that public health insurance does not equally cover state and private health services, however, in the peripheral zones, health care is generally not provided by the public sector.

Access to public administration is also a problem, as decentralisation is still in a transitional phase in Serbia. This is especially evident in towns and cities where government is centralised and the urban centre dominates the other municipalities within the urban area and, in particular, the smaller local communities (such as neighbourhood units, who can host several thousand up to tens of thousands of inhabitants). Municipal branch offices located in these local communities are assigned a small number of administrative tasks by the municipal government, such as issuing certain enactments and documents, instead of being part of an administrative system which is equally accessible to the inhabitants of the urban and the peripheral zones. In addition, these offices have no adequate human resources and equipment, not even for the limited range of services they provide. A special problem is also posed by poor access to postal and financial services, which for the residents of most peripheral zones are available only in the town. Peripheral urban zones also lack the basic material elements of an urban surrounding, from the arrangement of streets, parks and squares to children's playgrounds and sports and recreational facilities.

Possibilities for organising and financing activities for the improvement of living conditions and of the spatial arrangement of peripheral town zones are very limited, since they are confined to the funds of the very residents and the private sector in these zones. Financial support from the municipal budget is either very small, or lacking. The municipal government does not provide even minimum technical assistance to local actions with a view to improving living conditions, especially in peripheral zones. Another problem is that local communities do not enjoy the status of a legal entity, so that they cannot represent their interests before the municipal government, funding institutions or investors. In other words, small local communities have only the formal right to organise themselves, but no basic instruments to initiate any joint action and represent the citizens' interests. In this way, residents of peripheral town zones and town districts are denied the possibility to act in an organized way and to lobby for their interests at different levels of government.

As for the availability of basic public infrastructure and public services, it can be concluded that the residents of peripheral town zones are underprivileged, i. e., they are "second-class citizens" relative to those living in central town districts.

b) Spatial arrangement and construction
In peripheral town zones there is a great discrepancy between the method of arrangement and construction of settlements, on the one hand, and the size and quality of buildings and house plots, on the other.

The spatial organisation and arrangement of peripheral town zones are not carried out in a planned way, but spontaneously, without urban plans and regulations governing spatial arrangement and construction. As a result, the parcelling of large cadastral plots on private agricultural and forest land in peripheral zones is done as requested by the owners and with technical assistance by land surveyors, who thus become the chief "quasi-planners" of those zones. Since this land (agricultural and built-up land) is much cheaper, building plots are larger than those in the urban tissue. Land acquisition and development costs can be several times lower than in central or elite residential town districts, so that comparatively large financial resources are invested in buildings. Therefore, even the smallest new residential building (over 100 square meters) and mixed residential-business buildings in the peripheral zone have the same area as exclusive plots in the central town district. As for the quality of construction, the floor area per user of the building meets high standards, but the buildings are frequently irrational from the viewpoint of the user's actual residential and business needs, as well as of economic or energy efficiency.

The size of plot depends on its location (in relation to the central town district and the centre of the settlement, major roads, utility infrastructure, etc.), natural conditions, costs (price of land, taxes and other dues), and the owner's economic and social aims and interests (including safety, status and prestige). In addition to the factors mentioned, the organisation and arrangement of plots also depend on psychological factors (affinity, aesthetic experience and symbolic perceptions of the space and landscape, etc.) as well as the availability of information.

In peripheral town zones, there is a clear differentiation in the size and organisation of plots, depending on the households' core activities and sources of income. In other words, a distinction can be seen between the plots of households with non-agricultural income and households with mixed sources of income as well as agricultural households. Only the plots of the first type of owners resemble urban methods of spatial organisation. Availability of utility infrastructure and the size of plot correlate negatively: the lower the level of available infrastructure, the larger is the size of plot in the peripheral town zone. As a rule however, the smallest plots intended for housing construction in the peripheral zone equal the largest ones in the urban zones (about six hectares). On plots of households with mixed sources of income one can observe the combined influence of traditional rural methods of spatial organisation (for the part of the plot where auxiliary buildings, the garden, orchard and the like are located) and urban methods (for residential and mixed residential-business buildings). As for the plots of agricultural households, they are characterised by modernised rural methods of spatial organisation.

The geography of Serbia, especially its central part, is widely varied, ranging from lowlands and river valleys to mountainous regions. Such versatility exerted influence on the development and diversification of the traditional methods of spatial arrangement and building in villages and towns. With the abandonment of the traditional life style and its migration to towns or their peripheral zone, or the migration of some members or complete households to other countries, the population abandoned traditional patterns of spatial arrangement and construction and adopted and imitated new ones. Therefore, in peripheral town zones, as well as in some rural regions, one encounters, with respect to the regional particularities, a dysfunctional method of spatial construction, which refers especially to residential buildings, but also to various buildings for service activities, small businesses, etc. The traditional type of rural one-storey house, with its simple, functional and unpretentious form and hipped roof, built with local building materials (stone, wood, roofing tiles) and adjusted to the local spatial and climatic conditions, as well as being energy and economically efficient, and possessing aesthetic and environmental values, is abandoned.

Traditional folk architecture is neglected and abandoned, not so much due to an adjustment to the new housing and business needs and the provision of modern housing elements (e. g. modern indoor bathroom instead of the latrine), which could also be achieved by modernising the traditional house, but primarily due to ignorance and psychological factors: the wish to acquire the status of a citizen and new, vague symbolic ideas about urban housing and construction. New houses are multi-storey ones with an attic, which dictates the double-pitch roof. In other words, they adopt the functional and design elements of urban houses, which are extended vertically due to the small plots. Apart from the elements of modern housing, some other elements of the town house are also adopted, such as interior staircases, terraces and balconies as a replacement for the porch,[9] but without its functions.

The greatest negative influence on new architecture, primarily on the houses in peripheral town zones, was exerted by various tradesmen, so that it can be called a "contractor's" architecture. Another negative influence was exerted by migrant workers. One such example is Negotin, a distinctly traditional cultural region in Eastern Serbia, with a long and rich tradition of folk architecture. This is also a region with a high migration rate (over 12000 workers work abroad). The people migrated first to Slovenia, then to Austria and Germany and, finally, to Sweden, which became the final destination of almost 90% of migrant workers

[9] Porches were one of the basic functional and aesthetic features of folk architecture in Serbia. They covered the approach to the doorway and linked the interior of the house with outdoors.

from Negotin. On their return, migrant workers brought new designs for their houses, which were typical of the regions in which they had lived – this is the so-called "migrant worker's" architecture. Whole settlements, from houses to courtyards, have been arranged and constructed under the influence of mountain and Alpine-style houses – types of houses which have nothing in common with the Negotin region and its architectural legacy (Maksin-Mićić 2002: 147, Marković 2006: 248–250).

In the peripheral zones of small and medium-sized towns in Serbia, it is possible to make a differentiation of settlements and their constituent parts with respect to spatial arrangements and construction methods of residential and other buildings and how they fit into their environment:

1. The first type of settlement is characterised by urban spatial arrangement and construction methods, with fairly uniform plot sizes and building heights, a fairly uniform location of the buildings relative to the street, and a favourable location relative to the neighbours.
2. The second type includes settlements or their parts based on rudimentary urban methods of spatial arrangement and construction.
3. The third type includes settlements without the features of the urban spatial arrangement and construction, with distinctly disorganised and deregulated spatial arrangement and construction. There are usually two subtypes:
   a) Settlements with some urban features as for their spatial arrangement and construction, and
   b) settlements without any such features, where it is very difficult to provide for minimum urban control, spatial arrangement and provision of infrastructure, as well as building regulation.
4. The fourth type includes settlements or their parts which preserved the rural method of spatial organisation and arrangement but also know the modernised traditional method of plot arrangement and construction of buildings owned by agricultural or mixed households.

The greatest differences arise between those parts of the settlement located along trunk, regional and frequently used local roads on the one hand, and other parts of the settlement on the other. In the built-up part of the settlement, along the access road to the town, which has already merged with the urban tissue, one can observe the first three methods of spatial arrangement and construction, the most frequent being the second and third types. In the remaining part of the settlement one can find the fourth type or a combination of the second and fourth types.

c) Examples of spatial arrangement and construction in the peripheral zones of Valjevo and Knjaževac

Sedlari (see figure 3) is located about three kilometres away from the central urban district of Valjevo. It has relatively well-organised suburban public transport, with two bus stops in the settlement. Although it is located at an acceptable walking distance, the central town district of Valjevo is not accessible on foot to most residents of Sedlari, because there is no pavement along the regional road, and there are no special pedestrian paths (see figure 4). The system of streets, constructed spontaneously with private funds, has a good layout; the streets have mostly asphalt carriageways, but no pavement, lighting and parking lanes; in many places there are no spatial conditions for the widening and arrangement of residential and collector-distributor streets.

The settlement has local water supply and sewerage, which were installed with private funds. Sewerage was to be laid according to technical documentation and in agreement with the municipal government about connecting it to the municipal sewerage. However, this has not happened, because several citizens refused to give their approval for routing the sewer through their plots in Valjevo. As a consequence, local sewerage is not adequately maintained and is slowly losing its function. At the same time, waste waters are released directly into the Jablanica River, upstream from town. The problems relating to safe pedestrian movement, as well as to the repair and connection of the local sewerage to the municipal system are regarded as the most pressing by the inhabitants of Sedlari.

The settlement is adequately supplied with electric power and telephone lines and the same applies to the weekly removal of solid waste. The settlement has no public service facilities. There is only the unequipped municipal branch office building. The priority list of Sedlari's inhabitants with respect to the provision of public services, includes a kindergarten (the closest kindergarten is almost six kilometres away), a four grade primary school (the next is four kilometres away), a post-office, the expansion of services provided by the municipal branch office, and its proper equipment. The services provided by the private sector, in contrast, are well developed: the settlement boasts food stores, catering establishments, repair shops and an agricultural pharmacy.

The inhabitants complain about the excessive loss of time and money, as they have to go to the town centre every day for meeting their basic needs. This subjective evaluation is confirmed by the fact that the rate of commuters is the highest in Sedlari compared to other settlements in Valjevo's peripheral zone (over 60% of the economically active population and pupils commute daily). The residents of Sedlari also express their readiness to participate with their funds and labour to solve the priority issues and also to improve their living conditions in the future. They have no wish to live in the town and would be completely satisfied with their living conditions should the aforementioned problems be resolved. Several inter-

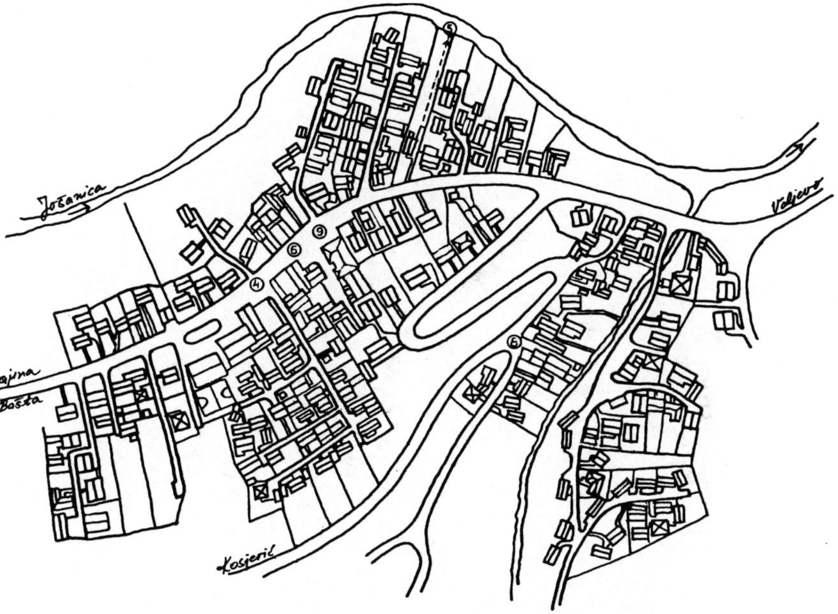

Figure 3. Construction of a part of Sedlari at the regional road

viewed persons even gave precedence to life in the village from which they came to Sedlari and Valjevo, if there were good local roads and employment opportunities.

The location, size and organisation of plots are differentiated according to the type of household. Households with non-agricultural sources of income are located along the regional and major local roads. The size of their plots is more than ten hectares. Plots are used for residential or mixed residential-business purposes. All buildings have been constructed without a building permit.

One of the households, using its plot by the regional road for residential purposes, falls into the group of households with mixed sources of income (see figure 5). The members of this household engage in construction as well as in farming as a secondary activity in the village of Jovanja from which the family originated. Their advantage is that Sedlari is located at equidistance from the town and the village. The house was built in the 1970s. In contrast to the traditional folk-style houses in Jovanja (see figure 6), or the modified folk-style house on the adjacent plot (built immediately after World War II), this household built a large two-storey house with an attic. Later, they added a porch alongside the façade as a functional element modelled after their old house. When asked why they built the house like this, the head of the household answered in a very illustrative way: "If one sheep leaps over the dyke, all the rest will follow." He also said that today

Figure 4. Unpaved centre of Sedlari

he would not have built a two-storey house. Otherwise, the household members say that living conditions here are better than in the villages thanks to the vicinity of the town centre and transport links, as well as the availability of basic utilities. The next example is a property with a building for business and residential purposes (see figure 7). Business is done on the ground floor, which has direct access to the local road. The building has been extended and has changed its use in step with the development of the household's business (baked goods).

In all examples mentioned, the buildings do not fit into the rural surroundings and can thus be classified as "contractor's" architecture, whose style is not recognizable. Only the agricultural household, which is located far from the major roads, has preserved and improved the traditional method of plot organisation and arrangement and building construction (see figure 8).

To sum up, the settlements in Valjevo's peripheral zone can be classified into two main types according to their patterns of spatial arrangement and construction:

1. Settlements with rudimentary presence, or lack of the features of the urban method of spatial arrangement and construction; these are suburban settlements which have physically merged with the urban tissue of Valjevo along the access

Figure 5. House with added porch on the regional road to Sedlari

roads to the town: Degurić, Petnica, Rađevo Selo, and some parts of Popučke, Beloševac, and Sedlari (see figure 3).

2. Preserved rural methods of spatial arrangement and construction, such as in Zlatarić, Jasenica, Gornja Grabovica and Bujačić, and some parts of Beloševac, Popučke, and Sedlari (see figure 8).

From the point of view of construction, the houses in the peripheral zone of Knjaževac are of high quality and large, in particular when considering the fact that households in the Timok region are usually small (with two or three members on average). Houses in the peripheral zone of Knjaževac, too, have been built without building permits. It is not known whether this happened by chance or whether there was an inspection, but all buildings follow the street regulation width and building line with only slight deviations. Courtyards are spacious, and their organisation is more rural than urban. Courtyards include an area for farming activities, with small lifts for cereals that are transported from the village in which the families had lived in the past. There are also mini pigsties, hen coops, etc. Adjacent to the house is a summer kitchen, since its residents spend summer mostly outdoors in the courtyard. As a rule, they have no sewage disposal system, but cesspits.

Figure 6. Old property and buildings owned by the same household (as in Figure 5) in the village of Jovanja

Concluding remarks

The peripheral zones of Serbian towns have been neglected from a social, economic as well as legal point of view, thus resulting in their unplanned, unregulated and uncontrolled construction. Over the past twenty years, new rings and agglomerations have flourished around the towns in Serbia. There are as yet no solutions or adequate experiences as to how to rehabilitate and, at least to some extent, improve the quality of life in these agglomerations.

One of the basic criteria for assessing the quality of life in peripheral town zones relative to central town districts and rural settlements is their level of inclusion in the municipal infrastructural and super-structural systems, as well as the system of government. On the basis of this criterion, it can be concluded that the living conditions and the quality of life are much better in peripheral town zones – especially with respect to the level of material equipment and the availability of utilities and social infrastructure – than in rural settlements in hilly and mountain regions from where the population of the peripheral zones has migrated. But they are less favourable in comparison to central town districts. Their advantage over

Figure 7. Business-residential building in Sedlari

rural settlements is primarily due to the vicinity to the central town district and the prospect of being merged with the urban area, thus acquiring a more favourable status and greater possibilities for urban improvements. From an anthropogeographic viewpoint, there are two major trends:

1. The immigrant population in peripheral zones acquires the habits and lifestyles of the residents in the central town districts very fast, wishing evidently to achieve an urban way of life as soon as possible, and
2. at the same time, immigrants also preserve some of the rural habits as regards lifestyle and the spatial organisation of their property.

Considering the possibilities and needs for improving living conditions and the quality of life, as well as the proposed typology of settlements and their parts in the peripheral zones of Serbian towns, it is necessary to establish the rules governing spatial arrangement, protection and construction, as well as to prepare programmes for the improvement and rehabilitation of those zones, especially with respect to their gradual integration into the municipal infrastructural and superstructural systems. In order to implement improvement and rehabilitation programmes, it is necessary to decentralise the municipal government system and transfer some of its competencies and access to public funds to small local commu-

Figure 8. Farming household in Sedlari

nities in the town and its peripheral zone. In order to direct and manage the development of peripheral zones, it is also important to formulate land use and housing policies, as well as to provide them with incentives and instruments of tax policy, thus encouraging the private sector investments into the arrangement of those zones, all the more so because their intensive development and growth are expected in the future. Special attention should be devoted to the dissemination of information and education of the population, so as to enable the preservation of the values of rural life and the improvement of peripheral zones, by adopting and adjusting the patterns of urban life, spatial arrangements, and construction.

References

European Commission 1994: Europe 2000+ – Cooperation for European Territorial Development. Luxembourg: EC Regional Policies.

Maksin-Mićić, Marija 2002: The Landscape in Serbian Spatial Planning Practice. In: The XIV European Council of Landscape Architecture Schools Conference. Budapest, 134–151.

Maksin-Mićić, Marija, Dimitrije Perišić 2005: Slabosti upravljanja, planiranja i izgradnje gradova u Srbiji [Weaknesses in the administration, planning and building of towns in Serbia]. In: Ružica Bogdanović, Miodrag Pralević (eds.), Planiranje i menadžment gradova i regiona [Planning and management of towns and regions]. Belgrade: Udruženje urbanista Srbije, 301–311.

Marković, Predrag 2006: Verloren in der Transmigration? Der Einfluss der serbischen "Gastarbeiter" auf das Alltagsleben in Serbien. In: K. Roth (ed.), Arbeitswelt - Lebenswelt. Facetten einer spannungsreichen Beziehung im östlichen Europa. Berlin, Münster: LIT, 239–256.

Perišić, Dimitrije 1985: O prostornom planiranju [On spatial planning]. Belgrade: Institut za arhitekturu i urbanizam Srbije.

Petovar, Ksenija 2003: Urbana sociologija: naši gradovi između države i građanina [Urban sociology: Our towns between the state and the citizen]. Belgrade: Geografski fakultet Universiteta u Beogradu.

Pušić, Ljubinko 1997: Grad, društvo, prostor: sociologija grada [The town, society and space: the sociology of the town]. Belgrade: Zavod za udžbenike i nastavna sredstva.

Saveljić, Branislava 1988: Beogradska favela. Nastanak i razvoj Kaluđerice kao posledica bespravne stambene izgradnje u Beogradu [The Belgrade favela: the emergence and development of Kaluđerica as a consequence of illegal residential housing construction in Belgrade]. Belgrade: Istraživačko-izdavački centar SSO Srbije.

Stojanović, Dragana 1990: Sociološki aspekti bespravne stambene izgradnje u Jugoslaviji [Sociological aspects of illegal housing construction in Yugoslavia]. PhD thesis, Belgrade University.

Živković, Miroslav 1972: Uzroci i nosioci bespravne izgradnje [The causes and bearers of illegal housing construction]. In: Akademija nauka i umjetnosti Bosne i Hercegovine. Posebna izdanja - Odjelenje tehničkih nauka 20, 4 (Sarajevo).

Abstract

The unplanned and unregulated construction of peripheral zones resulted in the formation of agglomerations around towns in Serbia. This paper analyses different lifestyles in these peripheral zones, and concentrates predominantly on the arrangement and construction of them. On the basis of the proposed criteria for assessing the quality of life in terms of the organisation, arrangement and construction of these zones, the paper also compares the lifestyles with those in central town districts and rural settlements, from which the population now living on the town periphery emigrated. The conclusions indicate that the quality of life in peripheral town zones is much better than in rural settlements in hilly and mountainous regions, but less favourable than in central town districts. The paper also presents a typology of settlements in peripheral town zones based on spatial arrangement and construction, and points to activities conducive to improving the quality of life in them.

Evaluating the Spatial Context of the Suburban

Katarina Višnar, Ljubljana

Introduction

The preservation of architectural heritage reaches Slovenia at a time when the importance of civic inclusion into its various segments is recognized – from heritage planning to actual physical work on the objects of historical value. This is true regardless of the heritage preservation system of a particular country, as the comparative analysis of three preservation systems of Slovakia, England, and Slovenia has shown (Višnar 2004).

The precondition for real civic inclusion into heritage preservation is the awareness and understanding of the social groups to be included. In practice it is obvious that every single case of heritage protection and enhancement was and will be more successful if it is inclusive and functions at ground level, that is, when the people who are inhabiting and using the objects are conscious of their value.

In order to achieve this goal it is necessary to widen both the concept of heritage and the right to evaluate space in order to increase awareness of its value, which would result in improved heritage preservation, and enable a holistic evaluation as a basis for spatial planning.

For the evaluation of built (heritage) space the question of value is central. The question of evaluation is not only of a theoretical or philosophical nature but directs our decisions in the field, through specific objects of heritage (or their parts), so that the values recognized in an object influence decisions on its preservation or destruction.

The following two stories may clarify my point. The first is the Biblical story of Jacob's dream. After Jacob woke up, he decided to place the stone he had laid his head on the night before vertically, in order to make it a reminder of what had happened, not only for him, but also for his sons. So, physically, the stone remained the same and only its microposition changed. In terms of meaning, or value, however, the stone had changed its very essence.

If the story of Jacob is also the story of the first monument in Western civilization, the second story is clearly an opposite in terms of what we understand as a monument. In 1967, Robert Smithson, the famous land-artist, visited his hometown and later published his in-situ impressions – together with photos – as an essay called "A Tour of the Monuments of Passaic, New Jersey". What we may find surprising is that his notion of "monuments" of Passaic is but an inversion of the usual meaning of this term. Shocking actually, because Smithson observed and described monuments which were in fact the ugly remnants of the margins of an industrial civilization such as pipes, wired fences, ugly empty spaces, but what is interesting, is that we can really recognize the moment – or "movement", for it is all but static – of an evaluation based on observing, seeing and understanding, as the crucial moments in rendering the space elements important or valuable in the sense of heritage.

Charging an object with a meaning means developing values, and this has to happen within a social context if it is to be widely understood. Who would have known of Jacob's stone had he not spread word about it? This is the lesson we get from the two stories: heritage values are anything but given. They need to be established through seeing and understanding which is a conditio sine qua non of a holistic spatial evaluation. All evaluation is dynamic and evolutive, hence, in order to make it as precise as possible, we need to broaden its context and make it holistic.

All heritage – and especially the built heritage which is an important part of our everyday lives – by definition undergoes this process of evaluation. And it is, in our time, the professionals who are most likely to be given the mandate to evaluate. Heritage professionals have developed tools for heritage evaluation; a sophisticated system of these tools is used to distinguish something from something else as having a value which does not necessarily coincide with economic and/or political profit, but reaches beyond that.

If there is anything missing in this elaborated evaluation system, it is the fact that it does not really work unless the people who are involved with and are using these heritage objects are willing to listen to the professionals. In practice this is almost impossible to attain. The problems arising are at least threefold:

1. Imposed evaluation triggers misunderstanding, perhaps even anger.
2. The laity will not necessarily identify with the things valued by the professionals.
3. From a practical point of view, heritage protection is very expensive if those who use it on an everyday basis do not sympathize with the cause, because misunderstanding is a major vehicle for doing wrong things.

The proposal that would bridge the gap, is to establish and open a space for dialogue which involves the local community from the very beginning in order to reach the goal of establishing the statement of values. The method to be used for such a dialogue is not the chaotic, all-involving debate until consensus is reached (which may never happen), but the structured approach of community-based conflict resolution.[1] If applied properly, (1) people can be led to develop a sense or even appreciation for "the local spatial values" by "opening their eyes", and (2) professionals can obtain field data and cooperate in this kind of evaluation, so

---

[1] As taught and practiced by the European Institute for Community-based Conflict Resolution, based in Salzburg, http://www.conflict-resolution.at.

that they establish social ties and are in a position to include the data into their plans and research.

Applying the evaluation tools to the suburban

Why should one apply these tools to a suburban context which has not much or no obvious heritage value? In the Slovenian context, the suburban is a mixture of urban and rural, middle-class and working-class lifestyles, which was physically incorporated into the city only recently, in Ljubljana mostly in 1985. Why should one consider the suburban as something particular and worth exploring? There are, indeed, certain points distinguishing the suburban from the urban on a practical level, namely: (1) there is less heritage, as the heritage is quantitatively concentrated in urban centres, not peripheries, (2) there is less identification with that heritage, and (3) there is less control and political will.

Suburban also means a clash of urban and rural values, of which Ljubljana East provides a nice example, where the urbanite habit of dog walking clashes with the rural right to plough the soil and harvest.

The suburban is much less defined and confined within meaning(s), making it much tougher ground for developing historical awareness. The hypothesis is that through the application of our tools we should be able to generate a different, better relationship and awareness of the three-dimensional space. This can be proved through stories of the raised sensibility of citizens who were included in non-governmental organizations concerned with heritage.

The suburban has, in the eyes of planners, politicians, conservation officers etc., fewer values and is less important. It is the site where lots of degradation takes place – because its evaluation is omitted. This opens an opportunity for people to define what they value in their local space, and what spatial parameters make up the quality of their living space. It is important to talk about local space as it is the space people know and cherish. The locals may see and understand their heritage differently from the professionals. This approach is, on the one hand, an attempt to operate with values beyond the purely economic and/or political ones, while on the other hand, it is an attempt to popularize the "right to evaluate" in order to develop values. By including the inhabitants in the process of preparing a statement on the values of their local space, it is possible to trigger their awareness, to help strengthen their social bonds, to start building stronger social networks for heritage protection, and to help induce and produce new, and often exciting ideas. In proceeding this way, one could develop tools for distinguished urbanization in the sense of planning, consensus, controlled development and growth, thus furthering sustainable development.

Conclusions

Problems arise if the spatial evaluation is imposed upon locals who are not included in the planning process; if the participants are not asked what they want, but are presented proposals and asked for their agreement, and in case they disagree, slight adjustments are offered to them, but not the chance to do the whole thing all over again. This would be the limit of professional engagement in what is called participatory approach.

Though requirements for the inclusion of civic participation in the planning and decision-making processes are growing (in Slovenia, they are incorporated into the Spatial Planning Law), one can see that real democracy is not really easy to practice. In countries with no relevant historical tradition of civic engagement (such as the Southeast European countries) it is hardly possible to count upon strong civic engagement and maturity for civic discourse. Is the declared participative approach merely the vehicle for enhancing the influence of those who are already in power?

The practical approach would be to actually avoid acting in a conflict-igniting manner. The first step would be to forget the differences and to build on the commonalities. In any case the bottom-up approach has to be applied from the very first stage of fieldwork on, and non-governmental organizations should be included to establish communication bridges with the professionals. The statement on the values (as a result of the dialogue process) should focus on the consensual. This procedure can make it possible for space elements to become valuable in the sense of "heritage" and open the social space to include laymen, i. e., the various segments of civil society, in the planning process.

References

Smithson, Robert 1996: A Tour of the Monuments of Passaic, New Jersey. In: Jack Flam (ed.), Robert Smithson: The Collected Writings. Berkeley: University of California Press, 68–74.

Višnar, Katarina 2004: Vloga laične javnosti v procesu revitalizacije stavbne dediščine Slovenije. Historiat, stanje in metodologija razvoja aktivne participacije. Ljubljana: Faculty of Architecture (doctoral dissertation).

Skopje: Nostalgic Places and Utopian Spaces[1]

Ermis Lafazanovski, Skopje

Introduction

Any attempt at a more individual definition of the urban culture of the city of Skopje which seeks to incorporate the array of notions resulting from recent theoretical and practical research in Europe in the areas of urban anthropology, ethnology and folklore (cf. Hengartner 1999a, 1999b; Rolshoven 2003, Augés 1995, Lefèbvre 1991) would need, first and foremost, to embark upon an adjustment of these notions to the cultural specifics of this city.

Such a procedure would demonstrate how these notions, which claim to be of universal application, could work in a specific urban environment, such as Skopje. They could also disclose a need – if such a need exists – to enlarge and enrich the research vocabulary itself. This is because all cultural research of Skopje carried out locally to date has not yet produced a conceptual approach to the research of the civic culture of the city. Most of this research has consisted mainly of philological studies based on rural and urban elements in oral tradition (Macedonian Folklore 1991), ethnographic and historical records, or ethnological exploration of the rural or folk culture of Macedonian towns (Lape 1992, Hadži-Vasiljević 1930, Filipović 1939).

However, there has been an evident tendency in Macedonia in recent years to research urban culture, and the urban culture of Skopje in particular (Kaćeva, Hristova, Gjorgjovska 2002). The need to explore urban culture became more pressing in the 20th century as Skopje, in this period, was in many ways an atypical European city and its citizens developed a specific attitude towards their lives there. These specificities came as a result of historical ordeals and destruction of every kind – both in terms of war and natural cataclysms – which the city has undergone in its eventful history.

Following the records of ethnographic, ethnological and folklore research on Skopje from the second half of the 20th century to the present day, we may reach the conclusion that from a historical and cultural perspective, the attitudes of the citizens towards their city – and, in this context, towards their urban culture – are

[1] The present article is based on the research project "Urban Folklore" carried out 2004–2006 at the Institute of Folklore in Skopje, and results from my special interest in the contemporary culture of Skopje. The ethnographic and folkloristic details presented in this article derive mostly from unpublished personal narratives about life in Skopje collected in this period.

to a great extent determined by two conflicting forms of their city's identity. On the one hand, we see Skopje as a city whose identity during this period has been based on the socialist and post-socialist Eastern European urban image. This image is also characteristic of other Eastern European cities of the same period; but in this particular case, it has been supplied with the specific ethnic diversity of its Macedonian, Albanian, Vlach, Roma and Serb inhabitants, together with their religious affiliations to Orthodox Christianity and Islam. On the other hand, the image of the city has simultaneously been defined by the key moment in its recent history: the earthquake of 1963.

The contemporary identity of Skopje shows tendencies towards a deconstruction of the historical ideological character of the city and the construction of a new image uncontaminated by ideologies from the past: encompassing multiculturalism and religious diversity on the one hand and post-earthquake modern urban history on the other. If we venture into a detailed exploration of this contemporary urban identity, we will reach an interesting conclusion that this modern image is confronted by two equally powerful proclivities which constantly meddle with the identity of the city and its spatial urban characteristics. One of these proclivities is the nostalgic yearning for the times past when life in Skopje was "better". The other is the utopian concept of a "better" life craved by the citizens. These two concepts can be observed as two sides of the same coin.

From a cultural and anthropological point of view, this short initial explanation of the contemporary identity and character of the city can be supported by an analysis of the theoretical notions of the two key terms that have been debated in European anthropology and sociology in recent years. These are the categories of *place* and *space*. These two categories appear fairly appropriate and applicable to researching the urban character of Skopje and the lifestyle of its inhabitants in the second half of the 20th century – a period in which the city experienced a violent change of identity when the catastrophic earthquake of 1963 created the need for its reconstruction on new foundations. As the identity of pre-earthquake Skopje was built upon meanings and a substance produced by specific anthropological places and spaces, it is logical that we should presume that the post-earthquake places and spaces preserved their initial connotations or even expanded them.

For these reasons, initial theoretical and, above all, empirical research of urban living in Skopje might serve as a kind of assessment of the value of the notions of *place* and *space* as well as of their derivatives, such as inter-space and non-place, in circumstances of their violent deconstruction caused by a natural catastrophe. In this context, the research of social discourse in architecture, politics and culture has demonstrated that, in relation to the earthquake as a key moment in the history of Skopje and the subsequent reconstruction of the city, there exists a close link between the ideological component of the space and place articulated through nostalgia as a component of the so-called collective social memory, and utopia as a manifestation of a desire for a new city life in the spirit of the new times.

1 Place, ideology, nostalgia

If an "anthropological place" may be represented as a series of isomorphisms drawn between human existence, action and the inhabitation of a certain place, or if it may be identified as a historical place or a place connected with identity (Augés 1995: 77 f.), then it might be presumed that the anthropological place yields easily to changes. These changes may be changes in the identity of the place, such as its construction or reconstruction, politicisation, or ideologisation; or its instrumentalisation; or a physical change caused by violence or natural catastrophe. If we analyse definitions of place, starting with Heidegger, who described place as something connected with building, and finishing with the definitions of Augés and Hengartner, we can see that all these descriptions demonstrate that place is primarily understood as a tangible phenomenon connected with humans and one which realises itself through the manifestation of the identity of the people and their history, as well as giving each of these substance and meaning. Because of this tangibility, a place might become a target of ideological and cultural conflicts. Let us just remind ourselves that places violently deconstructed or destroyed – in wars, for example – represent a good starting point to examine changes of cultural and ethnic identity (Povrzanović 1997: 153–163).

The role of the destructive power of natural catastrophes, as demonstrated in the case of Skopje, can also serve as a starting point for the construction or deconstruction of certain identities; the difference being that human hatred "towards the other" – incorporated in the essence of a place destroyed during a war – is made relative by the inaccessibility of the powers of natural catastrophes. For these reasons, the destruction of places by natural catastrophe can be understood as an opportunity to implement certain purposeful and ideologically founded changes. The gravest consequence in both cases is the total disintegration of the relationship between people and things, i. e. places, and the emergence of complete chaos in the mental maps of the individuals. Let us remind ourselves that mental maps represent the transformation of individual spiritual and historical experiences into abstract ideas of a city (Hengartner 1999b). These abstract images of a city are the ones that survive, even after destruction, and that persist in time and space because they exist in the minds of the people and are therefore not as easily destructible as physical places. In this respect, we can agree with those who claim that even when the buildings and the infrastructure of a certain city have ceased to exist, they remain recorded in the memory of its citizens (Lindner 1997: 319–328). Thus, if we accept that the mental image of a city survives its physical destruction, it is logical to presume that the territorially determined psychological concept of nostalgia emerges at this exact moment. Mental images thus transform into nostalgic images – images of a city in which its citizens felt much more confident than in the new place that is emptied of meaning. In this manner, their nostalgia and memories enter the concept of collective memory, which conserves the mental images of the destroyed place.

The cross-section of the specific ideological, political and social elements intersecting in a specific space or connected with a specific place can define the methods of construction and functioning of the mental images and consequently, of the collective memory. Péter Niedermüller cites Paul Komerton in asserting that mental images are constructed by the use of the cultural and ritualised metaphors of memory and remembrance for the spaces, which subsequently emerge as places for the representation of the past (Niedermüller 1997: 113–123). This claim begs the question as to whether the destruction of places for the representation of the past causes the destruction of their mental images. As we have already mentioned above, it appears that the destruction of a place itself does not contribute towards the destruction of its mental images, although there is a great probability that these will eventually be obliterated following the disappearance of the people who posses those images of the place before its destruction. In this respect, these remembered places represent leading forms of recollection of specific historical processes, which in the current social space are encompassed by political meanings and social and cultural differentiation; that is, by the social memory that organises the past with respect to the future.

These places can be incorporated into the newly constructed history and imaginary past, but this social memory also affects the colonisation of the future with reference to the imaginarily constructed past. In other words, when a certain place has been deconstructed, it creates its own space in the social memory from which it constantly feeds the future. There is a great probability that this future will be tinted with the ideological and political colours of the tradition characterising the place before destruction. These perspectives are applicable in many of the countries in transition in Eastern Europe which, according to Niedermüller, turn to the past because of the great insecurity of either their present or their future (Niedermüller 1997).

These concepts of space can be articulated in another kind of "transition', which is not mental, but physical, and which refers to the implementation of theoretical premises of place and space onto a place destroyed as a result of natural catastrophe. We can cite the case of the central Square in Skopje as a good example of a place and space suitable for the analysis of the concept of ideology of space.

The Square

The main Square in Skopje, from the beginning of the 20th century up until 1963, was conceived in the traditional manner applied to the construction of main squares in the larger European cities. It was supposed to reflect a three-dimensional image of power: political, financial and cultural. This image of the main Square in Skopje before the earthquake consisted of three very significant anthropological places in which most of the public and cultural life of the citizens took place. These were the National Bank and the Army Hall on the right bank of the Vardar River and the Skopje Theatre on the left bank. The objects were connected by an old Ottoman bridge. Within this three-dimensional image of political and ideological power, the Square in this shape represented a symbol of the rule of the Kingdom of Yugoslavia (1918–1941): that is, a symbol of the cultural domination of the Serbs in the period stretching from the immediate aftermath of the Balkan Wars and the First World War up until the Second World War.[2] In this context, the Theatre, the Army Hall and the National Bank were symbols whose role was to demonstrate the power of that political influence. It could be concluded therefore, that the physical image of the main Square in Skopje before the earthquake was represented in the mental maps of its citizens with architectural symbols of power.

The intensity of the meaning and symbolism of the ideological space of Skopje Square was only increased after the Second World War when people started parading "en masse" in this space, to honour both the victory over fascism and the establishment of communist ideology within the framework of the newly created Yugoslav federation (1945–1991). Thus, Skopje Square further confirmed its purpose as a place for gatherings of the people, as a place for manifesting the power of the masses (military parades), and as a space for honouring and celebration (celebrations of the Day of Youth and Tito's birthday), but it also affirmed itself as a medium for the public instrumentalisation and ideologisation of the masses (celebrations of the jubilees and anniversaries of important events from the recent history of the Communist Party of Macedonia). All these images represent an establishment of socialist and communist content (celebrations of the masses) in a bourgeois setting (the surrounding architecture as a symbol); or, in other words, the space was ideologically reconstructed. In this context, the pre-earthquake contents of the space of the main Square in Skopje were in no major aspects different from the contents of the spaces of other great Eastern European squares, whether in Moscow, Bucharest, Sofia or Belgrade.

The dramatic changes that occurred in the physical space of the city of Skopje after the earthquake in 1963 – in its central area in particular – contributed to-

[2] From 1912 to 1941, Vardar Macedonia – the territory of today's Republic of Macedonia – was annexed to Serbia and subjected to Serbianisation policies, grounded in the assumption by Serb nationalists that the Slavic population of Macedonia was actually Serbian [note by the editors].

wards radical changes not only in the identity of the city but also in the cultural identity of its population. These changes were much more radical than the aforementioned ideological changes in the rest of the Eastern European cities, where the architecture remained unchanged and only the symbolism of their squares was gradually altered. Quite the opposite was the case in Skopje: the image that the citizens of Skopje had of their city, or their so-called mental maps, underwent drastic, almost catastrophic changes.

Anthropological (or socio-cultural) places – where citizens were connected with one general, politically and culturally delimited space – were partly or completely destroyed. The three objects that had served as an axis, around which the decade-long identity of the space of the main Square had been established, were razed to the ground. The physical destruction caused by the natural catastrophe emptied the meaning of the previously replete anthropological places as well as the previously replete physical spaces. Nothing was left in this space, and the area itself lost its meaning and representative quality. In his oft-quoted essay on building, Heidegger says that before a bridge is constructed, there is no place as such. Therefore, it seems fairly logical to conclude that there will be no place again if the bridge disappears. But this can only refer to the anthropological place as such, to the physical place, as it is actually defined in Heidegger's philosophical concept (Hajdeger 1982). As far as the structure of the space satiated with meanings is concerned, the emptied place does not mean no place at all. Thus, the physical destruction of the three key buildings on Skopje Square did not imply that they had stopped being places forever.

Emptied of meaning, symbols, anthropological places and substance, Skopje Square acquired a new representative image – that of emptiness. If the citizens of Skopje based their cultural and economic identity on the identity of this space, then it is logical to conclude that a major transformation must have occurred in their urban and cultural identity. Bearing in mind that squares typically symbolise historical power, the case of the Square in Skopje represents a case of radical change in symbolic impact. The earthquake happened when Macedonia adopted socialism as a social and political system and was ruled by socialist ideology in every sphere of life. The destruction of the former symbols on the Square was accordingly instrumentalised and used to ideological ends. Namely, the reconstruction of the new centre of Skopje was used as a place where emptiness was filled with utopias – classic socialist utopias, to be more precise. All this was necessary to minimise nostalgia in favour of a "better and more beautiful tomorrow".

The most prominent characteristic of the change was the welcomed, total and radical – albeit forced – break with the symbolic bearers of tradition: a break which created favourable conditions for the symbolic construction of a new socialist and communist tradition which would leave its mark on subsequent times. But in this instance, too, the newly established tradition did not depart from the narrow boundaries of ideology. However, new symbols as physical architectural objects were not erected on the Square on account of the new conviction that Skopje should become an internationalist city, which enabled a gradual symbolic intrusion of globalism. This approach still seemed possible, despite the odds.

2 The utopias and globalised spaces of Skopje

Utopias are unities with no attachment to real place, but which are still connected with a certain unreal space in society. Utopias can be understood as completely "irreal" (Michel Foucault). In both a cultural-anthropological and ethnological sense, utopia can be defined in the process of its correlation to place and space. Despite arguments which claim that place is, above all, a real dominant of space, utopia cannot be associated with a real place but more with a certain material and real space such as the city or the state. Let us remind ourselves of the great utopian writers such as Thomas More, Robert Owen and Charles Fourier, who dedicated much of their work to the utopian spaces in which entire "future states" were placed and thus served as one of the pillars for the future communist ideologies of a Marxist type which projected such an "invented world". In this respect, the inability of utopias to be related to a certain place contributed towards an unreal definition of their possibilities for realisation.

Thus, if spaces can be utopian, the creation of the new Skopje after the earthquake was – in the larger context – supposed to be one such utopian space. The utopian semantics integral to the idea of a new European city were of a dual character. On the one hand, this utopia was encouraged by the socialist ideology, whose aim was to build a city for the workers regardless of their ethnic or religious affiliation, while on the other hand the reconstruction of Skopje was to be a factor in the attempt at the globalisation of spaces. The first component represented an intervention of ideology in the emptied space:

> "Skopje has endured a terrible catastrophe, but the city will be rebuilt with help of the whole society; it will become a symbol of the brotherhood and unity of the Yugoslav and of world-wide solidarity" (Tito).

"Brotherhood and unity" based on socialist principles was the first ideological component which was to fill the utopian space. This was an ideological dimension of a primary category as demonstrated in the new War in the Balkans after the dissolution of Yugoslavia at the end of the 20th century. It is a different issue as to whether the individual constituents of this "brotherhood and unity" experienced specific spaces or specific places as their own and not as general ones – as individual and not collective (in the socialist sense). In fact, the aim of this ideologisation was to integrate the phrase into space, not to create a sense of belonging. Therefore, in the reconstruction of Skopje, the accent was placed mainly on the right bank of the Vardar River and on the Square. These areas of Skopje acquired a character symbolic of Christian ideology after the demise of the Ottoman Empire and thus, automatically, the Muslim population of the city could not identify with the creations of "brotherhood and unity" on the right bank of the river. The same was true in reverse. The Christian population could not distinguish its identity in the old part of the city called the "Turkish Bazaar". This certainly demonstrates that places and spaces hold their own specifics – such as oft-cited religious and social differentiations.

The second component of the reconstruction of Skopje entailed globalisation of the space. Teams from all over the world took part in this process. In this context, a new city suited to new, modern – perhaps post-modern – humans was to be conceived and realised. In this sense, the architects – and Kenzo Tange as the main architect in particular – saw the space of Skopje as a container for human living. Jerry Sheerin, one of the participants in the team designated to carry out the reconstruction of Skopje, describes the ideas and the methods which served as a basis for the erection of the new city as follows:

> "The design phase took some six months with a team of young architects, 30–35 years old, and graduate students, in all about 25 persons, plus a number of consultants. We carefully reviewed all previous such undertakings in an effort to find a unique solution that would respond to Skopje, and at the same time to present a special image for the city. In general, urban planners do not seek urban form, but only a distribution of horizontal spaces, but Tange's emphasis is on urban physical form as a container for human activity that reflects the nature of the environment and of the people who live there. The resulting City Wall, the City Gate, the urban walkway along the Vardar River, the administration centre and railroad station sought to create a highly identifiable urban form that was a continuation of the 6th century walled centre and the 19th century radial city form, all incorporated into a new main access road and a new linear city defined by the mountains to the north and south and the Vardar River."

We can see that the idea of the planners included spatial planning of physical places as containers of human activities and surroundings for the people that were going to live in this city. Ethnologists disagree with such ideas: "Space should be regarded not only as a physical space, not only as a container of specific life forms, but also as a complex and specific process of *cultural and social differentiation*" (Katschnig-Fasch 1999: 283). This discord between the researchers of urban forms and the researchers of urban contents is in fact one of the reasons why a space becomes utopian. But as Katschnig-Fasch says, "Sandwiched between the ruling and law-making structures of high modernism and the utopian project of the 'other' city life of post-modernism, a process of experimenting in building started in the 1970s and this experimentation required certain reforms of space" (Katschnig-Fasch 1999: 282).

In this context of a new utopian city, the main Square was never reconstructed with its previous characteristics (the three objects-places). It remained as an empty inter-space and existed as a non-place of the most faceless kind. This facelessness resembles Augés's concept of non-places, a situation where anthropological places have been dispersed and, in fact, people are left to act and exist completely by themselves with no reference to their shared history or similar experiences: each of them separately taking their discrete place in the plane or in the train. Augés says that if a place can be identified as relational, historical and connected with identity, then space which cannot be defined as such represents a non-place (Augés 1995: 77 f.).

It is questionable whether a typical place such as the Theatre, brimming with spatial meanings, can really stop existing in its quintessence and transform into a non-place. The answer is provided by the fact that a bus station was erected in its place on the left bank of the Vardar: a typical place without historical or cultural identity. The fact that the Theatre was not re-erected in its old place but was replaced by a bus station implies that an ideological process of total profanation of the previously ideologised holy cultural places was at work. In this respect, we can argue in favour of a fluctuation of place and space between the holy and the profane as demonstrated with historical examples by Mircea Eliade. The attitude of the people towards the anthropological places and structured spaces in the city resembles the attitude of people towards holy and religious places throughout history, starting with pre-history and the places where people realised their religious identity.

Dislocation, relocation, actualisation

The three important objects, the three important symbols of the power of pre-earthquake Skopje, as well as the power of the bygone ideology of the Kingdom of Yugoslavia, were never re-erected in their previous places on the Square. This is understandable because this concentrated symbolic power was to be relegated to history and be replaced by a different political and ideological one. Therefore, destroyed places were dislocated, relocated and re-actualised in a context of newly invented and utopian places.

The dislocation of the Theatre as a place for spending leisure-time and its relocation to a place about a hundred metres further down the left bank of the Vardar River was an attempt not only to remove the ideologically replete anthropological place and space, but also to fill the substitute place with an alternate meaning appropriate to the newly established political doctrine and power, as well as to the spirit of the post-modern era. Total effacement of the place of the Theatre was achieved by the construction of an inter-city and international bus station on the site. The choice was typical as being the most suitable for the deletion of memories of the previous ideology.

In a cultural sense, theatres represent spaces for the realisation of leisure-time on the one hand, but on the other they can also represent spaces with many and various characteristics – or, to put it more precisely, they are structured. Theatres in their essence are places where various different spaces are represented and these spaces are usually incomparable between themselves. According to Foucault, the theatre represents a microcosm reflecting a macrocosm. The theatre is a heterogeneous space where several different spaces meet. The new Theatre in Skopje at the location where it was built represents an example of a realised utopia. In other words, it was a place that was supposed to start creating new meanings so that people could forget those of the old place, which in the meantime had become a non-place. The new Theatre was thus not only relocated, but in its substance represented a realised utopia.

The National Bank was relocated several hundred metres further down the Vardar River, on the right bank, and in close proximity to the place where the envisaged Gate of Skopje was to be built as a part of the realised utopia. This relocation of financial power was certainly symbolic. In other words, it meant a transformation of the place itself, because the centre of financial power in socialist Yugoslavia did not reside in Macedonia as one of its constituent republics but in Belgrade as its capital. The dislocation of the Army Hall and its relocation deep within the City Wall, as well as its renaming as the Hall of the Yugoslav People's Army, is self-explanatory. A completely new Yugoslav military power had entered the scene.

These three dislocations, relocations and actualisations were to decisively disperse the concentrated symbols of power on the Square for two reasons: to erase their every trace and to indicate that power was now concentrated in the Yugoslav centre Belgrade. The Square remained a place for gatherings of the masses, but these masses could no longer identify with a familiar cultural space. With the dislocation, relocation and re-actualisation of the three "anthropological places", an attempt to draw new mental maps was made. This was a difficult task because the older generation of Skopje citizens, who still remembered old Skopje and had preserved their old mental maps in their minds, persisted in their nostalgic reminiscences and even applied pressure on public opinion for the restoration of those buildings that not only had a close connection to their youth, but also to their ideology.

In fact, their nostalgia was not focussed on the buildings as such, but more on the memories they evoked of their childhood and youth, of celebrations in honour of the socialist past, which had all taken place on the Square. This nostalgic image of communism still survives in the mental spiritual maps of the older generation of Skopje citizens.

Conclusion

Our analysis demonstrates that the places and spaces in the central city area of Skopje affected by the key event of the earthquake in 1963 can define space in all its ideological configuration. Space structured in this way revealed the new collective awareness of the older citizens of Skopje in the form of nostalgic memories of socialism, i. e., communism, and its urban symbols within the framework of a larger utopian definition of the contemporary space called Skopje.

In support of this claim, we can refer to the recent aspiration to restore the Theatre again in its old location that had been occupied by a bus station. The strength of this nostalgic image has been confirmed by the official endorsement of an architectural design for the construction of the old Theatre in its original place. The bus station has already been relocated. According to the blueprints, the architectural appearance of the future Theatre is almost identical to that of the old one from the beginning of the 20th century. This is a perfect example of an invented tradition as recognised by Eric Hobsbawm who, in the introduction to The Invention of Tradition, cites as English examples of this phenomenon the choice of the Gothic style in the reconstruction of the House of Parliament or the decision to restore everything as it was before the bombardments of the Second World War (Hobsbawm 2002: 6).

Tendencies to reconnect with traditions of both older rural and urban types only emerged in Skopje after the establishment of the independent Macedonian state in 1991. This is entirely understandable after the radical rupture with tradition of the preceding fifty years. In other words, these tendencies towards the invention of a tradition emerged as a result of the total break with all previous traditions after the Second World War in the name of the totally new "socialist and communist tradition". This inventing of traditions intersects with nostalgic places only in the minds of the people who lived through the historic phase of the "former regime". The younger population – who has only known the modern cultural places bearing the new identity of the city, and is therefore free from nostalgic images of pre-1963 Skopje, except those gleaned from books about the old city – is better adapted to this situation and does not long for a return to the old. This reaction, all things considered, is to be expected. The younger generations do not suffer from nostalgia for the old buildings and accept the city as it stands. If anyone belonging to the younger population supports the restoration of the old Theatre – attracted by the grandiose European architectonic style – then their support is initiated more by their longing for a better future in which they envisage Macedonia as a part of the European Union.

Consequently, we can say that both nostalgia and utopia are fairly significant features of urban living in Skopje. Present mainly in the mental maps of the older population, they represent nostalgic and utopian annexes to the transformations brought about by our contemporary way of life.

Translated from the Macedonian by Matthew and Maria Jones

References

Augés, Marc 1995: Non-Places: Introduction to an Anthropology of Supermodernity, transl. John Howe. London, New York: Verso.

Filipović, Milenko 1939: Običaji i verovanja u Skopskoj kotlini [Customs and beliefs in the Skopje Basin]. In: Srpski etnografski zbornik LIV (= Život i običaji narodni, vol. 24).

Hadži-Vasiljević, Jovan 1930: Skopje i njegova Okolina: Istorijska, etnografska i kulturno-politička izlaganja [Skopje and its surroundings: historical, ethnographic and cultural-political treatises]. Belgrade.

Hajdeger, Martin 1982: Mišljenje i pevanje [Heidegger, Martin: Bauen, Wohnen, Denken. Pfullingen 1967]. Belgrade: Nolit.

Hengartner, Thomas 1999a: Forschungsfeld Stadt: Zur Geschichte der Volkskundlichen Erforschung städtischer Lebensformen. Berlin: Reimer.

Hengartner, Thomas 1999b: Zur Wahrnehmung städtischer Umwelt. In: Olaf Bockhorn, Gunter Dimt, Edith Hörandner (eds.), Urbane Welten. Vienna: Verein für Volkskunde, 9–43.

Hobsbawm, Eric 2002: Uvod: Kako se tradicije izmisljaju [Introduction: How traditions are invented]. In: idem, Terence Ranger (eds.), Izmisljanje tradicije [Invented traditions]. Belgrade: Čigoja štampa, Knjižara Krug (= Biblioteka XX vek).

Katschnig-Fasch, Elisabeth 1999: Im Wirbel städtischer Raumzeit. In: Olaf Bockhorn et al. (eds.), Urbane Welten. Vienna: Verein für Volkskunde, 279–297.

Kaćeva, Alla, Slavica Hristova, Tatjana Gjorgjovska 2002: Životot vo Skopje, 1918–1941 [Life in Skopje from 1918–1941]. Skopje: Muzej na grad Skopje.

Lape, Ljuben 1991: Makedonija vo XVIII, XIX i XX vek. Odbrani trudove [Macedonia in the 18th, 19th and 20th centuries. Selected works]. Skopje: Kultura.

Lefèbvre, Henri 1991: The Production of Space. Cambridge, Mass.: Blackwell.

Lindner, Rolf 1997: Perspektiven der Stadtethnologie. In: Historische Anthropologie 5, 2: 319–328.

Macedonian Folklore 1991: Rural-Urban Relations in the Folklore of Balkan Peoples. In: Macedonian Folklore 24/47: 27–169.

Niedermüller, Péter 1997: Politik, Kultur und Vergangenheit. Nationale Symbole und politischer Wandel in Osteuropa. In: Rolf W. Brednich, Heinz Schmitt (eds.), Symbole. Zur Bedeutung der Zeichen in der Kultur. Münster: Waxmann, 113–123.

Povrzanović, Maja 1997: Identities in War: Embodiments of Violence and Place of Belonging. In: Ethnologia Europea 27, 2: 153–163.

Rolshoven, Johanna 2003: Von der Kulturraum- zur Raumkulturforschung. Theoretische Herausforderungen an eine Kultur- und Sozialwissenschaft des Alltags. In: Zeitschrift für Volkskunde 99: 189–214.

Abstract

The places and spaces in the central city area of Skopje affected by the key event of the earthquake in 1963 can define space in all its ideological configuration. Space structured in this way reveals the new collective awareness of the older citizens of Skopje in the form of nostalgic memories of socialism, i. e. communism, and its urban symbols within the framework of a larger utopian definition of the contemporary space called Skopje. Consequently, we can say that both nostalgia and utopia are a fairly significant characteristic of urban living in Skopje. Present in the mental maps mostly of the older population, they represent nostalgic and utopian annexes to the transformations brought about by our contemporary way of life.

Socialist Humanism on Tour: Monuments, Public Spaces and Subjectivity in Haskovo, Bulgaria

Cristofer Scarboro, Urbana

The socialist humanist system, a period of late socialism from the mid 1960s to 1981, invested tremendous resources in directing the movement of its population, at least in part, to transform it subjectively. This article, part of a larger project on the creation and negotiation of socialist humanism in Haskovski okrăg (district of Haskovo) in southeastern Bulgaria, focuses on the narrative of the remade socialist city of Haskovo, written by Haskovians through small daily acts of proximate tourism: trips from home to work, walks in the park, or lunches eaten on monumental steps. The socialist humanist period, read through its urban monuments in Haskovo, was a period when the meanings of socialism were being re-written. The proximate tourist in the early socialist period walked with martyrs, murderers and victims of torture, graphically frozen in their moments of heroic anguish. Later tourists communed with resting granite workers, children chasing hoops and basketball players. Socialist humanism was about the establishment of small-scale private pleasure and personal meaning – heroism replaced by whimsy.

I use the term proximate tourism to convey a sense of the sacred movement and the importance of signs that are central to the tourist act – a sacredness that the city planners sought to bring from the mountains and historical sites into the daily lives of the people. While most tourism focuses on the authentic, singular and unusual – *the* Leaning Tower, the *highest* waterfall, *the* site of Botev's landing – Bulgarian socialist humanist tourism was essentially about making the spectacular a mundane experience (or, if you prefer, the mundane spectacular): extending the sacred into the everyday. Work sites became places of pilgrimage, trips to the mountains were to be understood as ordinary. Proximate tourism is emblematic of this distinction; socialist humanists were to experience touristic sacredness and witness the transformation of the space around them and themselves in the daily minutia of their lives. Boundaries of work and leisure, normal and extraordinary, were permeable under proximate tourism and limned by the larger socialist humanist project of subject creation.

Socialist tourism, as all tourism, was centrally a project for re-ordering space and people's relationship to it. Through tourism, newly socialist Bulgarians were encouraged by the state to commune with nature, to grow to love the land and its beauty, apprehend the accomplishments of socialism (which had created new opportunities for leisure and rural escape, though not an interest in organized tourism, which has a history in Bulgaria dating to the 19th century), and to grow into strong healthy bodies. Most importantly, they were to commune with newly formed ideas of sacredness, to understand the meaning of Bulgarian history and its relation to the socialist revolution and their place in it.

These notions were neither fixed nor static and transformed dramatically during the socialist humanist years. During this time tourism became paradoxically both an extraordinary and an everyday experience; the socialist sacred became accessible on trips to the mountains and to the grocery store. Socialist humanists took control of their tourist spaces and experiences and brought the idiosyncratic with them. Socialist understandings of the sacred also radically shifted: notions of work and suffering were replaced by leisure and frivolity, communal purpose by individual introspection and whimsy. Thus socialist humanist tourism was shaped as much by the understandings and expectations of the would-be socialist humanists as it shaped these understandings itself; as an investigation of the socialist humanist sacred, excursions physical and otherwise were spaces of contested meaning.

As Bulgaria became an increasingly urban country during the socialist years, proximate tourism came to be understood as a primarily urban phenomenon. Socialist planners sought to incorporate the sacred in the daily lives of the population and as Haskovo was remade during the 1960s and 1970s to accommodate the tremendous growth in urban population of the period, city planners sought to remodel the city to create a new type of urban socialist subject. Monuments played an important role in the planners' attempt to create this socialist orientation. By way of example, Reuben Fowkes, in his essay "The Role of Monumental Sculpture in the Construction of Socialist Space in Stalinist Hungary" (2002), understands public sculpture in Hungary as a process for educating Hungarian citizenry in the proper, that is, socialist understanding of history. Monuments were destroyed to erase signs of a retrograde past, new ones were erected to speak of a more glorious communist past and the progressive march of history towards communism and the stability and strength of the established political order. Monuments marked space in time and were erected to transform the people's understanding of both space and time. While walking around Budapest the pedestrian was, from the perspective of those who erected the monuments, to engage in a certain narrative understanding of the city, of its place in time and of a specific direction into the future.

Centrally organized proximate tourism was, of course, open to interpretation and contestation: the intentions of the regimes in erecting monuments were always mitigated and transformed by the visions and understandings of the would-be socialist flâneurs. The past was never completely erased; the transformation contingent upon its reception open to irony as well as to belief.

Linkages between space and subjectivity are, of course, not unique to socialism but are, rather, part of a larger modernist phenomenon. In his "Seeing Like a

State" (1998), James C. Scott speaks of the modernist city as a utopian project in which scientific housing and rational city planning were, from the perspective of the city planners, to discipline the crooked, disordered, non-modern city and the attendant slums of growing urban areas. These high modernist cities were to result in a symphony of right angles; easily readable from any perspective, where high-rise geometric buildings provide well constructed, sanitary, standardized housing – a city divided into districts and purpose. These intended high modernist cities were conceived as the imposition of the rational, in the belief that they would result in a new "modern" or "high modern" subject: as such they were to be a definitive break with the past. The requirements of the citizenry (carefully thought out by the central planners) were to be met in a "machine for living", as Le Corbusier famously called his cities – in carefully arranged grids of green space, working space, and living space – creating an ordered space in which people could behave rationally. The form of the city was to result in the correct function of the subject.

None of this will seem novel to students of socialist cities. Much recent scholarship has been devoted to the question of "socialist space" as an arena for negotiations of subjectivity. The socialist landscape has been seen as both an agent and an avenue for the creation of a socialist subjectivity and for its resistance and co-optation. Post-war Eastern Europe saw its landscape extensively remade under socialist rule, with the central intention of creating new socialist spaces to aid the creation of a new socialist subjectivity and as arenas in which this subjectivity could flourish. For Susan Crowley and David Reid (2002), the attempt to inscribe socialist meaning onto the ordinary makes socialist space unique – the transformation of ordinary spaces into "Great Spaces" transforms "a steel foundry into a 'forge of communism'; a housing commune into a microcosm for socialist order; and a children's after-school facility as a paradigm of the communist 'city of the future'" (Crowley, Reid 2002: 7–8).

Socialism was itself marked as a permanent and radical break from the past in part by its constant evocation of it. To be understood correctly from the perspective of the socialist planners, the landscape must be understood as firmly and inherently rooted in time – symbols and remnants of a decadent bourgeoisie or heroically resistant past, markers of a happy socialist present spent "building communism", or as harbingers of a shining communist future. Space was to be composed of a single unified narrative of time, in which the past, present and future were lived and felt simultaneously, through which one made sense of both the present and oneself.

Proximate tourism was a method for bringing the general "collapsing of time", and "communing with the sacred", affiliated with more traditional tourism, into the everyday world of would-be socialist subjects. People found their pedestrian apartment buildings transformed overnight into spaces of note and importance. Walking through their front door they were to be reminded that they followed in the footsteps and walked on the bones of martyrs. Lawyers entering the central courthouse on Georgi Dimitrov Boulevard were greeted by a plaque (affixed by their own union) dedicated to those jurists killed in the struggle against fascism.[1] Teachers and students at the Ivan Raikov Technikum were reminded of the sufferings of their forerunners in education, who were tortured to death by the previous regime.[2] Giant squares and statues dominated cities as well as tiny villages – old men sitting and chatting on benches were metaphorically joined with silent, granite interlocutors. Shopping in the market and drinking from the ubiquitous fountains *(češmi)* around the city, the socialist subject was surrounded with ghosts from the past and visions of the future.

During the summer of 1980, the Haskovo Regional History Museum catalogued every monument in the *okrăg* (district): archivists traveled to each site, photographed the monuments individually, transcribed their inscriptions, and noted both the effectiveness and condition of the monuments and their surroundings. This catalogue, created for internal use in the museum, provides both an interesting record of the monuments that once sat on the forest of empty plinths that now peoples post-socialist Haskovo, and also speaks of the negotiations and transformations that the socialist narrative wrote on the district through its monuments. At its heart, the catalogue is a map and evaluation of how well the monuments were performing their function in creating a lived historical space and proper socialist understanding of the regional past and its bearing on the present and future.

While Haskovo was far from an empty blueprint for socialist city planners, the city itself and its surroundings were extensively remade during the socialist period. The general post-war mass urbanization of Bulgaria was replicated in Haskovo itself, which almost doubled in size to a little less than 100000 people by 1980, and in the smaller towns of the region which all acquired block apartment housing *(panelki)* and some form of industrialization. Bulgarian city planners generally, with varying degrees of interest and success, sought to replicate the Soviet model for urban life on Bulgarian ground. This trend was most dramatically exemplified in Dimitrovgrad, "the city of youth", built by youth brigades on the site of three small villages along the Maritsa River as the first socialist city in Bulgaria. Throughout the region, streets and squares were renamed, monuments transformed, erected, and reinscribed to create a coherent and easily readable narrative of regional history within an appropriate socialist context.[3]

---

1 Haskovo, Marble Plaque, 1980 census "Haskovo: Monuments 19th Century to 1944", 52.

2 Ibid., 53.

3 Examples of physical destruction of pre-Revolutionary monuments were rare in the district – I encountered only one example in which a memorial to an unknown soldier in Derviška Mogila was destroyed in 1944 and the base of it left standing in the central square of the village between the village school and city hall to be recorded by the survey in 1980. Upon

Two periods of extensive monumental building frame the socialist period in Haskovski okrăg: the first lasting from the ascension of the Communist Party to political control in Bulgaria in 1944 until the early 1950s, and the second, longer period beginning in the mid-1960s and lasting until the celebrations for the 1300th anniversary of the Bulgarian state in 1981. The first set of monuments sought to explain the coming to power of the socialists as a story of purity and suffering against the forces of evil – of martyrdom in the face of terror. Death and torture were intended as the primary linkages in time between the would-be proximate tourist and the pre-socialist past – this central image of the sacred was the visceral emotive engine constructing the sense of simultaneous time. Execution spots were written into the landscape, marking these temporal nodes geographically. Walking across the central Ninth of September Square in Haskovo one was informed:

In this building Todor Velev Željazkov, 23, from the village of Gavranovo, Haskovo district, was mercilessly tortured and killed by fascist forces on December 1, 1934. And on this very square on May 1' 1925, Želju Diakov Panaukov, 32, from Gorski Izvor, Haskovo district, and Vălčo Pavlov Apostolov, 39, from Jabălkovo, Haskovo district, were executed by firing squad.[4]

The connection between death and space was specific, precise and immediate.[5] Execution spots became places of note and villages erected marble plaques and monuments to provide the where to go with the awful when.

Place also served as a linkage between the heroic era and the socialist era in the realm of deeds. Every village and city in the district sought to publicize its linkages to the anti-fascist struggle, noting the birthplace of those martyrs to the struggle, houses where partisans hid from "fascist executioners", or places where secret meetings occurred. Every plaque and monument noted the birthplace of the

---

speaking with older villagers, the 1980 survey ascertained that it had previously been a concrete cross with an inscription but offered no information as to why it had been torn down and not replaced (Derviška Mogila, "Ruined monument", 1980 survey, "Svilengrad Obština", number 5). While not destroyed outright, the pre-socialist monuments featured more prominently on the list of those monuments in need of repair, reflecting both their age and a general lack of attention as well as a commitment to their preservation. More common was the re-inscription of the space of the monument to include mention of socialist heroes and deeds. Often villages saw their monument to their dead in the Balkan Wars and World War I amended to include those killed in the battle against fascism and capitalism. This re-inscription regularly took place by erecting a neighboring monument to those socialist heroes of the anti-fascist struggle. In some cases monuments were physically re-written to include mention of partisans and martyrs for the socialist cause.

4 Ibid., 18.

5 Typical of this search for specificity is a plaque affixed to a central Haskovo building in honor of Končo Ivanov erected in 1952. It reads: "On the second floor of this building the fascist executioners captured and killed the selfless antifascist Končo Georgi Ivanov, 27 years old, from Haskovo" (ibid., 43).

hero as well as the place of his or her demise. Villages were often accorded their own martyrs and saints, often in conflict with one another much as medieval churches were over ownership of relics. Nikola Arnaudov, for example, was claimed both as a martyred citizen of Nikolovo and the neighboring villages of Bălgarovo and Široka Poljana. In all, five monuments to the young communist, "killed by fascists" in 1935, were erected in the district between 1953 and 1978, each claiming the hero as its own. It appears that there were some hard feelings: in 1965 the village council of Nikolovo placed a monument to Arnaudov "on the outskirts of Bălgarovo" on the road entering the town from Nikolovo identifying Arnaudov as "a son of Nikolovo".[6] The village of Izvorovo, apparently with no domestic partisans in whose honor to erect a monument, placed a marker at the entrance of the city hall stating only: "this town hid partisans 1934–35".[7]

Death and eternity were, however, the primary evocative narrative device used in the early monuments linking the past to the present in the mind of the idealized flâneur. The youth of those martyred was always mentioned, and the monument builders in the district paid special attention to members of the Young Communist League killed in "uneven" or unequal struggles with the forces of fascism. In their death, they were to be examples to those that followed them.[8] A tablet on the

---

[6] The monument outside Bălgarovo was commissioned in 1974 and completed in 1978 at the cost of 7000 leva and is much larger than any of the other plaques. Bălgarovo/Nikolovo free standing marble monument, 1980 census, "Haskovo Obština", 64; The Monument in Bălgarovo consists of a plaque on the house of Dimo Stalev Kirov where Arnaudov hid – he is identified as being from Bălgarovo. Bălgarovo, marble plaque, 1980 census, "Haskovo Obština", 14; Široka Poljana's monument was erected in 1975 on the 40th anniversary of Arnaudov's death where he is identified as being from the region of Široka Poljana. The monument did not meet the standards for cleanliness by the inspectors who noted that it "had not been cleaned for some time" and "was missing some letters". Široka Poljana, free-standing granite monument, 1980 census, "Haskovo Obština", 85; Nikolovo's monuments include a bust of Arnaudov in the village school explaining that he was killed in a shoot out with police and a monument in the central square of the village in honor of two young communists killed on September 2, 1935 including Arnaudov from Nikolovo, and Ljubo K. Penkov from Harmanli. Nikolovo, cast bronze bust and free standing marble monument, 1980 census, "Haskovo Obština", 63 and 65.

[7] Izvorovo, marble plaque, 1980 census, "Harmanli Obština", 20. Izvorovo was involved in a spat of its own with the village of Čerepovo over the Soviet pilot Ivan Andreevič Galjaškin who crashed and died on December 21, 1944. Two monuments were erected, one on the "exact spot where he perished" in Izvorovo and another in the competing villages. Izvorovo, free standing marble monument, 1980 census, "Harmanli Obština", 19 and Čerepovo, free standing monument, 1980 census, "Harmanli Obština", 32.

[8] The example of the young communist in the early monuments often tended to the melodramatic: "Like an eagle shot in the thunderstorm of battle a dear victim fell. Here was born and raised the brave fighter for freedom Ljubo Kirilov 1911–1934. After many days of illegal life filled with battle and brave deeds the young hero was shot by the fascist police."

house of Dimo Stalev Kirov in honor of the young Communist martyr Todorka Paunova stands as an example:

> "In this village house Todorka Paunova was born and spent her childhood in the service of red labor. Thus she and the people grew close together. Here is the birthplace of Todorka Paunova 1925–1943. She fell, not even 18, in the uneven struggle for national freedom near the city of Haskovo. Her name is a flag that marks the path of Communism."[9]

Death and stoicism were, however, the primary accomplishments of those memorialized. The deeds related in stone were birth (linking them to place), membership in some form of party organization, a generic fight or battle with police and then their own destruction in a specified location (again linking them to place).

Death accompanied every accomplishment memorialized on the streets of the district; in many cases it was *the* accomplishment. The village of Garvanovo made this clear in its memorialization of Todor Velev. A marble plaque on his house read: "In this house Todor Velev the wonderful *komsomolec* and student mathematician was born and raised. His thirst for knowledge and battle for the happy life of the working people was cut short by fascist murderers. All through his terrible inquisition he stayed true with all his soul to the great idea of Communism."[10] His accomplishments boiled down to the single purpose of steadfast loyalty and suffering for ideals. Death stalked even those whose accomplishments were more national than socialist. A monument erected on Vasil Levski Boulevard noted the spot where "on January 18, 1878, Russian soldiers were greeted by citizens of the city"[11], during the Russo-Turkish war that resulted in the creation of the first modern Bulgarian state. A plaque on the front of the store "Dimat" on the corner of Vasil Levski and 13th of March Street less than a block from the first monument provided the counterpoint: "Here on January 19, 1878, one of the first Russian Soldiers to enter the city was killed by Turkish Bašibazuci."[12] Death could reach from beyond the seemingly impregnable demarcation of *Deveti Septemvri* – the moment of rhetorical socialist transfiguration – as a monument in Ljubenovo made

[9] Haskovo, marble plaque, 1980 census "Haskovo Obština Monuments: Bălgarovo", 16. This house was also one of the earliest examples of attempts by private citizens to create monuments in the district. The house belonged to Paunova and was purchased by her cousin Dimo Stalev Kirov who sought to turn it into a monument to her. The tablet was attached to the house by the mayoralty in 1958.

[10] Haskovo, marble plaque, 1980 census, "Haskovo Obština Monuments: Garvanovo", 21.

[11] Haskovo, marble free-standing monument, 1980 census, "Haskovo: Monuments 19th Century", 10.

[12] Haskovo, marble plaque, 1980 census, "Haskovo: Monuments 19th Century", 11.

clear, claiming Bonju Ivanov Stoikov had died in 1947 in his native village from the "inhuman treatment suffered in a fascist concentration camp"[13].

Death recounted in the monuments of the 1950s was always presented in much more graphic detail than it was in later monuments – the malevolence of the "fascist executioners" or the "hunting dogs of the Cankov forces" demonstrated in the horrible nature of their actions a strong contrast to the stoic silent suffering of the communist heroes.[14] In the narrative of the early monuments, death was public:[15] entire families were killed by police burning down houses,[16] young Communists were beheaded,[17] police were murderers, and bodies were mutilated before their dispatch. Through the work of the monuments, death and its horrors was to remain public and immediate. Typical of the gruesomeness were the twin memorials to Gospodin Atanasov Šopov, Ljuben Delčev Patalov and Angel Dimitriev Petev erected by the District People's Council in 1953. The memorial plaques affixed to the entrance of the central *čitališe* (House of Culture) off the Ninth of September Square, and to the main children's policlinic on the corner of Georgi Dimitrov and Tolbuhin streets are graphic in their scenes of destruction. The narrative of both plaques is identical except for names and ages:

> "After a prolonged and terrible inquisition in which his bones were broken, parts of his body cut off, and his flesh and hair burned with gasoline, the bloody fascist executioners killed Gospodin Atanasov Šopov on August 24,

---

[13] Ljubenovo, marble plaque, 1980 census, "Haskovo Obština", 53.

[14] Invariably the deaths of Communist revolutionaries were attributed to fascist executioners. The Cankov hunting dogs are mentioned in the free-standing marble monument to Danjo Vasilev killed in a field just outside of the city in 1923. It reads: "Here on October 3, 1923 the hunting dogs of the Cankov forces killed the shining member of the Starazagora Uprising, Danjo Vasilev, from the village of Jastrebovo. Glory to the heroes". Svilengrad, marble plaque, 1980 census, "Svilengrad", 10.

[15] The public nature of the Communists' deaths under the pre-socialist authorities was often stated directly on the monuments. "Todor Vălčev Todorov leader of the Agrarian Youth Union and the regional Agrarian Union. A loyal single fronter, society man and supporter of the čitalište. Publicly killed by regional Cankovites October 27, 1927. Dălgičevo, marble plaque, 1980 census, "Dimitrovgrad", 10.

[16] In the village of Stojkovo a marble plaque speaks to this destruction. "On June 25, 1925, the bloodthirsty Cankov forces annihilated a whole family in the village of Stojkovo. After setting fire to the house the forces arbitrarily and cruelly killed Georgi Vălčev Gogov, 55 and his sons Dimităr, 27, Savo, 25, and Konstantin, 19, as supporters of the Hristo Botev Četa. Haskovo, marble plaque, 1980 census, "Haskovo Obština Monuments: Stoikovo", 74.

[17] "On this spot sat the house where Kosta Todorov Markov 1920–1944 was born. Member of the RMS Haskovo. Member of an illegal fighting organization. Cruelly killed and beheaded by fascist forces." Haskovo, marble plaque, 1980 census, "Haskovo Obština Monuments: Vojvodovo", 12.

> 1934 in the flowering of his youth at 22 years old. A fighter for national freedom"[18].

The explicit account of the three young communists' end proved too much for the sensitivities of the census takers three decades later who left the accounts of bodily torture on the second account marked by ellipses.[19]

Even while death was certain and graphically terrifying, by their very memorialization the heroes became part of the eternal landscape, active participants in the synchronicity of past, present and future. For all the corporal drama of the early monuments, the memorials themselves were remarkably free from notions of death as the end and the dissipation of the body were elided by socialist memorials. Graves did not factor into designs for memorials; the census noted only two instances where graves were included as monuments, both erected by private citizens and one self-consciously constructed as a memorial to the "undying" or "eternal" *(bezsmărten)*.[20] "Those who fall for freedom do not perish" was a common refrain closing the narrative of the monument. The most famous socialist memorial in Bulgaria, the mausoleum of Georgi Dimitrov, included a corpse, though one carefully mummified and preserved, thus speaking both to death and to an earthly, banal eternity as a marker of and agent in the transformation of socialist Bulgaria and its subjects.

During the mid-1960s, the monuments first began utilizing the active present tense. While they still sought to speak of the transformative project of socialism, to scenes of daily life, and of love, a shift to abstraction began to move among the monuments to fallen socialist heroes. Monuments like the one to Stoil Kosovski, a border guard passively "killed in the line of duty by enemies of the nation in 1952", erected by the border guard station in Vălče Pole in 1953,[21] were joined by more active present manifestations of border guard activity – a monument to border guards erected in 1972 in the center of Ljubimec is described in the census as consisting of: "Five border guards being led by a pioneer advance from the left and right towards the border with the intruder guns and dogs at the ready."[22]

---

[18] Haskovo, marble plaque, 1980 census, "Haskovo: Monuments 19th Century to 1944", 24.

[19] Haskovo, marble plaque, 1980 census, "Haskovo: Monuments 19th Century to 1944", 25. This is the only account of all the monuments where words were not written down in their entirety.

[20] The only crossing of monuments with graves in the Haskovo district were the grave of Dimităr Dulev Georgiev, erected in either 1947 or 1948 in Mladinovo and a marble free-standing monument to Captain Dimităr Nikolov Trifonov who died of wounds received in the Great Fatherland War in a Sofia hospital found in "the garden of the eternal" *(bezsmărtnite)* in Momkovo. Trifonov's grave-monument was erected by his two brothers and mother in 1968. Mladinovo, free-standing monument, census 1980, "Svilengrad Obština", 18, and Momkovo, free-standing monument, census 1980, "Svilengrad Obština", 22.

[21] Vălče Pole, marble plaque, 1980 census, "Ljubimec Obština", 7.

[22] Ljubimec, free standing marble monument, 1980 census, "Ljubimec", 10. The Haskovo

The creation of monuments of the active present tense was an innovation of the mid 1960s – previously the heroes of socialism were narrated as passive victims of torture, death and repression, generally represented narratively in the form of plaques – when presented in sculptures it was only in the form of life-size cast busts; heads without bodies, incapable of motion, icons of communism. By the 1960s those border guards killed in action were now represented as gigantic statues in heroic poses, guns at the ready gazing determinedly across the horizon to some ill-fated enemies of the nation.

This transformation is perhaps best exemplified by the erection of a monument to the three young communists Todorka Paunova, Ivan Rajkov and Kănčo Ivanov killed in the battle against fascists in 1943. Monuments to the three Communist Youth League members had been abundant in the district – Paunova and Ivanov each had three individual monuments, while Rajkov had two – before the construction of a larger shared monument in 1973. This monument replaced the earlier busts and narrative description of the Communist Youth League members – as direct objects killed and tortured by cruel inhuman enemies of humanity – with a representation of the heroes as subjects in action: a monumental sculpture of the three of them together rushing against their enemies. The size of the monument connotes both the power of the insurgents' movements (and the movement itself) and the power of the current system in memorializing them. The figures in the monument face certain death; indeed, the monument is entitled the "Destruction of the Three Young Communists". The figures themselves, however, are doing all they can to bring destruction to their enemies – Paunova leads her two comrades forward behind a presumably red banner held aloft in her hands; to her right Rajkov readies a grenade to hurl at his would-be executioners, while on her left Ivanov points a pistol at imaginary figures in the distance. This action is made more dramatic by the sheer monumentality of the figures; each is over seven meters tall – they dominate the setting in front of the Economic Technikum on Petăr Beron Street.[23] The monumentality of the sculptures spoke not only of the power and permanence of the socialist system but also removed their subjects from

---

district bordering both Greece and Turkey was well protected by stone border guards – there were no fewer than thirteen monuments to border guards in the district according to the 1980 census, six in the village of Vălče Pole alone. Of these memorials eight were busts and plaques erected in the 1950s and dedicated to border guards killed in action; five were erected in the 1960s and 1970s, of these three were to nameless border guards killed in action and two were statutes of Asen Iliev killed in action (in Vălče Pole) and the Soviet border guard Mihail Kozlov (in Kapitan Andreevo). See Vălče Pole, 1980 census, "Ljubimec Obština", 7–12; Ljubimec, 1980 census, "Ljubimec", 9–11; Svilengrad, 1980 census, "Svilengrad", 32; Kapitan Adreevo, 1980 census, "Svilengrad Obština", 8–9; and Generalovo, 1980 census, "Svilengrad Obština", 2.

[23] Haskovo, sculpture: "Gibelta na 3-ta remsisti", 1980 census, "Haskovo Monumental Decorative Monuments", 23.

human scale and distanced them from place (the Technikum as a setting, for example, had no relation to any of the three young communists killed). The past became in the monuments of the 1960s and 1970s less concerned with "past as disjuncture" – the motif of the 1950s; suffering in order to create an immediate break with a tormented past – but rather wrote monuments in which the heroic traditions of the communist past, covering the whole land, invited those of the present to follow them in building the future of communism. Frail human-sized busts gave way to strapping granite statues.

During the socialist humanist period, the subjects of monuments became not only active and oversized, but were also increasingly nameless and engaged in the prosaic activities of daily life under idealized socialism – a new and novel type of socialist humanist sacred. By leaving the subjects nameless and rooted firmly in the active present, the monuments invited the proximate tourist to participate vicariously in the activity – the statues became forms to be inhabited by those passing them. The temporal emphasis shifted to the present activities of those who passed the monuments on the street as the heroic past became a more distant and mythic arena.

Monuments to pioneers spoke to the activities of the members who are shown marching with flags, blowing trumpets, planting trees and reading books.[24] Statues of basketball, soccer players, and wrestlers waited outside sporting arenas, a statue of a village woman carrying water strode across a central square.[25] Rather than named and understood heroes, these were monuments to ordinary people engaged in everyday activities. These scenes of the commonplace in motion are perhaps best exemplified by a series of statues commissioned by the District People's Council under the rubric "Childhood theme" *(detska tematika)*. These monuments peopled the city of Haskovo with statues of children engaged in the activities of childhood. Those conducting the census tied the statues rather obliquely to the language of socialism – a statue entitled "Motherhood" consisting of a mother helping her child with its first steps is understood as a metaphor for socialist progress: "a mother sits in a low chair and is gently pushing her child on its first

---

[24] Haskovo, sculpture: "From the Life of the Pioneers", Evdokija Baldžieva sculptor, 1980 census, "Haskovo Monumental Decorative Monuments", 20.

[25] Haskovo, "Basketbolist", cast bronze statue, Veličko Menikov sculptor, 1980 census, "Haskovo Monumental Decorative Monuments", 19; Haskovo, "Futbolist", cast bronze statue, Veličko Menikov sculptor, "Haskovo Monumental Decorative Monuments", 18; Haskovo, "Borci" cast bronze statue, Professor Atanas Dalčev sculptor, 1980 census, "Haskovo Monumental Decorative Monuments", 17; "Selenka s kana", 1980 census, "Haskovo Monumental Decorative Monuments", 20. The village woman with pitcher further seems to reflect the idea of the "idiocy of rural life". It is recorded in the census thus: "This small sculpture features a village woman carrying a pitcher of water. The theme is that of village life. The expression of the figure is gloomy and the treatment of the form is amateur."

steps, who despite its unsteady gait, stretches its hands and head forward and steps boldly ahead".[26] A sculpture of two children with wheels is praised for its activity: "What is most pleasing about this sculpture is that it is in motion. It is dynamic. Both figures are rendered very well. One gets from both the theme – the association – with movement, with kinetic energy."[27] Childhood delight, the general theme of the series, is directly equated with the subject of motion – a symbol of socialism writ large. A statue of a girl on roller skates becomes a "symbol of childhood happiness. A girl plays on roller skates. The figure is in motion."[28] Motion in early socialism was a metaphor for the development of socialism, for sacrifice and hard work. Moving figures in the later monuments are in motion for no other purpose than the sheer personal pleasure of being in motion: individual pleasure, whose purpose resided in the personal, increasingly came to dominate the monuments.

These sculptures of the quotidian are also notable for their stillness and notions of the previously unimportant features of lived communism, of rest, contemplation, pleasure and pain among the advancement of the socialist state. Plaques moved to less dramatic events of the past: a movie theater in the city of Marica erected a monument noting Georgi Dimitrov's patronage of Bulgarian cinema;[29] a train station in Meričleri informed the reader that: "Here on August 9· 1944, the Partisan group led by Conju Ganev captured a typewriter for the use of the group."[30] Under a series of statues erected on the theme of work, Zlati Denčev composed a sculpture of a young "working woman taking a break from her work. She sits in long clothes with a kerchief on her head. To her left rests a hoe."[31] The working theme is conspicuous by its absence as the worker sits in quiet contemplation relaxing in the shade of a tree. The statues of the socialist humanist period often wait outside of time. Children sit and wait in a sculpture erected in front of the puppet theater. Two abstract figures of a man and woman twine into one in

---

[26] Haskovo, sculpture from the series "Childhood Theme", "Majčinstvo", 1980 census, "Haskovo Monumental Decorative Monuments", 21.

[27] Haskovo, sculpture from the series "Childhood Theme", "Deca s kolela", 1980 census, "Haskovo Monumental Decorative Monuments", 28.

[28] Haskovo, sculpture from the series "Childhood Theme", "Detska tematika", 1980 census, "Haskovo Monumental Decorative Monuments", 22. These monuments on the childhood theme could lead to some interesting creations. The village council of Konuš erected a well on the theme in 1967 which included the following figures: a stork, Mickey Mouse, Pinoccio (clearly modeled on the Disney film), a small mushroom, a small fish and a little boat. Haskovo, free standing monument, 1980 census, "Haskovo Obština Monuments: Konuš", 45.

[29] Maritsa, marble plaque, 1980 census, "Simeonovgrad", 21.

[30] Meričleri, marble plaque, 1980 census, "Dimitrovgrad", 13.

[31] Haskovo, sculpture from the series "Working Theme", "Žena", 1980 census, "Haskovo Monumental Decorative Monuments", 24.

"Embrace" *(pregrădka)*, oblivious to the passers by strolling on Car Osvoboditel in front of the city bath.

The figures themselves became less naturalistic and increasingly turned to abstract or abstracted forms to express the vision of the artist (and for a more idiosyncratic personalized connection between artist, work and audience). A monument such as Marica (representative of the eponymous river rather than product or producer of socialism, human or otherwise – and interestingly one of the few statues to survive in central Haskovo today) does not lend itself to shared interpretations.[32] Described in the census as a "horizontal figure of a woman representing the Maritsa River. She is wearing heavily pleated clothing which indicates the flowing water. The face of the woman is sculpted to resemble that of a woman underwater seen through the current and is formed by the sleeves of her clothing."[33] Even figurative monuments became highly stylized and particular. A statue of a violinist outside the House of Culture *(čitalište)* is barely recognizable as human (again this statue survives).[34] With their difficulty to untangle and enforce narratively, these monuments spoke to the individual in socialist humanism.

Importantly this also allowed for notable and, from the perspective of the city planners, broadly expressed idiosyncratic statements by sculptors on the ambivalence of the modern condition. Veždi Rašidov's sculpture "The Noise" *(Šumăt)* is perhaps the best example of this evolution. The census takers were struck by the sculpture, noting its high artistic qualities (the sculpture was purchased from Rašidov after it won note at a national exhibition of young sculptors in Sofia in 1979), and by its theme of deformation and pain. They describe it thus: "The sculpture is placed on three separate marble foundations. The composition is very compact. The figure is of a young man. His body is twisted in agony. The legs are pulled into the body and the head juts forward. The hands cover the head with their long fingers, the face is deformed from experiencing so much pain." Much as they were generally impressed with the quality of the sculpture, they were unnerved by its theme and treatment; they conclude: "The entire sculpture contrasts directly with the calmness of the area in which it is situated – the green grass of the square and the architecture surrounding it. This keeps one from fully appre-

[32] The monument's very difficulty to decipher is perhaps a reason for its survival. The sculpture sits outside the Haskovo History Museum (which conducted the census) in the central square of the city. I asked those working in the museum and people in the city about the monument. None knew the name of the sculpture or what it was to represent. Some complained that it had been placed near a much earlier Thracian monument and all thought it was ugly but it engendered none of the resentment that many other monuments brought forth.

[33] Haskovo, sculpture: "Marica", 1980 census, "Haskovo Monumental Decorative Monuments", 15.

[34] Haskovo, sculpture: "Violinist", 1980 census, "Haskovo Monumental Decorative Monuments", 16.

ciating the sculpture. We have yet to find the appropriate artistic space for the sculpture."[35]

This discomfort with the new, less traditionally socialist realist sculpture reflects a larger tension within the Bulgarian socialist humanist project. As work went the way of rest, the communal was replaced by the idiosyncratic, and meaning continually contested the socialist humanist system that was constantly in motion and increasingly disconcerting. Proximate tourism reflects this tension and the coming of leisure and the individual. The transformation in monumental narrative on the part of city planners reflects an important transformation in the manner in which the past was to be imagined by the tourists. The primary linkages to the past in earlier monuments – death, suffering and horror – increasingly gave way to more abstract representations of daily life under the successful socialist regime. Communism was built in the active rather than passive voice in the 1960s and 1970s. Torture gave way to monumental resistance and mothers who engaged with the past by picnicking at the feet of its heroes, saw those very actions turned into symbols of building a socialist humanist state.

References

Fowkes, Rueben 2002: The Role of Monumental Sculpture in the Construction of Socialist Space in Stalinist Hungary. In: Susan Reid and David Crowley (eds.), Socialist Spaces: Sites of Everyday Life in the Eastern Bloc. New York: Berg.

Reid, Susan, David Crowley (eds.) 2002: Socialist Spaces: Sites of Everyday Life in the Eastern Bloc. New York: Berg Publishers.

Scott, James C. 1998: Seeing Like a State: How Certain Schemes to Improve the Human Condition Have Failed. New Haven: Yale UP.

[35] Haskovo, sculpture: "The Noise", 1980 census, "Haskovo Monumental Decorative Monuments", 14.

Revealing the Historicity of Migrant Women: Moving from Mountain Areas to the Provincial Urban Centers of Greece. The case of Agrinio

Konstantina Bada, Ioannina

Introduction

During the last period of the 20th century, several historically defined factors such as globalization, the collapse of the social system in former socialist countries in South-East Europe, the emergence of nationalism, and other factors led to another strong flow of migration mainly towards countries in the southern part of Europe (Greece, Italy, Portugal), where people sought safety and a better way of life (Baldwin-Edwards 2002). The history of current types of migration demonstrates that the global economic transformation has formed a new division of labor (Psimmenos 1997: 367–377, Psimmenos 2001: 95–126). This is strongly determined by informal economic migration as well as informal work practices (King 2000: 3–18) and by a tendency towards feminization. The latter is limited to informal types of work like domestic assistants, private care for aged people, work in the entertainment business and the sex industry (Cambani 2000: 145–170, Psimmenos 2001: 109–111).

It is significant that the roads of migration are linked to the development of a new historiographic and anthropological discourse, which derives from the idea that migrants have gender, a particular ethnicity, and come from certain social classes. Therefore, they experience and comprehend migration differently, in both their departure from the place of origin and their life in the place of reception. Anthropology has already increased the degree of theoretical and empirical research devoted to the emersion of otherness and multiculturalism, integration strategies and practices, or the numerous and complex interconnections that exist between migration and the formation of migrants' communities, cultures and national identities in the countries of reception (Brettell 2000: 97–135, Vermeulen 2004: 175–194). A part of the cited anthropological research, as well as of historiography, investigates the phenomenon of migration and the process of integration through the scope of gender. In an attempt to trace the history of the changing types of male and female migration in time and place, contemporary research has refuted many of the existing stereotypes, in particular of women's inactivity, or the "male" nature of migration and mobility. In many cases it has been pointed out that female migrants are also subjects of action and carriers of social change

(Gabaccia 1989, Green 2004: 134–152, Anthias 2000; Markova, Sarris 1997, Chamberlain 1997: 87–108).

During the last decades, Greece has become a country of destination for an increasing number of migrants, especially women from Balkan countries, Eastern Europe, Africa and Asia (Linardos, Rulmon 1993; Psimmenos 1995, Iosifidis 1997: 26–50, Kasimati 1998, Vermeulen 2004: 178 f.). Greece is also a country with its own deep-rooted history of migration – both internal and external – which has been studied very thoroughly. Nevertheless, Greek migration studies did not focus on women until quite recently, missing an opportunity to understand the many faces of the migration process, including the crucial role that women play in it as active subjects (Ventoura 1993: 230–241, Psimmenos 2001: 95–126). If women were considered at all in anthropological studies, they appeared as passive followers of the initiating male migrant or as women who were waiting in the villages and were being responsible for the family, the household, the agriculture etc.

Therefore, it is necessary to break the historiographic and anthropological silence about women as migrants, in order to understand migration in Greece as a general process and to find out the similarities and differences across time and space, the continuities, and the intersections. In my opinion there is great historical depth to the Greek migration and immigration experience and, therefore, much to learn from this particular case, especially from the perspective of the impact of gender and of gender relations. I will turn my attention first to female rural-urban migration in Greece during the 1950–1970 period.

Female rural-urban migration in Greece

This essay will focus on rural-urban migration. More specifically, it is concentrated on the migration of rural women to the provincial urban center of Agrinio in the prefecture of Aetoloakarnania, western Greece. It will be an exploration of women's memories and their identities as former peasants who came to town, and as internal migrants. I also explore how they accommodated social changes in their life and how they responded to a series of situations and conditions they encountered (cf. Kotsamanis 1990: 97–126). I choose to approach this facet of migration for the following reasons. First of all, rural-urban migration has decisively contributed to the transformation of life in Greece. Therefore, it is necessary to broaden our understanding of the historical actors in this process. Secondly, I assume that the intrinsic characteristics of internal migration and urbanization in Greece (such as the massive urban concentration in Athens at the expense of provincial towns, the centralized state bureaucracy, the dependency on the economic and political forces of the national state and on the realignments of modern capitalism) constitute a recognizable and familiar pattern common to other countries of peripheral capitalism. Therefore we could use rural-urban migration as an analytic unit for the social and cultural study of societies of peripheral capitalism. In addition, my study complicates conventional wisdom, which considered rural-urban migration in Greece as synonymous with migration to Athens (Sutton 1983: 226). It is necessary to look also at the provincial urban environment. First of all, such studies would allow a comparative approach and deeper understanding of the phenomenon. Secondly, they could show that provincial centers have their own history and represent different responses to exogenous pressures. More specifically, I seek to shed light on the implications of local social and cultural history, putting into perspective the active historical subjects – women in this case – by investigating how social changes occurred and challenged their lives, how these changes corresponded to a series of situations and conditions these women encountered and how they integrated themselves under these new circumstances.

Anthropological research, also in Greece, of course many times expressed its interest for rural-urban migration[1] and for ensuing integration processes. This body of research has contributed to our knowledge of the strategies, the networks, the everyday life, the culture and the sentiments of the people who move into the cities (Sutton 1983: 225–252, Vermeulen 1983: 109–134, Damianakos 2002: 376–385). However, both these anthropological studies, along with historical research (cf. Chasiotis 1993, Glogg 2004: 23–62), portray men as the embodiment of labor mobility and of the search for more opportunities. Men were declared the solely active subject in the processes of migration from the village and search for work in urban centers. History itself and its sources, however, provide ample proof that women in Greece were part of all migration waves: beginning with women who, in the 19th century, arrived at the newly developed towns to become servants or workers; women who, at the turn of the century, crossed the Atlantic in order to find a job and, primarily, to get married; and more recently, women who, during the 1960s and 1970s, left their villages not only for urban centers but very often for Germany, Australia, Canada and other foreign destinations. According to evidence

[1] A period of rapid urbanization took place in the 1920s. It was caused by the settlement of Asia Minor refugees in Greece, and to a certain degree also by internal migrations. A first real wave of internal migration from the countryside to the urban centers was provoked by World War II and especially by the civil war. This phenomenon took massive dimensions during the period after the civil war. It is indicative that in 1928, 31 percent of the country's population lived in towns, in 1953, 38 percent and in 1971, 53 percent. Urban development after the war has been characterized on the one hand by a rapid population increase in the capital and the development of Saloniki, and on the other hand by the decline of provincial towns. Kayser calls this a process of synthesis (Athens) and disintegration (the provincial towns), which resulted in a changed national system (Kayser 1968, cf. Kayser, Pechoux, Sinignon 1976; Burgel 1976).

provided by the National Statistical Yearbook in 1971, the percentage of female migration towards urban centers and abroad had been about 34.3 percent in 1955, but had reached 46.6 percent by the mid-1960s (Petrinioti-Konsta 1981: 61).

In addition, those studies which referred to migrating women did not present them as actors in their own right but instead discussed their mobility and actions as the result of decisions and choices made by male migrants (a father or a husband), or from the family's point of view (Moustaka 1964, Lampiri, Dimaki 1965; Santis 1973; Allen 1973, Nikolaidou 1975: 54–64, Friedl 1976: 363–88, Dubisch 1977: 65–82, Sutton 1978: 135). Research neglected the gendered character of migration and did not focus on the changes migration might have brought to gender and family relations, to family structure and the division of labor. In fact, migrant women who, in the majority, became, in one or another way, part of the urban labor force and participants of urban activities, appeared only as supplements to men's economic activity: "Women's labour was widespread in Greece (...). That should not be attributed to the lack of the male working element but rather to a lack of society's prosperity ... The low daily income of man's work does not allow him to adequately provide for his family and fill the gaps of the family budget ..." (Zolotas 1964: 40).

The life history approach

The methods of anthropology for the study of migration involve eliciting data from individuals, including the collection of individual life stories. The particulars of the lives of the people allow anthropologists and oral historians to understand migration from the insider's perspective and to emphasize the multi-faceted nature of the migration process. Their works differ in the way of giving voice to the narrators and also in the extension to which the anthropologists introduce themselves collaboratively and analytically into the text (Herzfeld 1985). Nevertheless, all of them emphasize the story told from the active subject's point of view. They attempt to understand the narrator's life and its meaning to that person in the context of a wider history and culture (Ferrarotti 1980: 227–248, Langness, Frank 1985; Bertaux-Wianne 1979: 26–32, Okely, Callaway 1992; Brettell 2003: 24–25). The life history method enlightens the particular but also the general experience and allows us to approach personal experience as a shared and general one.

The narrative patterns of the individuals do not vary substantially. They are actually repeated self-representations and tend to create common stereotypes. This happens because people remember as members of the social group they come from (Halbwachs 1980, Rappaport 1990, Passerini 1998, Perks, Thomson 1998; Thomson 1999: 24–37). As Brettel also notes, "through individual stories we learn how the migration process is patterned and subjectively experienced. We also learn about how migration is part not only of an individual but also of a collective biography – something extremely important (...) Anthropologists, no matter what they study must be mindful of both the general and the particular" (Brettel 2003: 43–4).

The individual memory, therefore, identifies some common ground that reveals the social and cultural behavior of social groups. At the same time, it contains the individual's role in the historical process. In this context, the need to record and exploit an individual's memories becomes imperative, as the "eye witnesses" and ethnographic carriers who experienced the facts and gave them special meaning and interpretation, are reduced. More and more studies provide support to the idea that the dynamics of a social system cannot any longer be considered autonomous and independent of the way an individual acts, but are also shaped by the individual's reaction. E. P. Thompson notes that in this way women and men are now presented as subjects – not as autonomous subjects, or "free persons", but as individuals who experience the given conditions and relations of production, and then "process" this experience in the context of their consciousness and their culture, employing complicated and "almost autonomous" responses and finally, in their turn, "they intervene in their given role" (Thompson 1978: 356).

Motives and experiences of migration

This paper focuses on the life stories and testimonies of fifty migrant women who, between 1950 and 1970, left their villages in the mountains by themselves or as a family and settled in the town of Agrinio. Although the number of life stories is quite small it achieves its purpose to illustrate the context in which the individuals made their decisions and appeared as historical subjects. Most of the oral material comes from a collection of life stories from the research project: "On the cultural identity, collective memory and history of the Greek urban centers – the case of Agrinio."[2] The data from life stories has been complemented by other ethnographic data from my own fieldwork, and by written and published sources. The life narratives are used as a way of data gathering and as an analytical tool, which penetrates into the cultural practices, conceptions and social conditions. It also enlightens the way that historical subjects articulate and use memory, silence, cultural tradition and history for constructing their social and cultural identity (Benmayor, Skotnes 1994; Thompson 1999: 24–37).

[2] The research project, of which I was a principal investigator, was funded by the Greek Ministry for Culture and was conducted at Ioannina University in 2002–2003. The collected data of this project – a total of 200 interviews based on the life story method, and other ethnographic material – will be deposited at the Research Center of Local History and Culture of Aetoloakarnania.

The analysis of the life stories of migrant women in Agrinio allows me to argue that the integration of women in the history of migration leads to the assimilation process itself. This process includes the actions and presence of both men and women. It may be premature to argue that the history of internal migration in Greece brought about serious changes in gender ideology or in gender hierarchies. However, the oral data point to the fact that some changes in gender relations and roles definitely did occur. Increasingly more changes affected the family pattern (as it gradually became more egalitarian), kin relationships, the productive and reproductive roles of women, women's public activities and their role as wage earners.

Another seemingly obvious fact is that the experience of leaving the mountains and integrating into the new environment is different for men and women. Looking, for example, at the factors that motivate men and women to migrate, we can find similar – basically economic – motives but also many different motives between men and women. For women, a basic motive was to get married (so-called marriage migration). As Bertaux-Wiame noted, "while men move through the family network to find work, women move through job networks to find a family" (Bertaux-Wiame 1979: 29).

Another point is that women, as well as men, appear to have a noticeable sense of history in relation to the integration of the rural world into the wider society. Indeed, the analysis of their memories and life stories show that the peasants of Aetoloakarnania belong to that part of the peasant class that had not been favored by development and rural modernization, similar to what happened in other parts of Greece (Burgel 1986: 29–43, Kasimis-Papadopoulos 1999: 85–114, Damianakos 1999: 60 f.). They also depict a conscious will for adjustment to the new conditions, brought about by World War II, national agricultural policy and other factors, in order to survive outside the limits of their villages and to develop flexible methods and practices of integration into their new environment. Katina's life history (79 years old, inhabitant of Agrinio since 1962), for example, reveals her perception and historical interpretation of the way mountain peasants responded as individuals, as families and as a community to the process of integration into the wider society:

> "They were all leaving, so we left as well. What was left for us to do there anymore? With the few sheep we owned, was it possible to feed so many mouths? We, the girls, needed money in order to get married (you see, they were asking for money), the boys wanted to create families ... we were eight ... we had to muddle through somehow. You could ask me, of course, how it was done before ... Well, I think it was a bit better ... My family owned herds, there was enough land for pasture, it didn't cost much, later it was given for agriculture and gradually we reduced the herds. There were the emigrants, too ... my grandfather had gone to America, he lived there for

> years, but there were others left behind to support, so he was sending money. And when the emigrants were coming back, we had big feasts ... they were bringing goods. Then his brother left as well ... They managed ... Then, things changed ... The war, the rebel forces, we were losing all our land, we were doing worse day by day ... Even if you had ... cheese was almost for free, milk too, the money wasn't enough. Poverty, and we had many needs. So, everybody was leaving and so did we. And I had a desire, I wanted my children to go to school, to escape our fate."

From the women's point of view, the context of the migrating process takes various forms that are defined by age, social status, place and time. Certain patterns persisted in Greece into the post-World War II period, such as the waiting women, who nevertheless got to organize their departure; the absence and return of men as fathers, sons, husbands; women as the carriers of responsibility for anything concerning agriculture, household, family and everyday life. Through their words and their activities, their multiple actions as historical subjects that are conscious of their role in the family, the village, and the society, become apparent. These women, who finally left the village, remained captives of their world and the coherence and safety provided by its structures.

Life stories demonstrate that various factors, motives and reasons may have urged women to leave the village. The role of women differs in migration decision. We must take into account that gender ideology and gender hierarchies, as well as other factors – such as a woman's individual characteristics (age, stage in life-cycle), family characteristics, and external economic, social and cultural factors – might also play an important role in migration decision (Riley, Gardner 1993: 197–199). In most cases, the decision is taken by others, or is taken by the woman and other members of the family jointly. The majority of women relate their departure to their family's needs and expectations. There is an obligation to keep the family united and to contribute to its well-being (Green 2004: 42). But even when departure was accompanied by rejection or hesitation, the women express an active attitude and a sense of waiting to complement the husband.

Marriage was the most important reason and in some case the main strategy for moving to the city. At this point, the experienced story connects to the formal version. This is confirmed by written evidence (e. g. municipal records), where the movement of women from rural areas and their change of citizenship *"because of marriage"* were recorded. These decisions were not their own, but were taken in accordance with family commitments and strategies. In some cases, poverty appears as the only reason for the decision of marriage migration:

> "Poverty. We didn't even have a piece of bread. For a piece of bread, I left and got married. One night, the guy visited us with my cousin and he was to marry Sofia, who was older than me. She was a bit hard to get, and later

> he was given to me. I married him and came down here just for a piece of bread. He was widowed, at 55, with four children, he was old" (D. S., 82 years old, from Arahova).

Poverty threatened the survival of their family and neutralized any sense of social responsibility towards others. It appears to have been a very important parameter in their decision to leave:

> "What was I asked to give? I didn't have bread to feed the children, they were crying for some and they were coming to get it. I wanted to give, they were only children, they hadn't even grown face hair yet, they were poor, I wanted to give but I didn't have any, they came in and they didn't find anything to eat ... Then, we all left, we headed towards the south... My husband didn't want us to leave but I told him that I wouldn't stay here any longer to see our decadence. We will leave. Like that. We stopped at Avorani, we sowed tobacco and we lived. Our children, though, boys and girls, left this place and went to Athens."

It is interesting that *"us"* constitutes a standard narrating stereotype among the majority of women's life stories. It refers to the family and the village (Benmayor, Skotnes 1994: 2 –13). Another interpretive point for their migration was the war, specifically the civil war that traumatized their lives and memories (see Mazower 2000): "As if poverty wasn't enough, the brother-killing began ...". The following excerpts from three life stories reveal the memory of trauma and the decision to move:

> "From the place we were hidden I could see our house, the Germans were burning our village ... Then, I felt as if the mountain crumpled and fell as a rock over me and crashed upon me. We left. I never returned there, not for anyone ... I married a man from my village, he was telling me to go back ... but no ... I never went back ..." (K. X., 74 years old, from Arahova).

> "They were calling us rebel-stricken ... some of us went to the villages towards Agrinio, others at Nafpaktos and we were housed there ... some returned and then left again. I never returned, I begged my mother and she let me stay with my aunt. I never went back ..." (D. N., 77 years old, from Platanos).

> "My father died in 1947 in the prison of Mesolonghi and we were informed nine days later ... We had a sheepdog and he was going where my father used to sit, where his coat was and he was barking. We thought that something had happened to our father ... We went to find him at Mesolonghi, my mother and me, they didn't show us where they buried

> him ... My mother left the house and we moved to a small hut we had in Tragana, she was collecting others' olives, we lived ... Later we left, for different destinations ..." (K. M., 76 years old, from Katouna).

Other women indicate that leaving the village was due to their active participation in the civil war:

> "I and my two brothers had joined the rebel forces. Afterwards, we couldn't stay in the village any more. I left, I came to Agrinio and shortly after that one of my brothers came. I found a job at the tobacco storage area of Ilios" (G. D., 79 years old, from Thermo).

A major reason for moving to the cities, mostly among young women, was to seek a job, usually as maids, or as agricultural workers in the plains and on tobacco fields. Some of them decided to leave on their own and move close to a relative of the family, but usually the decision to move or not was made by a man, their father or brother. The decision to leave in order to find work was often made by men but resulted in additional income for the family, which generated reactions and doubts about the patriarchal family pattern. This led women to re-define their attitudes:

> "I stayed there until I was twelve, then I left for Athens to work as a maid for one year. It was nice there but my father wanted to take the money and to leave me there in torture. I returned to the village. Then I worked as a maid in the mayor's house in Platanos. I did all the housework. I have a secret complaint in me about that ... I married as soon as possible ... just to escape ... but fortunately my husband turned out to be nice ..." (K. M., 79 years old, from Klepa).

The construction of hydroelectric dams in the region caused a massive and compulsory exodus, upon which men and women comment in different ways. The experience of women is connected to the image of the abandoned village: the empty, non-social place. Men refer to the perspectives and better standards of life that the hydroelectric dam opened for them and to increased job opportunities:

> "They gave us compensation and we had to leave ... we had to leave that place where all our belongings were, our houses, our property, and our parents' graves. Now that area is gone, covered by water ..." (B. Z., 72 years old, from Sidira Kastraki).

We can also find self-representations of women who break the traditional rules by leaving and settling in the city (see Riley, Gardner 1993: 202 f.). These women consider themselves as protagonists of social change, especially of that which interests them:

> "I was fifteen when my parents forced me to marry a crazy man. Nobody from his family was with him. The marriage took place in my brother's house, without a wedding dress and clothes and stuff like that, as long as they could get rid of me. He took me and we left. We went to his house in Kalavrouza. His mother, [i.e.] my mother-in-law, and my brother-in-law lived there. I could not describe how horrible it was. I stayed there for one year and I had one child. I decided to leave. I didn't return to Arahova. I came to Agrinio, with a child in my arms, penniless, with nobody, walking. I stopped there, in the refugees' region. Bless her ... a woman took me under her protection, in her house ... Then, I struggled, I struggled a lot, I became a beggar ... I had dirt on my face and clothes so men wouldn't disturb me and I begged, I made it, I also got a divorce. I even got a house in the tenement houses. I got married again. In 1954 I got engaged, but who cares ... I lost my child, Kostakis. He drowned, he might have had psychological problems after everything he and I had been through ..." (K. P., 69 years old, from Agios Dimitrios).

Exclusion from the family and community because of the transgression of the code of honor and shame, was also a reason for moving (cf. Campbell 1964, Avdela 2002):

> "I couldn't stay in the village any longer. He fooled me ... My father and my brothers sent me away secretly, they brought me as far as the main road and left me there and told me never to set foot in the village again" (G. M., 68 years old, from Agios Dimitrios).

In the mid 1960s, the number of women who reacted against the violence of men, against adultery and abandonment, increased. They resolved their issues on their own, starting a new life in the more tolerant city (see Avdela 2002: 59–71):

> "I would not leave him like that. Who was I that he thought he could leave me because my father did not give him a damned piece of land as a dowry ... The meaning was that he used me and then left me ... I stood by and splashed acid on his face. I made him hard to look at ... I left. I came to Agrinio and rented a room ... leave the rest ... I was sentenced for a bit, but he became hard to look at" (K. D., 65 years old, from Thermo).

A new pattern that became more frequent among women in the 1960s was continuing education to secondary school. One of the most important motives of parents for moving to the city was education. In most cases, the woman made the decision, insisting on ensuring better life opportunities for her children (see Sutton 1983: 238–239, Tsoukalas 1977: 79–403):

> "Their father wanted us to move as well ... but my secret desire was stronger. I wanted my children to be educated ... to escape our fate ... I was clever at school but they stopped me from continuing. I had only attended for two years, my girls went to school too. I didn't want them to end up uneducated, to get married young and not have money of their own" (K. P., 73 years old, from Palaiokaria).

These interviews illustrate and illuminate what the written records have suggested about migratory activity. They provide us with a different perspective on these sources and infuse them with the personal sentiment and interpretation of experience. The interviews may not have uncovered something totally unknown, but they give a voice to the historical subjects themselves.

Settlement in the town

Migration describes the different levels of response and adaptation of people to a series of situations and conditions in which they are active subjects and try to change. The influx of migrants transformed the social and cultural physiognomy of the urban center of Agrinio, of the neighboring plain-land communities as well as that of the villages left behind by the internal migrants.

Agrinio's population appears to have grown due to in-migration. According to the census of 1961, the population of the town amounted to 24763 inhabitants, of which 6743 were registered as "foreigners" (the total population of the Agrinio town district was 27134). In 1971, the town was inhabited by 30973 persons, 10075 of whom were "foreigners" (the town district had a total population of 32654). The population of the communities in the plain around Agrinio (such as Kalivia, Dokimi, Megali Hora) also increased. The village Dokimi, for example, numbered 1541 inhabitants in 1951 and 2064 in 1971; the village Megali Hora (Zapant) 591 in 1951 and 1244 inhabitants in 1971. At the same time, the town became the departure point for its own inhabitants, who moved to the bigger urban centers or abroad. Nevertheless, and on the basis of census data from 1961, the town had a small positive migration balance (Kayser 1968: 56). It is noteworthy that Agrinio's development into a significant urban center since the last decade of the 19th century was due to tobacco cultivation and merchandise (Giannakopoulou 2003: 37–48, Patronis 2003: 61–170).

The fieldwork showed that the dominant economic and social groups in the town who made their money with tobacco (such as the Papastratos, Iliou, Matsagos, Keranis, and Karelia families), gradually left Agrinio, transplanting their activities and their investments into the capital. The relatively specialized workforce experienced a similar exodus after the transformation in tobacco processing in the 1960s. As a result, employment receded while unemployment figures increased, mainly among the male population. These facts had a negative effect on the commercial and industrial activities of the town.

Moreover, as concerns the social identity and dynamic of the incoming people, one discovers that Agrinio, a town linked to tobacco production, withheld those peasants who showed, by choice or by necessity, the least socio-cultural ambitions and possibilities to progress towards Athens or similar places. These people were unable to claim, at least in the first generation, an integration into urban life beyond their own familiar – traditional, so to say – socio-economic and cultural habits. Their situation and life in the fields urged them to develop adaptation strategies combining the socio-economical circumstances of the urban center with their own farming background. Retracing, in detail, the social and professional tissue of the town from 1950 until 1970, we find that an important part of its population were tobacco growers (small proprietors, leasers or *"sempoi"*). Older inhabitants and the new incoming workforce clearly made up this tobacco cultivating world. The new workers from outside also had the means, the technical knowledge and the experience to organize agricultural production that was based on self-exploitation of the family. This adaptation strategy constituted a continued tradition embedded in an active integration process, which served the requirements of the specific urban-agricultural environment much more than it was a simple survival of the past.

The final result was that Agrinio shifted from a developed urban center (Patronis 2003: 62–165) towards primary production in the post-World War II period, significantly restricting the commercial activities and urban characteristics of the town. The recession of the commercial sector and the regression of urban development in a town which was the center of an important agricultural region are expected results of the integration of the region, and in general the agricultural world, into the specific capitalist development of Greece during the period between the two World Wars (cf. Damianakos 1987: 13–26, Anthopoulou-Moisidis 2001). The previously decentralized economy became more centralized, resulting in two or more industrial and urban development poles. This process was explained by Burgel, who points to the fact that no provincial activity experienced real and continuous expansion and development, which would have become relevant at the level of demography (Burgel 1976: 185–227).

The other parameter of the social change affecting the economic, social and cultural physiognomy of the town concerned the forces and adaptation skills that the internal migrants from the mountain areas developed, as well as the tight relationships that the agricultural world had with the town. The adaptation to that particular town was made easier by the fact that, notwithstanding its older urban origins, it had a small level of urban life to reproduce and to offer.

Conclusions

The rural-urban migration in and around the area of Agrinio seems to have contributed in a significant way to the transformation of the social and cultural physiognomy of the town, wherein the female population played an important role. Oral and other ethnographic data reveal the increasing changes that occurred in the social and cultural profile of the town. The experience and memory of their integration into the town gives us the image of women that employ conscious adaptation skills to new living conditions by developing subtle ways of integration into the new community. Their settlement in the town together with their husbands and their families is related to the different social organization of the public and private space. It is related to the memory of the village that does not automatically coincide with the space of the town. On the contrary, the memory of the agricultural mountain space is in many ways interwoven with that of the urban space (Kenna 1977: 14–23). This feature comes forth when looking into the organization and functions of the home space, into neighbor relationships, into the culture of everyday life, gender relations, kin relationships, supporting networks and frequent communications with relatives from the village.

It is clear that a main component of this memory is women. The first generation, in particular, sustained itself more by necessity than by choice. They fought across the tried, fragmented but still homely traditional social and cultural tissue to adapt to the new place and its living conditions. These same women appear in their self-representations to be common women, in the sense that not many of them had yet succeeded to obtain even a small level of public recognition. In reality, though, these women feel that they have reached valuable achievements. As the story of their lives unfolds, it becomes clear to them that their contribution to family and society is not underestimated. In this case, migration seems to have improved women's lives and their social status. Paid labor (as tobacco workers, in textile industries), in particular, brought some important changes to women's lives (Bada 2003: 117–130). Their economic contribution to the household income gradually increased their domestic power and extended their influence in family decision making.

It probably gradually also brought, in the sphere of culture, changes to gender ideology, relations and practices. This problem, though, requires much more research into the impact of rural-urban migration on gender relations.

References

Avdela, Evi 2002: "Dia logous timis". Via, sinesthima kai aksies sti metemfiliaki Ellada ["A Matter of Honour". Violence, Feeling and Values in Post-civil War Greece]. Athens: Efeli.

Allen, Peter 1973: Social and Economic Change in a Depopulated Community in Southern Greece. PhD dissertation, Brown University.

Anthias, F. et al. (eds.) 2000: Gender and Migration in Southern Europe: Women on the Move. Oxford: Berg.

Anthopoulou, Th., A. Moisidis 2001: Apo ton agrotiko choro stin ipaethro chora. Metaschimatismoi kai sigchrona dedomena tou agrotikou kosmou stin Ellada [From the agricultural space to the open space. Transformations and contemporary facts of the agricultural world in Greece]. Athens: Gutenberg.

Bada, Konstantina 2003: Oi kapnergatries tou Agriniou [Women tobacco workers in Agrinio]. In: Konstantina Bada (ed.), I mnimi tou eparchiakou topou kai topiou: To Agrinio mechri ti dekaetia tou 60's [The memory of the provincial urban place and space: Agrinio until the '60s]. Athens: Metaichmio, Municipality of Agrinio, 117–130.

Baldwin-Edwards, Martin 2000: Semi-reluctant Hosts: Southern Europe's Ambivalent Response to Immigration. In: Brown Journal of World Affairs 8, 2.

Benmayor, Rina, Andor Skotnes (eds.) 1994: Migration and Identity. Oxford (= International Yearbook of Oral History and Life Stories).

Bertaux, Daniel (ed.) 1981: Biography and Society: the Life History Approach in the Social Sciences. Beverly Hills, Cal.: Sage.

Bertaux-Wiame, Isabelle 1979: The Life History Approach to the Study of Internal Migration. In: Oral History 7, 1: 26–32.

Brettel, Caroline B. 2000: Theorizing Migration in Anthropology: the Social Construction of Networks, Identities, Communities and Global Spaces. In: Caroline B. Brettel, F. Hollifield (eds.), Migration Theory: Talking across Disciplines. New York: Routledge, 97–135.

Brettel, Caroline B. 2003: Anthropology and Migration. Essays on Transnationalism, Ethnicity, and Identity. New York, Oxford: Altamira Press.

Burgel, Guy 1976: Athina. I anaptixi mias mesogeiakis protevousas [Athens. The development of a mediterranean capital]. Athens: Exantas.

Burgel, Guy 1987: Epistrofi stin agrotiki Ellada [Return to rural Greece]. In: S. Damianakos (ed.), Diadikasies koinonikou metaschimatismou [Procedures of social transformation]. Athens: National Centre of Social Research, 29–43.

Campbell, John K. 1964: Honor, Family and Patronage. A Study of Institutions and Moral Values in a Greek Mountain Community. New York, Oxford: Oxford University Press.

Campani, G. 2000: Immigrant Women in Southern Europe: Social Exclusion, Domestic Work and Prostitution in Italy. In: E. King et al. (eds.), Eldorado or Fortress? Migration in Southern Europe. London: McMillan, 145–170.

Chamberlain, M. 1997: Gender and the Narratives of Migration. In: History Workshop Journal 43: 7–108.

Chasiotis, Ioannis 1993: Anaskopisi tis sigchronis ellinikis diasporas [Overview of the modern Greek diaspora]. Thessaloniki: Vanias.

Clogg, Richard 2004: The Greek Diaspora in the Twentieth Century. London: MacMillan Press.

Damianakos, Stathis (ed.) (1987): Diadikasies koinonikou metaschimatismou [Procedures of social transformation]. Athens: National Centre of Social Research.

Damianakos, Stathis 1999: To disevreto montelo tis ellinikis georgias [The uncommon model of Greek agriculture]. In: X. Kasimis, L. Louloudis (eds.), Ipaethros chora. I elliniki koinonia sto telos tou 20^{ou} aiona [The Greek agricultural society at the end of the 20th century]. Athens: Plethron, 55–84.

Damianakos, Stathis 2002: Apo ton choriko ston agroti. I elliniki koinonia apenanti stin pagosmiopoiisi [From the peasant to the farmer. The Greek farming community confronted with globalization]. Athens: Exandas, National Centre of Social Research.

Dubisch, Jill 1977: The City as Resource: Migration from a Greek Island Village. In: Urban Anthropology 6, 1: 65–82.

Ferrarotti, F. 1980: Les biographies comme instrument analytique et interpretative. In: Cahiers Internationaux de Sociologie 69: 227–248.

Friedl, Ernestine 1976: Kinship, Class and Selective Migration. In: John G. Peristiany (ed.), Mediterranean Family Structure. Cambridge: Cambridge UP, 363–388.

Gabaccia, D. 1989: Immigrant Women in the United States. A Selective Annotated Multidisciplinary Bibliography. Westport: Greenwood.

Giannakopoulou, Eleni 2003: I diamorfosi tou koinonikou istou sto Vrachori (19os a – miso tou 20os [The transformation of the Agrinio (Vrahori) social tissue (19th until the first half of the 20th century)]. In: Konstantina Bada (ed.), I mnimi tou eparchiakou topou kai topiou: To Agrinio mechri ti dekaetia tou 60's [The memory of the provincial urban place and space: Agrinio until the '60s]. Athens: Metaichmio, Municipality of Agrinio, 37–48.

Green, Nancy L. 2004: Oi dromoi tis metanasteusis. Sigchrones theoritikes prosegiseis [The roads of migration. Contemporary theoretical approaches], transl. D. Parsanoglou. Athens: Avvalas.

Halbwachs, Maurice ^{2}1980: The Collective Memory. New York.

Herzfeld, Michael 1985: The Poetics of Manhood: Contest and Identity in a Cretan Mountain Village. Princeton: Princeton University Press.

Iosifidis, T. 1997: Immigrants in the Athens Labour Market: A Comparative Survey of Albanians, Egyptians and Filipinos. In: R. King, R. Black (eds.), Southern Europe and the New Immigrations. Sussex: Academic Press, 26–50.

Kambouri, Helen 2005: The Past and the Present in Migration Discourse: Nationals and Aliens in Greece. PhD thesis, London School of Economics.

Kasimati, K. 1998: Social Exclusion: The Greek Experience. Athens: Gutenberg.

Kasimis, X., A. Papadopoulos 1999: The Maintenance of the Family Farming Exploitation and the Capitalistic Development of Agriculture in Greece: A Critical Survey of Bibliography. In: X. Kasimis, L. Louloudis (eds), The Greek Agricultural Society at the End of the 20th Century. Athens: Plethron, 115–147.

Kenna, Margaret 1977: Greek Urban Migrants and Their Rural Patron Saint. In: Ethnic Studies 1: 4–23.

Kayser, B. 1968: Anthropogeografia tis Ellados. Stoicheia dia tin meletin tis astifilias [Anthropogeography of Greece], transl. T. Tsavea, M. Merakli. Athens: National Center of Social Research.

Kayser, B., Y. R. Pechoux, M. Sinignon 1971: Exode rural et attraction urbaine en Grèce. Athens: Centre National de Recherches Sociales.

King, R. et al. (eds.) 2000: Eldorado or Fortress? Migration in Southern Europe. London: MacMillan.

Kotsamanis, B. 1990: I kinitikotita tou agrotikou plithismou sti dekaetia tou 1940–50 kai I anadiarthrosi tou koinoniko - dimografikou charti tiw metapolemikis Elladas [Mobility of the farming population in the 1940s–1950s and the redesigning of the social-demographic map of post-civil war Greece]. Athens: Centre National de Recherches Sociales, 97–126.

Lampiri-Dimaki, Jane 1965: Social Change in a Greek Town: The Impact of Factory Work on the Position of Women. Athens: Center of Planning and Economic Research.

Langness, L., G. Frank 1985: Lives: An Anthropological Approach to Biography. Novato, Cal.: Chandler & Sharp.

Linardos-Rulmon, P. 1993: Metanastes ergates kai i agora ergasias stin Ellada [Immigrant workers and the labor market in Greece]. Athens: INE.

Markova, E., A. H. Sarris 1997: The Performance of Bulgarian Illegal Immigrants in the Greek Labour Market. In: South European Society and politics 2, 2: 57–77.

Marvakis, A., D. Parsanoglou, M. Pavlou (eds.) 2001: Metanastes stin Ellada [Migrants in Greece]. Athens: Ellinika Grammata.

Mazower, Mark (ed). 2000: After the War Was over: Reconstructing the Family, Nation and State in Greece. Princeton: Princeton UP.

Moustaka, Calliopi 1964: The Internal Migrant. Athens: National Center of Social Research.

Nikolaidou, Magda 1975: The Working Woman in Greece. In: Greek Review of Social Research 7: 54–64.

Okely, Judith, Hellen Callaway (eds.) 1992: Anthropology and Autobiography. London, New York: Routledge.

Rappaport, Joanne 1990: The Politics of Memory: Native Historical Interpretation in the Colombian Andes. Cambridge: Cambridge UP.

Passerini, Luiza 1998: Sparagmata tou 20[ou] aeona. I istoria os biomeni empeiria [Heartaches of the 20th century. History as a lived experience], transl. O. Baron-Vasar, I. Laliotou, Ioulia Pentazou. Athens: Nefeli.

Patronis, Vasilis 2003: I oikonomia tou kapnou kai to kapnergatiko zitima sto Agrinio tou mesopolemou [The economy of tobacco and the tobacco workers issue in Agrinio during the period between the two World Wars]. In: Konstantina Bada (ed.), I mnimi tou eparchiakou topou kai topiou: To Agrinio mechri ti dekaetia tou 60's [The memory of the provincial urban place and space: Agrinio until the '60s]. Athens: Metaixmio, Municipality of Agrinio, 161–170.

Perks, Rob, Alistair Thomson (eds.) 1998: The Oral History Reader. London: Routledge.

Petrinioti-Konsta, Xanthi 1981: Oi prosdioristikoi paragontes tis ginaikeias simmetochis sto ergatiko dinamiko stin Ellada 1961, 1971. Oikonometriki diereunisi, didaktoriki diatrivi [The parameters defining female participation in the labor force in Greece 1961–1971. Econometric research]. PhD thesis, Athens National and Kapodistrias University.

Psimmenos, Iordanis 1995: Metanasteusi apo ta Balkania [Migration from the Balkans]. Athens: Glorybook, Papazisis.

Psimmenos, Iordanis 1997: Globalization and Employee Participation. Avebury: Aldershot.

Psimmenos, Iordanis 1999: Metanasteusi kai ergasia: I dimiourgia neon koinonikon choron [Migration and work: the creation of new social spaces]. Athens: Athens National and Kapodistrias University.

Psimmenos, Iordanis 2001: Nea ergasia kai anepisimoi metanastes sti mitropolitiki Athina [New jobs and non-official migrants in the metropolis of Athens]. In: Ath. Marvakis, D. Parsanoglou, M. Pavlou (eds.), Metanastes stin Ellada [Migrants in Greece]. Athens: Ellinika Grammata.

Riley, Nancy E., Robert W. Gardner 1993: Migration Decisions: the Role of Gender. In: United Nations, Department for Economic and Social Information and Policy Analysis (ed.), Internal Migration of Women in Developing Countries. Proceedings of the United Nations Expert Meeting on the Feminization of Internal Migration. Aguascalientes, Mexico, 22 October 1991. New York: U.N., 195–205.

Santis, Eva 1973: Refugees and Economic Migrants in Greater Athens. Athens: National Center of Social Research.

Sutton, Susan Buck 1978: Migrant Regional Associations: An Athenian Example and Its Implications. PhD dissertation, University of North Carolina at Chapel Hill.

Sutton, Susan Buck 1983: Rural-Urban Migration in Greece. In: Michael Kenny, David I. Kertzer (eds.), Urban Life in Mediterranean Europe. Anthropological Perspectives. Urbana, Chicago, London: University of Illinois Press, 225–249.

Thomson, Alistair 1999: Moving Stories: Oral History and Migration Studies. In: Oral History 27: 24–37.

Thompson, E. P. 1978: The Poverty of Theory and Other Essays. London: Merlin.

Tsoukalas, Constantine 1977: Eksartisi kai anaparagogi: O koinonikos rolos ton ekpaedeutikon michanismon stin Ellada (1830–1922) [Dependence and reproduction: The social role of the educational mechanism in Greece (1830–1922)]. Athens: Themelio.

Vermeulen, Hans 1983: Urban Research in Greece. In: Michael Kenny, David I. Kertzer (eds.), Urban Life in Mediterranean Europe. Anthropological Perspectives. Urbana, Chicago, London: University of Illinois Press, 109–134.

Vermeulen, Hans 2004: Epistrofi oikoi me emmeso tropo. I anthropologia tis diethnous metanasteusis stin Ellada. Mia protasi gia mia istoriki kai sigritiki prosegisi [Back home in a roundabout way. The anthropology of international migration in Greece: Suggestions for a historical and comparative approach]. In: Greek Society of Ethnology (ed.), Elliniki Etairia Ethnologias, Opseis tis anthropologikis skepsis kai erevnas stin Ellada [Perspectives of anthropological thought and research in Greece]. Athens: Greek Society of Ethnology, 175–202.

Ventoura, Lina 1993: Metanasteusi ginaikon: gennisi kai ekseliksi tou epistimonikou endiaferontos [Women migrants: Genesis and evolution of a scientific interest]. In: Dini 6: 30–241.

Zolotas, X. 1964: I Ellada stin fasi tis ekviomichanisis [Greece in the face of industrialization]. Athens: Bank of Greece.

Urban Visions and Rural Utopias: Literature and the Building of a Nationalist Consensus in Croatia, 1924–1945[1]

Rory Yeoman, Peckham

Can cinema still be relevant in a time of war and destruction and, if so, how? This was the question posed in a competition for new screenplays launched by the Croatian State Film Institute in July 1944. The Film Institute was deluged with manuscripts of varying quality, which, if nothing else, at least served to answer the question that had been set. One of the winning scripts, entitled "Ašikovanje", written by Alice Horn, a female medical graduate, told the saga of a young Bosnian woman, Zejina, who abandons her quiet life in the countryside to live a life less ordinary in the city. Naturally, the exciting life she imagines for herself in Sarajevo is not matched by the reality of her new existence which she finds brutal and alienating. As a result of her isolation, though, she rediscovers her Bosnian patriotism and love of the natural beauty of her home region and this is expressed through her renditions of traditional Bosnian folk music, the *sevdalinka*. The screenplay, a combination of the national and the social, was a cautionary tale about pursuing shallow dreams in the metropolis and a paean to the virtues of village life. So impressed was the Film Institute with the screenplay, that it purchased it for the tidy sum of fifty thousand kunas.

The irony of a screenplay which sang the praises of rural conservatism while relying on the most modern technology that urban society could produce for its realisation, not to mention the intellectual and urban background of Horn herself, was apparently lost on the judges. Nonetheless, this contradiction reflected the ambiguity of the Ustasha Movement itself towards the respective roles of the city and the village in the new society and the relationship between them. As in many East European states, Croatian society had traditionally been riven not just by ethnic and national divisions, but also social divisions between the city and the countryside. Ending these fissures had been an important goal of all the major Croatian political parties, irrespective of their ideological orientation, at least since the end of the nineteenth century. While pro-Yugoslavist parties believed that this could best be achieved through the creation of a common state of the Serbs, Croats and Slovenes, more nationalist parties in Croatia argued that it was only after

[1] I should like to thank the anonymous reviewers for comments they made on an earlier draft of this paper. I would also like to thank Paul Jon Newman for obtaining documents and articles which I required for the revision of this paper. All errors of interpretation, fact and translation are solely my own.

social and national divisions had been over come that a strong confident Croatia would be in a position to join a common South Slav state. This position was perhaps best exemplified by the dominant Croatian party of the early twentieth century, the Croatian Peasant Party. Under the leadership of Stjepan Radić, at least, it pursued a moderate form of nationalism whose politics only rarely degenerated into chauvinism. Despite the name of the party, one of its guiding aims under Radić was to create a sense of solidarity between town dwellers and peasants and ameliorate the mutual distrust which often existed between them. From social conflict to national consensus: this was how Croatian nationhood and identity would be forged.

Moderate nationalism is not a label which was or ever could have been used to describe the ideological vision of the Croatian Ustasha Movement. Yet this terroristic, fanatically nationalist and violent organisation which ruled the satellite Independent State of Croatia between 1941 and 1945 claimed to be the ideological and political heir of the Peasant Party. Not only did the Movement's court writers and hagiographers constantly – and inaccurately – stress the peasant origins of Ante Pavelić, the leader and *poglavnik* of the Movement, but the Movement's leading activists also appropriated, and, in some cases, misappropriated many of the core ideas of the Peasant party as their own. This is perhaps not surprising when one considers that a significant minority of those who secretly joined the Ustasha Movement in the 1930s or who became members and activists of the Movement in the 1940s had formerly been members of the Peasant Party. Indeed, in 1941, not only did a group of parliamentarians from the Peasant Party very publicly join the Ustasha Movement, but local branches of the Party also joined the Movement en masse.

After coming to power in 1941, the Ustashas aimed to heal the ethnic and societal divisions in Croatia partly through the genocide of the Serbs, gypsies and Jews, the latter whom they blamed for introducing degenerate morals into Croatian society, and partly through the incarnation of the patriarchal and puritan peasant values which they believed represented the true values of the Croatian race. They despised what they perceived as the corruption, alienation and decadence of urban life; for them, it was associated with sexual licence, Marxism, bourgeois feminism and democracy. At the same time, however, they wished to embrace the technological advances and mass communication possibilities of modern city life and to utilise that very same urban culture to elevate the life of the peasant and to eradicate the gulf between city and village. Nationalist writers in Croatia played an important part in articulating this new vision of the city and the village and the relationship between the two in a future independent Croatian nation state. Not just novelists and poets, but also social theorists, political ideologues and anthropologists sought to reconceptualise notions of the rural and the urban in order to reconcile the two and build a unified nation and national consensus.

Pastoralism as student radicalism: the social visions of nationalist youth

Of all the fascist and extreme nationalist movements that emerged in inter-war Europe, few movements have been so intimately connected in the popular imagination with the cult of rural life and the peasantry as the Ustasha Movement. In the historiographies of the Movement that were produced in communist Yugoslavia, the Ustashas were perceived as a marginal and predominantly rural phenomenon, both in terms of their membership and in their worldview. Although most studies of the Movement noted the influence that fascism and national socialism had on their worldview, especially in the late 1930s, they nonetheless emphasised the peasant roots of the majority of its members and the influence that this had on their ideology, combining conservative patriarchal values with a blood and soil ideology which expressed hostility and suspicion of the city and elevated to an ideal the allegedly aggressive impulses of the peasantry. At the same time, such studies emphasised the lack of support the Movement experienced among the peasant masses (Jelić-Butić 1977; Colić 1973; Basta 1971). Relatively few historians and scholars in the West have studied the Ustasha Movement in any serious and objective manner and those who did have tended to interpret the Ustashas in the same manner as historians in Yugoslavia, with some, such as Aleksa Djilas, going as far as to suggest that the harsh and remote rural background in which many of the leading Ustashas had grown up could account not only for their semi-Rousseauist idealisation of nature, but also for the undeveloped and inchoate nature of their aggressive anti-urban violent ideology (Djilas 1996: 103–127). Even in the pioneering study of Martin Broszat and Ladislaus Hory which was, in many regards, a meticulous debunking of the myths surrounding the ideology and rule of the Ustashas, the authors were at pains to point out the impact of Pavelić's semi-rural childhood, as the son of a railway worker, on both his politics and his conception of the city when he arrived in "the new world" of Zagreb as a gauche law student in 1910. They suggest that his upbringing in nationalist Hercegovina explained his affinity to and identification with the radical nationalist student organisation, Young Croatia, among whose leaders was Mile Budak, like Pavelić from a semi-peasant background and later the author of stories which were paeans of praise to the enduring virtues of Croatian rural life (Hory, Broszat 1964: 13–14).

More recent discussions of the Ustasha Movement by Western historians have not essentially dissented from this interpretation. Thus, in Holm Sundhaussen's studies of the Movement, the Ustashas emerge as the heralds of a fanatical, extremist and "irrational" form of blood and soil nationalist ideology. Sundhaussen's interesting contributions note correctly the centrality of rural utopianism, the village community and a return to the simple life in the social visions of the ideologues of the Movement. The author also notes the visceral loathing of the Ustashas for the phenomena of contemporary life which they believed threatened the lives of the peasantry: Serbian rule, international Jewry, liberal democracy, capitalism and communism – all features, in their eyes, of a corrupt, modern urban society – as well as freemasonry and sexual and social licence. As the author points out, despite their contention that urban values had triumphed in the inter-war period at the expense of the peasantry, the Ustashas in fact inherited a largely undeveloped agricultural nation in which eighty per cent of the population worked on the land. However, despite the light that the author sheds on the ideology and outlook of the Ustashas, Sundhaussen's studies succumb to the same stereotypes as communist-era Yugoslav historians.

On the one hand, he sets out the heterogeneous nature of the support the Movement received from among others, clerical Catholic groups, dispossessed Muslim begs, retired Habsburg officers and radical student circles at the University of Zagreb and in Sarajevo, thereby implicitly suggesting that the Ustashas were not quite the unrepresentative and unpopular group of nationalist fanatics they were portrayed as being after 1945. Nonetheless, Sundhaussen maintains that, despite the strong intellectual support they received, most members of the Movement were illiterate and uneducated, "recruited from socially marginal groups, especially from the ignored worker and peasant groups who could be easily indoctrinated and who were looking for a kind of ersatz individual and social freedom in the carrying out of terroristic violence". In an attempt to explicitly emphasise that the Ustashas enjoyed no mass base of support, however, he confusingly argues that in contrast to the "more easily mobilised and indoctrinated" urban citizens, the majority of the peasantry were "conservative and reserved" and, as a result, rejected the radicalism of the Ustasha Movement (Sundhaussen 1995: 502–503, 507, Sundhaussen, 1983: 68–76, 102–107). Embodying all the negative traits of the peasant class while lacking any popular appeal to the very same peasant masses from which they had emerged: by such a paradoxical circularity of logic have historians interpreted the Ustasha Movement and the state they ruled.

Yet, as with many fascist and rightist movements, it was not as simple as this. While the Ustashas often expressed resentment, and hatred even, towards the city and urban life – as one would expect in a society in which the majority of the population lived in the countryside and enjoyed only isolated contact with the city – an anti-urban cultural ideology had relatively little to do with their vocalised hatred towards the city and urban values. Instead, as a viscerally anti-Yugoslav movement, the Ustashas' dislike of the city reflected their political opposition to the perceived urban values of Yugoslavism. Specifically, it reflected their contention that under Yugoslavism not only was the Croatian nation suffering persecution and torture, but that its national and racial identity was being systematically and deliberately destroyed. Since the urbanised Croatian man was too weak and "nervous" to attain liberty for his nation and destroy the corrupting influence of liberal democracy and its licentious ideas, the Ustashas aimed to be the progenitors of a new race of men who, imbued with militant, aggressive values, would liberate their country from the tyranny of Serbian and Yugoslav rule.

To understand the attitude of extreme Croatian nationalists to the city it is necessary to explain the cultural context of inter-war Yugoslavia and its own relationship to the city and the countryside, since much of the Croatian nationalist resentment towards the city and urban life and all that it entailed was predicated on this. The ideology of integral Yugoslavism presented itself as thoroughly modern and secular. It looked admiringly at countries such as the United States of America, Britain and France and aspired to replicate their liberal, modern and urban societies. The British writer David Footman, visiting Yugoslavia in 1935, wrote that Zagreb possessed "chic, well-dressed people" and that "everywhere you will find the most up-to-date ideas and appliances, including even penny-in-the slot-machines for contraceptives in the café lavatories" (Footman 1935: 278). Social and political ideas associated with the ideology of integral Yugoslavism included access to birth control, the secularisation of the Muslim community, and the embracing of racial eugenics as a means of national integration and social emancipation. Therefore, it was the specifically urban values of technological and scientific advance and social progress which were to inform the mores of Yugoslavia. Anxious to prove themselves "progressive", Yugoslav ideologues particularly emphasised the importance of the emancipation of women, and the liberated new Yugoslav woman of the 1920s and the 1930s, independent, physically athletic and intrepid became a potent symbol of the new state (Popović 1922).

By no means everyone was as enthusiastic about contemporary Yugoslav society. Some magazines and journals regularly mocked the New Yugoslav Woman, often reducing her to the stereotype of the chain-smoking decadent libertinage. Conservative writers also fretted about the burgeoning sexual freedom of the new society; sexologists and racial hygienists, even when they were writing official government sex education guides, were assailed for promoting pornography and morally corrupting young people. Writers also looked askance at the values of Yugoslav society. The Serbian satirist, Branislav Nušić, for example, penned a number of plays which poured scorn on modern metropolitan life. In one of his most famous pieces, *Beograd nekad i danas* (Belgrade in the Past and Today, 1923), he explored in typically humorous fashion the way in which a modern and youthful urban culture conflicted with the more conservative and rural values of the majority of the inhabitants of Yugoslavia. In this comedy, a wealthy upper-class couple come to visit their son and daughter-in-law in Belgrade. Much of the comedy is based on the striking differences between them: while the parents are dressed in traditional Serbian attire, their daughter-in-law wears trousers, smokes cigarettes and attends feminist meetings. Their grandson, meanwhile, paints naked bodies for newspapers. Nušić was suggesting that the aspirations of Yugoslavia to attain the level of progress and civilisation which it believed was already present in Western democracies, was predicated on an exclusivist and urban understanding of modernity which, in its emphasis on youth and metropolitan sophistication, was alien to the traditions and values of the older generation and especially to those who lived in the socially-dominant countryside.

Amusing and perceptive as Nušić's comedies were, ultimately they were larger-than-life satires and not strictly accurate. Yugoslav ideologues were far from blind to the plight of the villages, nor were they oblivious to the need for modernisation. On the contrary, throughout the 1920s and 1930s, anthropologists, scientists, psychologists and writers called for the transformation of the villages through public campaigns of hygiene, eugenics and universal education. In the 1930s, anthropologists began to talk with increasing despair of the crisis in the villages, highlighting the dangerous alienation of its youth which had become addicted to drink, violence and political extremism. Yet, for all this, the values embraced by integral Yugoslavists were those of urban liberal democracy. Not surprisingly, among writers and artists of both the socialist left and the nationalist right there emerged a strong cultural opposition to Yugoslavia's bourgeois character and this was especially the case after Yugoslavism became the official state ideology in 1930. Artistic and literary groups emerged that stressed the virtues of the honest worker and peasant, the much-fabled "little man". A younger and more radical group of artists and writers emerged, advocating that artists should produce art that more readily addressed social themes. Whether from the political left or the right, such an artistic agenda had an implicitly national and even nationalistic outlook. In one famous incident in November 1939, Croatian artistic circles split into two rival groups, and exhibited their work in two different galleries. One group continued to propagate the idea of art for art's sake and advocate that the value of art should be based on its technical quality, not the social background of the artists or the themes that they explored; the other main group maintained that art had a strongly social function and could express the national soul. They championed the idea of a national and people's art, based on a pastoral and peasant art form (M. K. 1939: 11).

One of the impacts of this new social art was that it brought to the attention of the public a new generation of peasant and worker writer, often self-educated, and championed by the salon, who wanted to write about their experiences. Even among those writers who emanated from respectable middle and upper-class backgrounds, there was a desire to write about the struggles of the worker and peasant and, much to the amusement of some critics, even to affect their dress. Although social literature and social realism were usually associated with the left in the European context, in Croatia, at least, the focus on the lives of the ordinary peasant and worker led to the emergence of a group of writers from the nationalist and separatist right. One of the most prominent of this new generation of nationalist self-educated writers was the novelist Ivan Softa, a manual labourer. Softa's first novel, written in 1935, related the experiences of an itinerant worker in 1930s Croatia as he travelled across the countryside looking for work. The novel described a Croatian countryside allowed to fester and collapse into moral depredation by a callous Yugoslav regime. By contrast, his later two novels celebrated life in the villages in the post First World War era, reserving venom only for the impact that urban elites had had on the rural way of life.

In addition to the literature of self-educated workers and peasants, a new generation of young nationalist intellectuals, often from middle-class and urban backgrounds, were also exploring themes of the city and metropolitan life. One of the most prolific of these was the young poet and novelist, Vladimir Jurčić, whose work explored contemporary social issues, in particular the plight of the Croatian worker and the peasant in 1930s metropolitan Croatia. In 1932, Jurčić's anthology of poetry about city life, *U metropolu* (In the Metropolis), was published to much acclaim in the nationalist press. In this collection of poetry, Jurčić presented the city in deeply unflattering terms, exploring its social dislocation and economic poverty, but also its social vacuity: alienation and isolation; poverty; and the stultifying effect of cosmopolitanism. The poems told the stories of peasants and their difficult lives and deaths in the urban jungle, the starving students exploited by unscrupulous businessmen, the alcoholics that congregated every day at the cafés and the lives of shift workers who toiled in bars, cafés, and the homes of the wealthy. Hostility towards the city as a symbol of the corruption of modern capitalist society was a preoccupation that nationalist writers shared with socialist novelists. Meanwhile, the ennui of bourgeois life and the crisis of contemporary society were explored in the novels of Miroslav Krleža and Ivo Kozarčanin. Despite the ambiguous reception that they received from nationalist critics, they struck a chord. Ivo Balentović was surely not alone in remarking that such novels were emblematic of the alienation of a cohort of Croatians living in a society where life had become "nervous" and "rebellious"; as a result, young Croatian writers were employing art to militate against "the small town spirit and its capricious and miserable soul". Given this, it is hardly surprising that nationalist youth groups through their underground literary journals and pamphlets also engaged in the literary rebellion against bourgeois urban values and the city in favour of the more natural and national life of the peasantry. Jerko Skračić's 1940 short story, in which the teenage protagonist rebels against his family by announcing his intention to drop out of school and abandon the anti-Croatian bourgeois world of exclusive bars, fast automobiles, Paris fashion collections and visits to the opera for a simple life in the village, nature and nationalism was one of many such stories.

The literary return to the village and the exploration of the life of the ordinary worker and peasant in Croatia also reflected the social ideas that nationalist writers were increasingly articulating. From the middle of the 1920s onwards, the ideology of Yugoslavism was being criticised not just for its national inequity, but also for its social injustice; the typical regime supporter was caricatured as a fat idle bourgeois businessman. By contrast, the little man – the Croatian peasant and worker – was eulogised as representing the best qualities of the Croatian nation. And this little man was fated to be economically exploited by the corrupt bourgeois rulers in Belgrade and their supporters. No wonder, one nationalist workers' newspaper commented, on the occasion of the opening of the lavish new premises of a state bank, that the peasants reserved such hatred for the city. Many other nationalist writers went further, declaring that bourgeois values were intrinsically anti-Croatian. Zbiljko Marks, writing in 1935, commented that capitalism was not just anti-social insofar as it enslaved the worker, but also anti-nationalist. It did not recognise the homeland, he complained, and was a "Semitic" concept, imported by "foreign aristocrats and the national bourgeoisie". Therefore, the Croatian peasant and worker would resist it as it did not emerge from their psyche or contain the essence of the national spirit, built on "blood and land" (Marks 1935: 291–293).

Nationalist writers also worried about the effect that the city and its attitudes was having on the rural youth who came to study at the University of Zagreb and had formed the vanguard of the nationalist movement in Croatia. Most of the thousands of students had arrived "full of idealism", aiming to become Croatian men which meant becoming "men of justice, ethics, idealism and Western culture". Instead, according to the nationalist intellectual Dušan Žanko, they had been presented with two kinds of intellectual role models – the rationalist intellectual, lacking humanity, and the "small town bourgeois materialist". This had resulted in "apathy and disorientation" among the students (Žanko 1939: 57–62). Another nationalist commentator agreed and blamed the apathy of contemporary Croatian intellectual youth on a fossilised education system both antiquated and worthless. This had produced a generation of youth which, rather than playing the role of pioneer in the national struggle for liberation, had only one ideal: the passing of university exams in order to pay for a house and become a businessman. Instead of nationalist militancy, the contemporary student, he noted contemptuously, wanted only to survive. In place of militant activism and national consciousness, the commentator continued, today's student exhibited "a lack of consciousness, indifference, apathy, solipsism, in other words nothing". Football was more likely to awaken his passion than nationalist politics (Ti 1939: 1).

This description surely did not apply to the extreme nationalist student circles at the University of Zagreb. By the late 1930s their violent and increasingly frequent confrontations with communist and leftist students were becoming a source of consternation to the university authorities. The rise of Nazism and the victory of General Franco's forces in the Spanish Civil War, a victory in which conservative Spanish students had played a crucial role, heightened their belief that the hour of the Croatian national revolution was imminent. As well as political protest, radical nationalist student circles were setting out their vision of the future

Croatian society, a vision in which peasant values and a return to the village would play an important part. In a radical student almanac published in Sarajevo in 1938, the editor, Emil Lašić, identified one of the most pressing social-political problems of a future Greater Croatia as the relationship between the village and the town, the peasant and the intelligentsia. According to Lašić, one of the main barriers was the difference in the mentalities of the city dweller and the peasant, and the perception among peasants that life in the city was easier and more comfortable. This had served to breed envy and antagonism between the city and the countryside and the only solution to this, he concluded, was the "cultural elevation of the village", involving the eradication of illiteracy, the introduction of hygiene to reduce the "catastrophic mortality rate" and better wages for the peasantry. For their part, the intelligentsia would have to abandon their urban rationalism and be imbued with a national understanding and a social conscience (Lašić 1939: 7–9).

Not all student contributors were prepared to be so accommodating about the city. In the future peasant state, Zvonimir Topali wrote, the peasantry by which he meant those that worked the land would be the source of Croatian national power. The peasants would be the leading element and all other social groups would act as its "representatives in those fields of work in which it is not represented". Unlike other writers, Topali was not sure that the village or the countryside could be reconciled with the city. They were two different worlds and represented a conflict of interests and culture. The city, he wrote, was cosmopolitan, represented the mass of the population that lived disconnected lives from each other, competed against each other and worked in professions not in harmony with morals. By contrast, the village was governed by patriarchal values and, since peasants' work involved cultivating the land, it involved the co-operation of all the peasants. In distinction to the city, too, the village was racially and nationally homogeneous and those that lived in the villages were not subject to "foreign influences which could arouse them to militate against their nation". The village, thus, represented "a kind of organic unity, as opposed to the organic chaos of the city".

In the future Croatian state, the city would become the village writ large and adopt its value systems and moral codes. Only in such a manner would the village and the city be harmonised and all differences eradicated. Of course, given the importance of the role of the educated classes, what was required was nothing short of a revolution in the thinking of the intelligentsia; they, as much as the city, needed to harmonise their attitudes with those of the village. They needed to cast away their materialism and demonstrate that they were not, as the peasant leader Stjepan Radić had once called them, "those corrupt gentlemen". Only in such a manner could the Croatian intelligentsia demonstrate that "at its heart lies the nation" (Topali 1938: 10–15).

Likewise, Spasoje Prcović, writing in the pages of a nationalist youth journal, defined one of the guiding social principles of the new generation in Croatia as the appropriation of the values of the village. "The new Croatian generation has placed before itself the village and not the city as its ideal," he explained. "But we must be clear what we mean! We are not pleading for primitivism or the absence of enlightenment, against education and culture. We are only asking whether we want the principles of the village or the city, and opting for the values of the village, in other words for those positive values that the village, as the bearer of conservatism, has protected in the Croatian nation for so many centuries" (Prcović 1940: 15).

Were radical young writers such as Prcović merely advocating a return to simple pastoral values? Not really. Nor were they the conservative rural nostalgists that their writing might have suggested. Most of the nationalist students that came to Zagreb in the 1920s and 1930s had grown up in remote rural communities where there were significant ethnic tensions and contestation. Therefore, it was hardly surprising that the utopian state they envisaged would have to be a peasant state. However, the vision of students like Prcović was rather more radical than a simple return to the values of the village and imagined a social and racial revolution to eradicate the traitorous bourgeoisie that had betrayed the nation. Prcović referred with disdain to that "layer of people among us" that had served the Belgrade regime for two decades, in the process aiding in the enslavement of Croatia. The characteristics of this layer "mostly of foreign origin, although there are enough native members among them", were their "servility, selfishness, their absolute lack of all ethical concerns, and their consistently anti-Croatian position". For this reason, the new generation of radical students was "the sworn enemy of this anti-Croatian materialistic class; it wants to destroy this class" (Prcović 1940: 15).

Paradoxically, at the same time, students were writing of a return to the mores of the village, in the late 1930s, nationalist student newspapers were talking with pride about plans for the construction of contemporary and modernist university buildings for their technical and veterinary faculties. Without the construction of "more modern and spacious" new buildings, it was argued, the intellectual life of the university as well as the material well-being of the students would suffer. Writers argued that this also applied to better buildings for the students themselves; Zagreb, as the capital of Croatia, also needed its own student quarter like Berlin, Paris and Madrid. Many in fact looked to the example of the University City that had been constructed in Rome, a tribute to the "Fascists' well-known agility and speed". They wrote with astonishment of the avant garde design of the city, with its car parks, statues and "absolutely contemporary, beautiful and monumental" buildings constructed to the most exacting standards of contemporary society and the highest standards of hygiene (Hondl 1937: 3–5; Šen 1938: 132–141).

Radical nationalist students were not the only ones that looked to the village as a cultural inspiration for the new state. Kamilo Križanić asserted that, rather than raising the standards of life in the village, as some had arrogantly suggested, the city with its cosmopolitan tendencies and its aesthetes, futurists and cubists should seek to learn from the culture of the village. "The town has to get to know the village," he insisted, "not through ownership of land or intrusive visits. Not through the foggy ideas of some Rosenberg; not in the perspectives of some foreign Marxist formulas. We must abandon all these foreign 'isms', which poison the heart of the city" (Križanić 1934: 401–403). In fact, the writer believed that a renaissance of the village was already under way and that a new generation of nationalists born in the villages would reinvigorate the dying and decaying cities. Unlike the cities, which had demonstrated their passivity and weakness through their compromise with foreign occupiers and their "cultural eclecticism", virile peasants had made the ultimate national sacrifice in the First World War. If the villages had become emptier after the War, then the manly sacrifices of the peasants had guaranteed that "the fields were green again, the land was reborn and the old houses remained faithful hearths". Far from the decaying city, a new generation full of élan had been born, replacing the lost generation of their dead fathers. However, he also believed that from the decaying cities a new virile generation would arise. Rejecting the craven urban values of the past, they would instead "hold a belief in the village and the peasant nation, breaking all false and artificial partitions between the village and the city" (Križanić 1935: 289 f.).

By no means all nationalist writers were content with this interpretation, however. Ivo Balentović, for one, cautioned against an overly-sentimentalised view of the village. Noting the popularity of the village as a literary theme, he nonetheless observed that most novels generally failed to present the village in a "cultured or objective" manner, since many of those that wrote about the village had never visited one. Either the village was perceived as "some idyllic paradise", or as a society in which everything was "black and grey, stupid and narrow minded" and "an immoral toddy shop [...] the source of debauchery, drunkenness and criminality". Pouring scorn on the young generation of Croatian writers and intellectuals who declared dramatically that they would go and live in the village, he pointed out that many of them had grown up in the village, left it for the city and were now embracing the village again, often for purely commercial reasons. Ironically, they sought all this at a time when "we wear silk underwear, English dinner jackets and French top hats (top hats on peasants' shoes as Dragoljub Jovanović says), Crepe de Chine, Crepe Georgette [...] we sprinkle ourselves with colognes and Coty perfume, we shave our moustaches, women's armpits and eyebrows with hypo-allergenic razors, we play bridge and football and, like snobs, arrogantly declare that we are Western and that we are striding towards European progress" (Balentović 1934: 345–347).

New lives for new men: peasant cults and the modernisation of the village

The Ustasha Movement was a movement not just of revolutionary nationalists, but also one of social revolutionaries. From the inception of the Movement, its chief ideologues sought to transform society in Croatia and one of its main concerns was to address the relationship between the cities and the villages. The Ustasha Movement claimed a significant part of its ideological inheritance from the Croatian Peasant Party of Stjepan Radić and after the founding of the State in 1941, they adopted him as one of their many martyrs. Moreover, although the peasant masses did not join the Ustasha Movement in 1941, the radical right faction of the party did and the Party's paramilitary units, the Citizens' Defence Force and the Peasant Defence Guard, joined the paramilitary units and death squads of the Movement en masse (Konjević 1971: 173–189; Konjević 1972: 104–112). Like the Ustashas, Radić too had spoken of the need to eradicate the division between the city and the village, had mistrusted the urban intelligentsia and had talked of an independent nationalist Croatia in which the peasantry would constitute the ruling class. As a nationalist movement dominated by activists of peasant origin and founded on the values of the village, the Ustashas developed a cult of the peasantry, claiming to have a unique understanding of them. Many members of the Movement surely agreed with the anonymous commentator who, in February 1945, declared that the peasant was the "protector of the Croatian land and blood and the purest expression of the Croatian nation", so much so that "Croatians are considered those whose direct descendants come from the village" (Anon 1945: 1).

In the period before the Ustasha Movement came to power, peasantism had played a central role in its political and social vision. The principles of the Ustasha Movement declared that the peasantry was the "basis" and "source" of everything, as well as the "true carrier" of state authority. Rejecting both "brutal" capitalism and Russian bolshevism, they aimed to create a "one hundred per cent peasant state", whose property relations would be structured on the model of the peasant *zadruga*, or village clan. However, the Ustashas argued that the workers too could live in the peasant state as workers were nothing else but peasants living in a city; for their part, intellectuals would form the guiding element of the state. As part of their peasantist vision, the Ustashas sought to create a new man, based on the virtues of the peasant population of the Lika region. Unlike the bourgeois passive Croatian gentleman who had failed to liberate Croatia, the new Ustasha man would employ "flame, iron and blood" to "smash the spine of the foreign oppressor". The Ustashas aimed to heal repression with aggression and the concept of "manly virtue" – violence in the cause of a free and independent Croatia – became a central tenet of their ideology.

After coming to power in 1941, the incarnation of this new Croatian man was one of the means by which the Ustashas aimed to remake society and nationalise the masses. The new Ustasha man, epitomised in the inhabitants of the inhospitable Velebit Mountains – a region from which many of the early Ustashas had hailed – reinforced the Ustashas' belief that the most natural instincts were to be found within the peasant population. As an anti-bourgeois movement, the Ustashas also utilised him as a counter-stereotype to the self-satisfied and urban businessman whose passivity and nervousness had kept Croatia enslaved for so long. His proximity to nature and a bleak landscape as well as the harsh nature of his existence had given him a healthier and more manly character as well as a more pronounced national consciousness than the bourgeois gentleman isolated in his luxurious apartment or barking orders at his secretary as he dashed out the door to play tennis. When Colonel Jure Francetić, fanatical commander of the elite death squad, the Black Legion, died in 1943 at the hands of the Partisans, nationalist writers such as Marko Čović and Karlo Mirth noted with pride that he had hailed from a village in the Lika Mountains. This accounted for his "manliness", "toughness" and "heroism". Francetić's qualities of rugged masculinity, asceticism, a yearning for death and love for his fellow soldiers could not be understood by the "effete and moribund" small town mentality (Čović 1943: 2, Mirth 1943, 2). Ivo Bogdan, a prominent nationalist ideologue, writing on the first anniversary of the foundation of the Ustasha nation state, declared that the Lika Region was the purest region of the nation, a Croatian Sparta unpoisoned "by the influence of foreigners", an area which "has given birth to healthy strong men, heroic and significant" (Bogdan 1942: 2).

As Mijo Bzik pointed out, the new Ustasha man was the antithesis of the interwar urban bourgeois Croatian gentleman. His era was over and he had been replaced by the Croat as revolutionary warrior, who would be modest, manly and Spartan, thinking more of his comrades than of himself, and not given to "chattering" about himself. He was not a ladies' man or a respectable gentleman and nor did he aspire to be: he was the son of peasants and workers. Swearing, drinking and "visiting questionable nocturnal haunts or consorting in the company of dubious women" were forbidden; instead, he would lead a life founded on the family. In fact for the new man, his first love and duty would be towards the nation, not the opposite sex. This was to be contrasted with the conduct of the decorous bourgeois youth who sat at a table in a café, writing a love letter to his girlfriend or at home in his silk dressing gown smoking a cigarette; moustaches, in particular, were manifestations of the mental meanderings of overly-intellectualised young men. "If you had to go into battle," Bzik acerbically observed, "the tempest would quickly remove your moustache" (Bzik 1943: 21–26, 108).

For some nationalist writers, the arrival of the Independent State of Croatia represented the defeat of a corrupt urban ruling class and a full-scale attack on urban values. Milan Ivšić, a leading nationalist academic, described Yugoslavia as a corrupt democracy that had been brought on the backs of the suffering of peasants "in prisons, under batons and in death on the gallows". By contrast, the Ustasha revolution had destroyed "Belgrade democracy, free masonry and capitalist corruption". In particular, the concept of individualistic rights, with its "selfishness" and "profiteering", had been replaced by the ethos of collective rights. In the new state, he argued, those exponents of selfish capitalism, who had done little work but had managed to build "villas and palaces and ordered luxurious apartments" would have to be expelled. The nation would pour scorn on parasites, those who "daily waste time in the cafés dawdling, chattering, in intrigues, in great political discussions and criticism – those who live off the living flesh of the Croatian nation and, like bloodsuckers, suck its blood" (Ivšić 1943: 369–376).

Not surprisingly, nationalist journals and newspapers also launched polemical attacks on the city, depicting it as a labyrinthine cess pit of racial impurity. For example, in the summer of 1941, after Aryan racial laws had been passed against the Jews of Croatia and after the campaign of genocide against the Serbs of Croatia had begun in earnest, articles appeared in the press pillorying the city as the centre of "the Jewish-foreign soul", those Croatian traitors who had served the nation's enemies "for a bowl of lentils" as well as those "representatives of the mongrel Serbian-Cincar-Gypsy-Armenian race" and "the Serbian-Cincar-Gypsy mentality". In order to build a new Croatia and protect its Aryan purity, the Croats should look to the example of the village. It had not been infiltrated by "foreign-Jewish" blood and so the migration of villagers to the city renewed the biology of the population of the city, "in whose veins flows ever more foreign-Jewish blood" (Anon 1941: 1).

They also lauded the racial and political effects of the arrival of peasants into the metropolis, a process they argued would renew the blood of the city. The Ustasha student commissar, Milivoj Karamarko, for one, boasted that those nationalist students who come to study in Zagreb in the 1930s and become the vanguard of the new nationalist intelligentsia "came from the nation, from the villages and the suburbs". In the overwhelming majority of cases, nationalist student activists "came directly from peasant hearths and workers' huts. There were no spoilt land-owning children from the circles of the affluent upper classes" (Karamarko 1941: 1). Yet, if many nationalist writers perceived the peasant influence in the degenerate city as a positive development, they worried about the influence of the morals of the city on the village. According to Eduard L. Miloslavić, modern urban ideas regarding birth control and abortion were corrupting the "most far-flung villages, and are gaining influence amongst our peasant people, who naively and ignorantly listen to and believe the criminally disposed pseudo-intelligentsia". If such notions triumphed, he warned, the survival of the family would be threatened and the village would collapse (Miloslavić 1943: 233).

Despite the polemical use to which the Ustasha Movement put its anti-urban rhetoric, the Ustashas recognised both the limited aspirations and values that village life could provide and the role that the city could play in preventing the village from becoming too narrow-minded and parochial. The Ustashas were under no illusions that the village was in decay. According to Franjo Lačen, social reality in the villages was "very difficult" and he wrote with disdain of those who romanticised the village and "popularised the idea that life in our villages was ideal". Of all the layers of society, he continued, the village had developed most slowly because daily life was monotonous. Peasants were not accustomed to the idea of social change and, therefore, were more inclined to embrace not only the innovations, but also the superficiality of city life. As much as he criticised the cities for importing degenerate ideas to the villages and impoverishing the village through economic exploitation, the writer insisted that peasants would also have to end their hostility to modern technology. On the contrary, he believed that it was only by using the most technologically-advanced equipment such as tractors and mechanised ploughs that the village would be reborn. From its foundations, the village would be remade, "starting from houses and farming buildings to the most modern peasant offices and to schools" (Lačen 1942: 168–170).

But this was not enough. When the ideologues of the Movement talked of the decay of the villages, they were not simply referring to its economic stasis and social torpor; they also had in mind the lack of a vibrant cultural life. How could this be rectified? One professor, writing in a students' journal in 1941, argued that peasant youth who had come to Zagreb to study could be the answer. By imbibing the cultural riches of the city alongside their university studies, they could return to the villages as pioneers "not only of technical but also cultural progress" and this would lift them above "the banality of parochial [village] society" (N. N. 1941: 172). More fundamentally, the Ustashas believed that modern cultural forms of communication, such as cinema, could be utilised to enrich and elevate cultural life in the villages. The State Commissariat for Film, headed by Marijan Mikac, sought to develop a mobile film department that would transport new Croatian cinema – both documentaries and feature films – to remote rural areas of Croatia. This reflected the Movement's belief that mass forms of communication such as film and radio should serve the "social and artistic needs" of the people as an antidote to the commercialism and elitism of liberal democratic and "Jewish" spirit (Mikac 1943: 22–23). Other plans were rather more ambitious and involved a campaign to educate the peasants and eradicate illiteracy which the Movement's ideologues believed could be achieved in six years. However, this would have to be implemented sensitively.

As Milan Ivšić pointed out, the project to educate the villages needed "distinctive peasant schools" to provide education in the village. What was important was that solutions provided by urban educators were not forced on the villages by urban professionals or distant cosmopolitans; peasants were to take an active part and they were not to be considered the "subjects of some scientific experiment".

Nor was the point of the education to ensure that the peasants received more opportunities in the city. Educational work in the village was rather to ensure the uniqueness of the peasants. To be successful, the peasant instructor had to be guided by an understanding of and connection with the village. Yet it was a fact that many members of the urban educated classes did not understand the conditions for the "economic and educational progress of the Croatian village". The same could also be said for many among the educated in the village. Such people had no feeling for the village or for the life of the peasant and they wanted to be the judges and critics of everything. "They would rather spend time in criticising their surroundings or spend hours and hours in some rural tavern and engage in endless wise conversations and discussions about politics" (Ivšić 1942: 217–221).

Nonetheless, the order and cleanliness of modern technology played an important part in Ivšić's vision of a village transformed. Women, as well as men, would be educated. In the new enlightened and progressive village, the lives of the peasants would be altered out of all recognition: the establishment of a clean home; the maintenance of hygienic standards and the introduction of electricity to the villages as well as the more rational breeding of livestock would all contribute to making life in the villages more cultured. Moreover, peasant educators would awaken in the peasants a desire for the reading of books and newspapers as well as the education of their children, not only in elementary but also in technical and secondary schools, "especially if those children are particularly talented or there are too many of them in the family, and there is too little land for them to continue to work as peasants." In addition, the peasant intelligentsia would help to construct educational institutes and to arrange, advise and lead peasant libraries, reading rooms and land communities (Ivšić 1942: 217–221).

Ivo Balentović imagined a similar transformation for peasant women. Noting the extent of emancipation enjoyed by urban women, and "their life of luxury", he wrote that life for women in the villages was distinguished by unhygienic conditions and massive illiteracy; in short, "dirty houses, dirty beds, bodies and surroundings," and an insufficient period between giving birth and going back to work had led many peasant women to an early grave. "Young fresh peasant women," he wrote "are entering into marriages as real beauties, full of strength and health, and after a few years of married life (and burdens) are falling to bits and looking like real old women." Yet, although he lauded the liberation of women in countries such as Turkey, where women could be factory workers, businesswomen, students, doctors and lawyers, he too saw a more negative side. In some rural parts of Croatia, especially in Slavonia, Medmurje and Podravina, there had been a "'rationalisation of sexual morals', a limiting of the number of children, an even greater number of abortions, and a death rate among young women which is frighteningly high" (Balentović 1941: 533–536).

Balentović's comments reflect the fact that some nationalist ideologues rejected the idea that the city was inherently morally inferior to the village. Eugen Sladović, another leading social theoretician, argued that the emphasis on the revival of the village should not be used as a stick with which to beat the city, but should be used to bring the city and the village closer. Just because in some industrially developed states, there was an increasing tendency in literature to explore the "tragedy and difficulty" which befell the town dweller who had settled in the village, this did not mean that city culture was not equal in the nation or in social morals. The city, as he pointed out, played the crucial role in the formation of the culture of the nation and the state.

True, there were many characteristics that divided the life in the city from the life of the villages, but the nation as a whole incorporated in itself the village and the city, the peasant and the city dweller. Sladović also lauded the advance of modern technology into the villages, arguing that modern cultural and technical advances made peasant work easier; the influence of the city could also provide the village with doctors, vets, agronomists, teachers and craftsmen. In any case, he wrote, despite the difference in mentality between the city dweller and the peasant, the city dweller made every effort to visit the village by going for week-ends in the countryside to feel closer to nature. The urbanite also attempted to create part of the countryside in his garden in the centre of the concrete jungle, not surprising since the majority of town dwellers were third or second generation descendants of the villages. At the same time, however, he recommended that when city dwellers came to the village they should respect the religious views of the peasant and not dishonour them (Sladović 1941: 283–292).

In the same way that the city could assist the village, so he believed that the problems of the city were also national problems which village and city needed to solve together as a national community. Since the city was the centre of arts, politics, science, education and sport, the city called to the village for assistance, from which emerged "streams of new fresh blood, new national strength and healthy new impulses". It was natural that the residents of the city should be proud of their urban culture, but the inhabitant of the new modern city rejected isolation and would offer a hand of friendship to the village in the aim of mutual work; in this way they would increase their understanding and deepen the ties of friendship.

For some, the modernisation of the village was the only means to create a cohesive organic nation. According to at least one anonymous writer, it was simply untrue to argue, as some demagogues "dizzily proclaimed" before April 10, 1941, that the village would lose its uniqueness if it served the appetites of the city, in other words the means and methods of contemporary technology. "As if our peasant would be less nationally conscious if, in place of a plough, he had a tractor!" On the contrary, the village in the Independent State of Croatia had to be progressive and had to have railway lines, post offices, farming devices, and veterinary and agricultural clinics. At the same time, the city dweller had to be imbued with the same thoughts as the Ustasha peasant. The regime had to reverse the gulf between the village and the city because the common good of the nation resided "in the physical and spiritual co-operation between peasant and urbanite" (Anon 1942: 1).

And, in fact, some writers were positively indignant about the depiction of the city in nationalist journals and popular fiction, being governed by "politicisation and demagogy" and "laughable" assertions. Nikola Peršić, a teacher at the Croatian Economic Commercial School in Zagreb, argued that the debate was dominated by "stories about deceitful gentlemen and parasites on the national body etc". In his opinion, harmony between the city and village and "mutual work for the national good" were the only proper process. The writer even argued that the emigration of villagers to the cities should be praised as long as it did not threaten to destroy the villages, as it helped to increase the birth-rate in the cities, which had been kept low as a result of social phenomena such as abortions and late marriages (Peršić 1941: 5). In the struggle for a national consensus, it appears that there was little intellectual agreement.

Degeneracy, suicide, renewal: Croatian writers envision the city

From its inception, the Independent State of Croatia adopted an ambiguous attitude towards the idea of the city and its place in national life. On the one hand, the cultural commissars of the state wanted to create a spectacular city capital that would be modern, technological and contemporary. Many of the Ustashas' architectural plans could even be interpreted as futuristic in that they envisaged a world of communal living and functionalism. Between 1941 and 1945, the Movement's cultural commissars formulated grandiose and utopian schemes to transform the capital. One such plan envisaged creating an underground railway system, skyscrapers as communal workers' homes and huge new thoroughfares. The Ustashas also aimed to construct an entire new suburb in the centre of the capital, with new streets, tram lines and buildings; the designs for the new offices, university facilities, sanatoria, workers' flats, and cafés of New Zagreb were clearly inspired by the functionalist ethos of experimentalist architects such as Le Corbusier and Mies van der Rohe. These concepts were also reflected in the schemes of the Ustashas to build workers' settlements, which envisaged electrification schemes, swimming pools, sports complexes and leisure facilities. The Movement's cultural visionaries also revived the demands of the inter-war Croatian nationalist student movement for the creation of a university city and announced an ambitious and monumental project to construct modern and monumental buildings for the technical, veterinary and medical faculties at the University of Zagreb (Jurišić 1943, Stahuljak 1943).

As part of their campaign to elevate life in the village and eradicate illiteracy, the Ministry for National Enlightenment announced an ambitious plan for the construction of educational centres and modern hygienic homes for peasants. According to the architect Aleksandar Freudenreich writing in the pages of the Ministry's journal, their design would be "in harmony with contemporary and up-to-date technological teaching". However, they were also to reflect the traditional ethos of the typical Croatian village which, according to Freudenreich was not simply a collection of houses, but a "community of the spirit". Those educated workers sent to the village to teach the peasants and advance national education would have to carry out their work in such a way that it did not disturb the harmony of the peasant approach, he continued. The peasant wanted to expand his horizons and realise his creative talents but he did not require an ideological or cultural frame from outside the village (Freudenreich 1942: 168–176).

The incarnation of a new nationalistic literature played a defining role in the cultural politics of the Ustasha Movement. Like the creation of a new man, the Ustashas argued that a new nationalist literature would help to build a national consensus. Like the new Croatian man too, the new literature would be in harmony with the intrinsic values and racial characteristics of the Croatian nation, epitomised in the rugged Lika region, with its codes of rural honour, militant nationalism and patriarchal conservatism. In his essay on the new Croatian literature, the poet and Ustasha cultural commissar Vinko Nikolić argued that a new man could only be created by a new nationalist literature. Setting out the regime's vision of the new literature, he called for an end to the old types of literature represented by men such as "[Milutin Cihlar] Nehajev's Andrijašević", much less "[Miroslav] Krleža's degenerates, sluts and drunks". Nor could he be represented by "various individuals created in sick fantasies, such as [Ivan] Kozarac's 'Duka Begović', a type of sexualised man, who thinks only of himself". In the new era that the Ustashas were inaugurating, heroes of various literary works who rejected "the will to live, destroyed enthusiasm, and are intellectually driven to spiritual or physical suicide", would not be allowed. It was ridiculous to imagine the Ustashas could create a new man without the purification of degenerate literature. A revolutionary new man could not be created from the young generation with "cosmopolitan" and "anti-Croatian" work (Nikolić 1944: 35 f.).

Instead, Croatian writers should take as their literary model the peasant novels of Mile Budak. This did not mean that the lives of the peasants were of any greater value than those of city dwellers, nor did Nikolić recognise any special kind of peasant literature. Nonetheless, the novels of writers from peasant backgrounds acted as a bridge between the ambitions of peasants on the one side and the urban artistic milieu on the other. It demonstrated the affection of the peasants for culture and art, which was exemplified in the large number of novelists in Croatia who had been brought up in the village (Nikolic 1944: 118–123).

However, themes of reconciliation between the village and the city in the writing of nationalist novelists were not prevalent. In student literary circles at the University of Zagreb, the city was often represented as bleak and depressing. Isolation and feelings of suicide were never far away and even the most pleasurable aspects of the city offered little respite. A vivid example of this is illustrated by the Jakov Ivastinović poem, published in the student almanac of 1942. In the poem, Ivastinović is living away from home, studying in Zagreb. He contrasts the familiarity of village life with the cold and sterile reality of life in the city. In this lonely world, even going to the cinema is unbearably bleak. "Outside it is gloomy / dark and / dense. / The rain pours down ... / And I was in the cinema / and gulped a look / at a girl with large breasts," he writes guiltily. "The village remained far away from me / from me, / who walks the streets / hungry, / while father shares out the food." In another poem, the young writer imagines spending a desolate Christmas Eve in the city while all his family gather at the family hearth and roast chestnuts. "Today is Christmas Eve," he writes, "and tonight father will carry in the straw. / And they will all be together for the evening / except me" (Ivastinović 1942: 187–189).[2]

Other literary interpretations of the city were rather less self-pitying. Mara Švel-Garmirsek's social realist novel, *Hrast* (The Oak Tree, 1942), was at once a eulogy of the peasant ideals which the Ustashas claimed to represent and a visceral polemic against the bourgeois values of the city. Telling the story of a peasant couple from Zemun, Marko and Nada Ivnatić, and their struggle to keep hold of their homestead from the banks in Belgrade, the novel was a perfect distillation of the social and the national. Set during the inter-war period, the novel took as its central motif the oak tree – resilient, natural and stoical, constantly renewing itself in unseen and almost mystical ways, like the Croatian nation. At the centre of the novel, however, was the clash of values between the city and the village. In the novel, social space and landscapes are completely nationalised, with the Croatian characters representing the guileless values of the village and the Serbs and Jews representing the degenerate and exploitative mores of the city.

Although the novel climaxes with Germany's declaration of war against Yugoslavia and the subsequent liberation of Croatia by German military forces, political events play a relatively minor role in the novel and far more of the narrative is

---

[2] An explanation: straw is an integral part of the Christmas celebrations in both Croatia and Serbia. "Badnjak" is the Serbo-Croatian word both for Christmas Eve and the traditional Yule log. In Croatia, this is brought in on 24 December and is placed on the hearth. Straw, upon which wishes are made, is also brought into the house and candles are lit for the departed. According to tradition, people spend Badnjak awake, burning candles and lighting the Yule log. The Christmas table is also set on Badnjak. It is covered with one or more ornamental tablecloths under which straw is placed. In both cases, the straw alludes to the manger in which Jesus was born and reminds believers why Christmas is celebrated.

given over to a depiction of the struggle that Nada and Marko face in attempting to persuade the bank to help them financially. In order to obtain assistance from the banks and the Ministry of Agriculture, they are required to venture into the city. And it is on one of these trips to the city that Nada meets her old school friend, Vera, who is living the life of an emancipated city woman. Vera, the reader learns, was married to a dissolute bohemian artist who has left her for another woman. "After a few years, marriage became boring for him," Vera tells Nada. "He rose quickly in his profession. He achieved fame as a writer and poet. He constantly sought new interests, new women [...] He talked about the freedom of the individual, about the right to life and enjoyment. One day, he said to me that he was going to an island with a girlfriend. He left and I did not wait for him at home. I sought a divorce and you see now I live alone."

For all the freedoms of the city, hers is effectively a miserable and barren life. "Don't pity me, Nada," she protests at one point. "I have my hobbies and my work." But this sounds as unconvincing as it is meant to. Vera and her wrecked life, which includes the death of her infant son, are a symbol not just of the degeneracy of urban life, but also its brutality. Underneath its gleaming skyscrapers and smart boutiques, life in the city is barren and empty. "If only you knew," laments Vera, "how great the difference was between this artificial image and our life. How great the difference was between his high forehead, his clear eyes – and his sadism and incidentally – even you remember – he worshipped Dorian Grey." At the same time that the novel exposes the reality of life in the city, through the character of Nada, it also angrily rejects the romantic view of the village as sensuous and unruly, a stereotype that exists only in the imaginations of urban novelists (Švel-Garmirsek 1942: 108 f.).

After meeting Vera, Nada goes to the cinema to watch the latest American film, but leaves halfway through bored by its emptiness. Indeed, everywhere she goes she is struck by the ennui of Belgrade and its moral bankruptcy, whether it is the pampered wife of the Jewish bank manager or the "hermaphrodite" Jewish secretary at the Ministry of Agriculture, who asks her out. Returning to the village is, not surprisingly, welcome. "When the train passed the bridge and left the luxurious lit-up city, Nada breathed a sigh of relief" and "felt how peace and sleep slowly came to her."

When her husband comes to the city to visit the bank, he is even less enamoured with the city than his wife. Having remembered Belgrade from his youth, he is appalled by the changes that have taken place, its cosmopolitan nature and the array of races and cultures that live side by side. Sitting in the Café Moscow drinking a cup of coffee, he stares out of the window at the "slim women dressed in French fashions, in short, narrow skirts, coiffeured hair, rouged cheeks, extremely high-heeled shoes, heavily made-up mouths, elegant men, fat matrons in Serbian clothes, slugs with baskets, shabby children, tramps, officers rattling sabres". Marko has not been in Belgrade for twelve years, and he hardly recognises "the elegant facades of the newly-built mansions or the chaotic suburbs". The cosmopolitan nature of the city and the mixing of different races are especially repulsive to Marko:

> "At the table next to his, they spoke Greek and at another Hungarian and, in one corner, a black man sat drinking tea. No, this was not the Belgrade of [Branislav] Nušić – as Marko remembered – a provincial city with an oriental character; the centre of the city gave an impression of an international citadel which had wiped away all its special traditions, and, with a downpour of gold, had built houses which had suddenly shot up in the same way that mushrooms sprout up after rain. [...] These Babylonian towers of the nouveau riche did not please Marko, did not mean as much as one morning on the cherished land. He felt physically as if a wave of hatred rose in him towards this modern Sodom which called itself the capital city of Yugoslavia" (Švel-Gamiršek 1942: 89–90).

However, it is the exploitation of the honest Croatian peasant by the affluent decadent citizens of Belgrade that most outrages Marko. Who has paid for the gleaming offices and homes for the Yugoslav elite he wonders. The answer is the ordinary Croatian peasant. The novel uses the contrast between the poverty and decay of the villages and the gilded opulence of Belgrade to emphasise that the suffering of the Croatian peasant nation is a result of a forced existence in a state that is not just racially but also culturally alien. Yugoslavia is anti-Croatian not simply because of its national policies, but also because of its bourgeois materialistic mentality, personified in the decay and degeneration of the Croatian village:

> "Somewhere in the cities they built skyscrapers and dreamed about asphalting and motorisation, sport and cultural life, and somewhere unwhitewashed and unkempt peasant houses rotted and were destroyed, wheels cracked under potholed roads. Somewhere women recuperated their tired limbs at public baths from energetic sports or dancing at nightclubs and looked after their slim figures, so that their fur coats fitted them [...] Somewhere Mother Croatia silently wept about her unhappy children, both the born and the unborn" (Švel-Gamiršek 1942: 161).

Ultimately, of course, the national values of the village triumph over the decadent values of the city. The novel climaxes with Germany's declaration of war against Yugoslavia and the subsequent liberation of Croatia by the Ustashas. Curiously, for a novel that is so preoccupied with the corruption and degeneracy of the city and the nationalist landscape of the Croatian village, it contains relatively little about life in the villages. However, the story ends on a note of idyllic pastoralism. On a beautiful spring day shortly after the national revolution, Marko and Nada sit under the oak tree in each others' arms and watch as their sons till the land, the next generation of Croatian peasants, suggesting a lineage as stable as that of the tree itself. Croatia, like the oak tree, will survive.

Many other nationalist novelists followed the lead set by Švel-Gamiršek and interpreted the city from a position of almost exclusive hostility, even if relatively few established writers interpreted the city from the distant perspective of the peasant. Indeed, images of the city as a degenerate and immoral underworld of exploitation and dishonesty were disseminated so assiduously in novels, poems and short stories that such accounts of the city almost became parodies of themselves. Ivan Triplat, for one, a self-educated worker and novelist, whose semi-autobiographical novels and short stories explored the lives of struggling workers and peasants in Zagreb, frequently used a grotesquely caricatured stereotype of upper-middle class life as a literary convention: vacuous starlets, caddish suitors, alcoholic ne'er-do-wells and duplicitous Jews as well as "fortune hunters, killers, fraudsters, adulterers, drunks, loose women, millionaires" all formed an important part in his narrative. His last novel, completed in 1945, shared its name with Jeremy Bentham's Panopticum, the utilitarian philosopher's architectural device which made it possible for a prison superintendent to continually observe the behaviour of inmates. In the city, Triplat suggested, all the inhabitants were locked in a prison, and those that were not – the affluent bourgeoisie – surely belonged in one (Triplat 1945: 217).

By no means all Croatian nationalist novelists used the city in this way. Zvonimir Remeta utilised the urban landscape of Zagreb as the location for all three of his novels and in the award-winning *Grijeh* (The Mistake, 1943), the story of how secrets and lies result in the suicide of the daughter of a middle-class couple, the landscape plays an important role in providing solace to the characters. Remeta also effectively employs the cityscape as a means of deepening our understanding of the emotions of the central protagonists. Likewise, in Zdenka Jušić-Šeunik's *Jedna žena* (One Woman, 1943), the city is employed in order to understand the feelings and internal conflicts of an educated middle-class woman who embarks on an extra-marital affair as an expression of her fundamental isolation from contemporary society. In the novel, it is life itself and an unhappy marriage, not the anonymity of the city, which pushes her to the brink of suicide.

A more complex treatment of the conflict between the village and the city than Švel-Gamiršek's appears in Ivo Balentović's short story *Kako je minula Buga* (How Buga Passed By, 1944), published as one of an anthology of short stories exploring the lives of peasants in the city. Balentović was one of the most politically-engaged of novelists during the existence of the Independent State of Croatia. Interned by the authorities in 1940 for his nationalist activism, this multi-faceted critic, novelist and journalist also happened to be the official biographer of the élite Ustasha death squad, the Black Legion, and a personal friend of

Francetić. Balentović's novella, written in 1944, is set in Zagreb on the eve of the outbreak of the Second World War and tells the story of a doomed love affair between the mysterious Buga and a young student, footballer and aspiring journalist, Marcel Marić.

The opening scenes present a society that is clearly in its last days. The novel opens atmospherically with a description of the weather in the city. The sky is overcast and grey and throughout the story the city and characters are bathed in an autumnal gloom from which there is no escape. Fog, mist, rain, hail: this is the meteorological scenery which accompanies the story. Decadence and suicide are also prevalent in this city. At the beginning of the story, a newspaper reports that a beautiful young female student, Milica Rajić, a former girlfriend of Marcel, has committed suicide by hanging herself. According to police reports, she had left three letters behind, one of them for Marcel. In the letter to him, she declares that she has taken her own life because she has lost "faith in everything in the world". There are a number of salacious stories in Balentović's novella. In Balentović's vision, the odd and excitable behaviour of citizens appears to reflect the nervous mood of the state. The deaths are emblematic of the decadent and degenerate nature of the city, emanating from the sexual and personal frustrations of its inhabitants. Conversations of passers-by discussing the outbreak of war in Europe are intertwined with bizarre and distressing anecdotes of suicide: a young man kills himself because he has been unlucky in love; two young people decide to jump from the roof of the cathedral under the influence of "erotic melancholy". It is in the midst of this dystopia that the protagonist appears.

When the reader first encounters Marcel, he is walking through the streets of Zagreb in the pouring rain with holes in his shoes. He walks into a café to escape the downpour, ordering a cup of coffee and the café serves as the microcosm of the economic deprivation of the city. The café is almost completely empty and is no longer full of "chattering guests" and music as it was in the past. Only on Sunday does it become full, yet its clientele consists of the unemployed, the hungry and "hard-up students, some because they were bored and others because they had a lack of heating in their rented attic rooms". The café also appears to reflect the depressing existence that Marcel himself leads, as, in the course of the story, he becomes increasingly alienated by the harsh reality of life in the city. Despite his many friends, he is alone and isolated. Near the start of the story, we are introduced to a number of Marcel's friends, all of whom are exemplary bourgeois gentlemen. Matija, for example, is a young ambitious novelist dressed smartly in a suit and immersed in the urban and "Western" vernacular of inter-war Yugoslavia. Affluent, unquestioning and self-satisfied, he is the polar opposite of Marcel. He also meets a friend from university, the editor of a political journal, who asks him if he could write a short story with a political theme. However, when Marcel informs him that he wants to be paid for it, the editor is surprised as he has never asked for payment before and the newspaper's budget will not stretch to this. Asked why he suddenly needs paying, Marcel gives an evasive answer and we share the humiliation and embarrassment that Marcel feels at having to ask for money.

In the life that Marcel leads in the city, all friendships can be sullied by financial concerns. The next day, Marcel visits his friend, Ivan Div, political editor of a daily mass-circulation newspaper, frequently at risk of being banned by the authorities. As the day before, he is forced to ask a friend to lend him money. It is at this point of the story that he first meets Buga. He has caught sight of her on a number of occasions: behind the counter of a stationery shop; on the tram; unlocking her apartment door. Now, he asks her out and she agrees. However, despite his elation, his frustration at the inconsequential nature of his life torments him. As he looks at the river, he feels like "an atom, a zero, a barely visible maggot". The sense of an unfulfilled young life is a constant and nagging theme of the story and in his most melancholy moments, it leads him to question his entire philosophy and outlook on life. Existential crises are a fact of his life. Returning to his dark and cold apartment one night, for example, Marcel bitterly recalls all the editorial doors which have been shut in his face in his attempts to establish himself as a writer and he reflects on the money which he could have earned as a professional footballer. Yet he also realises that a lavish apartment and a comfortable lifestyle would not bring him the satisfaction and peace of mind that he is searching for.

Marcel is not just set apart from most of his friends by his lack of money or his sense of alienation, but also by his social and national radicalism, a result, the author suggests, of questioning the urban lifestyle. To his friend Ivan, he rails against the small coterie of well-heeled students "muttering about dialectic materialism and doctrinaire Marxist evangelism while wearing a silk cravat!" with whom he, as a nationalist student, has come into open conflict at the University of Zagreb. His sense of justice is especially outraged by the fact that their privileged backgrounds have afforded them the protection of the Rector; his subsequent challenging of this support has led to him being labelled a troublemaker and his academic marks suffering. In a verbal tour of the city, he points out the opulent villa "constructed on corruption and speculation" and owned by an "embezzler, unscrupulous businessman and criminal" who has gained respectability and the state Order of Merit by his presidency of a humanitarian organisation. Modernist architects and town planners do not escape his withering censure either: he entertains satirical sallies about gentlemen "in gloves" giving lectures on modern architectural fashions while the urban poor live in tiny homes with no hygiene or fresh air. Ivan's pampered lifestyle – his dinner jackets, glamorous girlfriends and chic footwear, is also held up to uncomfortable scrutiny when Marcel compares it to his father's fifty years of toil in the village.

Marcel's greatest scorn is reserved for those affluent urban intellectuals who write articles in newspapers and journals glorifying the supposed culture of the village without ever having been near one, and one of the most interesting aspects of Balentović's short story is the manner in which he explores the conflicts that rural students faced in moving from the village to the city. Marcel's rugged masculine physique is one means by which the author conveys the virtuous nature of his national and political opinions. Unlike his friends, Marcel exhibits none of the soft and unmanly physical or behavioural characteristics of his bourgeois friends. Marcel is the epitome of the new man, a masculine man of action. When Ivan comes to visit his friend shortly before he plays an important football fixture, Marcel is in the process of getting changed. He walks towards him, and observing Marcel without a shirt, notices "how he rubs his hard muscles with water from a cold shower". Grabbing him by the arms, he "feels the swollen toughness of his muscles". He exclaims in an admiring manner:

> "You are a modern youth. See, how strong your arms are! Real athletic muscles. And you know, that is what women love. You think that you will be known as a result of the few journalistic articles that you have had published. Aah, no one is interested in a cub reporter. But, as a footballer, you are a man who is the object of women's fantasies and someone who has earned the adulation of ordinary citizens" (Balentović 1944: 23).

In this novel, however, muscularity equals virtue. As a new man, Marcel has no time for such shallowness. "Don't think for one minute that I count myself among those young athletes who, with a carnation in their buttonhole, drink in the smiles of women and feed off the vanity that comes their way from a talent in the nimbleness of their footwork. You really babble nonsense, my friend." His emotions are equally admirable. Although Marcel's name is again in lights above the football stadium and he is once more the idol of the adoring masses, he thinks – with some sadness – of all the people who have decided to go without dinner so they can afford to attend the football match. He also thinks, with disdain, of the women who have come to watch him play football, motivated by reasons other than an exclusive interest in the match itself. And he is made uncomfortable by the president of the club who thrusts banknotes into his hands for his contribution to the victory against the opposition. So, this is what it means to be a professional footballer. Women, money, adoration: is he repulsed or seduced? Later, in a café, he comforts himself with the thought that at least he is now able to buy himself a new raincoat to replace the tattered one which he currently has to make do with. The author also explores Marcel's conflict between his city existence and rural upbringing through his incipient relationship with Buga, a child of the working-classes. Unlike Marcel, who had spent his childhood "full of songs and the smell of flowers, imbued with the warm wide soul of the peasant", hers had been lived in the city, where she had endured a "dark and meagre childhood". In fact, one of

Marcel's most appealing characteristics is the fact that he is different from all the other city boys whom she has dated:

> "She loved him because of his coldness; because of his simple way of speaking. She loved his enthusiasm for the village, for peasant life, habits and songs. For hours he would regale her with fiery eyes and fists with a life of their own about the small houses in the valleys, the carts laden with wheat, about the meadows where one could smell the aroma of strawberries and hear crickets murmuring in the silent secret dusk" (Balentović 1944: 57).

This difference is also the cause of friction between them, however. There is a ferocious argument when Marcel sees Buga being overly friendly to a young man during the football match and gives his jealousy and suspicion full expression. Buga does not understand what she has done wrong; as she explains, the man she was speaking to was her former boyfriend whom she hardly had anything to do with and, in any case, she was only being polite. It is a collision between the liberalism and independence of the city and the inherent conservatism and possessiveness of the countryside. Although they are later reconciled, the argument leads to a lengthy disquisition on the nature of life and death at Marcel's depressing cold apartment in the company of his long-suffering friend Ivan. He decides to leave the city to spend sometime in the countryside – as he tells Ivan – to find peace and rest from the disappointments of his life.

The last part of the story is taken up with Marcel's decision to return to the village. On the train he begins thinking about his life and, considering the misery and struggle of his life, in particular his penniless existence and the fact that he is leaving the woman he loves behind, he momentarily considers how he could end it all, weighing up different methods including blowing himself up with a hand grenade or throwing himself under a train. As Marcel nears the village, a wave of nostalgia overcomes him, but on alighting, he is quickly seized by a feeling of profound disappointment as he steps off the train into a covering of soft, slippery mud. Life in the village is not "as he had anticipated and expected it". For Marcel, the whole life of the village is encapsulated in the mud he encounters. With the rain lashing down, "the filth of this life astounded Marcel" and as he gazes at the uneven streets and potholes, he "noticed how removed he was from this life". Misery was the "condition of life in the village".

The author explores the hopelessness of life in the village under the Yugoslav regime through the conversations that Marcel has with those members of the community he left behind when he moved to the city. Going into the local tavern, he meets many people he has not seen since he left the village, including a young man Galić, with whom he used to catch butterflies as a child. Galić was formerly a fiery nationalist and Radić supporter, but now works in a "political school" for "progressive rural youth" and engages in "political activism" under the guidance of a prominent local lawyer, Doctor Kitić. Affecting a pair of greasy glasses to demonstrate that he is now a gentleman, he harangues Marcel about the importance of youth being educated in "the national spirit", by which he means in an integral Yugoslavist spirit. Marcel looks at this former school comrade of his and wonders "what exactly in this man has remained that is peasant, national and human; how much profit this man with the glasses makes from his village, as a man who parasitically flatters those who are the most obese and most powerful". Fittingly, Galić then collapses into a drunken heap.

He also meets an old friend of his father's – Gabrić, a pensioner, confides in Marcel his belief that God will send the Saviour to save Croatia. As he looks around the café, he notices that the Jewish innkeeper, Weiss, is "picking his hooked nose with his index finger" and Galić is still drunk and asleep. The village has sunk into degeneration and filth. While modernity has not come to the village and the peasants lead lives of poverty and backwardness, the vices of urban society have infiltrated the countryside; not simply the Jewish owner of the local bar, but alcoholism and the unprincipled pursuit of money and power. As he steps outside, it is still raining and the streets are grey with mud. After receiving a letter from his best friend, Ivan, and another one from Buga, he decides to return to the city, completely disillusioned by the reality of life in the village. He departs for the city eagerly, unaware that in his absence, his girlfriend and his best friend have developed a close relationship after Ivan rescued her from a drunken attack by an acquaintance of hers, a doltish young shop assistant called Martin. Oblivious to this, Marcel arrives in the Croatian metropolis in exultant mood and exclaims "Hello, Zagreb!" in his happiness. It is like returning to an old friend and he delights in rediscovering the pleasures of the city. "It seemed to him that he had been here only days before. He recognised everything. Everything was the same. Life in the village now seemed far away and struck him like a dream" (Balentović 1944: 33–43).

He has rejected the life of the village and thinks about "those depressing autumn afternoons" as he stirs his tea and waits for Buga. "The mud nauseated him, the empty faces, movements, words ... he decided to take on work, to return to his old life and to return again to Buga" (Balentović 1944: 46 f.). However, the sound of an orchestra causes him to reflect on his life and the melancholy returns. Above the empty chatter, he asks himself what he has achieved, what has been great or sacred? Or has it been empty? Sadly, he admits that it has. However, Buga can give him back his life. How much more crushing then is the blow at the climax of the story when his friend Div arrives in a blind panic to deliver the devastating news that Buga has been shot dead by Martin, the youth who had previously attacked her. Like the city itself, which is gleaming and dazzling on the surface, the brief love affair and the promise of happiness which it held out has all been an illusion. Buga, embodying the city, has fallen victim to its dangerous charms.

With this one act, the narrator informs his readers, the whole of Marcel's world and his youthful hopes have been destroyed. However, there is no going back: not just physically, but also emotionally and mentally, he has fled the village. In fiction, at least, Marcel's attempt to navigate his journey between the two worlds of the village and the city does not bring reconciliation. Instead, he finds himself alienated by the city and disillusioned by the village and a defeated stranger in both.

Conclusion

The relationship of the radical right in Croatia to the city during both the inter-war period and the subsequent Independent State of Croatia is one of deceptive complexity and frequent contradiction. Although much of the official rhetoric of the radical right in the inter-war period referred to the city and its supposed values in disparaging terms, the situation was far more complex than this. Similarly, when the Ustasha Movement came to power in 1941, its activists and cultural commissars heralded a return to pure Croatian values which were to be found in the peasantry and the life of the village. Despite the fact that a key aspect of the Ustashas' social vision involved an attempt to elevate the social and cultural life of the village through the introduction of modern urban technology, at the same time, they aimed to preserve the conservative moral values of the village: sexual chastity, opposition to abortion and contraception, and the traditional patriarchal family unit. The Ustashas hoped, too, that with their accession to power as peasant rulers in the heart of the city – and the concomitant curtailment of degenerate Jewish and Serbian influence – a moral as well as spiritual cleansing would take place and the authentically Croatian values of the peasant would spread to the city.

The ambiguous and ambivalent attitude of the radical right in Croatia to the city means that post-war historians of the Movement in both communist Yugoslavia and the West need to question their own attitudes and conclusions. For decades, the Croatian radical right was dismissed as a marginal political phenomenon divorced from mainstream Croatian society: the uneducated rural proletariat. As early as the 1930s, leftist literary and political journals were stereotyping radical nationalist students at the University of Zagreb as clericalist, village-educated totalitarian dolts. In some regards, this replicated the propaganda of the Ustashas who saw themselves as the embodiment of the authentic values of the Croatian nation.

The contention that followers of the radical right in Croatia were rural uneducated men, marginal and disappointed, now needs to be revised. As we have seen, social inequality and the quest for social justice, rather than social inadequacy, fuelled their anti-urban bias. Their real resentment against the city was reserved for its role as the embodiment of liberal capitalism. This had resulted, so they argued, in the exploitation and impoverishment of the peasantry, the death of the villages and a widening of the gulf between the city and the countryside. However, the remedy that the radical right prescribed – the elevation of the village through the introduction of technology and mass culture – was not only a tacit acknowledgement of the supremacy of urban values, but also introduced peasants to the very metropolitan values which the Croatian radical right, led by the Ustashas, despised. Ultimately, the Ustashas aimed to elevate the economic and social life of the villages by importing modern urban ideas and, simultaneously, cleansing the degenerate morals of the city through the incarnation of peasant culture and attitudes, in order to create a national consensus. In pictorial terms, they envisaged the village in the city and the city in the village, both populated by a nation of Croats and peasant-urbanites.

References

Balentović, Ivo 1934: Vraćanje selu [Returning to the village]. In: Hrvatska smotra 3, 7–8 (July – August) 345–347.

Balentović, Ivo 1941: O teškom životu seljačke žene [About the hard life of women in the village]. In: Hrvatska smotra 11: 9 (September) 533–536.

Balentović, Ivo 1944: Kako je minula Buga [How Buga passed by]. Osijek: Hrvatski list.

Basta, Milan 1971: Agonija i slom Nezavisne Države Hrvatske [Agony and breakdown of the Independent State of Croatia]. Belgrade: Rad.

Bzik, Mijo 1943: Ustaški pogledi [Views of the Ustasha]. Zagreb: Glavno ravnateljstvo za promičbu.

Colić, Mladen 1973: Takozvana Nezavisna Država Hrvatska [The so-called Independent State of Croatia]. Belgrade: Delta Press.

Djilas, Aleksa 1996: The Contested Country: Yugoslav Unity and Communist Revolution, 1919–1953. Cambridge: Harvard UP.

Dragoslav 1925: Zemlja [The soil]. In: Hrvatska radiša 20, 15 (October) 161–166.

Footman, David 1935: Balkan Holiday. London: Heinemann.

Freudenreich, Aleksandar 1942: Prosvjetna ognjišta [Fire-places of education]. In: Prosvjetni život 1, 4–5 (October – November) 168–176.

Hondl, Stanko 1937: Koje nove zgrade treba sveučilište? [What new buildings needs the university?] In: Alma Mater Croatica 1, 1 (September) 3–5.

Hory, Ladislaus, Martin Broszat 1964: Der kroatische Ustascha-Staat, 1941–1945. Stuttgart: DVA.

Ivastinović, Jakov 1942: Gladan sam dok otac kolje hranjenike and Na Badnjak sam daleko od kuće [I am hungry until my father kills the foster-child and On Christmas I am far from home]. In: Zbornik hrvatskih sveučilištaraca 1: 187–189.

Ivšić, Milan 1942: Nova Hrvatska – novi čovjek [New Croatia – new man]. In: Hrvatska smotra 11, 6 (June) 369–377.

Ivšić, Milan 1943. Prosvjetni problemi hrvatskoga sela [Educational problems of the Croatian village]. In: Prosvjetni život 2, 12–13 (June – July) 217–221.

Jelić-Butić, Fikreta 1977: Ustaše i Nezavisna Država Hrvatska [The Ustasha and the Independent State of Croatia]. Zagreb: Liber.

Jurišić, Krunoslav 1943: Architekura [Architecture]. In: Filip Lukas (ed.), Naša domovina. Zagreb: Glavni ustaški stan, 579–585.

Karamarko, Milivoj 1941: Novi ustaški djački rod [The new generation of Ustasha pupils]. In: Ustaša 11, 8, 24 August, 1.

Konjević, Mile 1971: O nekim pitanjima politike Ustaša prema Hrvatskoj Seljačkoj Stranci 1941 [On some questions of the policy of the Ustasha against the Croatian Peasant Party]. In: Vojnoistorijski glasnik 3: 173–189.

Konjević, Mile 1972: O odnosu Ustaša prema Hrvatskoj Seljačkoj Stranci i Stjepanu Radiću 1941 [On the relation of the Ustasha to the Croatian Peasant Party and Stjepan Radić 1941]. In: Jugoslovenski istorijski časopis 2: 104–112.

Križanić, Kamilo 1934: Selo i grad [Village and City]. In: Hrvatska smotra 2, 11–12: 401–403.

Križanić, Kamilo 1935: Mrtvi gradovi [Dead cities]. In: Hrvatska smotra 3: 5–6 (May – June) 289–290.

Lačen, Franjo 1942: Rad, radnici i seljaci u Nezavisnoj Državi Hrvatskoj [Work, workers, and peasants in the Independent State of Croatia]. In: Ustaški godišnjak 1: 165–171.

Lašić, Emil 1938: Naše suprotnosti [Our controversies]. In: idem (ed.), Zbornik hrvatske omladine Herceg-Bosne. Sarajevo: Kranjević, 7–9.

Marks, Zbiljko 1935: Rad i radnici [Work and workers]. In: Hrvatska smotra 3: 5–6 (May – June) 291–293.

Mikac, Marijan 1944: Tri godine hrvatskog slikopisa [Three years of Croatian newsreel]. Zagreb: Hrvatski slikopis.

Miloslavić, E. L. 1943: Kobno spriečavanje poroda [The disastrous prevention of delivery]. In: Ustaški godišnjak 2: 227–233.

Nikolić, Vinko 1944: "Za novu Hrvatsku – nova književnost" and "Pitanje hrvatske seljačke književnosti" ["For new Croatia – a new literature" and "The question of the Croatian peasant literature"]. In: idem (ed.), Nacionalni zadatci književnosti: književni nacionalno-odgojni članci. Zagreb: Hrvatska školska knjižnica, 33–38, 118–123.

Peršić, Nikola 1941: Bijeg sa sela [Running away from the village]. In: Hrvatska gruda 1, 62, 6 September, 5.

Popović, Laza 1922: Jugoslovenska žena [Jugoslav women]. In: Nova Europa 4, 1, 1 January, 1–3.

Prcović, Spasoje 1940: Nekoliko naših socijalnih načela [Some of our social principles]. In: Plava Revija 1, 1 September, 13–17.

Professor, N. N. 1941: Sveuclištarči i umjetničke izlozbe [University students and art exhibitions]. In: Alma Mater Croatica 5, 4 (December) 172.

Šen, Edo 1935: Izgradnja tehničkoga fakulteta [The construction of the Faculty of Technology]. In: Alma Mater Croatica 1, 5 (January) 132–141.

Sladovic, Eugen 1941: Selo i grad [Village and city]. In: Hrvatska smotra 9, 5–6 (May - June) 283–292.

Stahuljak, Tihomil 1943: Architektura u XX. stoljeću u Hrvatskoj [Architecture in the 20th century in Croatia]. In: E. Lukas (ed.), Naša domovina. Zagreb: Glavni ustaški stan, 713–714.

Sundhaussen, Holm 1983: Wirtschaftsgeschichte Kroatiens im Nationalsozialistischen Großraum 1941–1945: das Scheitern einer Ausbeutungsstrategie. Stuttgart: DVA.

Sundhaussen, Holm 1995: Der Ustascha-Staat: Anatomie eines Herrschaftssystems. In: Österreichische Osthefte 37, 2: 497–509.

Švel-Gamiršek, Mara 1942: Hrast [The oak tree]. Zagreb: Matica Hrvatska.

Topali, Zvonimir 1939: Opravdavanje seljacke države [The justification of the peasant state]. In: E. Lasić (ed.), Zbornik hrvatske omladine. Sarajevo: Kranjević: 10–15.

Articles in newspapers

Anon 1941: Povijesna važnost zakonskih odredaba o zaštita arijske krvi [The historical importance of the legal decrees about the defence of the aryan blood]. In: Hrvatski branik, 10 May 1941, 1.

Anon 1942: Selo i grad [Village and city]. In: Hrvatska gruda, 14 February 1942, 1.

Anon 1945: Sviest hrvatskog sela [The consciousness of the Croatian village]. In: Hrvatski radiša, 1 February 1945, 1.

Bogdan, Ivo 1942: Poglavnik [Our leader]. In: Spremnost, 10 April 1942, 2.

Čović, Marko 1943: Vitez Francetić [Knight Francetić]. In: Spremnost, 4 April 1943, 1–2.

Mirth, Karlo 1943: Iskra ličkog krsa [The spark of the karst of Lika]. In: Spremnost, 4 April 1943, 2.

M. K. 1939: Zašto dio hrvatskih umjetnika izlaže u novom, a drugi dio u starom Umjetničkom pavilonju [Why a part of Croatian artists exhibits in the new, and the other part in the old exhibition hall]. In: Novosti, 30 November 1939, 11.

Ti. 1939: Naša učeća omladina [Our learning youth]. In: Nezavisnost, 12 May 1939, 1.

The Quarters of Shkodra in 1918: Differences and Similarities

Siegfried Gruber, Graz

Introduction

This article deals with a topic not yet common among anthropologists or ethnologists: social topography. "Although spatial thinking has long been a part of anthropological inquiry, it has waxed and waned in its perceived utility and centrality to the field," according to Aldenderfer and Maschner (1996: v). Historical research in social topography is directed to a localisation, as topographically exact as possible, of direct or indirect social characteristics or personal data. It deals also with the analysis of their spread, distribution, and position at a point in time or over a period of time. Through this, we get insights into the social organisation of space within a city, for example. The starting point is a topographical attribution of personal data to the place of residence, and this place is also often the place of occupation. The result is generally a mapping, as complete as possible, of the economic and social characteristics of a city's population, i. e., covering the whole area, and with a large scale.

These results enable a social and spatial interpretation of the distribution of characteristics within a city. Comparing different cities highlights the particular structures of social areas within them, as well as their duration and change over time. This method also establishes the connections between the structure of buildings, their function, and the economic and social status of their owners or users. The underlying assumption of social topography is that social relations, social organisation, structures and activities, all influence and shape space. The structure of a city at a special point in time is, therefore, the outcome of these processes during the preceding periods of time (Denecke 2005: 123 f.).

Shkodra in the late 19th, early 20th centuries

In the first half of the 19th century the city of Shkodra grew to 40000 inhabitants (Shkodra 1988: 22) and was composed of 25 neighbourhoods *(mahalles)* divided into three districts, Tophane, Terzihan and Tabaki (Kiel 1990: 227). In the second half of the 19th century the importance of the city decreased and at the beginning of the 20th century, Shkodra suffered heavily from an earthquake (in 1905), the dissolution of the Ottoman Empire, and the creation of new state borders. Montenegro, only a few kilometres away from the town, became independent in 1878 and tried to expand its territory at the expense of the Ottoman Empire, to which Albania still belonged. Shkodra, as the commercial centre of Northern Albania, attracted Montenegro's particular territorial interests. In the Balkan Wars and World War One Montenegrin and Serbian armies invaded Northern Albania and tried to shift borders. Only after the Balkan Wars did Albania become an independent state. However, its infrastructure was rudimentary and its economy underdeveloped. During World War One, the Austro-Hungarian army occupied most of Albania after Serbia and Montenegro had been defeated. During this time Shkodra was the administrative centre and, by far, the largest city in the Albanian territory under Austro-Hungarian occupation. Under occupation, more than 20000 inhabitants lived in 19 different parts of the city.

My article deals with the social topography of the town at that moment in time. Several questions direct my explorations: Were the town quarters similar to each other or were there decisive differences between them? Can we distinguish between living quarters of Catholics and Muslims? Were the newer quarters inhabited by higher percentages of immigrants to the city than the older quarters? Did people with the same occupation live near each other? Can we see spatial patterns of gradual differences between neighbouring quarters or of sharp contrasts? Is it possible to divide the city into several groups of districts according to their characteristics?

Overall such research has been rather neglected in Balkan studies. The classic book on the Balkan city (Todorov 1983) does not deal with these questions, but from this book we know, for example, of the separate living quarters of Muslims and non-Muslims in Istanbul in the early modern period (Todorov 1983: 58). Recent Albanian studies on Albanian towns in the past by Hamdi Bushati and Valentina Duka deal with Shkodra and the urban developments in Albania, but use a different research approach (Bushati 1998, 1999; Duka 1997). The use of statistical material for such research on Balkan cities has been rather limited due to the lack of existing data and adequate maps, and a hesitation to use quantitative research methods. Nevertheless, new methods using sources in different ways than before can help to shed light on the structure of living in a town such as Shkodra.

Geographic Information Systems

"Geographic Information Systems (GIS), as they became practical tools for spatial analysis in the early 1980s, were quickly seized upon by archaeologists, who immediately recognised their potential" (Aldenderfer, Maschner 1996: v). A GIS can be defined as "a sophisticated database management system designed for the acquisition, manipulation, visualisation, management, and display of spatially referenced (or geographic) data" (Aldenderfer 1996: 4). GIS can "make spatial analysis easier, more flexible, and more powerful" (Goodchild 1996: 241). This method of research depends on the quality of the geographic information it uses and the special character of geographic data. "Geographical information is primarily cross-sectional – that is, it represents a 'snapshot' at a point in time. Mechanisms of cause and effect, on the other hand, are strongly temporal, and it is consequently difficult or impossible to deduce cause and effect from patterns observed in geographical data. Spatial analysis is primarily analysis of form, whereas understanding requires analysis of process" (Goodchild 1996: 245). Furthermore, geographical information is multidimensional, requiring at least two coordinates to define location, which distinguishes it from other kinds of information (Knowles 2002: xii).

As GIS becomes more and more widespread and easy to use, this tool could be of interest to anthropologists and ethnologists as well, dealing with phenomena situated in space. The advantage of maps over the use of tables in the representation and research of spatial characteristics is that spatial patterns can be seen more clearly. The researcher is not forced to aggregate data to larger spatial units but can use individual data. Thematic maps are not only a means of representation of data but also a means of research. A written text has a linear structure which is less well suited for the discussion of places, regions and geographical connections. Maps can, in contrast to written or spoken text, submit several statements and connections at the same time and combinations of them can lead to new results (Steidl 2003: 28). However, the use of maps in ethnological and historical research is still rather limited. A rather new possibility, Historical GIS, can overcome this hesitation. An example for the application of GIS technology in historical research of social topography is a map of Stralsund of 1706/7 with the places of residence of sailors, indicating their sex and status as renter or owner of the flat.[1]

Project data base

The source used for the present research is the Albanian population census compiled by the Austro-Hungarian army during World War One,[2] when it occupied most of the territory of the newly created independent Albanian state and established a new administration. The 1918 Albanian population census registered 524217 persons who lived in about 1800 villages, towns and cities in the territory under Austro-Hungarian occupation (Seiner 1922: 5). The research project "The 1918 Albanian Population Census: Data Entry and Basic Analyses"[3] funded by the Austrian Science Fund *(Fonds zur Förderung der Wissenschaftlichen Forschung)*

---

[1] http://www.uni-rostock.de/fakult/philfak/imd/lehrbuch/kroll_pp/schiffer.htm.

[2] A description and evaluation of this source can be found in Nicholson 1999.

[3] http://www-gewi.kfunigraz.ac.at/suedost/seiner/index.html.

from 2000 to 2003, aimed at transposing data from the primary census sheets into machine-readable form. The data was processed on the individual level, which permits much more detailed analysis than aggregate data on the village level, which is frequently the data base used for similar research. The researcher is able to aggregate data according to his/her own research agenda and is not bound by the categories already established as a consequence of the prior aggregation of the primary data by statisticians (see Hall, McCaa, Thorvaldsen 2000: 9). Individually based data enables the researcher to combine different variables on this basic level for research purposes. In our database, information on 135 395 persons has already been included.[4]

This data has been combined with a city map of Shkodra from the year 1923 (see Bushati 1998). The geographical information on the map (streets) is linked with geographical information about the inhabitants of Shkodra. The information on streets is aggregated to the level of town quarters for this article since, as a first step, it would be too difficult to already do research on the street level.

The quarters of Shkodra

Shkodra was divided into 19 quarters at that time and they differed considerably in size: the smallest only had 126 inhabitants, while the largest had 4 045 inhabitants, as can be seen in table 1. In maps 1, 4, and 7 (see pp. 153, 154, 156), the size of the circle represents the population of the respective quarter.

Table 1: The quarters of Shkodra in 1918

	abbreviation on maps	inhabitants
Ajasma	AJ	353
Arra e madhe	AR	1,118
Badra	BD	1,836
Bahçelleku	BC	416
Ballabanja	BL	653
Dudasi	D	1,301
Mahalla e ré	M	413
Ndocaj	N	1,019
Parruca e katholikwe	PK	1,063
Parruca e muslimanve	PM	808
Perashi i poshtërm	PP	1,590
Perashi i sipërm	PS	1,492

[4] http://www-gewi.kfunigraz.ac.at/suedost/seiner/availability.html.

	abbreviation on maps	inhabitants
Qafa	Q	341
Rusi i madh	RM	3,214
Rusi i vogël (i katholikwe)	RVK	1,209
Rusi i vogël (i muslimanve)	RVM	4,045
Tabaku	TA	126
Tepja	TE	671
Top-hana	TO	1,922
Total		23,59

In the older parts of the city, population density was lower than in the more densely populated quarters in the east of the city. The most populous quarters were situated in the north of the city, but they also encompassed quite a large area.

Population characteristics

The population of the Balkan countries in the 19th century was characterised by a male surplus. Only the wars of the 20th century led to a female majority among the population. The male majority in the 19th century is explained by the under-registration of females by census-takers and by the patriarchal nature of Balkan society which treated women worse than men, leading to a higher female mortality rate. The official data published from the Albanian 1918 census has also shown that although the male majority of 1371 persons is very slight, only 100.5 men were counted per 100 women (Seiner 1922: 8), which is a quite exceptional result for censuses in the Balkans at that time, where male majorities were usually bigger. According to the original census sheets, the population registered in Shkodra also had a slight male majority (103.2 men per 100 women), as in all the other Albanian towns (with the exception of Elbasan, which had a slight female majority). Serbian cities in 1866, for example, had a slight male majority as well; only in Belgrade the male population amounted to almost 60 percent of the total (Todorov 1983: 333). Within Shkodra, there were five neighbourhoods with female majorities, and several quarters with a slight male majority, more or less divided across the city east to west. The quarters with a larger male majority can be found in both the east and west of the city. The largest male majority was in two southern quarters with a male surplus of 17 percent. These differences in the sex ratio between the town quarters can probably be explained by differences in occupational structures.

When considering only the population actually present at the time of the census, though, there was a slight female majority in the city (96.4 men per 100 women). We see quite a similar pattern when looking at the individual town districts; those with only a slight male majority turn into quarters with a slight female majority, when the population actually present is solely taken into account. Most of the quarters with a large male majority retain their male surplus, and the female surplus in the district of Badra increases to more than 18 percent.

These differences in the sex ratios were caused by the fact that many more men than women were absent at the time the census was taken. 7.3 percent of all male inhabitants of the town were not present, compared to only 0.7 percent of the women. In the southern part of the city no woman was absent, while in the eastern parts of the city up to 3.2 percent of them were somewhere else at the time of the census. The pattern for men was different with especially high rates of absence in the centre and the south of the city. In one southern town quarter, 14.1 percent of the registered men were absent. The reasons for not being in the city were different, such as serving as a soldier, working somewhere else (partly as a migrant worker), or political. Men had much higher mobility, especially over longer distances, and this accounts for the striking differences between the ratios of absent men and women. Note that all the following data is based on the population that was present.

The population of the city was relatively young: 41.8 percent of the population present were younger than 18 years. This proportion was similar to other Albanian cities and was only slightly higher in rural areas. In other Southeast European countries the share of the young population was even greater: in 1900, more than half the population in Serbia, Bulgaria, and Romania was under 20 years of age (Sundhaussen 1989: 116). In Shkodra, the proportion of young people was mainly lower in the east of the city. The highest share of young people was once again on a line dividing the east and west of the city, the quarter with by far the highest share being Tabaku in the south of Shkodra with 52 percent.

Almost the complete population of Shkodra was made up of Albanians; only 4.4 percent were Slavs and 0.7 percent of another ethnicity. The percentage of Slavs in Shkodra was higher than their share in the whole of the country since the border to Montenegro was near. These ethnic minorities were concentrated in the north-west of the city. 66.2 percent of the inhabitants of Shkodra were Muslims, 30.6 percent were Catholics and 3.1 percent were Orthodox. These percentages differed from the confessional affiliation of the overall population of Albania, the majority of which was Muslim (74 percent), with smaller Catholic (18 percent) and Orthodox (8 percent) populations according to the published census results (Seiner 1922: 10). A major part of the Orthodox Albanian population, though, lived outside of the territory administered by the Austro-Hungarian Army in Southern Albania and, therefore, their share in this census is smaller than the share of the Catholics. The Catholic population was concentrated in the north of the country, as evidenced by their higher than average share in Shkodra. Here, the Catholics were concentrated in six eastern neighbourhoods of the city, as presented on map 1 (p. 153), while the Orthodox population lived in the north-east of the city. The map presents an almost complete segregation of the Muslim and Catholic population within the city, which corresponds with the information given by Ippen at the beginning of the century, who claimed that the segregation of Muslims and Christians was especially sharp in Shkodra (Ippen 1907: 39). In addition, there were two town quarters divided along religious lines (see table 1).

Literacy was an almost completely urban phenomenon at that time in Albania; in the countryside almost nobody was literate. In Shkodra 40.4 percent of men and 12.3 percent of women were literate among the population older than 12 years. Only the coastal town of Durrës had similar rates of literacy in Albania; all the other towns had much lower rates. The highest rates of literacy could be found in the Catholic quarters (the highest, with 77.9 percent, in Parruca e katholikwe) and one Muslim quarter in the centre of the city. Overall, male literacy rates were higher in the eastern half of the city than in its western half, where the lowest rate was 1.7 percent in Mahalla e ré. The female pattern of literacy was even more accentuated: in the Catholic parts, literacy rates reached 50.5 percent in Parruca e katholikwe, while in the Muslim parts in the south and north-west of the city no woman was literate (map 2, p. 153). The reason for such an enormous difference can be found in the fact that education was seen as more important among the Christian population and, in addition, Christian schools had better trained teachers, some of whom were foreigners. The schools were run mainly by the confessions themselves, with additional funding from the state for Muslim schools, and from foreign states and religious orders for Christian schools (Detailbeschreibung 1900: 98–101). As already mentioned above, this cultural difference between Catholics and Muslims with respect to schooling, especially of girls, was an almost completely urban phenomenon, as practically the entire rural population was without any formal education.

22.1 percent of the male and 20.5 percent of the female inhabitants were not born in Shkodra, but somewhere else. In the town Durrës, for example, about a third of the Inhabitants of the city were immigrants and in the town of Kavaja about 15 percent. In the north of Shkodra the percentage of male immigrants was higher than in the south of the city. In some quarters their share rose to a third of the population. The female pattern of immigration was quite similar, and the newer quarters of the city obviously hosted higher percentages of people who had moved to Shkodra than the older quarters, which were dominated by people already born there. Immigration to Shkodra was mostly from the villages to the south-east of the city and the towns of Podgorica and Ulcinj in Montenegro (Gruber 2005: 139). This was related to the independence of Montenegro from the Ottoman Empire in the year 1878 and the acquisition of additional territories, e. g. Ulcinj in 1881, as a result of which many Albanians left Montenegro (Ippen 1907: 3).

Household characteristics

Let us now turn to the characteristics of the households in Shkodra. The average household size was 4.2 persons per household, the same as in Istanbul (Duben, Behar 1991: 49), the capital of the Ottoman Empire, to which Shkodra belonged up to 1913. Of all Albanian towns, only Durrës had a smaller average household size than Shkodra. Among Shkodra's quarters, the average household size ranged from 3.6 persons in Arra e madhe to 5.0 in Tepja. There existed a corridor of quarters with larger households extending from the north to the south-west (map 3, p. 154). East of this was another corridor of medium-sized households and in the east and west the smallest households were situated. Most of the Catholic neighbourhoods belonged to the parts with smaller households. Another criterion to classify households is to establish the type of household that the people were living in at that time. By using Peter Laslett's household typology (Laslett 1974: 31), the following results can be obtained:

Table 2: Household typology in Shkodra in 1918

	percent of households	percent of people
institutional households	0.2	1.3
solitaries	6.1	1.4
no family	4.2	2.9
simple family households	60.4	53.6
extended family households	19.4	22.5
multiple family households	9.6	18.3

These two columns clearly show the difference between counting household types in percentage of households or in percentage of people living in such households: only some 10 percent of the households were multiple family households, but almost 20 percent of the people lived in such households. Multiple family households were much larger than the average household and therefore they gain weight in the second column whereas solitaries as the smallest possible households lose weight.

In Shkodra simple family households were more common, and multiple family households less common than in the other Albanian towns, which corresponds to the smaller average household size. Institutional households were present only in the Catholic quarters in the east (map 4, p. 154). In the *mahalle* Perashi i sipërm even 11.3 percent of the population were living in such "households", which included two monasteries, one orphanage, and the police barracks. Solitaries were more frequent in the north-east and north-west of the city, "no family households" had a higher frequency in the centre or centre-east of the city, with the lowest percentages being found in the south. Simple family households show no clear pattern of differentiated frequency within the city: a line of quarters with lower percentages could be seen running from the north to the south-west surrounded by quarters with average percentages, while in the south there were quarters with both high and low percentages. Extended family households were more common in the north-east of the city and in two southern quarters, while in the south-west of the city they were less common. Multiple family households were more frequent in the western half of the city than in the eastern half of the city, while the highest percentages were in two southern quarters. A higher percentage of simple family households corresponded to a lower household size, while a higher household size didn't always correspond to a higher percentage of multiple family households.

Marriage patterns

Albania lies east of the so-called Hajnal line, which divides Europe in two halves with respect to marriage behaviour: in the western part age at first marriage was high in the past and a high proportion of people remained unmarried throughout life, while in the eastern part age at first marriage was low and almost all people got married (Hajnal 1965). We can now test this assumption with the existing data of Shkodra. The age at first marriage was low for women: 58.5 percent of them were married or widowed at an age of about 20 years (in the age group of 18 to 22 years). But there were considerable differences in the percentage of women married at such an age within the city: the lowest percentages were to be found in a zone extending from the Catholic quarters in the east (25.9 percent in Perashi i sipërm) to the south-west of the city (map 5, p. 155). In the north and north-west of the city more than 60 percent of the women were already married or widowed at this age. The highest percentage of women already married or widowed at the age of 20 was in the southern quarter of Bahçelleku (88.9 percent).

Age at first marriage was much higher for men: at an age of about 35 years only half of them were already married or widowed. This means that the percentage of married men at 35 years of age was lower than that of women 15 years younger! Hence, the average age difference of married couples was quite large. The majority of quarters had intermediate levels of married men. Higher levels of married men occurred in the west, south and east of the city, while in the centre of the city lower levels of married men prevailed (map 6, p. 155). The extremes were 20 percent of married or widowed men aged 35 in Parruca e muslimanve and 95.2 percent in Mahalla e ré.

At the age of about 50, around a tenth of all men were still unmarried. This rate was much higher than in rural areas of Albania, and also within the city there existed considerable differences. In three quarters in the south and one central quarter, all men were married or widowed at such an age. Low rates of unmarried men were prevailing in the east and west of the city. The highest rates of unmarried men can be seen in two Catholic quarters and one quarter in the north and one quarter in the south (Bahçelleku 22.2 percent).

Age at first marriage in Shkodra was the highest within Albania at that time (Gruber 2002: 12) and it is clear that this pattern does not fit into the usual marriage pattern east of the Hajnal-line. It is also evident that urban marriage patterns differ from rural ones, on which Hajnal has based his observations. In Istanbul in the late 19th century, for example, age at first marriage was a bit lower than in Shkodra, but rising and considerably higher than in other Islamic or Middle Eastern cities. In contrast to Shkodra, however, marriage was almost universal in Istanbul (Duben, Behar 1991: 123–126).

Occupational groups

Another important information for research about social topography is the occupational structure. In Shkodra, information is available for most of the adult men. Their occupations have been coded by us according to the HISCO-scheme (see van Leeuwen, Maas, Miles 2002). Until now, only those professions are coded, which occur at least 10 times. The occupational structure of the adult (18 years and older) male population of Shkodra appears as follows:

Table 3: Occupational groups for adult men in Shkodra in 1918

major groups	number	percent
white collar workers	258	4.3
sales workers	1,059	17.5
service workers	651	10.8
agricultural workers	267	4.4
production workers	1,807	29.9
others (domestic work, co-working relatives, not working)	464	7.6
missing	1,546	25.5
total	6,052	100.0

The proportion of white collar workers and service workers was especially high compared to the other Albanian towns of that time. People working in white collar jobs were more often living in three central quarters (9.4 percent in Perashi i sipërm) and one southern quarter (map 7, p. 156). Only two of these town quarters are among those with the highest literacy rates. The second largest group was the sales workers, who were living mostly in the west of the city, near the bazaar. The lowest percentage of sales workers lived in the east and south of the city. In the quarter with the highest percentage (35.5 percent in Mahalla e ré) the percentage of sales workers was ten times that of the quarter with the lowest percentage (Ballabanja 3.6 percent). Service workers were concentrated in the Catholic quarters in the eastern part of the city, while agricultural workers were most common in two eastern and two southern quarters of the city. In the east and centre of the city, quarters with low shares of agricultural workers dominated. In the west, low to intermediate levels of agricultural workers prevailed while in the north there were higher levels of such workers. Aside from people with agriculture as their main source of income, many craftsmen were still engaged in some farming activities (Duka 1997: 178).

Production workers were the largest group in the city of Shkodra, mostly engaged in small scale artisan manufacturing (Duka 1997: 178), and they were especially common in one quarter in the centre of the town (60.9 percent in Mahalla e ré) and one in the north-east. In the south-west of the city and in two other Catholic quarters they were above average, while they were less common in the centre of the city. The group of "others" was more common in a corridor from the north to the south in the centre of the city, and the quarters with the lowest percentages were interestingly very close to them. The group of missing occupations is mainly made up of people whose occupation has not yet been coded and a minority of people without recorded occupation. They were again more common in a corridor running from north to south in the centre of the city.

Conclusion: grouping the quarters

It would be fine to have some groups or clusters of quarters instead of 19 individual quarters. A cluster analysis revealed that there were not simply three or four groups of quarters according to their characteristics, but that there existed one large group of nine quarters, or about half of the city, which somehow represented an "average quarter" (map 8, p. 156). The Catholic quarters formed two clusters of four respectively two quarters and there was another cluster of two Muslim quarters. In addition there were two quarters which differed from all the others. The Catholic quarters were characterised by high rates of absent population, few young people, high literacy rates, and a great significance of workers in the service sector. The group of the two Catholic quarters of Parruca e katholikwe and Perashi i sipërm was additionally characterised by a high share of people in institutional households, a higher age of female marriage, and high rates of never married men. The other four Catholic quarters had small households and many solitaries. The two Muslim quarters of Qafa and Mahalla e ré were characterised by low literacy rates, small households, many solitaries, a low age at female marriage, few never married men, and an important production sector. The quarter of Tabaku had a very young population, low literacy, no absent women, many simple family households, few never married men, and an important trade and agricultural sector. Finally, the quarter of Tepja was characterised by few absent men, low literacy, no absent women, large households, many multiple family households, and an important production sector.

We can clearly say that decisive differences existed between the quarters of Shkodra in 1918. The spatial pattern of differences between neighbouring quarters, however, is not always the same: there were gradual distinctions and sharp contrasts, depending on the variable in question. The younger quarters did have higher percentages of immigrants to the city than the older quarters. The assumption that people of the same occupation lived close to each other can only be partly verified, as our analysis was done only on groups of occupations and on the level of quarters. The grouping of quarters was not as clear-cut as first assumed.

Religion can be seen as a major distinguishing factor within the city. A combination of occupation, literacy, and place of birth (Shkodra, other town, or village) may be of similar relevance, but this hypothesis still has to be proved. Future research should go one or two steps further in taking the street level or even single houses as units of investigation. In such a way it should be possible to reconstruct areas of different characteristics within the city apart from the administrative boundaries of the quarters, which have changed over time and could have been arbitrarily drawn as regards the cultural, social, or other differences within the city.

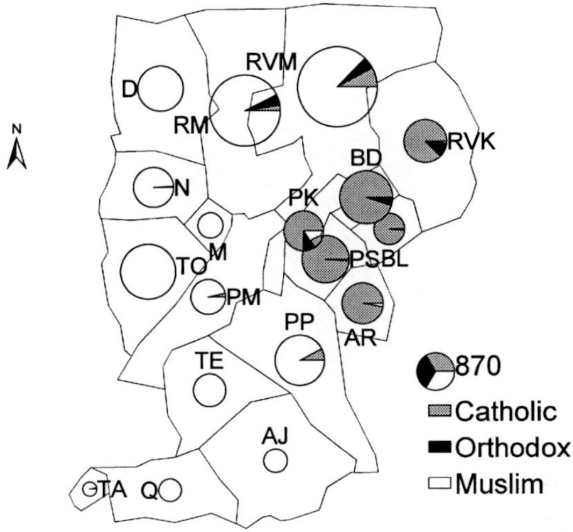

Map 1: Religion in Shkodra 1918

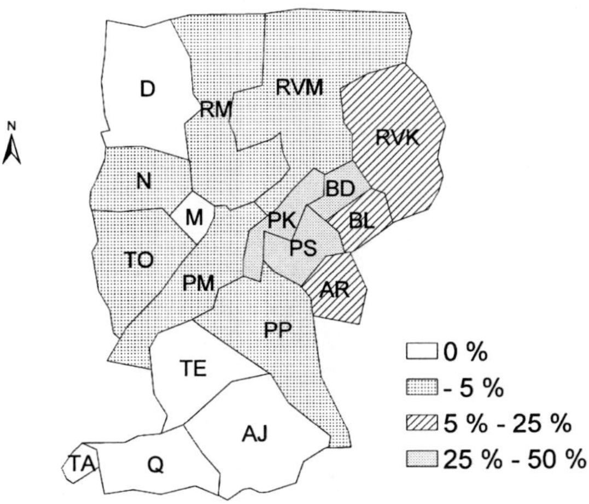

Map 2: Literacy of women in Shkodra 1918

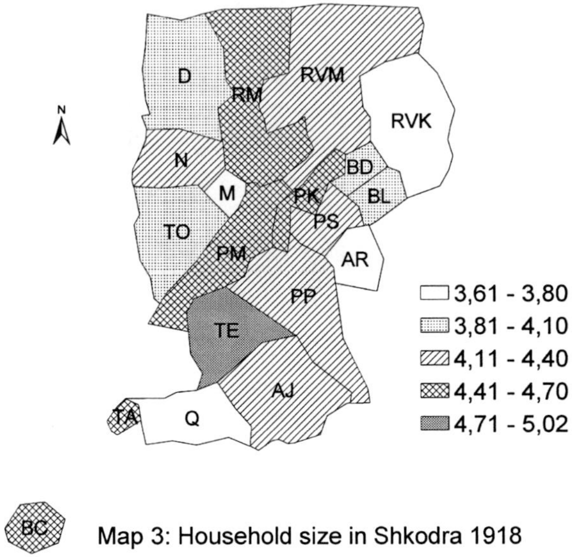

Map 3: Household size in Shkodra 1918

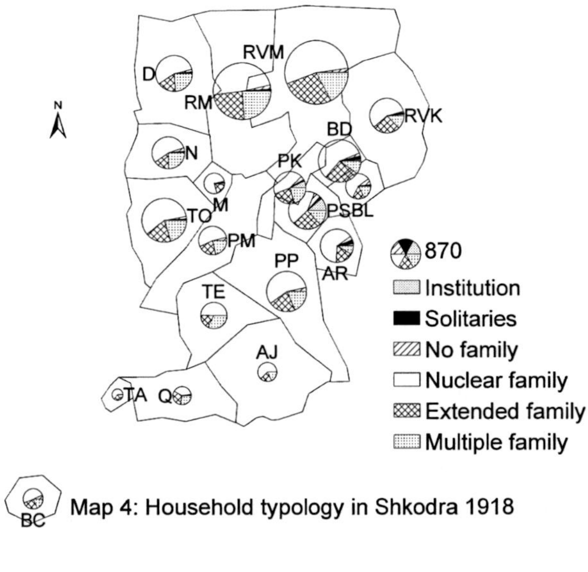

Map 4: Household typology in Shkodra 1918

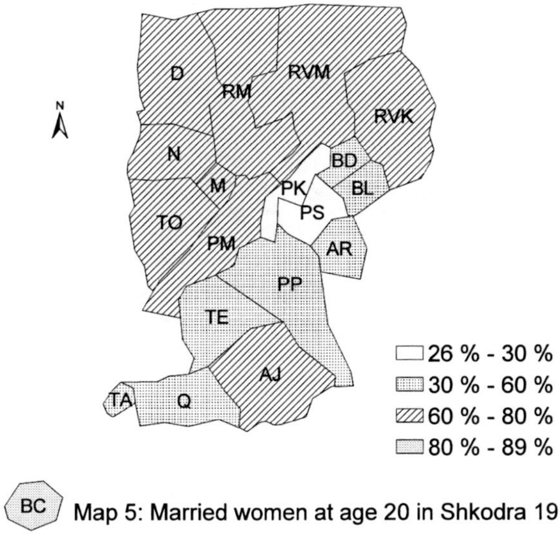

Map 5: Married women at age 20 in Shkodra 1918

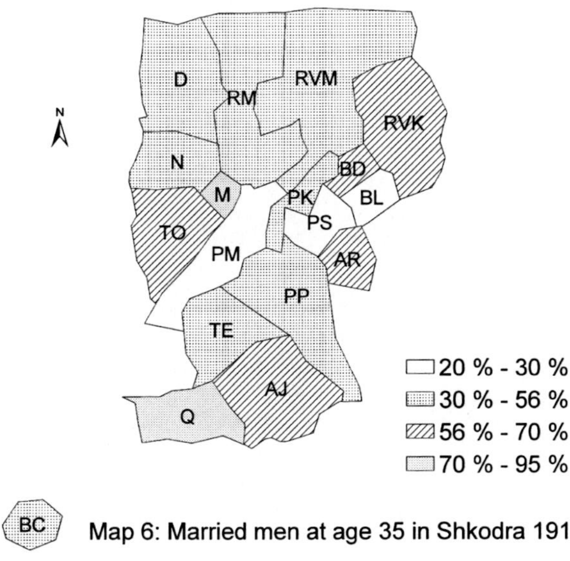

Map 6: Married men at age 35 in Shkodra 1918

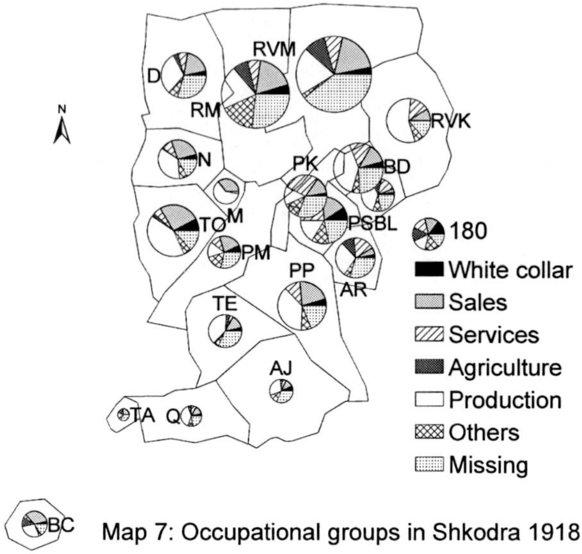

Map 7: Occupational groups in Shkodra 1918

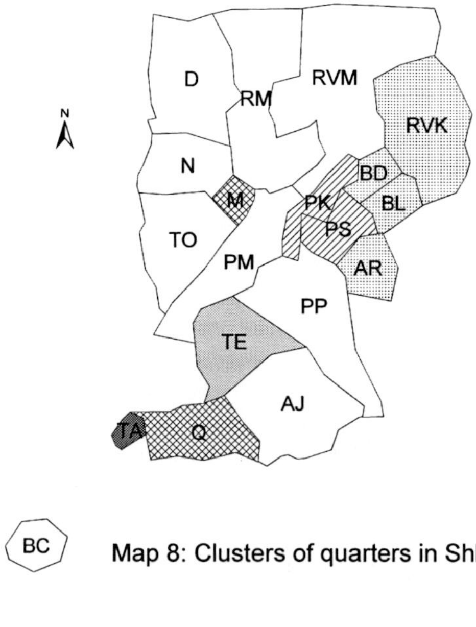

Map 8: Clusters of quarters in Shkodra 1918

References

Aldenderfer, Mark 1996: Introduction. In: Mark Aldenderfer, Herbert D. G. Maschner (eds.), Anthropology, Space, and Geographic Information Systems. New York, Oxford: Oxford UP, 3–18.

Aldenderfer, Mark, Herbert D. G. Maschner (eds.) 1996: Anthropology, Space, and Geographic Information Systems. New York, Oxford: Oxford UP.

Bushati, Hamdi 1998: Shkodra dhe motet (Traditë, ngjarje, njerëz) [Shkodra during the years. Tradition, incidents, people], Vol. 1. Shkodër: Idromeno.

Bushati, Hamdi 1999: Shkodra dhe motet (Traditë, ngjarje, njerëz) [Shkodra during the years. Tradition, incidents, people], Vol. 2. Shkodër: Idromeno.

Denecke, Dietrich 2005: Soziale Strukturen im städtischen Raum: Entwicklung und Stand der sozialtopographischen Stadtgeschichtsforschung. In: Matthias Meinhardt, Andreas Ranft (eds.), Die Sozialstruktur und Sozialtopographie vorindustrieller Städte. Berlin: Akademie (= Hallische Beiträge zur Geschichte des Mittelalters und der Frühen Neuzeit, Vol. 1), 123–137.

Detailbeschreibung 1900: Detailbeschreibung von Albanien. 1. Theil. Nord-Albanien mit den angrenzenden Theilen Dalmatiens und Montenegros. Wien: K. K. Hof- und Staatsdruckerei.

Duben, Alan, Cem Behar 1991: Istanbul Households: Marriage, Family and Fertility, 1880–1940. Cambridge et al.: Cambridge UP (= Cambridge Studies in Population, Economy and Society in Past Time, Vol. 15).

Duka, Valentina 1997: Qytetet e Shqip is n vitet 1912 924 [Towns in Albania between 1912 and 1924]. Tirana: Toena.

Goodchild, Michael F. 1996: Geographic Information Systems and Spatial Analysis in the Social Sciences. In: Mark Aldenderfer, Herbert D. G. Maschner (eds.), Anthropology, Space, and Geographic Information Systems. New York, Oxford: Oxford UP, 241–250.

Gruber, Siegfried 2002: Regional Variation in Marriage Patterns in Albania at the Beginning of the 20th Century. Unpublished conference paper, presented to the 2002 SSHA conference, St. Louis.

Gruber, Siegfried 2005: Occupational Migration in Albania in the Beginning of the 20th Century. In: Humanities, Computers and Cultural Heritage: Proceedings of the XVIth International Conference of the Association for History and Computing. Amsterdam: Royal Netherlands Academy of Arts and Sciences, 136–142.

Hajnal, John 1965: European Marriage Patterns in Perspective. In: David Victor Glass, David E. C. Eversley (eds.), Population in History: Essays in Historical Demography. Chicago: Aldine Publishing Company, 101–143.

Hall, Patricia Kelly, Robert McCaa, Gunnar Thorvaldsen (eds.) 2000: Handbook of International Historical Microdata for Population Research. Minneapolis: Minnesota Population Center.

Ippen, Theodor A. 1907: Skutari und die nordalbanische Küstenebene. Sarajevo: Daniel A. Kajon (= Zur Kunde der Balkanhalbinsel. Reisen und Beobachtungen, Vol. 5).

Kiel, Machiel 1990: Ottoman Architecture in Albania (1385–1912). Istanbul: Research Centre for Islamic History, Art and Culture.

Knowles, Anne Kelly 2002: Introducing Historical GIS. In: Anne Kelly Knowles (ed.), Past Time, Past Place: GIS for History. Redlands: ESRI Press, 1–18.

Laslett, Peter 1974: Introduction: The History of the Family. In: Peter Laslett, Richard Wall (eds.), Household and Family in Past Time: Comparative Studies in the Size and Structure of the Domestic Group Over the Last Three Centuries in England, France, Serbia, Japan and Colonial North America, with further Materials from Western Europe. Cambridge: Cambridge UP, 1–89.

Nicholson, Beryl 1999: The Census of the Austro-Hungarian Occupied Districts of Albania in Spring 1918. A Preliminary Note on the Manuscript. Newcastle upon Tyne: Centre for Scandinavian Studies (= Centre for Scandinavian Studies Papers, No. 5).

Seiner, Franz 1922: Ergebnisse der Volkszählung in Albanien in dem von den österr.-ungar. Truppen 1916–1918 besetzten Gebiete. Wien, Leipzig: Hölder (= Schriften der Balkankommission, Linguistische Abteilung, Vol. XIII).

Shkodra, Zija 1988: La ville albanaise au cours de la renaissance nationale (1831–1912). Tirana: Academie des Sciences de la RPS d'Albanie, Institut d'Histoire.

Steidl, Annemarie 2003: Auf nach Wien! Die Mobilität des mitteleuropäischen Handwerks im 18. und 19. Jahrhundert am Beispiel der Haupt- und Residenzstadt. Wien, München: Verlag für Geschichte und Politik (= Sozial- und wirtschaftshistorische Studien, Vol. 30).

Sundhaussen, Holm 1989: Historische Statistik Serbiens 1834–1914. Mit europäischen Vergleichsdaten. München: Oldenbourg (= Südosteuropäische Arbeiten, Vol. 87).

Todorov, Nikolai 1983: The Balkan City, 1400–1900. Seattle, London: University of Washington Press.

van Leeuwen, Marco H. D., Ineke Maas, Andrew Miles 2002: HISCO Historical International Standard Classification of Occupations. Leuven: Leuven University Press.

Center – Periphery: The Ethnicity of Serbs in Timişoara

Mirjana Pavlović, Belgrade

This paper seeks first to provide a relatively short revue of the historical development and most important contemporary features of the Serbian community in Timişoara. Secondly, it will explore the way in which complex processes of integration, acculturation, and assimilation influence the attitudes and values related to the maintenance of ethnicity as well as the dynamics within the group concerning the relations village - town and centre – periphery based on the community's point of view. The analysis is based on data gathered by field research in 2002 and 2003. A combined method of questionnaires, interviews, open discussion, and observation was used to obtain the data. Two questionnaires were used, the first for twelve pupils of the Serbian "Dositej Obradović" High School, the second involving fourteen male and female members of the Serbian community in Timişoara of differing ages and education levels. Around 40 people of various ages were interviewed in more detail, and open discussions were conducted with prominent members of Serbian minority organizations, and with their representatives at both state and local government levels. In addition, data was taken from various publications and from the weekly magazine *"Nasa reč"* (Our Word) published in Timişoara in Serbian.

Without providing a detailed analysis of the complex problems of acculturation and assimilation, it should be stated that in this paper a situational understanding of ethnicity is accepted, with emphasis on its symbolic and subjective dimensions (Pavlović 2003: 344–348). Successful assimilation means that a minority is absorbed into the dominant group, i. e., it disappears as an ethnic group. Acculturation, however, denotes the adoption of a foreign culture with a remaining consciousness of ethnic difference (Shibutani, Kwan 1965: 470–480, 504–51).

Timişoara is situated in Southwest Romania, in the Banat plain on the river Bega. It is an old city, first mentioned in historical sources as a fortress, "Castrum Temensiensis", in a diploma of the Hungarian King Andrew II from the year 1212 (Fenlački 2000: 138). Today it covers an area of 136 square kilometres in the middle of the Timiş-Torontine district. It has a population of 334081 (Secu 2002: 30). In the course of its long history the town and its inhabitants have been under the political domination and cultural influence of Hungary, Turkey, the Austro-Hungarian Empire and Romania. The latest major turnover happened with the fall of socialism in Romania after the end of the dictatorship of Cauşescu, whose dethroning started a revolution in this very town in 1989. Since then, the town as well as Romanian society in general have experienced a period of overall change, both economically and socio-politically.

These historical turbulences caused not only frequent changes in the ethnic structure, but also in the socio-political position, lifestyles and culture of the city's population.

The exact time in which Serbs settled in Timişoara has not been established, but it is certain that there were Serbs in the town before the Turkish conquest of 1552 (Popović 1933: 22). However, the majority of today's Serbs are descendants of the emigrants who fled from Serbia when it was occupied by the Ottomans from the 15th–19th century.

After the Turks had left and Habsburg rule was established, Timişoara experienced a great economic and cultural expansion, due to the accelerated development of industry and trade. In a few decades the small Turkish town became a central European city with wide urban streets and monumental buildings (Teleki 1959: 85). In this period there was both organized and spontaneous settlement in this area, firstly by Germans, then by Hungarians and Romanians. This resulted in a considerable increase in the population and changes in its ethnic structure (Cerović 1997: 79–81).

Life in the different town districts, which were for a time run by Serbian and German administrations, enabled the four groups of Germans, Hungarians, Romanians and Serbs to preserve their ethnic identity. At the same time the primary interest of the Austrian administration was social stability as the precondition for undisturbed economic development. This, combined with a long period of cohabitation, made integration through segregation possible, however paradoxical this may sound (Pavel, Popa 1999: 321). Parallel to the maintenance of cultural differences, a special civil, mercantile and cosmopolitan spirit was formed, which became the basis of inter-community cooperation. Timişoara was favoured more and more for its way of life and the patterns of its urban and central European cultural milieu (Nojman 2000: 2). At that time it was common for all inhabitants to know all four languages (German, Hungarian, Romanian, and Serbian) at an elementary conversation level. Correspondingly, the city has four names: Timişoara, Temesvár, Temeschburg, and Temišvar (ibid., 3).

After the incorporation of Timişoara into the Hungarian administrative districts and after the First World War in Greater Romania, integration through segregation was replaced by assimilation, first as Magyarization, then as Romanization. Credit for this can be given primarily to the establishment and development of nation states which, regardless of their structure, have always aimed at an open or quiet, inconspicuous assimilation of their minorities (Pavel, Popa 1999: 321).

As a result, at the end of the 19th and the beginning of the 20th century, the German, Hungarian and Romanian communities each made up approximately one third of the population, while in 1992 the Romanians represented 82% of the population, the Hungarians 9.5%, the Germans 3.9%, the Serbs 2.3%, and the remaining 2.3% comprised other ethnic groups (ibid: 322). Nevertheless, to this day, Timişoara has maintained elements of central European culture and urban spirit, not only in the architectural appearance of the city centre, but also embodied in the tolerance and peaceful cohabitation of its ethnic groups. It is still seen as a multiethnic, multicultural and multi-religious environment which guarantees the preservation and development of different ethnicities and their cultural cohabitation. "Why does the city government now insist that Timişoara should be multicultural? Timişoara is multicultural. It has always been. This is a fact. It is natural. Each community has its own life and its own holidays" (m, 45 years). "Between the First World War and the Second World War, Timişoara was a conglomeration. Nobody asked about nationality. Before the Second World War, all minorities lived together peacefully in this building [of the Serbian Eparchy which today is the seat of most Serbian minority organizations]" (m, 80 years).

Although in the past the Serbs represented a community rich in history, material and spiritual culture, and social life, nowadays in Timişoara they represent a minority ethnic community, largely because of assimilation and depopulation. Nevertheless, with its expanded network of minority organizations of various types, from educational to religious, from socio-political to cultural and sports, Timişoara still is a cultural, religious and political centre of the Serbian minority in Banat, and in Romania as well. Since the 17th century the see of the Serbian Eparchy has been in the city (Davidov 1990: 108 f.) which also hosts three Serbian Orthodox Church communities and the seat of the Serbian Association in Romania, the largest and most influential organization of Serbs in Romania. In Timişoara, the Serbs also have educational institutions in their mother tongue: two kindergartens, Serbian classes in Romanian primary schools, a primary school and the "Dositej Obradović" High School and a Serbian language department at the Faculty of Philosophy at the Western University. "Naša reč", a weekly magazine in Serbian, as well as the quarterly "Književni život" (Literary Life), are issued in Timişoara, and Timişoara Radio and TV broadcast a program in Serbian. There is also a Serbian Club, a Reading Room and various cultural artistic societies such as a choir, folk groups, tambour orchestras, etc.

Field research, especially the analysis of texts from the weekly "Naša reč", show that in the Serbian community in Timişoara there prevails a concept of ethnicity and/or ethnic identity in which the central place is reserved for tradition. More than 50% of the informants said that a person who had left the Serbian Orthodox Church or did not speak Serbian can not be a Serb. The community is also characterized by a common view of interethnic relations in which integration is seen either as only segregation or only assimilation, while adaptation and acculturation are considered as synonyms of assimilation. The picture of the life of the Serbs in rural and urban environments, in the past and present, has been formed and is demonstrated in accordance with this view.

Informants and especially journalists glorify the way of life of the past, particularly in the rural environment: villages which are considered to have been, until after the Second World War, inhabited, if not exclusively, then predominantly by Serbs, are idealized and presented as closed and compact ethnic environments where life was led exclusively in accordance with the traditional Serbian ethnic pattern. In families, but also in social communication, only the mother tongue was used. A rich social and cultural life went on, mostly in the form of numerous Serbian institutions, while the closed ethnic environment prevented to a great extent the adoption of foreign cultural elements. There was a particularly negative attitude towards mixed marriages which led to full assimilation. Thus, in the eyes of the present members of the Serbian community in Timişoara, villages were the keepers of unadulterated, "real" Serbian tradition.

It is clear that in such a stereotypical and polarized picture, the city, i.e., Timişoara, is viewed negatively. As a multiethnic environment it represents the basis for different foreign ethnic and cultural influences, and thus for the rapid and easy loss of roots, and inescapable assimilation. The signs are easily noticeable. The Serbs in Timişoara "have begun to stutter their language, and speak it with a German, Hungarian or Romanian accent" (Bugarski 2003: 55). In historical times it was considered "refined" to speak German or Hungarian, and Serbian declined in use, not just in mixed marriages but also in communication between members of the same ethnic group, or even in some homogeneous Serbian marriages. At the same time a number of elements disappeared from Serbian common practice and were replaced by traditions of other ethnic communities. Our informants considered that this led to the weakening, or even loss of national consciousness. They often quoted examples of neighbours whose first name or surname betrayed their Serbian roots but who were not aware of this.

The glorification of the past has, however, also led to a certain moderation of the negative image of the city. It is believed that in the past the Serbian community was much more homogenous even in the city. In this ethnic oasis of numerous Serbian institutions it was possible to maintain one's ethnic identity and its basic indicators. But the credit for this is again given to the villages from which a positive influence was spread to the urban environment. Thus the village to town migration, which at that time was not so significant, is viewed as a positive process, which contributed to the constant renewal and refreshment of tradition, enabling the Serbs in Timişoara not to "be lost".

However, in socialist Romania, agrarian reforms, land collectivisation, and industrialization led to the urbanization of a large proportion of the rural population who looked for work or, as they saw it, an easier life with a larger income. They left their villages and settled in towns. This process included members of the

Serbian community in Romania, among them a large number of so-called *kulaks* whose land had been confiscated, and others who found their rural dwellings destroyed after their captivity in Baragan.[1] This led to the depopulation of Serbian villages, leaving behind mostly the old or handicapped, and to the migration of many Serbs into towns, particularly to Timişoara, where their concentration is greatest nowadays. Members of the Serbian community would often say that Timişoara was "the largest Serbian village in Romania".

The post-war migrations completely changed the images of village and city. The departure of the younger, active population resulted in a reduction of social life, the extinction of Serbian institutions, and the fact that Serbian is heard less and less often, while common practices also disappear. "Once the young had left, there were no more *Slavas* [family celebration of its patron saint] and customs. In this village only the old are left. What will happen when we die, I do not know" (Perinac-Stankov 2002: 15). This gloomy picture changes only when "today's citizens and former villagers" drop into their villages in their spare time, or on holiday for a short time. "Only my elderly parents remained in the village. Every weekend I would travel there with my family, to help them about the house" (w, 60 years).

At the same time, and similarly, in Timişoara, it also happens that Serbian institutions are gradually being dissolved and social life is ceasing, although the town experiences an ever-growing concentration of its Serbian population. On the one hand, this is the result of the political conditions in which the minority communities and their institutions were subdued or at least not viewed kindly.[2] Villages and towns had only a few schools in minority languages and were confronted with a decreasing number of pupils, and the few churches were left almost without congregations. On the other hand, as most minority members were of rural origin, they did not practice their traditional customs in the city; they visited their villages, even if only for the important holidays, and tried at least to maintain the traditions in their parents' homes, under the patronage of the elders who were still familiar with them. "I have lived in Timişoara for thirty years, but I haven't left out one slava in my village. It's so beautiful. Everyone who lives in Timişoara comes. Guests from other villages come too. We gather. There's a big crowd outside the church in the afternoon, when we cut the cake, and in the evening there's a dance where we play our [national] music only" (Mišković 2002: 22).

Under such conditions the village retained its role as a centre of cultural and social life for the Serbs. In spite of this, the Serbs in Timişoara had a stereotypical, simplified and very gloomy picture of Serbian minority life and conditions

---

[1] In 1951 Serbs from villages along a 25 km border region with Yugoslavia were deported to Baragan, a sandy area in the Danube delta (Milin, Stepanov 2002).

[2] After WW II the oppression of ethnic minorities in Romania culminated in political processes and deportations to Baragan (Milin, Stepanov 2002).

both in the village and in the city until as late as the revolution of 1989. Then the picture changed once more. It was based again on the opposition village – city, centre – periphery, but in a different way. In the new situation of post-socialist transformation, aroused ethnic feelings, a renewal of tradition and of religiosity also affected the Serbian community in Timişoara. Thus in present Timişoara there is an extended network of minority institutions of various types, while reestablishing them in the villages where there are almost no Serbs left is very difficult, if not impossible. Nevertheless, members of the Serbian minority community and its institutions in Timişoara make great efforts to do this. Branch offices of ethnic institutions are opened in villages, local associations are promoted, celebrations or social events are organised not in Timişoara, but in villages, and so on. The city thus assumes the role of the village of the past and becomes the centre from where, paradoxically, Serbian traditional culture is spread.

Yet the nostalgic picture of the village and the past have not disappeared. On the contrary, they crop up very often and perhaps even stronger, mainly because the Serbian community in Timişoara is particularly heterogeneous (which it has probably always been) and variegated. For instance, a large number of the Serbian community members originate from villages, but from different regions of Romania, and thus numerous local variations appear in their culture, mentality, and even in customary practices. Furthermore, many Serbian community members were born in the city and their tradition, and their relation toward it, is also quite different; old ideological, political and religious divisions have not disappeared and new ones are emerging, for instance between democrats, globalists and nationalists. Moreover, the population of Timişoara has always had cosmopolitan orientations in all ethnic communities, including the Serbs, and has paid little or no attention to tradition and ethnicity. It is not irrelevant that all the above mentioned, as well as other differences which are today regarded in the Serbian community in Timişoara in a simplified way as cultural ones, are in fact only expressions of the struggle for better social positions of individuals and groups in the city within it.

The significant fact is that the small and mostly conservative group of Serbs in Timişoara, apart from all objective indicators, still has no power to open and to openly define its urban milieu as its centre and positive source of its culture and ethnicity. But this is precisely what it should do in order to survive and to develop its culture and tradition. For it is in the city where its cultural potential lies. Instead, the Serbian community in Timişoara still exhausts itself in social and cultural divisions, marking them symbolically as rural vs. urban, homogenous vs. heterogeneous, past vs. present, centre vs. periphery.

References

Bugarski, Stevan 2003: Srbi u Temišvaru [Serbs in Timişoara]. In: Izlaganja na naučnom skupu: Položaj i identitet srpske manjine u jugoistočnoj i centralnoj Evropi. Belgrade: Srpska akademija nauka i umetnosti, 52–62.

Cerović, Ljubivoje 1997: Srbi u Rumuniji od ranog srednjeg veka do današnjeg vremena [Serbs in Romania from the early Middle Ages to our days]. Novi Sad: Matica srpska.

Davidov, Dinko 1990: U temišvarskoj i aradskoj eparhiji [In the eparchy of Timişoara and Arad]. In: Velika seoba 1690–1990. Belgrade: BIGZ, 107–115.

Fenlački, Zdravko 2000: Temišvar - iz prošlosti i sadašnjosti grada [Timişoara - from the past and present of the city]. In: Globus 31, 24–25: 137–142.

Milin Miodrag, Ljubomir Stepanov 1996: Baraganska golgota Srba u Rumuniji 1951–1956 [The Baragan golgotha of the Serbs in Romania 1951–1956]. Temišvar: Demografski savez Srba i Karaševaka u Rumuniji.

Mišković, Srboljub 2002: Radost i uzdasi bivšeg štampara [Joy and sorrow of a former printer]. In Naša reč, 29. Novembar 2002: 17.

Nojman, Viktor 2000: Građanska kultura u Transilvaniji i Banatu. Uloga Temišvara u političkim promenama iz 1989. [Bourgeois culture in Transylvania and Banat. The Role of Timişoara in the Political Changes of 1989]. In: Habitus 1.

Pavel Sorin, Popa Nicolae 1999: Integration and Assimilation in the Urban Environment of Timişoara. In: Proceedings of the Regional Conference of Geography: Danube - Cris - Mures - Tisa Euroregion, Geoeconomical Space of Sustainable Development. Timişoara, Novi Sad, Szeged, Tübingen, 319–327.

Pavlović, Mirjana 2003: Etnički Identitet Srba u Temišvaru [The ethnic identity of the Serbs in Timişoara]. In: Tradicionalno i savremeno u kulturi Srba. Belgrade: Etnografski institut SANU, 339–348.

Perinac-Stankov, Ljubinka 2002: Moja generacija je ostala na selu [My generation stayed in the village]. In: Naša reč, 27. September 2002: 9.

Popović, Dušan 1955: Srbi u Banatu do kraja 18. veka [The Serbs in the Banat until the end of the 18th century]. Belgrade: Etnografski institut SANU.

Popovici, Virgil 1933: Ortodoxismul şi biserica naţională românească din Timişoara [Orthodoxy and the Romanian national church in Timişoara]. Timişoara.

Secu, Cornel 2002: Timişoara, Timiş ghid. Ghidurile Române.

Shibutani, Tamotsu, Kwan M. Kian (eds.) 1965: Ethnic Stratification. A Comparative Approach. New York, London.

Teleki, Dominik 1959: Putovanje kroz Ugarsku i neke susedne zemlje. Treće putovanje kroz južne prijedele Ugarske [Travels through Hungary and some neighbouring countries. Third trip through the southern parts of Hungary]. In: Zbornik za društvene nauke 23: 82–87.

Konstruktion von Identitäten in Grenzzonen. Interkulturelle Geschlechterbeziehungen am bulgarisch-griechischen Beispiel

Ana Luleva und Cvetana Bončeva, Sofia

Einleitung

Die Stadt als Kontakt- und Interaktionsraum verschiedener Gemeinschaften und Kulturen ist ein unerschöpflicher Gegenstand anthropologischer Untersuchungen. Das Thema unseres Beitrags widmet sich einem Aspekt dieses Problemzusammenhanges, nämlich der Beziehung zwischen zwei anthropologischen Hauptkategorien und ihrer Konstruktion im Milieu der Stadt: ethnische Identität und Geschlecht.

Unsere Überlegungen basieren auf Feldforschungen, die wir 2003 und 2004 in den Städten Sozopol, Pomorie und Nesebăr an der südlichen bulgarischen Schwarzmeerküste durchgeführt haben.[1] Wir wollten den Stand der Dinge hinsichtlich der Frage, ob eine „griechische Gemeinschaft" in Bulgarien existiert und wie sie konstruiert wird, vor Ort überprüfen. In der heutigen Vorstellung in Bulgarien werden diese Städte fest mit dem „Griechischen" assoziiert: Sie sind als antike griechische Kolonien gegründet worden und weisen eine lange historische Kontinuität als „griechische Städte" auf. Ein Teil ihrer Bewohner ist gemäß den bulgarisch-griechischen Verträgen über Bevölkerungsaustausch in den zwanziger und dreißiger Jahren des 20. Jahrhunderts nach Griechenland emigriert, ein anderer Teil aber geblieben – diese Menschen haben den „eigenen" Geburtsort dem „fremden" Nationalstaat vorgezogen.

Anfänglich war es unsere Absicht, die aktuelle Lage dieser Gruppe zu beschreiben; dieses Vorhaben wurde vor Ort korrigiert. Schon nach den ersten Gesprächen und narrativen Interviews wurde deutlich, dass es eine inadäquate Herangehensweise wäre, die „Griechen" abzusondern und „in sich selbst" zu untersuchen. Damit würden sie eine als in der Zeit konstante ethnische Gemeinschaft konstruiert werden; als ein geschlossenes Universum, das durch feste Grenzen von den Bulgaren getrennt ist. Dies entspräche weder der gegenwärtigen Realität noch dem Leben dieser Gruppen in den letzten Jahrhunderten. Andererseits inkludiert unsere Untersuchung auch die Identifikation der – für die Identi-

---

[1] Zu verschiedenen Phasen des vom Sofioter Institut für Minderheitenprobleme und Interethnische Beziehungen IMIR finanzierten wissenschaftlichen Projekts waren folgende wissenschaftlichen Mitarbeiter/innen des Ethnografischen Instituts der Bulgarischen Akademie der Wissenschaften beteiligt: Račko Popov, Ivan Nikolov, Svetla Rakšieva, Šterion Šerionov, Ana Luleva, Ženja Pimpireva und Cvetana Bončeva.

tätskonstruktion – *„significant others“:* in diesem Fall die bulgarischen Umsiedler, die sich in mehreren Wellen in diesen Städten niedergelassen haben. Somit wurde die Interaktion zwischen Einheimischen und Zusiedlern während der vergangenen rund achtzig Jahre, durch die neue Identitäten und Lokalkulturen entstanden, zum Gegenstand unserer Analyse. Diese neuen Identitäten und Lokalkulturen stehen sowohl dem „rein Bulgarischen“ als auch dem „rein Griechischen“ – Definitionen, die von unseren Interviewpartnern oft benutzt wurden – fern, denn ihr grundlegendes Kennzeichen ist Hybridität. Darüber hinaus stellten wir zwischen den drei betrachteten Städten Unterschiede fest, die sich vor allem aus den örtlichen Umweltbedingungen und wirtschaftlichen Verhältnissen ergeben.

Hybridität ist in diesem Fall nicht als mechanische Mischung von essentialistisch definierten Kulturen von Einheimischen und Zuwanderern zu verstehen, sondern eher als Gegenbegriff zur Vorstellung des Substantiellen, der festen Dichotomien, des Statischen. Als Muster kultureller und sozialer Organisation lässt sie sich definieren als Art, in der die Formen sich von den herrschenden Praktiken unterscheiden und sich von neuem in neue Formen und neue Praktiken zusammensetzen (Rowe, Schelling 1991: 231, zit. nach Niederveen Pieterse 2004: 75).

Der Akzent der Analyse liegt auf dem prozessualen Charakter der Interaktionen und ihrer Untersuchung in historisch unterschiedlichen Kontexten, womit die „Kinderkrankheit“ der Kulturanthropologie vermieden werden soll: die ethnografische Beschreibung des täglichen Lebens als spezifische lokale Welt, konstruiert als „Mosaik diskontinuierlicher, scharfer kultureller Unterschiede, statt als Netz untereinander verbundener und verflochtener kultureller Varianten“ (Dženkins 2001: 23). Im Prozess der Hybridisierung werden Identitäten konstruiert, die auch durch Beziehungen von Macht, Ungleichheit und Asymmetrie verbunden sind. Dabei ist die individuelle Ebene von grundlegender Bedeutung für das Verständnis der Bildung von ethnischen Identitäten, die nicht als monolithisch, abgeschlossen, sondern als flexible, sich verschiebende betrachtet werden (Brunnbauer 2002: 7–11).

Wir werden uns hier mit zwei Aspekten der Konstruktion ethnischer Identitäten beschäftigen: Geschlechterkonstruktionen einerseits und Mischehen in der ersten Hälfte des 20. Jahrhunderts andererseits. Bei der Untersuchung wurden zum einen qualitative ethnografische Methoden angewandt (autobiografische Interviews und teilnehmende Beobachtung), zum anderen Daten aus den kommunalen Eheregistern, Pressematerialien (lokale und nationale Presse) und historische Untersuchungen über die Region ausgewertet.

Der historische Kontext

Dramatische demografische, ökonomische und politische Veränderungen im 20. Jahrhundert machen die südlichen Schwarzmeerstädte zu einer Grenzzone in anthropologischem Sinne, was zu verstehen ist als „nicht scharf umrissene Linien, sondern Zonen, wo Dinge allmählich in etwas anderes übergehen, wo Unbestimmtheit, Ambiguität und Unsicherheit besteht“ (Hannerz 1998: 9). Die Grenzzone als solche wird unter den Bedingungen der nationalistischen Politik der Balkanstaaten konstruiert, die in ihrem Bestreben, die „eigene“ ethnische Nation politisch zu einigen, feste Grenzen errichten (vgl. zum Zusammenhang von Ethnizität und Territorium Giordano 1999). Erreicht werden soll das nicht realisierbare Ziel der ethnischen Homogenität durch den Ausschluss der ethnisch „anderen“ vom nationalen Körper (d.h. durch „ethnische Säuberung“) oder durch deren Assimilierung. Ein direktes Ergebnis dieses Vorhabens und der nationalistischen Politik waren Migrationen der ethnischen Gemeinschaften zwischen benachbarten Balkanstaaten. Die Kulmination in den Umsiedlungsbewegungen nach Bulgarien setzte nach dem Ersten Weltkrieg im Jahr 1919 ein. Damals strömten nach drei aufeinander folgenden, im Namen des nationalen Ideals geführten Kriegen zur Vereinigung der bulgarischen Nation in den Grenzen des eigenen Staats (Balkankriege 1912–1913, Beteiligung am Ersten Weltkrieg, 1915–1919) - nach verschiedenen Quellen - zwischen 253 000 und 350 000 Flüchtlinge aus den außerhalb der Grenzen Bulgariens gebliebenen Gebieten ins Land: aus Ost- und Westthrazien, dem griechischen und serbischen Makedonien, den so genannten „westlichen Grenzgebieten“ *(zapadni pokrajnini)* und der Dobrudža (Kosatev 1976: 262, Dimitrov 1985: 262). Viele von ihnen ließen sich in der Hoffnung, in ihre Heimatorte bald zurückkehren zu können, in Grenznähe nieder.

In Sozopol, Pomorie und Nesebăr siedelten sich in einigen Wellen Flüchtlinge an.[2] Bis zum Beginn des 20. Jahrhunderts von einer kompakten griechischsprachigen Bevölkerung bewohnt, waren diese Städte von den Bulgaren als Inseln der „Gräzität“ in der jungen bulgarischen Nation aufgefasst worden. Die Politik der nationalen Homogenisierung des Staates und der verschärfte ethnonationale Gegensatz zu den Nachbarn wegen der ungeklärten bulgarischen nationalen Frage trugen zur Konstruktion der griechischsprachigen Bevölkerung als ethnisch – folglich auch national - „fremd“ bei. Diese Bevölkerung erfuhr damit eine unaufhörliche Abwertung ihres sozialen Prestiges.

---

2 Die Frage der genauen Zahl der Ansiedler in den drei Städten müsste gesondert untersucht werden. In den Untersuchungen zur Flüchtlingsfrage in Bulgarien wird hervorgehoben, dass der Kreis Burgas (zu dem die drei Küstenstädte gehören) einer der Kreise mit der größten Anzahl von Flüchtlingen war. Im Zeitraum 1913–1931 wurden dort am meisten Flüchtlinge untergebracht: 14 910 Familien, insgesamt 64 504 Personen (Kosatev 1976: 53).

Nach dem Ersten Weltkrieg wurde mit dem Friedensvertrag von Neuilly zugleich eine „Konvention zwischen Bulgarien und Griechenland bezüglich der gegenseitigen Aussiedlung“ unterzeichnet, welche der jeweiligen griechischen beziehungsweise bulgarischen Minderheit die Option der „freiwilligen Auswanderung“ eröffnete. Ergänzend wurde eine Vereinbarung bezüglich der Entschädigung der Auswanderer erzielt. In der Praxis fungierte die Konvention über freiwillige Auswanderung als Instrument zur Durchsetzung von zwangsweiser Aussiedelung der entsprechenden Gruppen und in der Folge wurde unausgesprochen die Position akzeptiert, dass es in den beiden Ländern keine entsprechenden Minderheiten mehr gebe.

Diese Übereinkunft und die folgende Aussiedlung vor allem von Griechen aus den Schwarzmeerstädten Ende der 1920er Jahre waren der Schlüssel für das weitere Schicksal derer, die in ihren Geburtsorten blieben. Sie wurden nicht als Minderheit zum Objekt staatlicher Politik (weder seitens des bulgarischen noch des griechischen Staats), was ihre Möglichkeiten reduzierte, ihre kollektive Identität aufzubauen und zu erhalten. Die einzige Ausnahme war die Zeit des Zweiten Weltkriegs, als die Griechen in den Schwarzmeerstädten als (fremde) ethnische Gruppe Objekt einer diskriminierenden Politik wurden – eine Tatsache, die im kollektiven Gedächtnis der Gruppe zu einem Pfeiler der Auffassung von einer ethnischen Gemeinschaft wurde. Das damals verhängte Verbot, Griechisch zu sprechen, sowie eine Sperrstunde für Griechen stärkten die kollektive Identität als „andere“, von den Bulgaren unterschiedene Gruppe. Dies ist das sich wiederholende, fast legendäre Motiv in den Erzählungen unserer Gesprächspartner, das sie als Argument für ihr „Anderssein als die Mehrheit“ vorbringen.

Aber die Politik ihrer Nichtanerkennung als Minderheit, das Fehlen jedweder – positiver oder negativer – Gruppendiskriminierung, die sich auch in der Periode des Staatsozialismus fortsetzt, ließ keine Alternative für die Wahl einer nationalen Identität zu und hatte die unmittelbare, nicht durch die Gruppe vermittelte Bindung des Individuums an den Staat und seine Institutionen zur Folge. Die erzählten „sozialistischen Normalbiografien“ dieser Leute zeigen, dass sie die Bedingungen der neuen politischen Realität akzeptierten und sich als Individuen um Integration in die sozialistische Ordnung bemühten, indem sie ihre Gruppenzugehörigkeit verdrängten. Bei der für die Periode charakteristischen Entzweiung zwischen öffentlichem und privaten Leben wurde öffentlich eine bulgarische nationale Zugehörigkeit demonstriert. Das ethnisch und kulturell „Andere“ blieb in den Rahmen von Haus und Familie eingeschlossen. Auf der Ebene der alltäglichen Interaktion wurden aber die kulturellen Unterschiede der Griechen zu den „Anderen“ als Ausdruck ethnischer Unterschiede aufgefasst.

Geschlechterkonstruktionen

Geschlechterkonzepte und -beziehungen sind von großer Bedeutung für die Interaktion von Einheimischen und Zusiedlern. Sie beeinflussen nicht nur die Prozesse der Interaktion, sondern sie werden durch sie konstruiert und ausgehandelt. In solcherart Prozessen ist Geschlecht nicht allein wirksam, sondern wird gleichzeitig mit und durch andere Strukturkategorien, Subjektpositionierungen und Differenzen geschaffen (wie ethnische, religiöse und Klassenzugehörigkeit, Bildungsniveau, Lebensalter) und von politischen und ökonomischen Verhältnissen sowie institutionellen Einflüssen mitbestimmt (Schlehe 2000: 8). Da Gender soziokulturell konstruiert wird, werden die Unterschiede zwischen Geschlechterbildern und -arrangements in beiden Gemeinschaften als Ausdruck kultureller und ethnischer Unterschiede und Grenzen aufgefasst. So wird den Gender-Unterschieden zusammen mit den übrigen „Kulturmarkern" (Smith 2000: 38) Objektivität und Natürlichkeit (Essentialität) beigemessen. Sie bauen auf stereotypen Bildern der Anderen auf und verwandeln sich leicht in solche. Nach Strebe und Insko sind Stereotypen „a set of beliefs about the personal attributes of a group of people" (zit. nach Roth 1998: 23). Oft stehen sie in Verbindung mit Vorurteilen, d. h. mit bereits vor der eigenen Erfahrung mit dieser Gruppe existenten Urteilen, die ungeprüft übernommen werden. Vorurteile ergeben sich jedoch erst aus dem Zusammenspiel von affektiven Einstellungen und den eher kognitiven Stereotypen. Vorurteile sind affektive, emotional geladene, meist schon früh erworbene bzw. unkritisch übernommene, verhaltensrelevante Einstellungen (Roth 1998: 23).

Stereotypen und Vorurteile haben Einfluss auf den täglichen Umgang zwischen Griechen und Bulgaren, werden durch ihn bestätigt, aber auch erschüttert. Hinsichtlich der Geschlechterbilder ist oft ein Auseinanderklaffen der narrativen Ebene und der Ebene der Interaktion zu beobachten: Mitgeteilt werden Ansichten über die Andersartigkeit und die spezifischen negativen Züge der Männer und Frauen von der „anderen" Seite, aber es stellt sich heraus, dass in Wirklichkeit verwandtschaftliche und freundschaftliche Beziehungen zu ihnen bestehen.

Die ethnischen Charakteristika werden benutzt, um Probleme in den Familienbeziehungen zu erklären – wenn es keine Probleme in der Ehe gibt, wird die Tatsache, dass einer der Ehegatten von der „anderen" Seite stammt, nicht vermerkt und wenn sie doch erwähnt wird, werden sofort die guten Eigenschaften der Gemeinschaft seiner Herkunft hervorgehoben („es gibt keinen Unterschied zwischen uns, wir sind alle Christen"; „sie sind auch gute Menschen, sie sorgen für ihre Familien, sie sind fleißig"). Wenn es aber Spannungen in der Ehe gibt oder gar zur Scheidung gekommen ist, wird der Konflikt „ethnisiert" und werden die mit negativen Stereotypen behafteten Eigenschaften der „anderen" hervorgehoben: „die bulgarischen Männer sind Grobiane, sie schlagen ihre Frauen"; „hör bloß auf – Griechen!". Die ethnischen wie auch die ethnisch determinierten Gender-

Stereotypen verändern sich nur langsam im Laufe der Zeit. Der Ursprung vieler stereotypisierte Geschlechterbilder, die den beiden Gemeinschaften zugeschrieben werden, kann auf die Zeit ihres ersten Aufeinandertreffens in die 1920er und '30er Jahre datiert werden. Statisch durch die Zeit transportiert sind sie Teil der kollektiven Erinnerung geworden und werden heutzutage benutzt, um die kollektiven Züge und Unterschiede zu bezeichnen; so werden diese Abbilder zu Stereotypen. Derart sind zum Beispiel die Vorstellungen von der griechischen und der bulgarischen Frau – erstere sei eine *„Kokona"*, d.h. eine aufgetakelte Frauensperson, letztere eine *kaciveli* (Bäuerin). „Kokona" ist nicht nur eine Bezeichnung für Griechinnen und das Bild von Griechinnen, sondern der Ausdruck umfasst all das, was die bulgarischen Frauen nicht sind. Er umschließt ganz allgemein die Mentalität, Lebensart, die Position in der Familie, die äußerlichen Eigenschaften u.ä. der griechischen Frauen. Es geht um eine im Vergleich zur bulgarischen Vorstellung und Manifestation andersartige Form von Weiblichkeit.

Nach Fredrik Barth akzeptieren wir eine Kultur, indem wir ihre Verschiedenheit akzeptieren. Der wesentliche Unterschied zwischen Einheimischen und Zusiedlern in der Repräsentation von Geschlecht ist auf die Tatsache zurückzuführen, dass sie verschiedenen Kulturen angehörten. Die einheimischen Bewohner waren Träger einer alten Stadtkultur und verdienten ihren Lebensunterhalt als Fischer und kleine städtische Handwerker, die neuen Siedler hingegen waren Dorfbewohner und Bauern gewesen. Sie kamen mit ihren Ochsenkarren und ihrem landwirtschaftlichen Inventar und ließen sich mit ihrem Vieh am Rande der Ortschaften nieder, wo sie begannen, das Ödland zu bearbeiten, um sich vor Hunger und Elend zu retten. Ihre ersten Behausungen waren niedrige Erdhütten, die von innen und außen mit Lehm bestrichen waren. Alle, auch Frauen und Kinder, arbeiteten auf dem Feld. Davon setzte sich das Bild der griechischen Häuser ab – obschon sie nicht reich waren, sicherten die Männer doch den Lebensunterhalt mit Fischerei und Kleinhandel, und die zweistöckigen Holzhäuser waren in städtischer Manier gehalten – mit schmucken Vorhängen, gewebten Teppichen, Spitzen. Die Hauptaufgabe der griechischen Frauen war, sich um Haus und Familie zu kümmern.

Dieser soziolkulturelle Unterschied wurde mit Werten beladen: Die Stadt war das Symbol für Prestige, Zivilisiertheit, gute Erziehung und Umgangsformen, gewöhnlich durch das türkische Wort *„tertip"* bezeichnet, wohingegen das Dörfische für Primitivität, Zurückgebliebenheit, Grobheit, „Wildheit" stand. Die Griechinnen waren die Verkörperung der urbanen Vorstellung von Weiblichkeit – zart, mit schöner städtischer Kleidung, während die Bulgarinnen, in dicke Trachten *(sukmani)* gekleidet, das traditionelle Leben des Dorfes personifizierten, in dem die für die landwirtschaftliche Arbeit notwendige physische Ausdauer geschätzt wurde.

Aus einer derartigen Perspektive ist es interessant, wie sich die Informantinnen heute mit den beiden Gemeinschaften identifizieren. Gegenwärtig gibt es nicht eine

„griechische“ Familie, die Ergebnis ethnischer Endogamie ist. Die Offenheit der griechischen Gemeinschaft für Ehen mit Partnern von außerhalb ist ein charakteristisches Merkmal, das auch in Fallstudien über die Griechen in anderen Städten Bulgariens konstatiert wurde (Vălčinova 1999, 2001). In jeder Familiengenealogie ist die Rede von Ehen mit Bulgaren und Bulgarinnen, die aus dem Landesinneren stammen oder Umsiedler waren. Wenn sie ihre Familiengeschichte erzählen, unterstreichen unsere Gesprächspartner und -partnerinnen stets, dass sie „gemischter“ Abstammung sind. Im Laufe des Gesprächs identifizieren sie sich mal mit den Bulgaren als Nation („wir Bulgaren ...“), mal betonen sie voll Stolz ihre von den „örtlichen Griechen“ ererbte Würde („bei uns Griechen ist es so“). Gewöhnlich ist das „Griechische“ mit Haus und Geschlechterbeziehungen verbunden. In ihren Erzählungen schaffen unsere Gesprächspartnerinnen eine narrative Identität, indem sie aus den zahlreichen Möglichkeiten ihrer Zugehörigkeit jene zum prestigeträchtigen „Griechischen“ wählen, das sie mit einer idealisierten Vorstellung von der griechischen Frau der Vergangenheit verbinden: „Die Griechinnen haben sich nur um das Haus und die Kinder gesorgt. Sie sind perfekte Hausfrauen und sauber ... Ich bin es auch so gewohnt – ich schlafe auf spitzenbesetzten Laken. Meine Großmutter war [auch] so.“ Das Haus war der Raum der griechischen Frauen. Ihre heutigen Nachfolgerinnen stellen sich gleichfalls durch ihr Heim dar, durch Handarbeiten und Konfitüren, durch die hausgearbeitete Aussteuer.

Der Unterschied in den Geschlechterkonstruktionen ist in den verschiedenen Ehetypen begründet, die für die beiden Gemeinschaften charakteristisch sind. Die Griechen praktizieren ein uxorilokales Modell der postmaritalen Residenz („Die Griechen geben ihre Töchter nicht weg, sie behalten sie zuhause, und ihre Söhne wohnen bei den Schwiegereltern“, „die Jungen gehen als Schwiegersöhne fort“). Diese Sitte hat die neuen Siedler beeindruckt, bei denen das umgekehrte virilokale Modell die Regel war. So wurde das Residenzmuster nach der Eheschließung zu einem ethnischen Unterscheidungsmerkmal, das sowohl die Eigenen als auch die Fremden als solches auffassen. Es hält sich hartnäckig bis in unsere Tage, ungeachtet der Tatsache, dass die Ehen seit Generationen gemischt sind.

Die Unterschiede im Ehemodell sind mit der unterschiedlichen Stellung der Frau im Haushalt verbunden. Während die Griechen die Vormacht des Mannes und die untergeordnete Position der Frau in den bulgarischen Familien betonen („die Frauen tragen große Garben und vor ihnen reitet der Mann auf dem Esel her“), heben die Bulgaren die größere Macht der griechischen Frau in Haushalt und Familie und die ihr gegenüber mehr oder weniger untergeordnete Stellung des Mannes hervor. In der Tat aber dominieren in beiden Fällen die Werte der männlichen Überlegenheit und seiner symbolischen Macht; die Redensart „der Mann ist Gast im Haus“ ist in beiden Gemeinschaften gleich populär.

Die Bulgarinnen identifizieren sich mit der neuen Familie, in die sie eingeheiratet haben, die Griechinnen hingegen mit der Familie, aus der sie stammen, und dem Geburtshaus, in dem sie weiterhin leben. Für die traditionelle bulgarische Kultur ist die Beziehung zwischen Schwiegertochter und Schwiegermutter aufgrund des praktizierten virilokalen Ehemodells kennzeichnend; hier ist der Unterschied zum „Griechischen“ beachtlich, denn unter den Griechen ist Mutter-Tochter-Beziehung die grundlegende Beziehung. Die Informanten und Informantinnen sind einmütig darin, dass dies eine konfliktfreie Beziehung darstellt und sie auf der Autorität der Mutter und dem Respekt der Tochter gegenüber der Mutter gründen sollte. Dies entspricht einem Modell der von der Mutter dominierten häuslichen Ordnung (in direktem und übertragenem Sinn). Die starke Mutter-Tochter-Beziehung drückt sich in der Unterstützung der jungen Frau bei der Wahrung der Familientradition aus; als die griechischen Frauen in den fünfziger Jahren anfingen, außer Haus zu arbeiten, übernahmen ihre Mütter auch Sorgepflichten für den Haushalt und die Beaufsichtigung der Kinder.

Die griechischen Frauen unterstreichen ihre größere Religiosität im Vergleich zu den Bulgarinnen, die sich in der größeren Konsequenz beim Befolgen der ansonsten gemeinsamen religiösen Feste und dem längeren Tragen von Trauerkleidung ausdrückt. Da die Welt der erwachsenen Frauen geschlossen und konservativ ist, erhält sich das „Griechische“ dort am längsten – sie sprechen untereinander Griechisch (das oft als Art Geheimsprache vor den Kindern gebraucht wird), pflegen Familienbande, „verabreden“ Hochzeiten, sitzen zum Schwatz vor den Häusern und üben moralische Kontrolle in der Gemeinschaft aus. Dazu kommt die räumliche Abgesondertheit der Altstädte von Sozopol, Nesebăr und Pomorie, die auf Halbinseln gelegen sind, mit dicht aneinander gebauten alten Häusern, was ein besonderes „Zusammensein“ der Bewohner schafft; all dies hat die Vorstellung der griechischen Frauen und ihrer Heime als etwas Andersartigem, den anderen Unbekanntem genährt. In der sozialistischen Periode haben sich aber die Geschlechterkonstruktionen geändert. Als Teil der erzwungenen Modernisierung wurden die Frauen in die Sphäre der gesellschaftlichen Arbeit einbezogen. Sie internalisierten dabei ein neues Bild von Weiblichkeit, nämlich das der arbeitenden Mütter. Mit der drastischen Veränderung der herrschenden Normen („alle Frauen arbeiteten außer Haus“) begannen auch die griechischen Frauen außer Haus zu arbeiten: in der Konservenfabrik, in militärischen Einrichtungen, in Erholungsheimen.

Das Bulgarische und das Griechische hörten auf, als gesonderte Räume zu existieren. Infolgedessen wurden die traditionellen Bindungen und die Zugehörigkeit der Frauen zur Familie und zur lokalen Gemeinschaft durch einen „institutionalisierten Individualismus“ ersetzt, der einen Wandel der Identitäten stimulierte. Die nach den dreißiger Jahren geborenen Bulgarinnen und Griechinnen präsentieren sich in ihren Erzählungen über ihre Arbeit und Familie. Alle haben „Normalbiografien“ der „sozialistischen“ Frau vom gleichen Typ. Der vereinheitlichende Einfluss der sozialistischen Staatspolitik und gemischte Ehen führten zur

Hybridisierung der Kulturen, zur Angleichung der Rollen von Mann und Frau in beiden Gemeinschaften sowohl in der Familie als auch in der öffentlichen Sphäre.

Die Mischehen

Die nächste Frage, die wir erörtern wollen, ist, wie sich die Spezifika der Beziehungen zwischen Griechen und bulgarischer Mehrheitsbevölkerung auf den Aufbau, die Reichweite und die Struktur des den beiden Gruppen gemeinsamen Heiratsmarktes und die Ehestrategien ausgewirkt haben.

Die statistische Perspektive zur Analyse dieses Problems basiert auf der Analyse der aus den Heiratsregistern in Pomorie und Nesebăr aus der ersten Hälfte des 20. Jahrhunderts gewonnenen Daten. Die Tatsache, dass in den kommunalen Heiratsakten erst seit den dreißiger Jahren konkrete Angaben über die Nationalität der Ehewilligen gemacht wurden, spiegelt sich in der Konzentration auf die Heiratsjahrgänge der letzten drei Jahrzehnte des behandelten Zeitraums wider. Die Auswahl dieser Kohorten - von 1934, 1946 und 1950 - zielt nicht auf Repräsentativität ab, sondern ist vielmehr darauf ausgerichtet, grundlegende Entwicklungstendenzen in den Mischehen zwischen den beiden Gemeinschaften sichtbar zu machen. Die tabellarischen Daten zeigen sowohl für Pomorie als auch für Nesebăr zwischen 1934 und 1950 die allmähliche, aber in der Zeit beständige Verringerung der ethnisch homogamen Eheschließungen unter Griechen, wobei dieser Trend in Pomorie gleichmäßiger und in Nesebăr etwas sprunghafter verlief (siehe Tabellen 1 und 2).

Der Koeffizient, der das Niveau der Endogamie[3] unter den untersuchten Gemeinschaften in Pomorie angibt, ist während der drei beobachteten Jahre ziemlich hoch, aber seine Verminderung in der Untersuchungsperiode dennoch evident. Von 13,71 im Jahr 1934 fällt er auf 8 im Jahr 1950 (siehe Tabelle 1). Das Fehlen einer Möglichkeit zur Berechnung eines entsprechenden Koeffizienten für Nesebăr ließe sich als Hinweis auf eine drastische Disbalance im Austausch von Partnern beiderlei Geschlechts zwischen der bulgarischen und der griechischen Gemeinschaft interpretieren, insoweit dieser quantitative Indikator einerseits die Spezifik der Proportionen zwischen matrimonialem (Ehe-)Austausch von Männern und Frauen zwischen den Gruppen und andererseits die Ehetransaktionen innerhalb jeder einzelnen Gruppe ausdrückt. Die verzeichnete Besonderheit wirft die Frage der soziokulturellen Motivation für Ehen zwischen einem Bulgaren und einer Griechin bzw. einem Griechen und einer Bulgarin auf.

---

[3] Der Koeffizient für das Niveau der Endogamie drückt die folgende Korrelation aus: (Ehen unter Bulgaren/Ehen zwischen Bulgaren und Griechinnen) bezogen auf Ehen Grieche – Bulgarin/Ehen unter Griechen (für weitere Details dazu siehe: Kalmijn 1998: 405).

Bezüglich der griechischen Gemeinschaften in den bulgarischen Städten – Sozopol, Pomorie und Nesebăr – die kompakt von Griechen besiedelt sind, konstatieren ethnografische Daten eine starke Verbreitung der Ehen vom Typ Griechin-Bulgare. Für die Griechinnen waren diese Ehen eher hypogam (d. h. sie heirateten Partner aus einer niedrigeren sozialen Schicht) und für die Bulgaren umgekehrt hypergam. Durch solche ehelichen Verbindungen überwanden die Männer die soziale Distanz zwischen Dorf und Stadt und schufen sich Möglichkeiten zur Nutzung des bedeutenden, von den Griechen akkumulierten sozialen und wirtschaftlichen Kapitals. Insbesondere reizten die Bulgaren auch die Spezifika des traditionellen Erbprinzips, das zuließ, dass ihre griechischen Ehefrauen Eigentumsrechte auf Haus und diverse Immobilien erhielten (Vălčinova 1999: 34 f., Luleva 2004: 257–274; Popov 2004: 2–4). Ein solcher Ehetyp kann kaum als Beweis für die Annahme, dass die Bulgaren die Griechen als Minderheit nicht akzeptiert haben, behandelt werden. In diesem Fall haben wir es vielmehr mit einer niedrig stehenden Schicht der Mehrheitsbevölkerung – Bauern, Flüchtlinge, Umsiedler – zu tun, die bemüht waren, ihre soziale Position zu verbessern, indem sie bestimmte Heiratsstrategien benutzten. Für alle drei fraglichen Ehen in Nesebăr im Jahr 1934 kann man mit großer Wahrscheinlichkeit annehmen, dass sie zu diesem Typ gehörten – alle drei bulgarischen Männer waren in Dörfern geboren und offensichtlich Zusiedler in Nesebăr; die Eltern von zwei dieser Männer lebten weiterhin auf dem Dorf, die Eltern des dritten waren verstorben.

Der Umstand, dass die Bulgaren eine Rolle übernahmen, die im Kontext der traditionellen patriarchialischen Kultur als stereotyp weiblich angesehen wurde (nämlich in einen Haushalt einzuheiraten), kann als Indikator der höheren Stellung angesehen werden, welche die Mehrheit der griechischen Minderheit im Vergleich zu den anderen Minderheitsgemeinschaften auf der sozialen Werteskala einräumte. Dieser Aspekt der Ehestrategien kann auch dazu dienen, die der Frau zugeschriebene essentielle Charakteristik eines permanenten Objekts von Ehetransaktionen und der Übergeberin von kulturellen Werten in der Gruppe zu hinterfragen.[4] Die sozialen, ökonomischen und politischen Dimensionen des konkreten historischen Kontextes konnten diese Differenzierung der Geschlechterrollen mehr oder weniger dauerhaft verändern. Kurz gesagt, die Frage ist, warum die Griechinnen mit solchen für sie hypogamen Ehen einverstanden waren.

Die Suche nach einer Antwort macht es unumgänglich, das Problem des demografischen Verhältnisses zwischen den Geschlechtern im heiratsfähigen Alter im Rahmen der lokalen griechischen Gemeinschaft zu beleuchten. Gemäß ethno-

---

[4] Diese essentialistische Auffassung der Rolle der Frau wird im Übrigen auch durch Daten aus den hier betrachteten Heiratsregistern aus Pomorie und Nesebăr in Frage gestellt, die eine Reihe von eine uxorilokale Heiraten unter den Bulgaren verzeichnen. Vgl. in diesem Sinne auch Luleva 2002: 217–226.

grafischen Angaben über die Situation in Sozopol „verheiraten die Griechen ihre Töchter mit Bulgaren, weil sie nicht genug Männer haben“ (Popov 2004: 2). Wenn wir den ziemlich breiten Kreis von Heiratsverboten in Verbindung mit Blutsverwandtschaft, Verschwägerung und Patenschaft vor Augen haben, welche die orthodoxe Kirche verhängt, ergibt sich die Frage, ob eventuell die ethnische Endogamie ihre Ressourcen schon erschöpft hatte: „Die Griechen führten ein gutes Leben, weil alle Familien miteinander verwandt waren – die Stadt [Sozopol] war klein“ (ibid., 4). Durch Ehen vom Typ Bulgare-Griechin rekrutierte die griechische Gemeinschaft Angehörige der Mehrheit. Dieser Typ der Integration war für die Griechen selbst in der ersten Hälfte des 20. Jahrhunderts günstig, weil die Akkulturation der bulgarischen Zuwanderer in den eigenen Umkreis leichter war als die Versuche ihrerseits, sich an das bulgarische Milieu zu adaptieren: „Eine Griechin konnte nicht in Černomorie heiraten, weil sie die Sprache nicht konnte“ (ibid.).

Die in Tabelle 1 und 2 reproduzierten Daten für Pomorie und Nesebăr zeigen, dass sich in den drei betrachteten Jahren der Ehetyp Grieche-Bulgarin auf Kosten des Typs Bulgare-Griechin durchsetzt. Dieser Wandel in der Dominanz der Ehetypen geht in Pomorie eher allmählich vor sich und ist in Nesebăr abrupter. In jedem der fraglichen Jahre sind für Pomorie Ehen vom Typ Bulgare-Griechin registriert, auch wenn ihre Zahl konstant abnimmt, während für Nesebăr eine solche Ehe nach 1934 nicht mehr verzeichnet worden ist. Die deutliche Dynamik der Heiratstypen ist zugleich ein Anzeichen für die Veränderungen in der Beziehung der bulgarischen zur griechischen Bevölkerung. In allen drei betrachteten Jahren waren die meisten der Bulgaren, mit denen sich Griechinnen in Pomorie verheirateten, Einheimische und in dem Fall, dass der Mann nicht aus Pomorie stammte, war die Ehe vom virilokalen Typ; d. h. das „traditionelle“ Muster des Ehetyps Bulgare-Griechin, bei dem der Mann in den Haushalt der Frau übersiedelt und die nacheheliche Residenz uxorilokal ist, löste sich auf. Nunmehr mussten sich die Griechinnen in die bulgarische Umgebung integrieren. Vor dem Hintergrund dessen, was zu jener Zeit mit der griechischen Gemeinschaft geschah, kann dies als eine Form der Suche nach Sicherheit angesehen werden. Die Bulgarinnen, die Griechen heirateten, kamen in den drei Untersuchungsjahren aus verschiedenen Dörfern, meistens in der Nähe von Pomorie.

Im so umrissenen Bild bietet sich folgende Interpretation an: Unter den neuen konjunkturellen Bedingungen in den dreißiger und vierziger Jahren zeichnete sich eine Neudefinierung des Charakters der Ehen von Griechinnen mit Bulgaren ab: Zu einer Zeit, in der sich ein drastischer Wechsel in der axiologischen Aufladung der kategorialen Identitäten Bulgare und Grieche vollzog – konkret, die ausgesprochene Abwertung des Prestiges des „Griechischen“ – wurden solche Ehen aus hypogamen zu hypergamen. In Anspielung auf das, was Bourdieu über Béarn schreibt (Bourdieu, Waquant 1993: 106) könnte man schließen, dass die griechische Gemeinschaft für ihre Töchter keine Partner aus den eigenen Reihen haben wollte, sondern danach strebte, den weiblichen Nachwuchs möglichst schnell mit einem Bulgaren zu verheiraten, wobei die Töchter nach der Eheschließung ihren Wohnsitz wechselten, d. h. die Stadt verließen. Die griechischen jungen Männer mussten ihre Frauen außerhalb suchen, wobei die Dorfmädchen bulgarischer Herkunft am besten geeignet waren. Für diese Mädchen wurde die Ehe mit einem Griechen aus der Stadt aller Wahrscheinlichkeit nach als hypergam gewertet, da diese für sie einen sozialen Aufstieg, verbunden mit dem Übergang von Dorf in die Stadt, sicherte. Es ist nicht ausgeschlossen, dass hier auch die weit verbreitete Vorstellung, die Frauen der Griechen würden keine Arbeit auf dem Feld verrichten, sondern sich nur um den Haushalt kümmern, eine Rolle spielte (Popov 2004, Luleva 2004: 257–274).

Natürlich könnte das Hinzuziehen anderer Quellen zu einer neuen Lesart der Daten führen, die in den kommunalen Heiratsakten enthalten sind. Im Licht der vorgeschlagenen Interpretation der soziokulturellen Absicht der Ehen vom Typ Grieche-Bulgarin könnte das klare Überwiegen dieses Heiratstyps in Nesebăr auch als mögliche Folge der stärkeren Marginalisierung der Griechen in dieser Stadt angesehen werden. Die Abnahme der griechischen Bevölkerung in Nesebăr in Folge von Migration kann zugleich als Ursache und als Folge dieser Marginalisierung angesehen werden.

Die betrachteten Mischehen, unabhängig davon, ob sie auf die Integration von Angehörigen der Mehrheit in die Minderheit oder der Minderheit in die Mehrheitsbevölkerung abzielten, spielten eine wesentliche Rolle für die Wahrung der Vitalität der sozialen Beziehung Minderheit–Mehrheit. Dieser Typ Ehen zog die feinen, aber festen Fäden, welche die Minderheitsgemeinschaften mit der Mehrheit verbanden, die es ihnen nicht erlaubten, sich abzukapseln und zu isolieren, was für die Minderheit unter den Bedingungen des ablaufenden Modernisierungsprozesses verhängnisvoll gewesen wäre. Im Rahmen der Modernisierung wäre die strikte Einhaltung der konfessionellen und ethnischen Endogamie nicht der Preis für das Überleben gewesen, sondern vielmehr die Garantie für die Destruktion der jeweiligen Gemeinschaft.

Die Verwirklichung der Mischehen kann dabei nicht eindeutig als Assimilationsstreben interpretiert werden. Man könnte sie vielmehr als eine der Formen zur Erreichung von Verständnis im Prisma des Unterschieds, wovon Calhoun spricht (Calhoun 2003: 120–129), verstehen. Im unmittelbaren Umgang innerhalb der gemischten Ehen ergibt sich die Möglichkeit eines interkulturellen Dialogs, bei dem jede der Seiten in der Interaktion mit der jeweils anderen etwas in sich verändert, um Verständnis zu erzielen. So entstehen neue kulturelle Formen, die weder „ganz bulgarisch“ noch „ganz griechisch“ sind. In ihnen lebt sowohl etwas von der Majoritäts- als auch von der entsprechenden Minderheitskultur. Die Mischehen mit Bulgaren und Bulgarinnen waren einer der Mechanismen, durch die das „Griechische" es geschafft hat, bis heute zu überleben, und wir heute – nach dem Ende der realsozialistischen Periode – Zeugen einer neuen Identitätspolitik der Vertreter der griechischen Gemeinschaft bei uns werden können.

Resümee

Diese kulturelle Synthese und das neue Niveau der „Hybridisierung" der Kultur, entstanden aus dem Ineinanderübergehen der Kulturen der beiden betrachteten Gemeinschaften, bieten ihren Trägern auch entsprechende „Argumente", mit denen sie – durch die Spezifika des Kontextes evoziert – die Präferenzen hinsichtlich ihrer Identität begründen und ihre Identität in der einen oder anderen Richtung instrumentalisieren oder auch symmetrisch behandeln können. Mischehen könnte man also als Handlungen des taktischen Typs (im Sinne de Certeaus) betrachten, wodurch die Minoritätsgemeinschaften in einer Situation des Fehlens einer offiziellen Politik, die auf ihre reale Anerkennung als kollektive Subjekte und ebenbürtige Teilhaber im öffentlichen Dialog gezielt hätte, ihr Überleben sichern konnten.

Nach fast acht Jahrzehnten gemeinschaftlichen Lebens der Einwohner von Sozopol, Nesebăr und Pomorie erscheinen die kulturellen und ethnischen Unterschiede imaginär, retrospektiv und übertrieben angesichts der Zugehörigkeit zu einer gemeinsamen, gemischten und gut verkäuflichen Lokalkultur. Die Tourismus-Werbung präsentiert die Städte als antike (griechische) Kolonien, und nicht als kleine griechische Häfen des 18. oder 19. Jahrhunderts – ein Bild, mit dem sich die Einwohner nicht identifizieren würden. Gemäß dem Projekt ihrer persönlichen und kollektiven Identität leben sie an einem außergewöhnlich schönen Ort und sind Nachfahren des Besten aus dem Kreis der alten Kulturen.

Tabelle 1: Bulgarisch-griechische Mischehen – Pomorie

Jahr	1934	1946	1950
Heiraten insgesamt	57	89	121
Heiraten unter Griechen			
absolut	8	6	4
in Prozent aller Heiraten	14	6,7	3,3
Heiraten unter Bulgaren			
absolut	36	64	91
in Prozent aller Heiraten	63,2	71,9	75,2
bulgarisch-griechische Mischehen			
absolut	10	16	18
in Prozent aller Heiraten	17,5	18	14,9

Jahr	1934	1946	1950
Heiraten Bulgare-Griechin			
absolut	7	4	5
in Prozent aller Mischehen	70	25	27,8
Heiraten Grieche-Bulgarin			
absolut	3	12	13
in Prozent aller Mischehen	30	75	72,2
Koeffizient der Endogamie	13,71	8	5,6
sonstige Heiraten			
absolut	3	3	8
in Prozent aller Heiraten	5,3	3,4	6,6

Quellen: Heiratsregister der Gemeinde Pomorie (Anchialo) von 1934, 1946 und 1950, aufbewahrt im Gemeindearchiv der Stadt Pomorie.

Anmerkung: Unter der Rubrik „sonstige Heiraten“ sind für 1934 im Register zwei Eheschließungen von Russen mit Griechinnen und eine unter Türken aufgeführt; 1946 eine Eheschließung unter Juden und je eine zwischen einem Roma und einer Türkin bzw. einem Bulgaren und einer Armenierin; 1950 eine Heirat zwischen einem Türken und einer „türkischen Zigeunerin“, zwei Ehen unter Türken, zwei Ehen von Türkinnen mit „türkischen Zigeunern“, eine Ehe von einem Bulgaren mit einer Russin und zwei Ehen von Armeniern mit Bulgarinnen.

Tabelle 2: Bulgarisch-griechische Mischehen – Nesebăr

Jahr	1934	1946	1950
Heiraten insgesamt	13	24	53
Heiraten unter Griechen			
absolut	1	2	3
in Prozent aller Heiraten	7,7	8,3	5,7
Heiraten unter Bulgaren			
absolut	8	19	44
in Prozent aller Heiraten	61,5	79,2	83
bulgarisch-griechische Mischehen			
absolut	3	1	4
in Prozent aller Heiraten	23,1	4,2	7,5
Heiraten Bulgare-Griechin			
absolut	3		
in Prozent aller Mischehen	100		

Jahr	1934	1946	1950
Heiraten Grieche-Bulgarin			
absolut		1	4
in Prozent aller Mischehen		100	100
Koeffizient der Endogamie			
sonstige Heiraten			
absolut	1	2	2
in Prozent aller Heiraten	7,7	8,3	3,8

Quellen: Heiratsregister der Gemeinde Nesebăr (Mesemvria) von 1934, 1946 und 1950, aufbewahrt im Gemeindearchiv der Stadt Nesebăr.

Anmerkung: Unter der Rubrik „sonstige Heiraten“ ist im Jahr 1934 im Register eine Eheschließung zwischen einem Russen und einer Bulgarin aufgeführt; 1946 und 1950 jeweils Ehen von Türken mit Türkinnen.

Literatur

Barth, Fredrik (ed.) 1969: Ethnic Groups and Boundaries. The Social Organisation of Culture Difference. Bergen: Universitetsforlage.

Bourdieu, Pierre, Loic Wacquant 1993: Văvedenije v refleksivnata anthropologija. Sofia: KH [franz. Original: Réponses: pour une anthropologie reflexive. Paris: Ed. du Seuil, 1992].

Brunnbauer, Ulf 2002: Einleitung. In: Ulf Brunnbauer (Hg.), Umstrittene Identitäten. Ethnizität und Nationalität in Südosteuropa. Frankfurt am Main: Lang, 11–29.

Calhoun, Craig 2003: Kritičeska socialna teorija [Critical social theory]. Sofia: KH.

Dimitrov, Georgi 1985: Nastanjavane i ozemljavane na bălgarskite bežanci (1919–1939) [Die Unterbringung und Landzuteilung der bulgarischen Flüchtlinge]. Blagoevgrad: Otečetstven front.

Dženkins, Ričard [Jenkins, Richard] 2001: Etnicitet u novom ključu. Belgrad: Biblioteka XX vek.

Giordano, Christian 1999: Ethnizität und Territorialität. Zur sozialen Konstruktion von Differenz in Mittel- und Osteuropa. In: Ethnologia Balkanica 3: 9–35.

Hannerz, Ulf 1998: Flows, Boundaries and Hybrids: Keywords in Transitional Anthropology. Internet: http://www.transcomm.ox.ac.uk/working-papers.htm.

Kalmijn, Matthijs 1998: Intermarriage and Homogamy: Causes, Patterns, Trends. In: Annual Reviews of Sociology 24: 395–421.

Kosatev, Todor 1976: Bežanskijat văpros v Bălgarija sled părvata svetovna vojna (1919–1932) [Die Flüchtlingsfrage in Bulgarien nach dem Ersten Weltkrieg]. Diss. Sofia, unpubliziert.

Loizos, Peter, Evthimios Papataxiarhis 1991: Gender and Kinship in Marriage and Alternative Contexts. In: Peter Loizos, Evthimios Papataxiarhis (Hg.), Contested Identities. Gender and Kinship in Modern Greece. Princeton: Princeton UP, 3–29.

Luleva, Ana 2002: Ženite v malkija bălgarski grad (XIX - načaloto na XX vek) [Die Frauen in der bulgarischen Kleinstadt am Ende des 19./Anfang des 20. Jh.s]. In: Zorica Divac (Hg.), Običaji životnog ciklusa u gradskoj sredini [Lebenslaufbräuche im städtischen Milieu]. Belgrad: Etnografski institut SANU (= Pozebna izdanja, Bd. 48), 217–227.

Luleva, Ana 2004: Meždukulturni otnošenija pres prizmata na polovete: slučajat gărci-trakijci [Interkulturelle Beziehungen durch das Prisma der Geschlechter: Der griechisch-thrakische Fall]. In: Račko Popov, Georgi Gramatikov (Hg.) Trakiecăt i negovijat svjat [Der Thraker und seine Welt]. Sofia: EIM, 257–275.

Niederveen Pieterse, Jan 2004: Globalizacijata kato hibridizacija [Die Globalisierung als Hybridisierung] In: Mike Fatherstone, Scot Lash, Roland Robertson (Hg.), Globalni modernosti [Global modernities]. Sofia: Kritika i humanizăm, 70–104.

Popov, Račko 2004 (= AEIM No. 582-III).

Rakšieva, Svetla 2000: Istinskite trakijci [Die echte Thraker] In: Bălgarska ethnografija 26, 2: 2–15.

Roth, Klaus 1998: „Bilder in den Köpfen“. Stereotypen, Mythen, Identitäten aus ethnologischer Sicht. In: Valeria Heuberger, Arnold Suppan, Elisabeth Vyslonzyl (Hg.), Das Bild vom Anderen. Identitäten, Mentalitäten, Mythen und Stereotypen in multiethnischen europäischen Regionen. Frankfurt am Main: Lang, 21–43.

Rowe, William, Vivian Schelling 1991: Memory and Modernity. Popular Culture in Latin Amerika. London: Verso.

Schlehe, Judith 2000: Einleitung. Gender als transkulturelle Konstruktion. In: Judith Schlehe (Hg.), Zwischen den Kulturen - zwischen den Geschlechtern. Kulturkontakte und Genderkonstrukte. Münster, Berlin: Waxmann (= Münchener Beiträge zur Interkulturellen Kommunikation, Bd. 8), 4–16.

Smith, Anthony. 2000: Nacionalnata identičnost. Sofia: Kralica Mab [engl. Original: National Identity. Reno: University of Nevada Press, 1993].

Vălčinova, Galja 1998: Gărci [Griechen]. In: Obštnosti i identičnosti v Bălgarija [Gemeinschaften und Identitäten in Bulgarien]. Sofia: Petekston, 207–221.

Vălčinova, Galja 1999: „Melniškijat gărcizăm“: za bračnite strategii v konstruiraneto na ethnokulturnata identičnost [„Die Melniker Gräzität“: über die Heiratsstrategien bei der Konstruktion von ethno-kultureller Identität]. In: Bălgarska ethnografija 25, 3–4: 34–55.

Vălčinova, Galja 2001: Ökologie, Familienstruktur und Konstruktion der ethnokulturellen Identität. In: Ulf Brunnbauer, Karl Kaser (eds.), Vom Nutzen der Verwandten. Soziale Netzwerke in Bulgarien (19. und 20. Jahrhundert). Wien, Weimar: Böhlau, 355–380.

Abstract: Constructing identities in a border area. Intercultural gender relations: the Bulgarian - Greek case

The paper presents results of the research project “Greeks in Bulgaria - Cultural Interactions and Identities”. The aim of this article is to analyze identity constructions and gender relations between Greek and Bulgarian inhabitants of the towns along the southern Bulgarian Black Sea coast. The paper focuses on gender symbols and images as signifiers of cultural and ethnic differences, the variation of gender relations in a changing social and political context, and mixed marriages. The unifying impact of socialist state policy and mixed marriages effected a hybridization of cultures, and a unification of the roles of men and women from both communities, in their families as well as in the public sphere. The cultural and ethnic differences appear imaginary, retrospective, and transformed into a sense of affiliation to a common, mixed, and well-selling local culture, whose pillar is the ancient Greek tradition.

Geschlechterrollen in einem internationalen Unternehmen in Sofia

Ivanka Petrova, Sofia

1. Einleitung

Die Mehrheit der städtischen Bevölkerung in Bulgaren verbringt heute einen Großteil ihres Alltags als Arbeiter oder Angestellter in einem Betrieb. Durch die regelmäßige Zusammenarbeit dort bilden sich soziale Regeln und kulturelle Formen heraus, die sehr gut aus ethnologischer Perspektive erforscht und analysiert werden können. Ein konkreter Arbeitsvorgang ist durch berufsbezogene Kenntnisse, Techniken und Verhaltensweisen gekennzeichnet, die der zu leistenden Arbeit angemessen sind, sowie auch durch soziale Beziehungen, die sich zwischen den Kollegen am Arbeitsplatz herausbilden. Jede Wirtschaftsorganisation stellt Anforderungen an Arbeitshandlungen, die als geeignet für ihr erfolgreiches Funktionieren gelten und die mit Hilfe des Sozialisationsprozesses bei der Arbeit weitergegeben werden (Applebaum 1984: 3). Außer den vom Betrieb vorgeschriebenen formellen Handlungsnormen wirken sehr oft auch ungeschriebene Regeln am Arbeitsplatz, die man als Ergebnis des kulturellen Erbes und der Anwendung tradierter Denkmuster und Handlungsweisen in der Arbeitswelt bezeichnen kann. Die Ursache dafür ist, dass die Berufstätigkeit stark von der Persönlichkeit der Menschen beeinflusst wird. Im Arbeitsumfeld bringen die Mitarbeiter sowohl ihr berufliches Wissen und ihre berufseigenen Fähigkeiten sowie auch die bei ihrer früheren Sozialisation erworbenen Werte, Anschauungen und Lebenserfahrung mit. Im Arbeitsvorgang richten sich die Beschäftigten mehr oder weniger bewusst nach bekannten Stereotypen, die ihnen dazu helfen, ihrer Arbeit einen Sinn zu geben und besser die Herausforderungen der Arbeitswelt zu bewältigen.

Die Organisation der Geschlechterverhältnisse, die oft als ein grundlegendes Prinzip der Strukturierung der Gesellschaft aufgefasst wird, spielt z. B. eine wichtige Rolle beim Strukturieren der Arbeit in den Betrieben (Hengstenberg 1994: 539). Im Prozess der Lösung von beruflichen Aufgaben sind oft eine Weitergabe und eine Aktualisierung von solchen Verhaltensweisen zu beobachten, die mit der Zugehörigkeit zum einen oder zum anderen Geschlecht in Verbindung stehen (cf. Buhr 1998: 59). Die ersten Schritte der geschlechtsspezifischen Zuteilung erfolgen zuerst in der Familie, wenn die Kinder an bestimmten Arbeitsrollen gewöhnt werden, die als möglich und geeignet für das jeweilige Geschlecht betrachtet werden (Applebaum 1984: 3). Später setzt sich dieser Vorgang in unterschiedlichen gesellschaftlichen Institutionen fort, wo die weitere Sozialisation erfolgt. Dazu gehört auch der Beruf. Das Familienmuster mit den bekannten und mit dem Geschlecht verbundenen Einstellungen wird oft auf die Erwerbsarbeit übertragen und so wird das Geschlecht zu einem kulturellen Faktor in der Arbeit und im Beruf.

Im vorliegenden Beitrag wird die geschlechtsspezifische Arbeitsteilung in einem internationalen Unternehmen in Sofia dargestellt und analysiert sowie die Konstruktion der Geschlechterrollen in der urbanen Arbeitswelt erforscht. Dabei habe ich zu untersuchen, welche Rolle die in der bulgarischen Gesellschaft vorhandenen Geschlechterstereotypen für die beruflichen Chancen im unternehmerischen Umfeld spielen. Die mit der jeweiligen Arbeit verbundenen geschlechtsspezifischen Anforderungen an Leistung und Verhalten in der Arbeitswelt sollen auch thematisiert werden.

Meine Ergebnisse basieren auf empirischen Untersuchungen einer Gruppe bulgarischer Mitarbeiter eines international operierenden Unternehmens.[1] Die Organisation ist im Direktvertrieb von Nahrungsergänzungsmitteln und Kosmetik tätig und ist auf dem Prinzip des *Network Market* aufgebaut. Die Feldforschungen dauerten von Anfang 2001 bis Ende 2004. Die Erhebung der empirischen Daten erfolgte mit Hilfe ethnographischer Methoden in Form von Leitfadeninterviews und informellen Gesprächen mit den Mitarbeitern in der Gruppe. Eine weitere Methode, die teilnehmende Beobachtung, konnte ich durch mehrmalige Teilnahme an unterschiedlichen Arbeitsaktivitäten anwenden. Zudem wurden auch verschiedene Schriftquellen wie Fach- und Werbebroschüren sowie das „Handbuch für Berater“ gründlich ausgewertet, also jene Materialien, die die offizielle Ideologie des Unternehmens darstellen. Anhand der guten Kenntnis dieser Ideologie kann man Schlussfolgerungen auf die im Betriebsumfeld relevanten und mit dem Geschlecht verbundenen Leistungs- und Verhaltensanforderungen ziehen. Auf diese Weise sind aufgrund der Kombination verschiedener Forschungsmethoden die individuellen Handlungen, Beziehungen und Vorstellungen im Bezug auf das Thema der Geschlechterrollen besser zu erfassen und zu analysieren.

Nach den offiziell vorgegebenen Normen des Unternehmens, die in den Schriftquellen deutlich zum Ausdruck gebracht sind, sollen die sog. „Berater“ gleichzeitig in drei Richtungen aktiv sein: im Verkauf der Produkte an Kunden, bei der Anwerbung und Schulung neuer Berater und in der Veranstaltung von wöchentlichen Arbeitsaktivitäten (z. B. Parties, Verkaufswerbung, Seminare). Als spezielle Vorzüge des Unternehmens werden die Möglichkeiten der Teilzeitarbeit, des Einkommens nach den individuellen Leistungen und der Organisation der

---

[1] Es handelt sich um die Firma *Herbalife International*. Die untersuchte Gruppe von Mitarbeitern umfasst 17 Frauen und 8 Männer im Alter zwischen 26 und 60 Jahren, von denen vier unverheiratet, neun geschieden und zwölf verheiratet sind, wobei es in der Gruppe drei Ehepaare gibt, die ihre Arbeit zu einem Familiengeschäft gemacht haben.

Arbeit als Familiengeschäft dargestellt. Aus meinen Forschungen ergibt sich, dass die Berater, die mit diesen „Vorzügen“ ausgestattet sind, auf bekannte Geschlechterstereotypen zurückgreifen, um in der Arbeitswelt hierarchisch organisierte Männer- und Frauentätigkeiten zu konstruieren, deren Ausübung von dem anderen Geschlecht als eine Störung der symbolischen Ordnung aufgefasst wird.

2. Weibliche Tätigkeiten und Frauenrollen im Unternehmen

a) Die Teilzeitarbeit als Frauenarbeit

In der untersuchten Gruppe hat sich das geschlechtsspezifische Arbeitszeitmodell bei dem Leisten unterschiedlicher Tätigkeiten durchgesetzt. Eine 34-jährige Beraterin sagte: *„Die Teilzeitarbeit ist sehr geeignet für uns als Frauen, sie könnte aber einem Mann nicht angeboten werden“*. Auf meine Frage, warum im Produktverkauf hauptsächlich Frauen tätig seien, weisen die Berater beider Geschlechter an erster Stelle auf die Möglichkeit der Teilzeitarbeit hin. *„Für ein paar Stunden kann ich von einer Hausfrau zu einer Geschäftsfrau werden, ohne meine Familienpflichten zu vernachlässigen,“* sagte eine 36-jährige Frau. Ein Berater in einer höheren Position im Unternehmen erklärte in diesem Zusammenhang: *„Eine Frau kann nur 3–4 Stunden pro Tag arbeiten und dabei das Wohlgefühl haben, dass sie nicht nur ihrer Familie nützlich ist ... aber ein Mann soll nicht nur als einfacher Verkäufer arbeiten. Er soll sein eigenes Geschäft mit einer Vielzahl von Beratern aufbauen und dazu braucht er viel mehr Zeit und Kraft als eine Frau bei der Teilzeitarbeit“*. Seiner Meinung nach ist Teilzeitarbeit ideal für Frauen, sie ist aber gar nicht für Männer geeignet.

Die Teilzeitarbeit wird im Grunde von vielen Frauen nicht nur in Bulgarien bevorzugt. Seit den 1960er Jahren leisten viele verheiratete Frauen solche Tätigkeiten, weil sie ihnen eine attraktive Alternative zur Familien- und Hausarbeit bietet und die Möglichkeit der individuellen Gestaltung der Arbeitszeit gibt (Hausen 2000: 353). Wissenschaftler stellten fest, dass die Teilzeitarbeit in zunehmendem Masse als eine Anpassung der Arbeitszeit an den Familienrhythmus akzeptiert wird (Dülfer 1991: 217). Die Ehepartner, die im erforschten Unternehmen zusammen tätig sind, verwenden einstimmig Teilzeitarbeit für die Ehefrau und eine verlängerte Arbeitszeit für den Ehemann. Die Hauptverantwortung für die Hausarbeit bleibt dabei bei den Frauen und die Männer können sich endgültig davon distanzieren. Auf ähnliche Weise gestalten auch die anderen verheirateten Frauen im Unternehmen ihre Arbeit als Teilzeitarbeit und es scheint ihnen, als ob sie damit die Vereinbarkeit zwischen Beruf und Familie gesichert hätten. Andererseits kann dies einen Kompromiss zwischen Männern und Frauen in ihren vertrauten Geschlechterverhältnissen darstellen: Die teilzeitige Berufstätigkeit der Frau behindert nicht die Rolle des Mannes als „Familienernährer“. Diese Rolle kann oftmals die notwendige Voraussetzung für sein berufliches Engagement mit Überstunden sein.

Durch solche Arbeit bleibt jedoch die volle Belastung der Frauen mit Haushaltspflichten erhalten und ihre finanzielle Abhängigkeit vom Ehemann verfestigt sich. Somit ergibt sich, dass dieses Modell der Arbeitszeit für die Frauen nicht ideal ist. Mit ihrer Teilzeitarbeit opfern sie im Unternehmen ihre berufliche Weiterentwicklung: Sie richten ihre Arbeit nach der Beschäftigung des Mannes, ordnen sich den Familienangelegenheiten unter und geben ihre Kariere auf. Die Frauen sind sich bewusst, dass sie bei der Teilzeitarbeit keine Leitfunktionen einnehmen können. Dazu sagte eine 31-jährige Beraterin: *„Wenn ich ausschließlich im Bereich des Verkaufs ein paar Stunden arbeite, kann ich eigentlich kaum mit der Schulung neuer Berater anfangen. Dafür sind mehrere Stunden erforderlich, aber meine Engagements in der Familie erlauben es mir garnicht.“* Darüber hinaus bedeutet die Teilzeitarbeit in der Regel den Abschied vom beruflichen Aufstieg (cf. Goldmann 1986: 155 ff.).

Eine 34-jährige Frau hat völlig bewusst den Karrierenaufstieg aufgegeben, trotz der von ihrer Schwiegermutter angebotenen Hilfe bei der Kindererziehung: *„Die Erhöhung meiner Qualifikation würde mir die Möglichkeit bieten nach Amsterdam zu fahren. Das würde aber bedeuten, dass ich zweimal für zwei Jahre ins Ausland reisen würde, während mein Mann, der als Leiter einer Privatfirma tätig ist, für dieselbe Zeit nur einmal im Ausland gewesen ist. Ich dachte, das wäre nicht ehrlich ihm gegenüber und so behielt ich die gleiche Stelle im Unternehmen.“* Die Beraterin empfand ihren möglichen beruflichen Aufstieg als störend für die familiäre und berufliche Autorität ihres Ehemannes und hat deshalb freiwillig auf die Chance einer Karriere verzichtet. Sie erklärte ihr Verhalten im Interview sogar zu etwas Selbstverständlichem. Auf diese Weise vermeidet sie einen potentiellen Konflikt zu Hause, unterstützt dadurch aber eigentlich die Verfestigung eines Männerstatus in erstrangigen sozioökonomischen Positionen sowie des Status der verheirateten Frau, für die die Teilzeitarbeit nur genügend Zusatzeinkommen bringen soll.

Auf diese Weise gestaltet sich im Unternehmen die Teilzeitarbeit als weibliche Arbeit. Obwohl durch diese Zeitorganisation die Hauptverantwortung für die Hausarbeit bei den Frauen bleibt und die beiden Geschlechter weiter in den vom familiären Muster gut bekannten Rollen gehalten werden, haben doch viele Frauen in der Hauptstadt die Möglichkeit, beruflich tätig zu sein und ihre Tageszeit so zu verteilen, dass darin auch die Erwerbsarbeit zum Zuge kommt.

b) Die Anwendung von Hausfraueigenschaften im Betriebsumfeld

Die Verkaufsarbeit erhält ein weiteres Merkmal, das sie als weibliche Tätigkeit gestaltet und deshalb von den Beratern als eine typische Frauenarbeit gekennzeichnet wird. Bei den vom Unternehmen vorgeschriebenen Anforderungen an

Leistungen und Verhalten beim Verkauf wird am meisten mit solchen Eigenschaften und Qualifikationen gerechnet, die meist als quasi-natürliche Fähigkeiten der Frauen in ihrer Rolle als Mütter und Hausfrauen gelten und welche sie sich bei ihrer früheren Sozialisation in der Familie angeeignet haben.[2] Aus den schriftlichen Firmenmaterialien und Schulungen geht hervor, dass für den erfolgreichen Verkauf gute Kenntnisse der menschlichen Bedürfnisse, Herzlichkeit, Sensibilität, Verantwortungsbewusstsein, Hilfsbereitschaft, ständige Fürsorge und gute Kommunikationsfähigkeit notwendig sind. Diese Anforderungen, die eher als persönliche Eigenschaften formuliert werden, werden den Frauen als im privaten Umfeld erworbene zugeschrieben. Sie werden als Eigenschaften erwartet, welche die Frauen im Unternehmen aus ihrer Familien- und Hausarbeit mitbringen. Also erwartet man von den Frauen, dass sie eine solche Tätigkeit ausüben, die der weiblichen Hausarbeit sehr ähnlich ist.

Die Beraterinnen selbst ziehen oft Vergleiche zwischen ihrer Berufsarbeit in der Firma und der Hausarbeit: *„Wir sind wie Mütter, wir testen zuerst die Produkte, um von ihren Eigenschaften überzeugt zu sein und danach empfehlen wir sie an Kunden. Und genau wie Mütter sollen wir den Kunden zur Verfügung stehen,“* erklärt eine 42-jährige Frau. Eine andere Beraterin bewertet ihre berufliche Tätigkeit folgendermaßen: *„Unsere Arbeit ist typisch weiblich – wie zu Hause gibt es auch hier ständig etwas zu tun und die Bedienung ist wirklich eine reine Frauensache. Wir treffen uns mit Kunden und besprechen ihre Bedürfnisse. Danach bereiten wir ein Nahrungsprogramm vor, welches die Kunden wirklich brauchen ... Bei der Arbeit müssen wir praktisch wie Hausfrauen denken.“* Auf diese Weise wird die Erwerbsarbeit von den berufstätigen Frauen im Unternehmen nach den aus dem Haushalt vertrauten Mustern interpretiert. Nach diesen Mustern zählen die Aufgaben der Erfüllung von Wünschen, der Hilfe und Fürsorge zu den vertrauten Arbeiten der Hausfrau. Es fällt auf, dass die Berufstätigkeit der Beraterinnen in einer Firma in der Hauptstadt als Fortsetzung des alltäglichen Dienens der Frauen in ihren Familien erscheint. So erhält diese Erwerbsarbeit einen ausgeprägt routinierten Charakter. Bei den Forschungen habe ich kaum bemerkt, dass sich irgendwelche Beraterin über diese Ausnutzung ihrer Hausfrauqualifikationen beschwert. Im Gegenteil, die Frauen sind sicher, dass im Beruf ihre Fähigkeiten als Mütter und Hausfrauen letztendlich eine gesellschaftliche Anerkennung gefunden haben. Wärend die in der Privatsphäre geleistete Hausarbeit immer noch eine ziemlich geringe öffentliche Anerkennung hat, findet sie eine gute Bewertung durch die Tatsache, dass sie von den Frauen in ihrem Beruf benutzt werden kann. Vielleicht ist die Tatsache, dass niemand sich beklagt, auch dadurch zu erklären, dass den

---

[2] Zu solchen Schlussfolgerungen ist auch Irene Götz gekommen, wenn sie das Brotverkaufen in einem Betrieb in München darstellt, das zu einer Frauenarbeit erklärt wurde (Götz 1997: 92–125).

Frauen von zu Hause aus die Selbstverständlichkeit bekannt ist, mit der diese Tätigkeiten von ihnen erwartet werden (cf. Götz 1997: 115).

c) Die Ausnahme: Frauen in Männerrollen

Auf den höheren Qualifikationsniveaus der Verkaufs- und Organisationstätigkeit sowie im Leitungsberech arbeiten zwar auch Frauen, doch diese brauchen in ihrem privaten Leben die üblichen Frauenrollen nicht zu erfüllen. Es sind unverheiratete oder geschiedenen Frauen, die die Funktion des Familienoberhaupts übernommen und ihren Unterhalt ganz allein zu verdienen haben. Gerade wegen dieser Funktion, die für verheiratete Frauen nicht sehr üblich ist, werden sie vom vertrauten weiblichen Handlungsmuster am Arbeitsplatz ausgeschlossen und als ganz unterschiedlich im Vergleich zu den anderen Frauen betrachtet. Man spricht davon, dass ihre Arbeit und ihre Leistungen auf keinem Fall hinter den Leistungen und Fähigkeiten der Männer im Unternehmen zurückbleiben dürfen und dass sie ähnlich wie die Männer berufstätig sein sollen. So werden sie einer anderen Kategorie zugeordnet und zwar den Familienernährern. Solche Frauen sagten in den Gesprächen, dass diese Arbeit nur vorläufig sei, bis sie eine Familie gründen, bzw. bis die Kinder selbst ihr Einkommen verdienen und bis sie später als Großmütter beim Erziehen der Enkel helfen sollen. Wenn sie also ihren familiären oder Lebensstatus verändern, sind sie bereit, die Karriere und die beruflichen Chancen wieder der Familie unterzuordnen; eine solche Handlungsweise betrachten sie als ganz normal.

Diese Aussagen stimmen völlig überein mit den Erwartungen, welche die Kollegen beider Geschlechter an sie haben. Deshalb vertiefen sich die Konflikte mit solchen Frauen kaum. Die zwischen Frauen auf hohen Qualifikationsstufen und anderen Mitarbeitern entstandenen Auseinandersetzungen werden hauptsächlich aus der Perspektive der unvermeidlichen, zukünftigen Berufsaufgabe dieser Frauen bewertet, wenn sie im Unternehmen nicht mehr leitende Funktionen ausüben werden. *„Ich weiß, nach ihrer Heirat wird sich die Lage verändern: sie wird nicht so viel Zeit haben, um immer Anordnungen zu treffen, zu befehlen und uns in Spannung zu halten“,* sagt ein Berater über das Verhalten seiner unverheirateten Kollegin, die in höherer Position tätig ist. Ihre leitende Funktion wird insoweit akzeptiert, als sie die Frau in einer anderen Rolle darstellt – sie hat noch keine Familie und muss allein ihr Einkommen sichern. Wenn sie aber die Rolle der verheirateten Frau übernimmt, darf nicht zugelassen werden, dass sie eine führende Rolle im Unternehmen einnimmt. Solche Auffassungen der Mitarbeiter im Unternehmen zeigen eindeutig, dass die ökonomische Tätigkeit der Frau nicht sehr mit ihren persönlichen und beruflichen Ambitionen und Fähigkeiten in Verbindung gebracht wird, sondern vielmehr und grundsätzlich der Familie und ihren Bedürfnissen unterstellt ist. Wenn die Frau Ansprüche auf Führungspositionen stellt, bewerten die Berater dieses Ansinnen als etwas Ungewöhnliches.

3. Konstruktion von Männerrollen im Unternehmen

a) Verkaufsarbeit und männliche Berufsidentität

Bemerkenswert sind die Anschauungen der Männer über die Arbeit, die nur auf den Verkaufsbereich begrenzt ist. Ein 48-jähriger Berater teilte mit: *„Als ich zusammen mit meiner Frau vor 8 Jahren im Unternehmen zu arbeiten begann, wollte ich nicht auf der Verkaufsebene bleiben. Hier konnte meine Frau soviel arbeiten, wie sie wollte, das war aber nichts für mich als Mann ... Ich bin nicht unbedingt überzeugt von den Produkten, ich kann nicht die Menschen beraten und überzeugen. Mich interessierte damals die Marktstrategie der Firma und nicht etwa die Kosmetik und die Nahrungsmittel.“* Hier finden wir eine schlecht verhüllte Missachtung der Verkaufstätigkeit, die der Mitarbeiter seiner Frau überließ, weil er diese Arbeit als eine geeignete Fortsetzung der routinemäßigen familiären Tätigkeiten seiner Frau bewertet.

Im Gespräch mit einem 45-jährigen Berater ist mir nicht nur seine Geringschätzung der Verkaufsarbeit, sondern auch der ausgesprochene Gegensatz zwischen der männlichen Berufsidentität und der Verkaufstätigkeit aufgefallen. Er hat mit der Arbeit in der Firma zusammen mit seiner jüngeren Schwester vor neun Jahren angefangen, wobei beide die Produkte verkauften und gemeinsam die Arbeitsaktivitäten veranstalteten. Etwa ein Jahr später entwickelte das Unternehmen eine Reihe von Kosmetikwaren. *„Als sich herausgestellt hat, dass wir auch Kosmetik verkaufen sollten, geriet ich in eine Stresssituation, denn ich weiss, Kosmetik ist für Frauen und für Homosexuelle.“* So schließt der Berater die Möglichkeit des Kosmetikverkaufs aus seiner beruflichen Identität völlig aus, weil er als Mann nicht in eine „Frauenwelt“ eindringen möchte, in der die Sorge um gute Kosmetik einen wichtigen Bestandteil ausmacht. Das, was für Frauen notwendig und praktisch ist, betrachtet er als unzulässig für einen Mann im beruflichen Umfeld, weshalb er den Kosmetikverkauf ganz seiner Schwester überließ.

In Bezug auf die Geschlechterrollen in einem Unternehmen in der Hauptstadt ist es wichtig zu erforschen, welche Einstellung die Berater und Beraterinnen zu den Männern haben, die auf der niedrigsten Qualifikationsstufe der Verkäufer zu arbeiten beginnen. Alle Kollegen erwarten von ihnen, dass diese Arbeit für sie nur eine vorläufige Tätigkeit ist und dass sie nach einigen Monaten eine höhere Stellung im Unternehmen erreichen werden, wo das Einkommen höher und die Arbeit intensiver und mehrstündig ist. Eine 60-jährige Beraterin sagte dazu: *„Männer haben keine Affinität zu Nahrung und Kosmetik. Von einem Mann kannst du nicht erwarten, dass er sich nur mit dem Verkauf beschäftigt. Er ist so erzogen, eine Karriere im Beruf anzustreben und mehr als seine Frau zu verdienen“.* Vor dem Hintergrund dieser ererbten geschlechtsspezifischen Rollenmuster ist zu erklären, warum Frauen und Männer die Verkaufstätigkeit des Mannes als vorläufig bewerten und sie ausschließlich als eine Stufe zum beruflichen Aufstieg akzeptieren.

Die Männer auf der niedrigsten Qualifikationsstufe werden als Ausnahmen angesehen; für die Frauen sind sie etwa wie „gute Söhne", die zum baldigen Aufstieg im Unternehmen angeregt werden sollen, damit sie so schnell wie möglich die als Frauenarbeit bewertete Verkaufstätigkeit aufgeben können. Auf diese Weise werden im beruflichen Kontext die von der Arbeitsteilung im Haushalt bekannten Geschlechterstereotypen reproduziert und gefestigt.

b) Legitimierung der männlichen Dominanz

Die Rolle der Männer im Unternehmen ist durch tradierte Geschlechtsmuster geprägt, wobei die männliche Kompetenz und Priorität bei der Familienernährung als grundlegend und legitim gelten. Deshalb suchen die männlichen Mitarbeiter auch Legitimationsgründe dafür. So erzählte ein 55-jähriger Berater: *„Ich habe mit dieser Arbeit wegen des Geldes angefangen und das war meine erste Motivation. Als Journalist verdiente ich nicht viel, aber hier ist es so: je mehr du arbeitest, um so größer ist dein Einkommen."* Gerade im Sinne des Familienoberhaupts bemühen sich die Männer, ihre gesellschaftliche Dominanz gegenüber den Frauen auch im beruflichen Umfeld zu bestätigen. Sie konstruieren eine offensichtlich geschlechtshierarchische Struktur der Berufsarbeit, indem sie die Arbeit auf den höheren Stufen zur männlichen Tätigkeit erklären, die größeres Einkommen sichert und mit der Leitung von ein paar Beratern verbunden ist. Andere Aussagen von Männern bestätigen die Beobachtung, dass ein Mann im Unternehmen nur auf einer Führungsposition zu akzeptieren sei und dass Männer in die oberen und Frauen in die unteren Positionen gehören. Dadurch bekommt die Verkaufsarbeit den Status einer unqualifizierten, sogar marginalisierten Arbeit. *„Damit du aufsteigst, musst du riskieren, du sollst Geld ausleihen, großen Ehrgeiz haben, organisieren und leiten – und das ist genau etwas für einen Mann",* sagte ein 39-jähriger Berater.

So wird die Arbeit auf den höheren Stufen von den Männern zu einer Stelle ihrer Dominanz umdefiniert und die aus dem Privatleben bekannten Geschlechterrollen werden am Arbeitsplatz legitimiert. Das vollzieht sich durch die symbolische Erniedrigung der Frauenarbeit, wobei sie eine Benachteiligung im Vergleich zu der Männerarbeit erfährt, sowie durch die Konstruktion der übergeordneten Position der Männer in der Hierarchie. Die Bewertung der weiblichen Arbeit als Routine und als Ergänzung der Hausfrauenfunktionen und der Männerarbeit als qualifizierte und höherrangige Tätigkeit ideologisiert die Verbindung zwischen Beruf und Geschlecht (cf. Becker-Schmidt 1994: 533). Es scheint als ob das konventionelle Geschlechtsmuster auf diese Weise Sicherheit und Konfliktreduktion verspricht. Die Sicherung des hierarchischen Status tritt an die erste Stelle. Karrierenaufstieg, hohe Leistungsanforderungen und besseres Einkommen erscheinen als charakteristisch für das männliche Geschlecht und erfordern kaum eine Vereinbarung mit Hausarbeitstätigkeiten.

4. Zusammenfassung

Die geschlechtsspezifische Teilung und Bewertung der Arbeit sowie die mit ihr verbundenen Verhaltensmuster sind kulturell verankerte Eigenschaften, die jahrhundertelang bei der Konstruktion von Männlichkeit und Weiblichkeit im Arbeitsprozess reproduziert wurden (cf. Hausen 2000: 347). Sie erweisen sich bei der gegenwärtigen Umstrukturierung der Arbeit unter marktwirtschaftlichen Bedingungen als sehr anpassungsfähig. Bei der Erwerbsarbeit sind die Geschlechterdifferenzen für einzelne Tätigkeiten und für die Bewertung der Arbeit gültig, was sich auf die Herausbildung von Männer- und Frauenrollen am Arbeitsplatz auswirkt. Trotz der dynamischen Veränderungen in der bulgarischen Wirtschaft und Gesellschaft in den letzten 15 Jahren ist die ungleiche Verteilung von Berufs- und Hausarbeit, von beruflichen Chancen, von Macht und Ansehen, von materiellen und kulturellen Ressourcen auf die beiden Geschlechter nicht abgebaut worden. Im Gegenteil, sogar im Bereich der Erwerbsarbeit in den die Entwicklung bestimmenden Großstädten Bulgariens stellt sich heraus, dass die traditionellen Geschlechterstereotypen bei der Verteilung der beruflichen Aufgaben auch bei neuen Arbeitsplätzen große Auswirkungen haben.

Im erforschten Unternehmen in Sofia setzt sich die geschlechtsspezifische Arbeitsteilung in weibliche, hauptsächlich durch die Vereinbarkeit von Beruf und Familie definierte und in männliche Arbeit fort, die als eine grundsätzliche persönliche und gesellschaftliche Pflicht des Mannes gilt. Diese Rollenverteilung äußert sich im großen Anteil der Frauen, die sich nur mit Verkauf und Teilzeitarbeit beschäftigen, wohingegen die Männer nach Führungspositionen und Organisationsarbeit streben, die mit einem mehrstündigen Arbeitstag verbunden sind und eine weitgehende Entlastung von der Hausarbeit voraussetzen. Der volle, sogar verlängerte Arbeitstag gilt als Norm für das männliche Arbeits- und Lebensmuster, er gewährt den Männern Distanz zur Teilzeitarbeit des Verkaufs, die als unqualifiziert aufgefasst wird. Dadurch sichern sich die Männer eine dominierende Stellung im Unternehmen in Bezug auf Hierarchie und Einkommen. Sogar wenn Männer und Frauen die gleichen Funktionen ausüben, sind die Arbeitsverhältnisse von den geschlechtsspezifischen Verhaltensanforderung beeinflusst.

Die geschlechtsspezifische Arbeitsteilung im unternehmerischen Umfeld reflektiert die sozialen und kulturellen Bedingungen und hat wenig mit den persönlichen Eigenschaften und der Ausbildung zu tun. Die Konzeptualisierung von Männer- und Frauenrollen erweist sich als ein Versuch der Berater, sich im Arbeitsumfeld zu integrieren. Das Geschlecht wird auf diese Weise zu einem identitätsstiftenden Faktor im Unternehmen, wodurch die Organisation eine Gestalt erhält, die auf der Identität der Berater als Geschlechtswesen gründet: der Mann, gänzlich seinem Beruf gewidmet, und die Frau, zwischen Beruf und Hausarbeit balancierend, wobei diese Balance nur schwer zu halten ist.

Literatur

Applebaum, Herbert 1984: Work in Market & Industrial Societies. New York.

Becker-Schmidt, Regina 1994: Geschlechterverhältnis, Technologieentwicklung und androzentrische Ideologieproduktion. In: Soziale Welt, Sonderband 9. Umbrüche gesellschaftlicher Arbeit. Göttingen, 527–538.

Buhr, Regina 1998: Unternehmen als Kulturräume. Eigensinnige betriebliche Integrationsprozesse im transnationalen Kontext. Berlin.

Dülfer, Eberhard 1991: Internationales Management in unterschiedlichen Kulturbereichen. München, Wien.

Goldmann, Monika, Ursula Müller 1986: Junge Frauen im Verkaufsberuf. Berufliche Sozialisation, Arbeits- und Lebensperspektiven. Stuttgart, Berlin, Köln, Mainz.

Götz, Irene 1997: Unternehmenskultur. Die Arbeitswelt einer Großbäckerei aus kulturwissenschaftlicher Sicht. Münster, New York, München: Waxmann.

Hausen, Karin 2000: Arbeit und Geschlecht. In: Jürgen Kocka, Claus Offe (eds.), Geschichte und Zukunft der Arbeit. Frankfurt am Main, New York, 343–360.

Hengstenberg, Heike 1994: Geschlechtsverhältnisse und Ingenieurarbeit. In: Soziale Welt, Sonderband 9. Umbrüche gesellschaftlicher Arbeit. Göttingen, 539–555.

Gender Roles in an International Enterprise in Sofia

Many people in Bulgarian cities spend a significant part of their everyday life as employees in new business establishments. Work in these enterprises requires social rules and cultural forms. Ethnological analysis shows that work is regulated by formal norms of behaviour in an organization and – more importantly – by unwritten rules derived mostly from traditional mental and behavioural models. Gender roles and relations are a case in point. They play an important role in structuring work activities and in defining the contents of work. The paper investigates the gender divisions in a group of Bulgarian salespersons and consultants in an international firm in the city of Sofia. The interviews and observations reveal a strong influence of traditional stereotypical gender roles and relations regarding the definition of male and female work and the different requirements and opportunities for men and women in the company's hierarchies.

Insights into Urban Life, Cultural Change, and Modernization in the Kingdom of Serbs, Croats and Slovenians, 1918–1928

Aleksandar R. Miletić, Belgrade

In the last ten years much has been written on the phenomena of modernization and urbanization in the Yugoslav inter-war society. In Serbian historiography, books by Ljubodrag Dimić (1996), Predrag Marković (1992), Vladan Jovanović (2002) and Radina Vučetić-Mladenović (2003) brought a new methodology and broadened the scope of interest and research of these phenomena. Historical research became more focused on "long-lasting" historical structures, cultural history and the history of private life and everyday life in the Kingdom of Serbs, Croats and Slovenians (SCS)/Yugoslavia. Belgrade University professors Ljubodrag Dimić and Andrej Mitrović contributed significantly to the development of these new tendencies in Serbian historiography. However, one of the best monographs on the social history of Serbian inter-war society was written by German historian Marie-Janine Calic (2004). This short article is a small contribution to these studies.

This paper will shed light on the phenomena of urbanization and certain cultural transformations that took place in the main cities of the Kingdom of SCS. Most of the referenced material originates from newspapers and other publications of that time. The author of the present article is aware of the methodological advantages as well as limits which derive from these kinds of sources. Due to these limits the study is more descriptive than analytical, but has the advantage of filling in several gaps that cannot be approached otherwise. Its main focus is on the overall impact that the First World War had on psychology, morals, and changes in the everyday life of people in the Yugoslav provinces.

The first three sections of the study concentrate on economic and social conditions that emerged during and after the First World War, and the reflection of these circumstances in the life experiences of the urban population of Yugoslavia. State intervention in the economy and a profound upheaval in pre-war standards of living (e. g., restrictions and control of prices, adjustments in housing, state government intervention in relations between employer and employee, between landlord and tenant, etc.) are some of the phenomena examined in these sections. The fourth section deals with particular problems of urbanization in Yugoslavia, with an emphasis on wide-spread urban poverty, lack of hygiene, and disease. The fifth section examines the position of women in Yugoslav inter-war society. The sixth section focuses on newly emerging urban vices and modes of social behavior in Yugoslav cities between 1918 and 1928.

Immediate Consequences of the War

The violence of the First World War undermined the psychological and material basis of the prosperous European capitalism of 1871–1914 (Keynes 1971: 11–13, 110, 147 f.). War efforts and interruptions in production and distribution created hunger, misery, inflation and revolutionary fever all over Europe. A 1919 report by Herbert Hoover, the president to the Paris Peace Conference's Economic Council, estimated that there was a "surplus" of around 100 million people in Europe in relation to its production and distribution facilities. According to data collected from the national employment offices it was considered that some 15 million families in Europe supported themselves primarily through various forms of public welfare. Fear of general Bolshevik insurrection and revolution preoccupied national cabinets throughout Europe in terms of the social welfare of their citizens. Even the official phraseology of European politicians changed and became more sympathetic to the suffering of the poor. The ingenious organizer of the German war economy, Walther Rathenau, wrote in a 1917 pamphlet:

> "A more equal distribution of possessions and income is a commandment of ethics and economy. Only one in the State is allowed to be immeasurably rich: that is the State itself. (...) The monopolist, the speculator and the millionaire heir have no longer a place in the new order of economy" (Bruck 1938: 142).

Social policy and other forms of state intervention in the economy became the leitmotif of European policy during the 1920s.

German writer Erich Maria Remarque created a powerful image of turbulent post-war times in his country in his novel "The Road Back". It is hard to forget the image of trains overcrowded with hungry people who had left the cities in search of food in the countryside. Although one can suppose in hard post-war times it was much easier for the Yugoslav population to survive in the countryside, a great influx of people into the cities was, in fact, recorded. The population of the Kingdom of Serbs, Croats and Slovenians overcrowded urban areas in spite of the fact that there was no available employment. The statistical data for Belgrade is noteworthy. They indicate a rise in Belgrade's population of 24% (between 1910 and 1921), while the total population of the pre-war Kingdom of Serbia decreased by 24% (calculated here as the sum of persons died during the war and demographic losses of population) in the same period (Đuričić, Tošić

1927: 30). Statistical data on the populations of major cities in the Kingdom of SCS are shown in table 1.

Table 1: Population of major towns in the Kingdom of SCS 1921 and 1931 (Timet 1961: 58)

Town	1921	1931
Belgrade	111739	238775
Zagreb	108674	185581
Subotica	90961	100058
Sarajevo	66317	78173
Skopje	40666	68334
Novi Sad	39122	63985
Ljubljana	53294	59767

Housing problems

The basic problem for Yugoslav urban populations after the war was housing. Belgrade was devastated as the result of the war operations. Zagreb and Ljubljana also had a shortage of flats due to the small scale of housing construction during the war. It would be senseless to consider any more subtle aspect of urban life without considering the basic problem of "the roof over one's head". The shortage of adequate apartments was a long lasting problem in post-war Zagreb and Belgrade. People were living in the most incredible places: in 1923 a long time after the end of the war the daily newspaper *Politika* reported on a Zagreb family to whom the authorities had given an empty prison cell to stay in for a few days (Beda udovice, 1923).

During the 1920s approximately 1500 railway carriages all over the Kingdom were used as "suitable" flats for the Yugoslav railway workers (Predgrađe 1923). There was a small Belgrade "suburb on wheels". About 400 men, women and children lived in that particular settlement without basic hygienic facilities, water supply or electricity. One newspaper reporter mentioned an unpleasant smell coming from pigs, which the families kept under their improvised homes. These poor inhabitants complained about their "housing" conditions by noting that during the summer it was unbearable to stay inside the red-hot metal structure of the carriages, whereas in the winter the situation was even worse as they could not heat them. Two children died of the unhealthy wintertime conditions.

This was not only an inadequate housing situation but also a great financial loss for the state economy. According to a journalistic investigation any one of these railway carriages employed in transportation would have made a profit of about

500 dinars a day (Železnički vagoni 1925). In Belgrade at that time this was equivalent to the average monthly rent for a small flat. With a single day's profit the railway authorities could have provided their workers with decent homes for a whole month.

Housing policy of the Kingdom of Serbs, Croats and Slovenians

In the years after the war the leasing of flats or rooms was the most lucrative business in the country. *Politika* reported in 1919 on a citizen of Belgrade who complained about his salary. A graduate of two faculties, his salary totaled only 18 dinars a day. His mother-in-law had no education but she had one available room with three beds from which she could earn about 36 dinars a day (Šta se govori, Nov. 1919). However this kind of business was possible only in the case of so called new tenants who rented their flats after the enforcement of the Housing Act of April 1919 (Zakon 19 April 1919). The law was designed to help old tenants to survive the hard times following the war. There were no restrictions in leasing contracts for new tenants in order to encourage people to rent all available flats and rooms.

The executive and legislative power of the Kingdom of SCS tried to intervene in the relations between landlord and old tenant using basically the same measures as those implemented in Italy, Austria, Hungary or Germany.[1] The amount of money tenants paid to their landlord before the war could not be raised without approval from the designated state institution or official. Due to inflation these amounts had already been drastically decreased so the regulation must have had a strong impact on the social conditions of poor citizens. According to the Yugoslav Housing Act, a landlord could not cancel a contract with a tenant as long as he was paying the prescribed amount of rent. Yugoslav authorities not only neglected the principles of free market bargaining between landlord and tenant, but also prescribed the conditions under which apartments could be requisitioned for purposes of the State. Such a settlement made it impossible to cancel a contract between landlords and "old tenants" and stimulated the production of new houses.

It is not surprising that landlords were very nervous and embittered by these regulations. In free market bargaining they could get two or three times more money than under the Housing Act. They tried by all possible means to get rid of unwanted tenants. This often caused conflicts and other incidents. Newspapers reported on one anxious Belgrade landlord who took the tiles off the roof of his own house in order to force the tenants out of the rented apartment. Another tried his luck with a (little) bit of drama and superstition. In the dead of night he

[1] Les problèmes 1924; see also Guye 1931.

Table 2: Number of buildings in the major towns of the Kingdom of SCS (1918–40) (Timet 1961: 103 f.)

Town	1918	1930	1940
Belgrade	9538	25179	37556
Zagreb	5310	13668	24704
Ljubljana	4949	7478	10347
Sarajevo	6307	8452	10714
Skopje	6548	10164	12339

"acted" under the window of his elderly lady tenant disguised as a vampire. He wanted either to frighten the old lady or to accuse her in front of other neighbors of impurity (Šta se govori, Oct. 1919).

For two decades, the Yugoslav authorities encouraged construction by tax-exempting the rents paid for the newly-constructed apartments. The entrepreneur's building investment would pay off within only five years of rentals (Ognjanović 2000: 73, 77 f.). After this period he could enjoy the entire profit without any limitations. For this reason the largest share of investments in the Kingdom of SCS was in the construction sector. During the 1930s it was estimated that the amount of these investments was seven times higher than that of all other investments in the Yugoslav economy (Marković 1992: 96). However, in spite of the large scale of construction activities (see table 2), social and hygienic standards in Yugoslav urban housing were unsatisfactory and unbearable during the 1920s and 1930s. By this time, fundamental problems were already apparent in the housing legislation itself.

There were two separate pieces of housing legislation in the Kingdom of SCS. In fact, due to the different historical heritage of Yugoslav provinces there were six different Civil Code and Law systems in the Kingdom of SCS, but in this particular case different laws had been passed in 1920 for the former Kingdoms of Serbia and Montenegro (Uredba, May 1920) and for the former Austro-Hungarian provinces (Uredba o pomaganju, July 1920). When regulations valid for the whole country were introduced in 1921, they preserved all the differences in the previous legislation (Uredba, June 1921; Zakon, 23 February 1922). In the provinces of the former Austro-Hungarian Empire it was prescribed that tax-exemption would be reserved only for small (so called "workers") apartments, consisting of one or two rooms. In this way, the city of Zagreb was provided with a large number of small, affordable apartments (see table 3). However, the average number of persons living together in these apartments presented a problem. During the 1920s this number was estimated at about 2.5 persons per room, and verged on social pathology (Timet 1961: 219). Almost all new constructed houses in Yugoslavia were

Table 3: Structure of flats built in Zagreb (1918–1930) (Timet 1961: 117)

separate rooms	4659
one room apartments	9364
two room apartments	5456
three room apartments	2170
four room apartments	753
five room apartments	278
total	*22860*

built by private entrepreneurs. During the period of greatest need for flats between 1918 and 1923 the Yugoslav government financed construction for no more than about 150 workers' flats. In addition, approximately 100 improvised wooden flats were delivered by Germany as a part of war reparations (Arhiv Jugoslavije -39-8-22). Neither the central government nor local communities had sufficient financial means for such a project.

On the other hand there were no such limitations in the former Kingdoms of Serbia and Montenegro. All newly constructed apartments were tax-exempted. Belgrade entrepreneurs built large and luxurious apartments which were so expensive (for instance: 1000 dinars monthly when a top qualified worker could earn only 50 dinars a day) that as a result no one could rent them. During the 1930s there were 1500–5000 of these flats without tenants. That is why a significant number of Belgrade citizens lived in improvised wooden houses on the outskirts of the city, something very similar to the modern-day South American favela. The most famous Belgrade slum area was the so called Jatagan-Mala. An inspection by the Ministry of Social Policy in 1923 has afforded us some statistical data. Of 294 houses, only 68 (or 23%) were made of solid material, such as bricks. All other houses were constructed using a combination of wooden and paper materials, as well as traditional Balkan unbaked bricks. There were also four dugouts. More than half (167 or 57%) of these houses were covered only by paper. In most of them (234 or 80%) the floor was made of compressed earth (Potpuna slika 1923). One could even see the same type of slum house in the very center of the city, the so called yard-house. A view of the main entrance of the building facing the street presented an elegant facade and splendor, but on entering the yard from the opposite side one glimpsed a group of small, dreadful wooden houses.

Urbanization and social conditions of the Yugoslav urban population

If we consider urbanization in the Kingdom of SCS as a process measured by statistical data and compare data changes between the census of 1921 and 1931, the results are disappointing. We can see that the proportion of the nonagricultural population had risen by approximately four percent (19.63% – 23.7%). For example, the same percentage of urban population was estimated for the Italian part of the Roman Empire in the 2nd century AD or for entire Europe, Russia excluded, at the beginning of the 19th century.[2] Moreover, less than half of these urban dwellers were employed in industry and crafts (9.91% of all employed persons in 1921 and 11% in 1931) (Dimić 1996, I: 81).

The living conditions of poor citizens in the major Yugoslav cities were horrible, so one cannot be surprised by the rates of tuberculosis infection and mortality in urban areas. In 1918, 46.5% of all urban fatalities succumbed to tuberculosis. In the same period in the countryside, tuberculosis mortality was 31.76%. It is likely that an overall higher standard of hygiene in cities eventually contributed to a faster decrease in the rate of tuberculosis mortality (see table 4). Statistical data of 1926 referring to tuberculosis mortality by profession in the Kingdom are also indicative. Tuberculosis mortality of state administration employees was four times higher than that of the agricultural population (Hahn 1929). According to school reports on conditions of child nourishment, some 35% of the children in schools in Skopje and some 9% in Zagreb were malnourished, and the percentage of properly nourished children in these two cities was about 40%. About 71% of the children in Skopje and 24% of those in Belgrade had rotten teeth (Dimić 1996, I: 63, 72).

There is an unusual story about public action by the Yugoslav Ministry of Health against malnourishment of new-borns, providing insight into the state of the infrastructure and material means of the Yugoslav state. The Ministry was under-staffed at the local level, so they requested that priests handle questionnaires in an effort to collect what was quite intimate and subtle information. In addition to basic questions regarding infant nutrition (breast-feeding or artificial, or the kind of food), there were also questions concerning "whether the breasts or nipples were proper for breast-feeding or not", and so on. Of course, the orthodox priests found the whole case very amusing, and the whole "project" was abandoned (Među nama 1923).

Ljubodrag Dimić often argued that warmth was probably the only luxury Yugoslav villagers of the inter-war period could provide for themselves (Dimić 1996, I: 51). Inhabitants of slum houses in the cities could not afford even that kind of luxury. Every winter was a new challenge for them struggling against the cold. In the winter of 1927, a Zagreb newspaper reported on poor people standing

---

[2] Bairoch et al. 1988: 253–255; see also Malanima 2005: 97–122.

Table 4: Tuberculosis mortality (percentage of all deceased persons per year) in the Kingdom of SCS (ibid: 67).

Year	Urban areas	Countryside
1918	46.50	31.76
1919	40.53	26.88
1920	32.48	26.15
1921	30.85	25.14
1922	33.52	25.74
1923	31.76	25.44
1924	33.75	25.13
1925	29.91	23.31
1926	29.72	23.71
1927	30.78	24.02
1928	30.72	24.20
1929	30.76	24.29
1930	25.50	22.52

for long periods in local grocery shops just to catch a little bit of warmth there (17,2 ispod, 1927).

The nutritional standard of the population of Belgrade was quite low. Meat consumption per capita in Belgrade was about half that of Germany. It was estimated that about ⅔ of the proteins in the nutrition of Yugoslavs were of vegetable and wheat origin. Consumption of milk in Belgrade for 1928 was 50% less than in Germany in 1913. However, the bad nutritional value of food was compensated by a large proportion of vegetables in the diet, and the caloric deficit may have been compensated by strong alcoholic drinks. Consumption of the famous Serbian "rakija" was higher than that of milk (Marković 1992: 103).

Apart from a campaign for the public glorification of Serbian military heroism in the First World War, the Yugoslav authorities did very little to support the basic living needs of the war invalids. In the 1920s when the price of 1 kg of bread was about 4 dinars, the average monthly amount of war invalid pension was 40 dinars. The children of war invalids had 7.5 dinars of additional monthly social aid (Robovi 1920). The income of an average war invalid family with two children living on welfare would buy only 13 kg of bread. The Zagreb *Novosti* reported on an interesting case of the War Invalids Association in Zagreb which applied to the city authorities for some offices where they could have their library and hold meetings. But very soon after they received these offices, some of them figured out a better way to support their members financially. They turned the library into a Casino. A roulette was bought abroad and everything was prepared for the opening of the Casino Club, when the police received information about it. As a consequence, the War Invalids Association was deprived of their "offices" as roulette and gambling in the Kingdom of SCS could not be performed without a special license (Ruleta, policija, 1927).

The position of women in society

In spite of the lack of basic living conditions of housing and nutrition, Yugoslav cities in the inter-war period proved to be places of dynamic modernization and numerous cultural transformations. I will focus on the social position of women and on transformations which occurred in family and intimate life in Yugoslav cities. Women in the Kingdom did not have the right to vote. According to Article 920 of the Serbian Civil Law, they were treated like underage or mentally retarded persons not capable to dispose of even their family property. In order to do so a woman would need to have authorization either from her father (if she was single) or from her husband (if she was married):

> "As underage persons are considered all those who cannot or who are forbidden to dispose of their own property, including: mentally retarded persons, spendthrifts, as designated by the courts, persons heavily in debt with mortgaged property, married women during their husband's lifetime" (§ 920 of the Serbian Civil Law).

Even a woman's citizenship was defined by male patronage. Unfortunately there is no room to elaborate on the complexity of this question, but in many cases if she married a foreigner she would automatically lose Yugoslav citizenship. Belgrade newspapers wrote about an interesting case of a girl who married an American. He was a Yugoslav immigrant from Dalmatia but had an American citizenship. Problems appeared when they wanted to leave for America. By the act of marriage the girl had lost her Yugoslav citizenship, while she could not obtain American citizenship automatically. In the end she could not leave the country because she did not have the right to have either an American or a Yugoslav passport (Naša žena, 1924).

The decision of the Yugoslav government to employ three women in the Office of General Budget Control caused great opposition from male personnel. In an assembly they threatened the government with collective resignation if the appointments were to be authorized. They argued that these appointments should be withdrawn "for the sake of the authority of the institution of General Budget Control". After a few months, however, only a minority of employees in the General Budget Control still opposed these appointments (Mogu li, 1923; Žene, 1924).

Although the social and political milieus were conservative, women of great Yugoslav cities were gaining more and more self-confidence and influence. The Belgrade daily *Politika* delivered a story about Ksenija Atanasijević, the first woman to become professor at Belgrade University in 1924 (Prva nastavnica, 1927). My Belgrade colleague Ljiljana Lazarević provided me with an article about Belgrade women written by the famous Serbian comedy writer Branislav Nušić in 1924:

> "Before the war everything was long or long lasting: long skirt, long hair, long-lasting marriage. Now, after the war everything is short: skirts are short, hair is short and marriage is short-lived. Before the war a woman was giving birth once a year, today she gives three births a year but with no increase of population. Before the war it was insulting even to mention that a woman had been divorced, today it's a kind of compliment for her."

Lazarević also found interesting information on over 2000 unofficial marriages noted in one Serbian community alone in 1920. In patriarchal pre-war Serbia it was almost unimaginable to live in concubinage. There is an incredible story about a married woman who married one more time and whose husband got married two more times while serving at the front. So at the end of the war it turned out that the woman had two husbands while her husband had three wives.

The popular Belgrade novelist and journalist Milica Jakovljević Mir-Jam wrote many articles about changes in the everyday life of Belgrade women. She also noted great discrepancies between the pre-war and the post-war ways of life in Belgrade:

> "There on the promenade one can see the difference between pre-war and post-war generations. I remember the girls from high school before the war. They were sitting on the lonely benches away from the other people. They had their books with them in order to check each other's homework, discussing literature or solving mathematical problems. The girl of nowadays doesn't like those things, in fact she has no time for it. What she likes is to sit, to watch and she also likes to be watched by the others. If there are two of them they comment in a low voice, if there are four of them they are very noisy and insolent. They are capable of confusing even a grown up man. They are not shy; in fact, shyness is regarded not as a virtue but as a defect according to 20th century attitudes ... they are very loud and they want to be heard and noticed by the men ... They often fall in love and can do a lot of crazy things. They are afraid neither of their teachers nor of their parents. In fact they have no feeling of fear at all" (Portreti beograđanski, 1927).

Owning your own phonograph or car became a status symbol in Belgrade in the 1920s. The home piano went out of fashion as the "wild sounds" of jazz and Charleston entered Belgrade living rooms through radio and phonograph records. Milica Jakovljević wrote about everyday preoccupations of the "hyper-modern Belgrade girl":

> "She has bobbed hair, she wears short skirts, she smokes cigarettes. She is not any more interested in the cavalry second lieutenant. Her mind is becoming more and more occupied by the car driver (...) the hyper-modern Belgrade woman can identify every car's trademark. Even from a great distance she can tell you whether it is a Dodge, Mercedes, Cadilac, Fiat, Benz, Chevrolet, Ford, Citroen ... etc (...) In the modern age, literary education is not as important as the knowledge of different automobile brands. A young lady is very proud when there is a conversation about cars and when no man can answer the question for instance: what is the traffic signal when the driver wants to back up? Then she would stand up and as proudly as if she had solved some great problem, would say: – He should sound a horn four times. And all the gentlemen are surprised by such a knowledge of the young lady" (Četvrta brzina, 1927).

Drugs, prostitution and love-games

During this period of changes and modernization Belgrade experienced some new and exotic vices. *Politika* reported in 1923 on exciting police action against the "underground organization" of drug peddlers in Belgrade. It was the first time that Yugoslav police discovered a chain of the cocaine trade and a significantly large number of drug abusers in the city (Beli otrov 1923). At the same time Belgrade police were making a much greater effort to combat prostitution. There were so many prostitutes that one journalist for *Novosti* reported on "an army of immoral women", comparing Belgrade with the Biblical city of Sodom. A special police squad ("sanitation police") was formed in Belgrade in 1925 with the sole task of suppressing prostitution and its effects. About 20 men and 10 women patrolled the city streets trying to find the prostitutes and take them into custody. Actually the clinic was the first place where they were taken. A similar police unit with the same task was formed in Zagreb ("social department"). According to Belgrade and Zagreb newspapers most of the prostitutes were already infected by venereal diseases. In 1927 the Zagreb police arrested a girl of Polish origin who had no less than four contagious venereal diseases.

Despite their importance in terms of social and medical services, members of these police units also caused many problems and incidents. Guided by primitive police logic they would often start to follow or to sneak up to ordinary couples walking on the street. During the night hours, people and especially women felt insecure on the streets of the city. Belgrade *Novosti* reported on a man sitting with his wife in the park in the center of Belgrade when a policeman of the squad appeared, pointed his flash light at their faces and ordered them to leave the park. When the man tried to explain the situation they were warned: "Leave the park, otherwise I will take you to the clinic."[3]

Belgrade authorities combated prostitution by targeting night cafés, so called Variétés, as they suspected that night performances were only a pretext for prostitution. A few establishments were closed down and a strict seven-point regulation was instituted for those that remained:

> "1. The owners of the Variétés are obliged to submit details of all performances for authorization by the Belgrade authorities.
> 2. The price list must be posted in a conspicuous place.
> 3. Performances and all other forms of entertainment may last only until midnight and the restaurant may remain open until 2:00 AM.
> 4. Female personnel cannot reside in the same building where they perform.
> 5. There must not be a separate meeting room on the premises.
> 6. All female personnel must be subjected to screenings for skin and venereal disease, and no one can be seated together with the guests.
> 7. The owners of the establishment must submit a list of all female employees to the Clinic for Skin and Venereal Disease as this clinic will exercise control over them" (Beogradskih varijetea, 1923).

The Zagreb newspaper *Novosti* reported in 1925 on an interesting incident provoked by Ljubljana girls and women who were swimming in the Sava River near the village of Rateča. Wearing bathing suits the Ljubljana girls attracted the attention of the local male population. One morning, jealous and embittered local women awaited and attacked them with nettles, which caused a real incident. The breakdown of traditional society brought individual freedom to men and women alike. Marriages were no longer arranged by parents. City streets became the scene of love-games and the art of courting. Sometimes the police had to intervene. In Zagreb and Belgrade in 1925, newspapers often reported on incidents provoked by courting women in the streets. Arrested culprits in Zagreb were punished with eight days in prison. It is interesting that most of the arrested were students (Opet zadirkivanje 1927). But some young men were not so courageous.

[3] Beogradska 1925; see also: "Plesačica" 1927 and Strašna slika 1923.

They tried to approach women through personal advertisements in the newspapers which read as follows:

> "To the lady who gave me the eye near the Stone Gate and then turned and left: I ask if I can make her acquaintance."
>
> "To the girl who traveled from Novimarof to Zagreb on Thursday: I ask her if I can make her acquaintance."
>
> "Two prosperous and intelligent young gentlemen are seeking for young, modern and intelligent girls up to 24 years old for the purpose of a party in a provincial town where they should stay for a month. Please send un-anonymous answers with photos."

The women also tried to find mates for dating or marriage through such advertisements:

> "Rusalka and Bosiljka, good-looking and nice girls who are very bored are seeking two gentlemen for correspondence and to shorten boring winter nights ...
>
> "A young passionate woman unhappily married is interested in acquaintanceship with a prosperous older man ...

Some of these "love" announcements were strictly financial, in many cases like business proposals:

> "A retired woman, financially independent, with regular income and house, unhappily married, asks an intelligent and kind gentleman to help her with a short-term loan of 4000 dinars. Acquaintanceship is not excluded ..."
>
> "An academician, 28 years old, reserve officer, speaks German, Croatian and French, is looking for a discreet female acquaintance that would be willing to support him with financial means. Discretion is guaranteed by honor ..." (Poznanstva, 1927).

Final considerations

The final breakdown of traditional society in Yugoslavia came only after the violence of the Second World War and the revolutionary reforms of the Yugoslav communist authorities that followed. Throughout the Kingdom of SCS, the processes of cultural change and modernization in society were slower and their development was gradual. They were accelerated only at the beginning of the inter-war period due to the chaotic conditions after the First World War. Later on, the modernizing changes became less remarkable. Very often it is not easy to identify them. Therefore, the record of even small changes in everyday habits, morals, and ways of life are of great importance for studies of the cultural history of the Kingdom of SCS. The large Yugoslav cities like Zagreb, Ljubljana and Belgrade were only small islands in the agrarian ocean of traditional society. Conflicts between tradition and modernity usually occurred on the suburban margins where these two worlds met each other. Prostitution and the dissolution of the traditional concept of marriage jeopardized family life. Relaxed attitudes between the genders, especially among the younger urban population, emerged during this period. Although the social and political milieus were conservative, women in the large Yugoslav cities gained more and more self-confidence and influence. But in spite of modernization and numerous cultural transformations, Yugoslav cities were marked by a permanent housing crisis and desperate living conditions.[4]

References

Anon. 1924: Les problèmes du logement en Europe depuis la guerre. In: International Labour Review (1924) 480–499.

Bairoch, P. et al. 1988: La population des villes européennes 800–1850. Geneva: Centre d'histoire économique internationale, Université de Genève, 253–255.

Bruck, W. F. 1938: Social and Economic History of Germany from William II to Hitler. Cardiff: Oxford UP.

Čalić, Mari-Žanin 2004: Socijalna istorija Srbije 1815–1941 [The social history of Serbia 1815–1941]. Belgrade: CLIO.

Dimić, Lj. 1996: Kulturna politika Kraljevine Jugoslavije (I vol.) [Cultural policy of the Kingdom of Yugoslavia]. Belgrade: Stubovi kulture, 51.

Đuričić, V. M, M. B. Tošić 1927: Naša narodna privreda i nacionalni dohodak [Our national economy and the national product]. Sarajevo.

Guye, R. 1931: Post-War Building Difficulties and Housing Policy in Europe. In: International Labor Review (1931) 213–241.

Jovanović, Vladan 2002: Jugoslovenska država i Južna Srbija 1918–1929: Makedonija, Sandžak, Kosovo i Metohija u Kraljevini SHS [The Yugoslav state and Southern Serbia 1918–1929: Macedonia, Sandžak, Kosovo and Metohija in the Kingdom of Serbs, Croats and Slovenes]. Belgrade: INIS.

Keynes, John Maynard 1971: The Economic Consequences of the Peace. London: Macmillan.

[4] I wish to thank John Venham of Indiana University and Thomas Szerecz of the Central European University for their assistance in editing this paper.

Malanima, Paolo 2004: Urbanization and the Italian Economy During the Last Millenium. In: European Review of Economic History 9, 1: 97–122.

Marković, P. J. 1992: Beograd i Evropa (1918–1941) [Belgrade and Europe (1918–1941)]. Belgrade: Savremena administracija.

Ognjanović, V. I. 2000: Porodica Ivana Vić [The family of Ivan Vić]. Los Angeles, Belgrade: Ognjanovića.

Timet, Tomislav 1961: Stambena izgradnja Zagreba do 1954 [The construction of residential buildings in Zagreb up to 1954]. Zagreb: Jugoslavenska Akademija Znanosti i Umetnosti.

Vučetić-Mladenović, Radina 2003: Evropa na Kalemegdanu: "Cvijeta Zuzorić" i kulturni život Beograda 1918–1941 [Europe on Kalemegdan: "Cvijeta Zuzorić" and the cultural life of Belgrade 1918–1941]. Belgrade: INIS.

Articles in newspapers

Beda udovice i majke [The Misery of the widow and the mother]. In: Politika, 2 November 1923.

Predgrađe na točkovima [Suburb on wheels]. In: Politika, 26 September 1923.

Železnički vagoni [Railway carriages]. In: Privredni pregled, 16 April 1925.

Šta se govori [What they talk about]. In: Politika, 2 November 1919.

Šta se govori [What they talk about]. In: Politika, 30 October 1919.

Potpuna slika Jatagan male [The complete image of Jatagan mala]. In: Politika, 12 June 1923.

17,2 ispod ništice [17.2 below zero]. In: Novosti (Zagreb), 21 December 1927.

Dr Zeljko Hahn, Bolest i zanimanje [Dr Zeljko Hahn: Disease and profession]. In: Socijalna misao, 1 May 1929.

Robovi u slobodi [Slaves restored to freedom]. In: Ratni invalid, 11 June 1920.

Ruleta, policija i invalidi [Roulette, police and the invalids]. In: Novosti, 6 January 1927.

Naša žena u Americi [A woman from our nation in America]. In: Novosti (Belgrade), 2 June 1924.

Milica Jakovljević Mir-Jam 1927: Portreti beograđanski – Kiki sa beogradskih ulica [Belgrade's portraits – Kiki from the streets of Belgrade]. In: Novosti (Beograd), 18 April 1927.

Milica Jakovljević Mir-Jam 1927: Četvrta brzina u životu beograđanke [Fourth gear in the life of a Belgrade woman]. In: Novosti (Beograd), 11 May 1927.

Beogradskih varijetea kraj [The end of Belgrade's variétés]. In: Politika, 19 September 1919.

Beli otrov u Beogradu [White poison (cocaine) in Belgrade]. In: Politika 22 November 1923.

Beogradska noć [Belgrade's night]. In: (Belgrade) Novosti, 3 January 1925.
"Plesačica" Sonja [The "dancer" Sonja]. In: (Zagreb) Novosti, 26 Ožujka 1927.
Strašna slika iz sveta propalica [A horrible picture from the world of beggars]. In: Novosti, 16 August 1923.
Opet zadirkivanje u žena [Again about women]. In: Novosti (Zagreb), 6 November, 1927.
Poznanstva [Acquaintances]. In: Novosti (Zagreb), 21 April, 12 March and 12, 14 and 16 Dec. 1927.
Prva nastavnica na Univerzitetu [The first woman university professor]. In: Politika, 21 October 1923.
Mogu li žene biti računoispitači [Are women able to be accountants]. In: Politika, 7 October 1923.
Žene računoispitači [Women as accountants]. In: Politika, 4 August 1924.
Među nama [Between you and me]. In: Politika, 21 September 1923.

Sources

Uredba o stanovima [Regulation on Housing]. In: Službene novine, 31 May 1920.
Uredba o pomaganju produkcije novih stanova [Regulation on the Support of Housing Construction]. In: Službene novine, 23 July 1920.
Uredba o stanovima [Regulation on Housing]. In: Službene novine, 23 June 1921.
Zakon o stanovima [Law on Housing]. In: Službene novine, 23 February 1922.
Zakon o stanovima [Law on Housing]. In: Službene novine, 19 April 1919.
Arhiv Jugoslavije (Archive of Yugoslavia, Belgrade, Fond of the Ministry of Social Policy) –39–8–22

Abstract

The paper sheds light on the phenomena of urbanization and cultural transformation in major cities of the Kingdom of SCS. The processes of cultural change and societal modernization were accelerated at the beginning of the inter-war period due to the chaotic conditions after the First World War. Prostitution and the dissolution of the traditional concept of marriage jeopardized family life. Relaxed attitudes between the genders, especially among the younger urban population, emerged in this period. In spite of the conservative social and political milieus, urban women gained self-confidence and influence. Yugoslav cities were marked both by dynamic modernization and numerous cultural transformations but also by a permanent housing crisis and desperate living conditions.

ASFALT: The Construction of Urbanity in Everyday Discourse in Serbia

Ivana Spasić, Belgrade

Urban life and urbanization in the Balkans, in addition to being treated as historical and sociological facts, have lately also been addressed from a symbolic/discursive/rhetorical vantage point. As part of a general interest in "symbolic geography", especially – where the Balkans is concerned – following the lead of Maria Todorova's (1997) pioneering work, "urbanity" (and its counterpoint, "rurality") has been viewed as an element in various discursive strategies and a topos in narratives of individual and collective identity. Such studies have focused mainly on public discourse, analyzing past and present usages of the urban–rural opposition in academic and essayist writings or political communication,[1] while interest in the place of "urbanity" in non-institutionalized, everyday discourse has been more restricted.[2]

The present paper[3] deals precisely with such mundane constructions: how ordinary people in Serbia refer to "urbanity", what it means to them, how they use it – in their daily talk about themselves, their life, and their society. The argument is built on a secondary analysis of qualitative data collected for the study "Politics and Everyday Life" conducted in 2002 by the Institute for Philosophy and Social Theory, Belgrade, and focusing on people's experiences and interpretations of the downfall of Milošević's regime in 2000. The study was designed by sociologists Zagorka Golubović, Đorđe Pavićević and myself.[4] The data consisted of 300 interviews in 19 Serbian cities and towns by qualified researchers residing in the respective communities. A multistage proportional sample was employed allowing for systematic variation on all major socio-demographic variables, such as gender, age, education, occupation, (un)employment, marital status, geograph-

---

1 For the ex-Yugoslav context, see Žanić 1998; Vujović 1997: 71–105; Naumović 1995; 2002: 19–31; Čolović 1993: 47–59, 83–92; 2000: 113–155; Rihtman-Auguštin 1997: 167–192, 211–236; Živković 1998; 2001: 57–92, 146–153, 168–173, 221–230.

2 Full-length analyses include Jansen 2006; 2005: 109–167; Brown 2001; important insights are to be found in Živković 1998 and 2001.

3 The paper is part of Project No. 149029, supported by the Ministry of Science of Serbia.

4 Main findings are reported in: Golubović, Spasić, Pavićević (eds.) 2003. An English summary is available at: http://www.afebalk.org/rencontres2002/textes/I.Spasic.pdf.

ical region,[5] and ethnicity. In addition, elements of quota sampling were introduced for the two most important ethnic minorities – Bosniaks in Novi Pazar and Hungarians in Subotica.

The interviews were semi-structured and based on a guide containing a list of "political" and "everyday life" thematic areas, but *not* including any questions related specifically to "urbanity". Discussions of urbanity emerged as a by-product of the conversational flow, since interviewees were encouraged to talk freely and to elaborate on any point they felt appropriate.[6]

The starting point for the present analysis is precisely the fact that people invoked the theme of urbanity completely spontaneously in their responses to a range of questions. This demonstrates that constructions of urbanity, and self-identification with these constructions, represent an important part of how people situate themselves in their social world.

In spite of this evident importance, ordinary definitions of urbanity in Serbia have so far not been a subject of systematic sociological study. Unlike other forms of self-perception (class, professional, or political) this topic has never been part of survey questionnaires amongst large representative samples. Thus the body of work examining lay meanings of urbanity is composed of studies by anthropologists (see footnote 2). Though my own findings mainly coincide with theirs, as will be seen throughout the paper, this difference in disciplinary frameworks perhaps explains some of the divergences, discussed in the concluding section.

1. Verbalizations and what they imply

Let me start from the interview questions that most frequently triggered references to "urbanity". Some were expected in this context, such as the one concerning the feelings about one's place of residence: *Do you like the place where you live?* Some others were more surprising, like class self-positioning: *To which social class or stratum do you think you belong?,* and general self-identification: *If you were asked – who are you, what would you say first?* But the most surprising, and most indicative, were questions seemingly completely unrelated to the topic, such as various political ones: *Are you a member of a political party? Are you satisfied with the new local government? Did you join the anti-Milošević protests during the*

[5] Research sites were sampled so as to obtain an even distribution between Vojvodina (the northernmost part of the country), Belgrade, and western, eastern and southern subregions of Central Serbia.

[6] It may be argued that a social science interview is not quite identical to mundane talk. However, a relaxed, conversational mode of conducting interviews produced data that strike a reasonable compromise between mundanity and a degree of formalization, necessary to achieve comparability across the sample.

1990s? What is it that bothers you the most about the current situation? Should all war refugees be allowed to return? This disparate list shows the areas in which "urbanity" functioned to help people make sense of their social setting and their place within it.

This becomes evident in the verbal form, or "names" for urbanity that people used. The analysis has to start from the complicating fact that in the Serbian language there is no separate word for "urban". In just a handful of cases, the internationalism *urbano* appeared. Its infrequency indicates that this is a very marked word in social and cultural terms. It distinguishes its users; but rather than simply implying the level of education, its usage reflects the self-positioning of the speaker as having a modernized, sophisticated outlook and a well thought-out attitude to one's social environment, for instance:

> Q: What does this society need to improve? – *We need urbanization, modernization of consciousness and of some basic principles, a new way of thinking, a new taste* (Paraćin, f, 18, high school student).

> Q: If you could choose, where would you prefer to live? – *In Barcelona. This has been my dream lately ... And in Japan. I'm attracted to places with a mixture of urbanity and aesthetic.* – Q: Have you ever been to Barcelona or Japan? – *No, but ...* (Belgrade, f, 31, incomplete college, secretary).

Another "name" denoting urbanity is *asfalt* (literally: asphalt). It implies being urban by birth and family background, and generations of work in a non-farming occupation.

> Q: To what class/stratum do you think you belong? – *Bourgeois.* – Q: What does class membership depend on? – *On your background – whether you are from the asphalt or from the plough field* (Niš, f, 47, sociologist).

Asfalt is thus not just the physical matter used to pave streets and roads, but a metaphor for an urban way of life. This metaphorization is obviously not of domestic origin but imported, yet it has long been part of local usage. Ever since there has been asphalt in Serbia, the phrase "born on *asfalt*" has carried a distinct bundle of meanings. The despised counterpart to *"asphalt"* is, of course, "mud", the foremost visual and tactile representation for all that the village stands for.[7]

Kaldrma is the Balkan equivalent for *asfalt*. This somewhat outdated word for cobblestone retains, both linguistically and symbolically, strong traces of its

---

[7] For illuminating discussions of how "mud" figures in discourse in today's Serbia see: Jansen (2005: 110 f., 118 f.) for the dichotomy "mud : asphalt", and Živković (2001: 13–23) for "mud : *kaldrma*".

Turkish origin and hence points to a more specific, and more intimate, "Balkan" urbanity. It is not so cosmopolitan and "modern" as *asfalt*, but conveys the same message with a stronger regional flavor: *We have no land, both my wife and I are cobblestoners* [kaldrmaši] (Čačak, m, 51, secondary school, clerk).

Urban things were conveyed most frequently, however, by the word for city – *grad,* and its derivatives: the adjective *gradsko* (of the city), the noun *građanin* (city dweller, as well as citizen) and its adjective *građansko*, etc. In Serbian, these words mean many things in addition to "urban": they may denote "municipal", "civic", or "bourgeois".[8] It is important to note that respondents relied on this semantic ambivalence, though not always completely consciously. I will come back to this later.

Thus the substance covered by "urban" in English appeared in the data under the headings *gradsko, građansko, naš grad* (our town) or the name of the town, *ljudi odavde* (people from here) etc. Frequently it was implicitly defined through the use of opposite categories such as *seljaci* (peasants), *ljudi sa sela* (people from the country), *polutani* ("half-breeds", peasant-workers or peasant-urbanites), *došljaci* or *pridošlice* (newcomers), *ljudi sa strane* (people from the outside), *izbeglice* (refugees). The surest way to discern the "urban" layer of meaning within the ambiguous *grad* is to look for cases when it was used within a binary opposition to something else, to something that is non-*grad.*

Hence, to examine what "urbanity" implied in symbolic terms it is best to start from its intersection with social classifications where a connection was established between urbanity and social superiority, in its broad sense. For, while the *"asfalt"* quotation above identified urbanity unmistakably with the bourgeois class, the connection was by no means always that simple:

> Q: What is the basis of difference among social strata in Serbia? – *It is generally believed that money decides, but my criteria are education and behavior.* – Q: What does "behavior" mean? – *There is, say, peasant behavior. ... For example, when people keep changing their mind* (Kruševac, m, 36, elementary school, phone operator).

In the interviews, the discussion of class, in addition to individual self-positioning on the social ladder, almost invariably contained a version of "lay sociology", i.e., a vision of the basic principles of social stratification in today's Serbia. As Bourdieu (1979) teaches us, to propound visions of the social structure is never

---

[8] In socialist times, official rhetoric made *građansko* a pejorative label for undesirable phenomena: in the social and political realm, it meant "bourgeois" as opposed to the "working-class"; in the realm of ideas, it referred to false non-Marxist thought as opposed to the veracity of the Doctrine. These sedimentations of meaning still linger on in the background of current usages, especially when the insistence on *građansko* serves to assert the post-socialist reversal of values.

simply to describe what there is, but also a performative move to carve out an appropriate place for oneself. In our research "urbanity" often figured within these strategies:

> *I belong to the middle stratum, which has been thinned down completely. It comprises 10% of the population, at the most. It is people who have a cultural level, who are not so much tied to the country* (Pančevo, m, 30, technician).

> *I won't refer to peasants* [seljaci] *here, peasants are farmers* [zemljoradnici], *and yokel* [seljačina] *is a character trait* (Sremska Mitrovica, m, 27, unskilled worker).

Urbanity was thus identified with a host of commendable personal and social qualities – cultivation, politeness, competence, personal integrity, self-restraint – while rurality was used as a synonym for their undesirable opposites. This, of course, is nothing very new: the association of "urbanity" with civilizational progress is of long standing and reaches far beyond Serbia. It reflects some general cultural themes from the history of European modernity, acquiring particular acuteness in peripheral societies of "belated modernization". In Serbia, it is ubiquitous and very much taken for granted (Jansen 2005: 155–158).

Incidentally, rurality fared somewhat differently. Though it was often keyed as negative, it was not always so: there were many neutral references to the village and to peasantry as well. But it was in literally *one* out of three hundred interviews that we found the extremely positive and romanticized construction of "the Serbian peasant" as a sort of noble savage:

> *In the late 1980s ... I felt that genuine national spirit, the archaic one – you know, Serbia, plums, hospitality ... the warmth of the people, of the peasant, who is not primitive, but just uneducated, who will give you everything and welcome you any time* (Novi Sad, m, 31, historian).

That this was the only case is intriguing, given the prominence of the "peasant trope" as a favorite propagandistic tool of different political and social ideologies propagated in Serbia over the past two centuries (Naumović 1995; Živković 2001: 226–228). This raises some interesting questions concerning the segmentation of discourse into public (academic and political) and private spheres, possibly indicating that the celebration of the "ideal peasant" as representative of the Nation has basically remained limited to the former and failed to take firmer hold in the latter. The fact that the speaker here is a university-educated urbanite, and a historian by profession, is not insignificant.[9]

---

[9] Analyzing discursive strategies of constructing images of the nation in the same interview

In the next section, I further discuss the symbolic content of "urbanity" by delineating specific local experiences of it.

2. Local stories of urbanity

Ways of talking about the urban experience gave rise to a series of "local stories of urbanity". Three broad regions will be distinguished: Central Serbia, Vojvodina and Belgrade.

In Central Serbian towns people were generally anxious to express their emotional bond to the place they lived in and to list all the positive features of local life they found reassuring. This insistence can be interpreted as part of a reactive symbolic "defense" of their place, as we shall see later on. The intensity of local identification varied greatly, however. Contrary to what we would perhaps expect, the prominence of "urban" reference in individual accounts depended less on the respondent's externally measurable characteristics such as education completed or class membership, and more on one's personal trajectory and the importance of local identification for one's overall identity. Thus to people born in a town, and especially those with a long-standing urban family background, these facts mattered very much:

> *I was born in Leskovac. It would be an even nicer place to live in if it were run by its own townsfolk* [građani] *instead of peasants and people from the outside* (Leskovac, m, 27, student).

It was in Central Serbian towns that we found the strongest resentment against "newcomers", especially those from the neighboring villages; and to a lesser extent, from elsewhere (subsumed under the general label of "people from the outside").[10] The newcomers have settled here (we are *too* hospitable); they are well-off; they hold the best jobs and the most important positions; they have taken over the control of the town:

> *I love Čačak, I'm the fourth generation here. But this Čačak of today, it is not the Čačak of my childhood ... There are very many newcomers who,*

material, Đerić (2005: 148) concludes that the incidence of stereotypes actually rises with the respondent's level of education, and is the highest among professionals in the "national" sciences like Serbian language and literature, history, and ethnology.

[10] Interestingly, there was also an alternative way of viewing urbanity precisely as openness to "people from the outside". This was, understandably, the option of respondents who were themselves of non-urban background. This infrequent and submerged variant of the "local story" was characteristic of Niš, where the latter's warmth and hospitality were contrasted with the alienated and "soulless" Belgrade.

instead of merging with Čačak people, and in spite of living here, do not feel Čačak to be their town (Čačak, m, 51, secondary school, clerk). *Požarevac is no longer the Požarevac that used to be. Požarevac today is full of people who have come in from somewhere, who lack culture ... There are very few of us, genuine Požarevac people, who were raised here in this town, who love it really ... Nowadays it is fashionable that moms and dads from the country buy apartments in cities for their kids. They throw garbage out of their windows, there's dirt everywhere* (Požarevac, m, 56, secondary school, clerk).

This strongly felt rootedness in the local urban milieu, along with bitter complaints against "peasants", expressed self-identification not with "urbanity" in the abstract but with the *local* urbanity of the particular place where the speakers happened to be born and raised. Parallel to this, there was widespread resentment against what they called the "Belgradization" of Serbia – the concentration of funds and decision-making in the capital. Local urban pride was thus constructed through a double rejection – of both "the countryside" and "Belgrade".

This position ought to be contextualized historically and sociologically. Massive rural depopulation due to rapid industrialization and urbanization after 1945[11] made the cleavage between urbanites "with pedigree" and recent migrants culturally salient in Serbian towns. But at the same time, and perhaps more importantly, socialism meant centralization and a highly asymmetrical pattern of development.[12] While Belgrade was exposed to the same intense immigration that resulted in what is sometimes called "rurbanization", it could compensate for it by deriving symbolic profits from the growing economic and political ascendancy over the rest of the country. The so-called "province", on the contrary, was for the most part robbed of its one-time urban dignity.[13] Matters only became worse in the 1990s, when centralization tightened, rural immigration continued, and the post-socialist ruin of many industrial plants exacerbated local despair. Thus scant resources remained to build a positive local identity. The emotion with which interviewees defended local urbanity was proportional to its fragility.

---

[11] Between 1948 and 1981, 6.5 million people moved from village to city in former Yugoslavia. The percentage of urban population rose from 21.9% after WW II to 46.5% in 1981 and 58% in 1991 (Vujović 1995: 112 f.).

[12] Urban sociologists have termed the imbalanced growth of republican capitals, especially Belgrade, alongside neglected medium-sized cities and towns "a major developmental failure in Yugoslavia" (Vujović 1990: 37).

[13] To illustrate the vitality of local cultural life in earlier times, it is instructive to know that in 1910 almost every town from our sample was publishing 2–5 newspapers or magazines of its own (Skerlić 1911: 79). One hundred years later, despite urban growth and overall modernization, the figures are, at best, the same.

In comparison with Central Serbia, local stories in Vojvodina exhibited a similar baseline (positive identification with the town, resentment against newcomers and Belgradization) but remarkable differences as well. Here, the chief "culprits" were not peasants from nearby villages, but immigrants from distant regions:

> *I don't like it that retired army officers now occupy important places in our town, without having lived here before. They should go back to where they came from, and be chairmen of executive boards over there, not here* (Kikinda, f, 42, preschool teacher + farmer).

But most importantly, the target of resentment were refugees of the ex-Yugoslav wars. They were seen as bearers of primitivism, lack of culture, and a different (inferior) set of values. They were often depicted not just as war victims but as actually benefiting from their status.[14]

It is peculiar for Vojvodina that the urbanity under threat from refugees, apart from the usual "civilizational" features, also included multiethnic coexistence and tolerance[15]:

> Q: Who is responsible for nationalist incidents? – *Politicians, and citizens as well. There are so many refugees. It's mostly them* (Subotica, m, 38, secondary school, entrepreneur, ethnic Hungarian).

This attitude interacted strongly with ethnic memberships (of the speaker and of the persons talked about): for some ethnic Hungarians from Subotica, refugees – who are almost exclusively Serb – became the convenient scapegoat for all social ills.

In Vojvodina, local urban identification was less particularly *local* than in Central Serbia; one is tempted to say it was rather identification with Vojvodina, as a culturally specific region within Serbia. This perhaps explains also the relatively low antipathy against local peasants: Vojvodina villages are (considered to be) culturally similar to their regional centers. Refugees, on the contrary, originating from Croatian and Bosnian highlands, were said to belong to a completely different world:

> *They* [refugees from Croatia and Bosnia] *cannot get accustomed to the urban ways, to the street* [šor], *to the house. They are used to open space*

---

[14] During the 20th century, Vojvodina received several waves of immigration from mountainous regions of Yugoslavia, with particularly intense ones in the wake of the two World Wars, making this image just an updated version of the older "uncultivated highlander" identity ascribed to such newcomers.

[15] Outside Vojvodina, a similar construction of local urbanity as multicultural was noted in Bor, a languishing mining town in East Serbia, whose population has been characteristically multiethnic for over a century due to the specific exigencies of the mining industry. There, however, its "destroyers" were again local peasants, like in the rest of Central Serbia.

(Novi Sad, f, 45, secondary school, librarian; of Vojvodinian rural background).

This is not accidental. In intra-Serbian cultural distinctions, or "nesting orientalisms" (Bakić-Hayden 1995), Vojvodinians – thanks to their Austro-Hungarian past – have the special possibility to identify "their" peasants not with primitivism and barbarity but rather with culture and civilization. Živković (1998: 85–86) coins the name of "peasant-cosmopolitan" for this figure, whose chief opposite is not the sophisticated urbanite but the barbarous Dinaric highlander (embodied, in our data, by the refugee).

Let us finally have a look at Belgrade, Serbia's metropole. It was almost exclusively in Belgrade that local identification might have overridden all others[16]: when asked "How would you present yourself?", many respondents replied: "I'm a Belgrader". It is important to note that this often appeared in conjunction with explicit rejection of the primacy of ethnic belonging within one's identity.[17]

> Q: You don't recognize any sort of ethnic identity in yourself? – *No, I don't.* – Q: You don't even feel Yugoslav? – *No, I don't feel Yugoslav, I declare myself to be Yugoslav, but I feel more a Belgrader.* – Q: So you feel Belgraders to be your people? – *Yes, because I don't even know the others* (Belgrade, m, 28, incomplete secondary school, taxi driver).

Belgrade identity was often seen as incompatible with nationalism, and self-evidently so:

> *In the beginning, I went often to these rallies* [organized by Vuk Drašković], *but you know, this Chetnik thing was pushed to the foreground. I'm a Belgrade kid, you know, these things are not for me ... I'd rather support some pro-European movements* (Belgrade, m, 28, postman).

Resentment against "peasants from around" who invaded the city did not figure so prominently among Belgraders as it did in Central Serbian towns. We may hypothesize, firstly, that over the past decades Belgrade received migrants from more diverse places in the former Yugoslavia, so that the nearby villages were not felt to be such an immediate danger to its urbanity.[18] Secondly, Belgraders might be so

---

[16] The only two other places where this happened in individual cases were Čačak (Central Serbia) and Novi Sad (Vojvodina). Both exceptions can be explained. Čačak's local pride has recently been boosted by the universally acclaimed role its activists played in the anti-Milošević revolt of October 5, 2000. The prestige of Novi Sad on the contrary dates much farther back, due to its centuries-old role of cultural center, or "Serbian Athens" as it was called before 1918.

[17] The same point is made by Jansen (2005: 142 f.).

[18] Another recent process has been experienced as a serious threat to Belgrade's integrity: the intense brain-drain of young urban dwellers during the 1990s (Bolčić 2002: 162–164).

secure in their urban identity that they need not invest so much passion in its defense as old-time town dwellers. While the latter defined their urbanity predominantly negatively against the *arriviste* culture of the peasant-newcomers, the urbanity of Belgraders was more often defined positively, as a route to participation in the cosmopolitan culture of "the world". If there is an opposite to being a "Belgrader", it is the narrow outlook of chauvinistic isolationism. Moreover, for Belgraders the fault-line went simply between Belgrade and "the rest", and they made few distinctions within this "rest". They were completely insensitive to the complex reality outside of their city, and unwilling to accept there were urbanites in other places as well. This is another aspect of the factual and symbolic centralization of Serbia: from the center, nothing is seen but the center itself. At that, Belgraders did not care much about the obvious fact that they themselves were overwhelmingly of non-Belgrade origin, only a generation or two back; it was enough to be born in Belgrade, or even just to have lived there for a dozen years, to adopt the contemptuous, deliberately ignorant stance of a Belgrader.

3. Urban decay and urban nostalgia

Let us now consider one point that runs right through the interviews, irrespective of region, gender, profession or age. It is captured in the phrase, "This place is no longer what it used to be". In other words, the stories of urbanites were almost always stories of local urban decay and nostalgia for times gone by. This motif was present in previous excerpts and can also be found in other instances:

> *For the past couple of years, or even dozen years, I see a sort of decay. I see that many people I used to associate with, who were for me the milieu of this town, have disappeared, moved away, fled* (Novi Sad, m, 39, B. Sc. electrical engineer).
>
> *In the times of the former Yugoslavia, Mitrovica was something. It used to be a town, and now it is a backwater with no future* (Sremska Mitrovica, f, 55, retired clerk).

In temporal terms, this change for the worse, this loss of the authentic "soul" of the cities was most frequently located in the 1990s. The causes of urban deterioration ranged from abstract and generalized (wars, crisis, impoverishment) to concretized – embodied either in "Milošević's regime", or in particular social groups: peasants, newcomers, refugees.

Another point that repeatedly appeared was the criticism of the socialist policies of "pulling people out of the villages". Their result – a mass of peasant-urbanites, people who are "neither here, nor there", equally uncommitted to either setting – was seen as the cause of various developmental mismatches in post-WW II Serbian/Yugoslav society[19]:

> *We may expect social unrest. The main reason is surplus labor. Over the past sixty years, the wrong policy was implemented of pushing peasants into factories on a massive scale* (Sremska Mitrovica, m, 27, unskilled worker).

This is not a simple eulogy to "the city" and devaluation of "the country"; it is rather advocating the necessity of keeping the two apart. If we inspect more closely some of the previously quoted excerpts on self-ascribed urbanity, we see that negative feelings were generally not aimed at "the village" *per se* but at the peasants who had moved to the city. If they stayed in the country, that is, "where they belonged", peasants were not so problematic. These demands for "unmixing" country folk and city folk may be interpreted as the popular, lowbrow version of the Serbian "culture wars" of the 1990s, in which the peasant-urbanite appears as the "rider of the cultural apocalypse" in the eyes of sophisticated urban elites (Živković 1998: 90–94).

4. The politics of urbanity

Several threads in the foregoing analysis converge in what may be termed the politics of urban labeling. This particular theme concerns most directly the overlapping of urban symbolism with the strategies of political positioning.

Other authors (Jansen 2005: 138–145; Živković 1998; Naumović 2002: 25 f.; Bougarel 1999: 157) have shown that "urbanity", with its connotations of "culture", "modernity" and "cosmopolitanism" has served as a major resource for constructing identities and political positions alternative to the nationalist collectivism that dominated Serbia in the 1990s. This comes as no surprise bearing in mind the centrality of populist appeals in the official propaganda of Milošević's regime.[20] From the self-consciously "urban", and simultaneously anti-Milošević and anti-nationalist standpoint, the Yugoslav wars of the 1990s are explained by an

---

[19] The sociological import of the Yugoslav peasant-urbanite has been widely acknowledged in literature – Simić's (1973) classical study being only the best-known example – so much so that, according to Brown (2001: 419), the category acquired undue conceptual dominance.

[20] In one famous statement among many, Milošević, responding to the challenge raised by the 1992 demonstrations of Belgrade students and intellectuals solemnly declared that, for him, the opinion of a university professor was no more important than that of any farmer. During the protests of 1996/97, the regime itself insisted on framing the pro/anti-Milošević divide *as* a rural/urban one, deliberately playing up the latter, sociological cleavage in order to deepen the former, political one (Pavićević, Spasić 1998).

expansion of "peasant primitivism" of culturally backward "highlanders". In academic discourse, the view of the wars as a "revenge of the countryside" against the city and the urban spirit has been echoed rather widely.[21] While providing valuable insights into the rhetoric of Serbian nationalism and into the mechanisms by which the regime secured support,[22] such accounts have had as their secondary – and sometimes primary – function to help the speaker distance themselves at once from the nationalist wars *and* from "peasant primitivism".

Within Serbia itself, the Milošević regime has often been accused of "peasantizing" the society. This was reflected in the interviews: *The past ten years have strongly contributed to this peasantization* (Pančevo, m, 29, technician).

From the perspective of urbanites, the "peasants" referred to were usually recent newcomers. But sometimes, they were somehow "internal" peasants, peasants *in spirit* who lived in hiding within the entrails of the city itself all the time, without "us" noticing them:

> *Those people who surfaced in 1987, 1988, all that was going along with Milošević, that bunch of socialists, for me they were demi-monde, something that had suddenly crawled out of hidden holes, literally ... and I felt they were threatening me awfully* (Belgrade, f, 53, university professor).

Such instances of close articulation between urbanity, class and politics lead us back to the point raised in section 1, concerning the strategic possibilities residing in the Serbian-language words denoting "urbanity". Our data contain clear illustrations of how the equation nationalism = Milošević regime = peasants, complemented by the opposite self-construction cosmopolitanism = democracy = urbanity, utilized the welcome ambiguity of the word *građanski*:

> *I'm a member of the Civic Alliance of Serbia* [Građanski savez Srbije] ... *It is a party of citizens* [građana], *and I am of urban background* [ja sam gradsko dete] *and all my family were born in the city* (Niš, f, 47, sociologist).

> *The civic* [građansko] *conception of society is in the minority in Serbia ... I am a member of the Democratic Party because its program is civic* [građanski koncipiran], *urban* [gradski], *"from asphalt", which is not true for 99% of the other parties* (Niš, m, 37, theater director).

---

[21] Emblematic in this regard is the treatise by the architect-philosopher Bogdan Bogdanović (1994). Sociological, ethnological and political-scientific elaborations may be found in Vujović 1997: 23–105; Prodanović 2000; Ramet 1996; Žanić 1998. In his critical review, Bougarel (1999) provides historical and sociological arguments for rejecting this view in its simplistic version.

[22] Throughout the 1990s, the countryside remained Milošević's electoral stronghold.

Here a "civic conception" evidently becomes an *urban* conception, designed by, and for, urban people. Country folk seem to have no place in it; it is not at all intended for them. The official programmatic statements of democratic parties define their "civic orientation" *[građanska orijentacija]* in purely political terms: it implies a political outlook based on the established principles of Western liberal democracy and has nothing to do with a person's occupation or residence. But unofficially, just beneath the surface lurks the other semantic strand of *građanski* as *gradski* that comes openly to the fore in the quoted statements. I believe this unofficial identification (democracy = urbanity) has played a major role in political commitment to "civicness", and the parties embodying it in Serbian political life, and has accounted for much of the emotional force invested in these allegiances.

Lay discourses are assisted by academic ones here. Scholarly analyses of Serbian politics in the 1990s frequently contain a shift from sociological description to normative evaluation. The presentation of facts on the disproportionate participation of urban middle strata in anti-Milošević mobilizations – most notably, in the winter 1996/97 protests – imperceptibly slides into an identification of the democratic potentials of Serbian society with these strata alone, with the implication that, quite simply, urbanity equals democracy and vice versa.[23]

Grasping this implication helps us to paint a more nuanced portrait of the dynamics of political choice in contemporary Serbia than the one put forward in the "heroic" accounts of anti-Milošević resistance. It allows us to acknowledge the significance of democratic politics in Serbia's recent past or near future, without losing track of its – sometimes contradictory – symbolic underpinnings.

5. Conclusions

On most points the analysis presented here agrees with what other students of everyday meanings of urbanity in the post-Yugoslav context – Jansen (2005, 2005a), Živković (1998, 2001), and Brown (2001) – have arrived at. Yet there are also some departures, modifications and qualifications which merit attention. They basically stem from the nature of the data on which my analysis is based. The three cited authors, following anthropology's commitment to studying particular communities, and guided by the specific objectives of their own projects, focus on inhabitants of the capital (Belgrade and Zagreb for Jansen, Belgrade for Živković, Skopje for Brown[24]). Furthermore, their prime interest lies with the liberal intelli-

---

[23] Such descriptions, with various degrees of the normative ingredient, can be found in: Vujović 1997: 15–17, 167–180; Lazić 1999; Mimica 1997; Dragićević-Šešić 1997; Čupić 1998; Gordy 1999; Collin 2001; Prošić-Dvornić 2002; Milić, Čičkarić 1998; Golubović et al. 1995.

[24] Brown, in his book-length study of the town of Kruševo (Brown 2003) does indeed leave the capital, but again concentrates on a single community.

gentsia within those capitals. Therefore, for the first time, the data used here provide an insight into the constructions of urbanity among a more diversified selection of people: residents of smaller cities and towns, and belonging to various social groups. This enables us to identify how definitions and pragmatics of "urbanity" differ across regions and social strata.

So the first point of divergence refers to geographical variation. In Central Serbia, "urbanity" was strikingly localized, and entailed an experiential rootedness in a particular local lifeworld composed of a bundle of sights, smells, and daily trajectories. This lifeworld could be incorporated in the "right" way only by imbibing it through lifelong personal exposure. In consequence, local urban oldtimer status was uniquely important here. The chief Others that urbanity was aimed against were peasants from the neighboring villages, and Belgraders.

In Vojvodina, on the contrary, urbanity was based on rootedness in the Vojvodinian lifeworld, with particular urban communities within the region being more or less symbolically interchangeable. The main Others were highlander immigrants and, to a lesser extent, also Belgraders.

Where Belgrade is concerned, my picture most closely resembles that of other authors. Belgrade's urbanity was constructed through a double paradox: one concerns the logic of essentialization, the other the logic of distinction (cf. Jansen 2005: 112–118; 2005a). With regard to the first, on the one hand, urbanity here entailed a refusal to restrict oneself to narrow attachments (ethnic, local, regional). What was required instead was cosmopolitanism, an openness to and understanding of the wider world. In this anti-essentialist move, Belgrade's urbanity was considered comparable to that of any large city on the globe. But on the other hand, a "proper" Belgrade identity was completely closed to the rest of Serbia, which was written off as indiscriminately not-urban-enough. This is the essentializing move. The second paradox points to the almost magical power of Belgrade identity. Unlike in Central Serbia, in Belgrade oldtimer status did not matter greatly: as soon as one had a Belgrade address, one could claim the status of a Belgrader which, moreover, became one's master status. Thus a personal link to Belgrade was at once easy to obtain, and inordinately weighty.

The second point of divergence tackles the link between urbanity and class. The data invite us to relativize the self-understandable correlation of urban distinction with certain stratificational features. In Bourdieu's original formulation (1979: 293–364), the strategy of distinction is tied to the upper or dominant class. Within it, thanks to the connection between urbanity and "culture", the specifically urban distinction would most closely fit into the strategies deployed by what Bourdieu calls "the dominated fraction of the dominant class", i. e., intellectuals, endowed with more cultural than economic capital. But our data suggest that strategies of urban distinction were by no means restricted to the educated classes. The feature that marked the boundary between this group and other strata was the utilization of the politicized version of "urbanity", through the equation urbanity = democracy. Yet as the stories of urban decay and the prominence of the peasant-urbanite figure showed, a non-political form of urban distinction was amply used by urban dwellers of most diverse social statuses. One is tempted to conclude that, in internal cultural hierarchies of contemporary Serbia, "urbanity" is a most broadly applicable identity/discursive resource to build strategies of asserting one's own superiority against "others".

References

Bakić-Hayden, Milica 1995: Nesting Orientalisms: The Case of Former Yugoslavia. In: Slavic Review 54, 4: 917–931.

Bogdanović, Bogdan 1994: Grad i smrt [City and death]. Belgrade: Beogradski krug.

Bolčić, Silvano 2002: Iseljavanje radne snage i "odliv mozgova" iz Srbije tokom 90-ih [Emigration of workforce and "brain drain" from Serbia in the 1990s]. In: Silvano Bolčić, Anđelka Milić (eds.), Srbija krajem milenijuma [Serbia at the turn of the millennium]. Belgrade: ISI FF, 159–166.

Bougarel, Xavier 1999: Yugoslav Wars: The "Revenge of the Countryside" between Sociological Reality and Nationalist Myth. In: East European Quarterly 33, 2: 157–175.

Bourdieu, Pierre 1979: Distinction: Critique sociale du jugement. Paris: Minuit.

Brown, Keith 2001: Beyond Ethnicity: The Politics of Urban Nostalgia in Modern Macedonia. In: Journal of Mediterranean Studies 11, 2: 417–442.

Brown, Keith 2003: The Past in Question: Modern Macedonia and the Uncertainties of Nation. Princeton: Princeton UP.

Collin, Matthew 2001: This Is Serbia Calling: rokenrol radio i beogradski pokret otpora [This is Serbia calling: Rock'n'roll radio and Belgrade's underground resistance]. Belgrade: Samizdat B92.

Čolović, Ivan 1993: Bordel ratnika [Warrior's brothel]. Belgrade: XX vek.

Čolović, Ivan 2000: Politika simbola [The politics of symbols]. Belgrade: XX vek.

Čupić, Čedomir (ed.) 1998: Duh vedrine. Kultura protesta – protest kulture [Spirit of cheerfulness: Culture of protest – protest of culture]. Belgrade: FPN.

Dragićević-Šešić, Milena 1997: Street as a Political Space: The Space of Carnivalization. In: Sociologija 39, 1: 95–110.

Đerić, Gordana 2005: Pr(a)vo lice množine. Kolektivno samopoimanje i predstavljanje: mitovi, karakteri, mentalne mape i stereotipi [Speaking (of) "we". Collective self-conceptions and presentations: myths, characters, mental maps and stereotypes]. Belgrade: IFDT.

Golubović, Zagorka, Bora Kuzmanović, Mirjana Vasović 1995: Društveni karakter i društvene promene u svetlu nacionalnih sukoba [Social character and social change in the light of national conflicts]. Belgrade: IFDT.

Golubović, Zagorka, Ivana Spasić, Đorđe Pavićević (eds.) 2003: Politika i svakodnevni život: Srbija 1999–2002 [Politics and everyday life: Serbia 1999–2002]. Belgrade: IFDT.

Gordy, Eric D. 1999: The Culture of Power in Serbia: Nationalism and the Destruction of Alternatives. University Park, PA: Pennsylvania UP.

Jansen, Stef 2005: Antinacionalizam: etnografija otpora u Beogradu i Zagrebu [Antinationalism: Ethnography of resistance in Belgrade and Zagreb]. Belgrade: XX vek.

Jansen, Stef 2005a: Who's Afraid of White Socks? Towards a Critical Understanding of Post-Yugoslav Urban Self-perceptions. In: Ethnologia Balkanica 9: 151–167.

Lazić, Mladen (ed.) 1999: Protest in Belgrade. Budapest: CEU Press.

Milić, Anđelka, Lilijana Čičkarić 1998: Generacija u protestu. [Generation in protest]. Belgrade: ISI FF.

Mimica, Aljoša 1997: The Awakening of the Civil Society? The 1996/97 Protest in a Sociological Perspective. In: Sociologija 39, 1: 5–14.

Naumović, Slobodan 1995: Ustaj seljo, ustaj rode: simbolika seljaštva i politička komunikacija u novijoj istoriji Srbije [Peasants, people, stand up: the symbolism of peasantry and political communication in modern Serbian history]. In: Godišnjak za društvenu istoriju [Social history annual] 2, 1: 39–63.

Naumović, Slobodan 2002: The Ethnology of Transformation as Transformed Ethnology: The Serbian Case. In: Ethnologia Balkanica 6: 7–37.

Pavićević, Đorđe, Ivana Spasić 1998: Situirana ksenofobija: opaska o građanskom protestu u Srbiji [Xenophobia situated: a note on the civil protest in Serbia]. In: Božidar Jakšić (ed.), Interkulturalnost vs. rasizam i ksenofobija [Interculturality vs. racism and xenophobia]. Belgrade: Forum za etničke odnose, 419–428.

Prodanović, Milan 2000: Regional Wars and Chances for the Reconstruction of Balkan Cities in a Global Information Society. In: City 4, 2: 277–287.

Prošić-Dvornić, Mirjana 2002: Srbija: priča iznutra [Serbia: the inside story]. In: J. M. Halpern, D. A. Kideckel (eds.), Susedi u ratu [Neighbors at war]. Belgrade: Samizdat B92, 396–421.

Rihtman-Auguštin, Dunja 2000: Ulice moga grada [The streets of my city]. Belgrade: XX vek.

Ramet, Sabrina Petra 1996: Nationalism and the "Idiocy" of the Countryside: the Case of Serbia. In: Ethnic and Racial Studies 19, 1: 70–87.

Simić, Andrei 1973: The Peasant Urbanites: A Study of Rural-Urban Mobility in Serbia. New York: Seminar Press.

Skerlić, Jovan 1911: Istorijski pregled srpske štampe 1791–1911 [A historical survey of the Serbian press 1791–1911]. Belgrade: Srpsko novinarsko udruženje.

Todorova, Maria 1997: Imagining the Balkans. New York: Oxford UP.

Vujović, Sreten 1990: Ljudi i gradovi [People and cities]. Budva: Mediteran.

Vujović, Sreten 1995: Urbana svakodnevica devedesetih godina [Urban everyday in the 1990s]. In: Silvano Bolčić (ed.), Društvene promene i svakodnevni život [Social change and everyday life]. Belgrade: ISI FF, 109–134.

Vujović, Sreten 1997: Grad u Senci Rata [City in the shadow of war]. Novi Sad, Belgrade: Prometej/ISI FF.

Žanić, Ivo 1998: Prevarena povijest [History deceived]. Zagreb: Durieux.

Živković, Marko 1998: Too Much Character, Too Little *Kultur*: Serbian Jeremiads 1994–1995. In: Balkanologie 2, 2: 77–98.

Živković, Marko 2001: Serbian Stories of Identity and Destiny in the 1980s and 1990s. Ph. D. dissertation, University of Chicago, Department of Anthropology.

Abstract

On the basis of interview data, this article analyzes how “urbanity” is constructed in informal, everyday discourses of ordinary people in Serbia, what meanings are ascribed to it, who uses it, and to what purposes. A review of the forms of verbalizing urbanity and their symbolic implications (1) is followed by an analysis of how urbanity is experienced locally (2) and couched in terms of urban nostalgia (3), concluding with the political aspects of the issue (4). In the final section I compare the findings of my own analysis with other studies treating the same topic (5).

Corso as a Total Social Phenomenon: the Case of Smederevska Palanka, Serbia

Vesna Vučinić-Nešković and Jelena Miloradović, Belgrade

Introduction[1]

How did the study of Corso come about?

While studying spatial behaviour in the old town of Dubrovnik in the early 1990s, the evening promenade in the main town street, generally known as the corso, was spotlighted as an important social phenomenon. An analysis of the corso at Stradun showed that its space was segmented, both lengthwise and crosswise, by the positioning of specific social groups who differed by their rural/urban origin, age, gender, social status and ethnicity. Those segments were the mirror image of the social structure of the town, but were also the channels through which the processes of enculturation (of the younger into mature youth) and acculturation (of the rural incomers into the town) were taking place (Vučinić 1994, 1999).

Intrigued by its complexity and, at the same time, the absence of interest in the topic in the immediate scientific community,[2] the study of the corso continued with the aim of investigating its constant and variable features in the towns of Serbia and Montenegro.[3] The question was whether other geographically and temporally

1 This paper presents results of research on the theme "Everyday Life and Rituals in Serbia and Montenegro" as part of the project "Cultural Identities in the Processes of Globalization and Regionalization", supported by the Ministry of Science and Environmental Protection of the Republic of Serbia. The authors of this text are grateful to colleagues from the Department of Ethnology and Anthropology of the School of Philosophy, University of Belgrade for their support, to the participants of the 3rd InASEA Conference held in Belgrade (at which the general points of this paper were presented) for asking questions which helped clarify some of the important issues of the corso problematic, as well as to the anonymous reviewer of *Ethnologia Balkanica* for valuable suggestions and comments, especially on the concluding part of the text. In addition, we appreciate Rayna Gavrilova and Katja Jerman sending us their work as well as Smiljana Antonijević, Sándor Horváth, Onur Inal and Ljupčo Risteski for help in finding further references on the corso. Finally, we owe thanks to Francesca Opačić and the other faculty of the Active English School in Belgrade for assistance with those terms and idioms that only the English native speakers living in Serbia would know.

2 At the time the Dubrovnik corso was studied the only piece of anthropological research devoted to the contemporary corso in former Yugoslavia was the text by Ljiljana Gavrilović (1984) "Korzo – iskazivanje generacijske polarizacije u strukturi grada" [Corso – the expression of generational polarization in the urban social structure], which dealt with the generational split imbedded in the corso of Novi Pazar, a town in Southwest Serbia.

3 A few detailed and insightful seminar papers on the corso, produced by students of the

distant corsos shared a similar type of socio-spatial segmentation. The same method of research was thus applied to the study of the Belgrade corso during the period of the Kingdom of Yugoslavia. Knez Mihajlova Street of the 1930s proved to be the promenade of the middle-class exclusively, and its segmentation reflected the distinction between its lower and upper strata (Vučinić, Antonijević 1998).

The next step in the study of the corso was to follow the dynamics of a specific corso through different epochs, starting from the times captured in the reminiscences of our oldest interviewees to the present. Using identical questionnaires this approach was applied to the investigation of the corso in two small towns of Serbia and Montenegro. Smederevska Palanka, a typical town in Serbia proper was chosen as the first, while Pljevlja, a North Montenegro town was chosen as the second such locality.[4]

Aim and basic concepts

This paper presents the main features of the youth corso in Smederevska Palanka in the period between 1930 and 2001 with the aim of showing that it can be perceived as what Marcel Mauss called a *total social phenomenon*. The corso is analysed through the characteristics of temporal, spatial and social behaviour of its participants. Each decade is approached from a synchronic perspective. With the consideration of the age, gender, and town/country origin of its participants, the following features of the corso are studied: the space occupied and time spent at the corso, the walking routes, the standing places, the male-female relations, and the dress codes. The static and dynamic aspects of spatial behaviour at the corso are accentuated, the first encompassing standing places, while the second includes

---

Department of Ethnology and Anthropology of Belgrade University, supervised by V. Vučinić-Nešković, provided proof of a wide-spread existence of the corso in Serbia proper and Vojvodina in the 1990s as well as of similarities and differences in their socio-spatial segmentation.

[4] The relatively scarce literature on the corso does not avail any comparative studies of the contemporary forms and structures of this informal social institution. The only two texts of anthropological nature discovered in electronic library databases are on the promenade in Split, Croatia (Mišetić 1997), and on *passeggiata* in a central Italian town (Del Negro, Harris 2001). The other references tell of the prevalent interest in the historical promenade, primarily noted as a 19th and early 20th century phenomenon, discussed from the point of view of urban or cultural history. The institution is tied either to the elites in the cultural capitals of Europe such as Paris or Vienna (Lawrence 1988, Rottenberg 1992), tourist sea resorts such as Nice, Cannes, Trouville or Brighton (Debie 1993), or the middle classes in small towns such as in Norway (Telste 2002). In Southeast Europe, historians have written about the promenade as a sign of modernity and Westernization of Budapest (Gyaeni 2004), Istanbul (Çelik 1986), Ljubljana (Jerman 2003), and Bulgarian cities (Gavrilova 2003). Across the Atlantic, the promenade was studied as a novel tradition of the 19th century New York elite (Scobey 1992).

walking routes, i.e., their length, shape, direction and path. By widening the perspective to a period of seventy years, the diachronic dimension is hoped to reveal which of the corso features have persisted, changed, disappeared or were introduced as novelties.

Being vague and inconclusive enough to leave open space for creative remodelling, the definition of the total social phenomenon given by Mauss will be treated as the starting point for the working definition for this study. The *total social phenomenon* is here understood as a complex phenomenon which simultaneously reflects different religious, political, economic, legal, moral, and social institutions that produce specific aesthetic and morphological effects. In order to make these institutions and their effects visible, the corso is traced throughout most of the 20th century.

Corso is a word originating from Latin *cursus* and Italian *corso* with the basic meaning of running, race, running track, flow, circulation, street promenade.[5] In medieval Italian towns, corso used to be the space for sports competitions within certain public celebrations of the carnival type, which were later added to the religious celebrations organized in honour of the city's patron saints.[6] In the Serbian linguistic domain the word has two contemporary meanings: first, it denotes the part of the town in which people come out for a leisurely walk, but also the activity of walking of a large number of people in the main town street.[7] In this paper, the corso is defined as a dual category, standing for the space in which interaction at the town level takes place passively, from a distance, and actively, in more intimate social contacts. At the same time, corso denotes the social interaction itself, which takes place during the promenade in a well-defined open public space (Vučinić 1999: 196).

The leisurely promenade that takes place on the main town street in the evening hours, most generally known as the *korzo,* is represented in its local linguistic forms. For example, the inhabitants of Dubrovnik and other cities along the Adriatic coast, would use the term *djir,* a word borrowed from Italian (from Greek *gyros*), meaning "to go back and forth, to turn around, to circulate".[8] In most Serbian towns in which the corso has survived, the term *korzo* is well recognized, but not commonly used for the promenade itself. Our research in Smederevska Palanka, for example, shows that the phrase "I am going into čaršija" was used in the period between the 1930s and 1960s, while in the following period, the phase

---

5 Milan Vujaklija: Leksikon stranih reči i izraza, Belgrade 1972, s.v. korzo.

6 Communication of Maurice Aymard, director of La Maison de Sciences de l'Homme, Paris, June 1998, with V. Vučinić.

7 Rečnik srpskohrvatskoga književnog jezika 2. Novi Sad 1967, s.v. korzo.

8 Petar Skok: Etimologijski rječnik hrvatskoga ili srpskoga jezika 1. Belgrade: Yugoslav Academy of Sciences and Arts 1971, s.v. agirat.

"I am going into town" took its place. In this town, the only explicit (and visible) association with the "korzo" exists in the name of a pastry shop, situated at the promenade since the late 1960s.

Research Methodology

Fieldwork in Smedrevska Palanka took place in the period between June and October 2001. Beside the implementation of a carefully designed survey, the fieldwork encompassed observation of the present corso as well as collection of written documents and photos which told of the changes in the urban structure of the whole town as well as in the street used as the corso. The survey was implemented through interviews based on a questionnaire containing 30 standardized, mostly open questions. Specific groups of questions were related to: (1) socio-demographic characteristics of the interviewees, (2) temporal and spatial characteristics of the corso, (3) social characteristics of the corso participants (4) motivation for participation and modes of socializing during, before and after the corso, (5) standing places along the corso, (6) establishing romantic relationships at the corso and norms of public behaviour of young couples, and lastly (7) the corso dress codes.

The primary sampling principle was temporal, with the aim of covering every decade between 1930 and 2001 with the same number of interviewees. Each decade, thus, was to be ideally represented by ten interviewees who would narrate their experiences from the corso of their youth. The exceptions were the 1930s for which only six respondents were found as well as the 1940s that were, owing to radically different political and social circumstances during and after WW II, divided into two periods, each represented with ten interviewees. Interviewees were found among the researchers' friends and relatives, with special attention paid to the balanced representation of men and women as well as of persons with varied social and professional profiles. All in all, 76 interviewees participated in the research.

About Smederevska Palanka

Smederevska Palanka sits in the heart of Serbia known as Šumadija, in the region known as Donja Jasenica. Its origin as an urban settlement, mentioned in written sources as Bela Crkva, stems from the 11th century, the period of the Serbian medieval kingdom (Novaković 1970: 19–42). Part of the name it has at present comes from the Turkish period, when it was called Hasan Pašina Palanka after its founder, *beğlerbeg* of Timişoara, Hasan Paša (Perunišić 1980: 13). The settlement served as a fortress along the Constantinople road, one of the main thoroughfares of the Balkan Peninsula. In the mid-18th century, after peace had been established between the Ottoman and Habsburg empires, Serbian migrants from the south settled in and mixed with the few remaining native residents, thus establishing the demographic profile that lasts until the present. The liberation from Ottoman rule, especially visible in the regulations of Hatišerif of 1833, brought about the planned removal of the fortress and the resettlement of the dominantly peasant residents from the old to the new čaršija. From this time on, more peasants and craftsmen moved in, transforming the village into a small town called *čaršija* [market]. The *old čaršija* was the residential heart of Palanka, settled by traders, craftsmen and administrators, while the *new čaršija* was becoming its commercial heart, with *kafanas* [coffee houses/pubs], shops and other entertainment establishments; the street that would later on become the town corso.

Palanka was officially pronounced a small town, *varošica*, in 1866 (Ristić 1993: 9). Signs of modernity came with the arrival of the first steam train in 1884. The first four-year private high school was established by king's decree in 1919, while ten years later the same institution moved to a new building not far away from the new čaršija (Ristić 1993: 10). In 1937 Palanka had 5 188 inhabitants, mainly involved in agriculture, craftsmanship and trade. In the period following WW I it had 130 craft shops. During the 1920s, the town developed industry – a steam mill and three brick factories. In 1921, *Lorraine,* a Paris investment fund, founded a company for the repair of trains belonging to the Yugoslav Railways called *Jasenica Inc.,* with both French and Yugoslavs being members of the governing and supervisory boards. *Jasenica* was in operation until 1940, when a number of the French owners returned to their home country; the others did the same after the nationalization of the company after WW II. In 1947 *Jasenica* started to invest in housing and accompanying infrastructure for its workers in the city outskirts, the location presently known as *Kolonija* [Colony]. In 1950 the factory changed its name to *Dragoslav Djordjevic-Goša*, a WW II hero originating from this region. Employing 7000 workers, the factory continued to be the primary force in the economic development of the city (Ristić 1993: 92–103). According to the 1991 census Smederevska Palanka had 25 146 inhabitants, the majority (97%) declaring themselves as Serbs.

The corso in Smederevska Palanka

Spatial and temporal features of the corso

The space of the corso in the entire period examined did not change. The corso remained in the main town street in which commercial, entertainment, cultural and administrative objects were concentrated. This is the street known as King Aleksandar Street in the pre-WW II period, Marshal Tito Street in the socialist period and, since the early 1990s, the Street of the First Serbian Uprising. Until the 1950s, it was one of the two cobblestone streets in town, which allowed easier movement of pedestrians. In the early 1970s the street was permanently closed to traffic.

The temporal features of the corso in Smederevska Palanka depended on the season, day of the week, and age of the participants. In the whole period under scrutiny the corso took place all year round. Only since the 1990s, it has become more crowded in the summer, while almost nonexistent during the winter.

Until the 1960s the promenade was an everyday activity, although it was busiest on Saturdays and Sundays. The interviewees point to the introduction of television as the main reason for the reduction of the corso to weekends. Another reason was the shift of corso time to somewhat later hours (as a consequence of the weakening of school authority), which then resulted in less willingness to stay up late because of early school or working hours the following day. In the period after the 1960s, going for a promenade on a daily basis continued during the summer holidays, but even then the corso was most populous towards the end of the workweek.

During the 1960s, the most frequent participation in the corso moved from Saturday and Sunday to Friday and Saturday, the main reason being that at that time the workweek was officially reduced from six to five days.

It should also be noted that in all the studied periods, the corso began one hour earlier in the winter than in the summer. This means that the corso for everyone started at 6 p.m. in the summer and at 5 p.m. during the winter period.

Youth participating in the promenade from the 1930s to the 1960s can be divided into two categories, related to whether they were secondary school pupils *(srednjoškolci)*[9] or graduates *(maturanti)*. Until this period the school authorities had prohibited staying out on the street after 8 p.m.[10] Only the second category of youth stayed at the corso until 10 p.m., and this in the warmer period of the year. From the 1960s onwards, the time of leaving the corso was no longer determined by the school authorities, but by the parents. The earlier institutional control over students' public time was abandoned. As a consequence, the times which the secondary school pupils and the graduates spent at the corso began to merge. Since then, every decade has experienced the shifting of the corso time to half an hour later, reaching its maximum in the 1990s, with the youth coming out at 10 p.m. and leaving at about midnight.

---

[9] *Srednjoškolci,* as used here, is a general term for secondary school pupils. However, later in the text this term will be used in its narrower sense, referring to vocational school students, to be distinguished from high school students, called *gimnazijalci*.

[10] The only exception, with the same kind of restriction for the whole population though, was enacted by the German occupation forces during WW II, when everyone had to return home before the police hour started, which set the 8 p.m. limit.

The corso participants

The most numerous participants in the corso in all decades are secondary school pupils. Until the 1950s, with the four-year elementary and eight-year secondary school educational system, the corso is joined after the so-called *Mala matura* [Little Graduation], which means after the fourth year of secondary school. With the introduction of eight-year elementary education, the corso is joined after enrolment in secondary school. In both cases, participation in the promenade begins at about the age of sixteen. Younger pupils do not join the corso because it is prohibited by the authority of both the school and the parents. After the 1950s, the age limit of pupil participation in the promenade moves gradually downwards. The corso is now being "entered" at the end of elementary school. At first, only a small number of individuals join in, after which this number grows, but even so the generation as a whole is not completely integrated in this informal social institution. The youngest participants spend less time at it, which means they form a smaller number of circles, have less acquaintances they meet along the way, still do not stop at the standing places, nor do the boys have the right to occupy them. Until the end of WW II the corso is the only place for the secondary school youth to gather in the evening hours. Besides the corso, young men who have finished school, frequent the *kafanas*. Young women seldom go with them, and if so, this is usually for special celebrations. Thus, the corso is mostly frequented by secondary school pupils and female graduates, while male graduates spend more time in pubs than at the corso. From 1945 to the 1960s, after promenading, secondary school youth and graduates go to dances, which start at 8 p.m. From the 1960s onwards, female graduates also go to *kafanas* more regularly and without male companions, so that in this period the corso is primarily occupied by the secondary school pupils. The older youth now use the corso as a place to make plans about where to go out later. Since the 1980s, a new leisure time institution appeared, the *kafić* [café]. Both the upper grade secondary school pupils and older youth frequent them. Starting to hang out at the cafés means the beginning of departure from the corso. The youth go to the promenade only before or after the time spent at the café. The most frequent participants of the corso are now the youth from the lower grades of secondary school. For them, the corso is the main gathering place. A generational cohort withdraws from the corso after the age of 20, when generational bonds weaken due to moving to another town or establishing marital ties. A participant of the corso in this phase has the same pattern of socio-spatial behaviour as when he/she first joins in. The time spent at the corso is shorter and the number of circles made is smaller. The number of acquaintances is reduced, and there is no need for stopping at the standing places simply because some new people occupy them. Only a few young men still use their "right" to standing places because almost one whole age group disappears from the corso. For the complete withdrawal from the corso the entrance into marriage is of crucial significance. Upon marriage and birth of the first child the young married couple withdraws from the corso completely.

Until the 1960s, adults also participated in the corso. The time of their arrival and participation in the promenade was the same as that of the youth. These two corsos, however, took place at opposite sides of the street. The introduction of television in the 1960s led to the withdrawal of most adults from the corso. The starting time of the youth promenade moved to later hours while for the adults it remained the same, thus, the two corsos became temporally detached.

In all the periods studied, contacts at the corso were made on the basis of the generational cohort and related to the same school grade, workplace, neighbourhood, class and subcultural affiliation. Going out on the corso was done mainly within the same gender group. Until the 1960s the patriarchal morale did not allow for youth to go out in mixed groups. However, in the decades preceding this period, adults have an increasingly weaker control over the behaviour of the youth in public places, so that their conduct becomes more liberal and they are more frequently seen going out in mixed company. Until the same period, couples went out together only if in a "serious", i.e., socially accepted relationship. The intimacy of romantic relationships was not exhibited in public. In the 1960s, the situation changed. A girl could now go out with a group of male friends without causing a scandal in the local community. The possibility of physical contact between new couples on the corso, such as holding hands (1960s), and a man walking with his arm around a girl (1970s), also became a novelty.

Even though, generally speaking, everyone went to the corso "to see and to be seen", its main implicit function in all the periods was "networking" among the youth, who were interested in establishing friendly and romantic relationships.[11] There were, of course, other places to meet a boy or a girl. In the 1930s, youths regularly frequented dances organized in hotels or by officials, traders, craftsmen, hunters or other associations. During WW II they met at the movies (in *Kafana Stara Srbija*), theatre plays (kafanas *Central* and *Kruna*) or at home gatherings, such as those traditionally organized for the second day of Slava, the family saint's day. In the late 1940s and 1950s, dances were organized at the Officials Club, Students Association, the movie theatre hall, or the Abrašević Society summer garden. Throughout the 1960s dances were organized in the Army Hall and the Youth Hall. Going out to *kafanas* was the dominant leisure activity in the 1970s, with *Kafana Turist* being the most popular place. From the 1980s onwards the café became the principal leisure time institution, where youth groups either sat in their "favourite café" or moved between a few such places.

[11] "Networking" is defined as "the developing of contacts or exchanging of information with others in an informal network" (Webster's Dictionary).

From the 1930s to the early 1960s, contacts at the corso were established through an intermediary, a person both parties would know. There was also a more direct, ritualized way to make a contact, which has remained a tradition until today. The gist of it is that the girl who wants to attract the boy's attention shortens her walking route and thus passes with friends as many times as possible in front of his standing place. If a boy wants to make a pass at a girl he walks behind her and tries to start a conversation. Since the 1960s, the boys began to approach the girls even more directly, and since the 1980s, this "ritual" has been transferred to the cafés, where either side may be making the first approach.

Romantic relationships were established within the same age group, maybe with a two or three years difference, and more or less the same social class, thus "a high school girl could rarely be seen with a member of the working class; if this happened, he would have to be extremely handsome", an interviewee noted who participated in the corso in the 1950s.

Dynamic features of the corso

The dynamic features of the corso encompass the *travel routes* of the circulating participants, which are characterized by the specific route length, shape, direction, and path. For most of the studied periods, the length of the corso route remained constant. The corso took place along the main street presently known as the Street of the First Serbian Uprising, covering two blocks, from Karadjordjeva Street and Heroes Square to October 10th Street. Only since the mid-1980s has the route of the youth corso been shortened and reduced by half, extending from Karadjordjeva Street to Saint Sava Street (previously known as November 29th Street), thus keeping only its northern part. The elliptical shape of the corso route as well as the counterclockwise direction of the participants' movement remained, without exception, the same in the whole period. This means that the corso participants walk on the right side of their elliptical route no matter which end of the street they are facing at that moment. It can thus be concluded that the length, shape and direction of the route are not influenced by the age of the participants nor by the time of day at which the corso takes place (see figures 1 and 2).

The path which corso participants took, however, changed over time. Before and during WW II the youth walked on the street pavement. The *kafanas* frequented by the older generation are located along the southwestern pavement, so the adults used this side of the street space during the corso. The northeastern pavement, on the other side of the street, is a thoroughfare used by those who are in a hurry, but also by younger couples that are in publicly acclaimed relationships. The interviewees who participated in the corso of that period said that the reasons for the prevailing use of one of the pavements were: lesser isolation, better

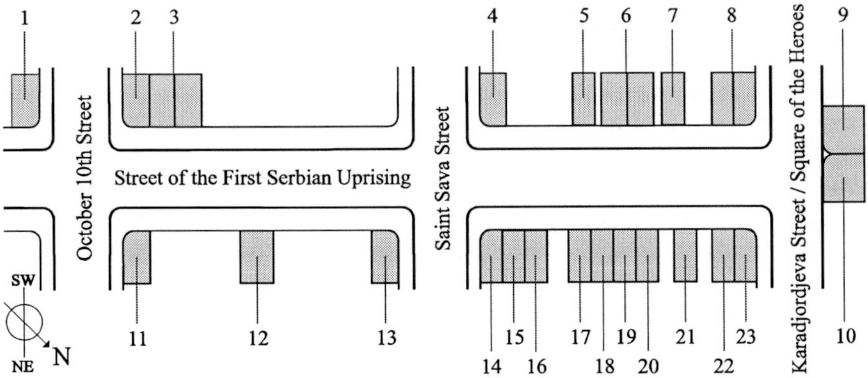

1. Kafana *Stara Srbija* (Grocery store *Uzor*)
2. Kafana *Mala Kasina* (Kafana *Turist*)
3. Tailor's shop and a bakery (Military staff apartment building)
4. Kafana *Central* (*Goša*)
5. Kafana *Kruna* (Store *Nama*)
6. Private objects (Department store *Uzor*)
7. Pharmacy *Krstić* and a soda shop (Store *Ateks*, shoe store)
8. Kafana *Narodna gostionica* and Kafana *Djurišić* (Park)
9. Regional court (*National Museum*)
10. Regional government (Kafana *Konak*)
11. Store *Arandjelovac* (Outpatient clinic, Communist Party Committee)
12. Kafana *Terzibašić* (*Army Hall*, *Yuth Hall*, *Robna kuća Beograd*)
13. Pharmacy (*Jasenica Inc.*, Bookstore *Zmaj*, Store *Ateks*)
14. Kafana *Ilija Vlaj* (Kafana *Lovac*, *Invest banka*)
15. Bistro *Petrović* (*Foto Bora*)
16. Hairdresser *Šarlo* (Bookstore *Nolit*, Café *Vizantija*)
17. Private house (*Radio Jasenica*, Pastry shop *Pelivan*)
18. *Džogina Kafana* (*Workers Hall*, Shoe store *Peko*)
19. Private house (Café *Bravo*)
20. Tailor's shop (Pastry shop *Korzo*)
21. *Students Hall* (Post Office)
22. Kafana *Albanija* (Summer garden *Abraševič*, Parking)
23. Municipal government (Parking)

The order of naming the buildings is in accordance with their successive uses, starting from the 1930s until the present.

Figure 1: Building uses at the corso in Smederevska Palanka (1930–2001)

preserved stones built into the pavement surface and a larger number of entertainment places. The other pavement, even though less used, was not negatively characterized. In fact, it was not completely excluded from the corso activities – the young couples used it on a regular basis, and the whole corso moved there after a rain shower, because it was the sunny side of the street.

In the early post-war period, between 1945 and 1954, the youth corso took place on the northeastern pavement, the part of the street previously used as a thoroughfare. The main reason for this shift of the corso away from the street, the interviewees say, was the irregularity of the Turkish cobblestones paving it, which didn't make leisurely walking as pleasant. The choice of this particular side of the street is explained by a higher concentration of communist youth organizations.

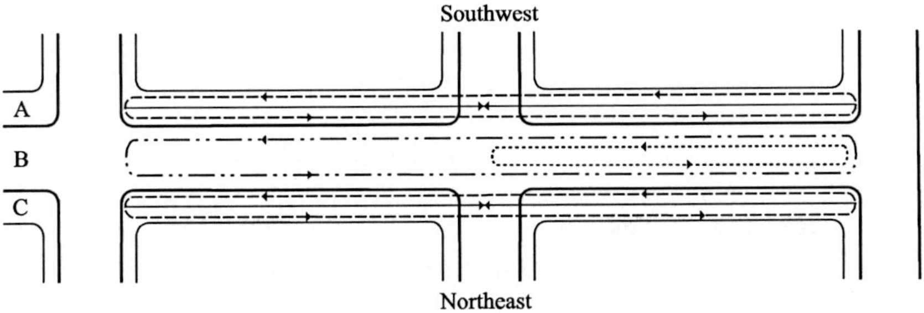

A_1 ----- 1930-1945 Grownup corso path
A_2 ——— 1946-2001 Walk through path

C_1 ——— 1930-1945 Walk through path
C_2 ----- 1946-1954 Youth corso path
1961-1970 Younger youth path

B_1 —··— 1930-1945 Youth corso path
1954-1960 Youth corso path
1961-1970 Older youth path
1971-1985 Youth corso path

B_2 ·········· 1986-2001 Youth corso shortened path

Figure 2: Paths of the corso participants in Smederevska Palanka (1930–2001)

The opposite pavement now served as a thoroughfare, used by those who had not yet joined the corso (children) and those who had already withdrawn from it (adults) or who wanted to pass in a hurry. The interviewees characterized this side as the one where "the peasants" went. Relating its use to the country people gave the side a negative image. This same attitude towards certain longitudinal segments of the corso (i. e., the space of the southwestern pavement) as well as the reasons mentioned, were perpetuated in the periods to come. In the accounts of corso participants of different age groups, the negatively assessed part of the street was related to the rural population from the vicinity, which in fact, was not present at the corso, but could be seen in town usually by day, when they came to the market or performed other commercial or administrative chores. The few youths from the vicinity of Smederevska Palanka who participated in the corso actually lived and attended school in town and went out with their school friends (the town youth), sharing their rules of spatial and temporal behaviour at the corso.

Some of the interviewees explain this "connection" between the rural folk and the southwestern pavement by referring to objects or places located near this part of the corso. Bus and train stations are the nodes to which the arrival of the rural population into the town is connected. It is curious that none of the interviewees mentioned the open market (where the "rural" is constantly present), situated near the stations and on the same side of the corso. These objects may be viewed as signs of the rural. If, in contrast, we look for objects that are in the opposite part ("half") of the town, the one "gravitating" to the northeastern part of the corso, we can notice numerous signs of "urbanity", such as the Municipal Government, the Regional Court and the Regional Government (since the 1970s), the high school, and other administrative, medical and cultural institutions. We can thus suggest that differentially viewed parts of the corso are associated with the objects situated in the "part of the town" representing the "rural" or the "urban" in the mental/symbolic maps of Smederevska Palanka residents.

In 1954 the street was repaired and layered with new, regularly shaped cobblestones, which brought the youth corso back onto the street, where it would remain until the present. The later part of the 1950s is characterized by the use of the northeastern pavement for standing places, while the southwest side is used as a thoroughfare for those in a hurry.

During the 1960s, all three lanes become actively used during the promenade. The youth corso is now divided into two segments, differentiated by age group. The street is now the corso of the secondary school graduates who are still part of this informal institution, while the northeastern pavement is the corso of the youths still attending secondary school. The northwestern pavement is a thoroughfare, usually used by adults and children.

In the 1970s and onwards, the use of the street segments shifted back to what it was in the period before 1960. This means that the street remained the youth corso, the northeastern pavement was used for standing places and the southwestern pavement used as a thoroughfare.

As regards the paths used in the promenade throughout the whole period, one can conclude that the logic of longitudinal segmentation of the corso changed. Until the end of WW II, the corso was divided into three segments. This division entailed a differentiation into youth, young couples and adults. From this period to the 1960s the promenade was divided into two segments, differentiating between the real corso of the town youth and the imaginary corso of the rural youth. From this time on, the second segment, which was the lesser used part (the southwestern pavement used as a thoroughfare) was negatively viewed and correlated with the rural. This "symbolic" segmentation, we may suggest, probably had the function of delimiting town and country folk, or stressing the significance of the urban origin of the townspeople. The corso of the 1960s was divided into three segments. Preserving the imaginary rural segment, the other two belonged to urban youth, differentiating between older and younger groups. In the following period (1970–2001), the corso preserved the distinction between the "imaginary urban" and "rural". As mentioned earlier, since the mid-1980s, keeping the same spatial arrangement of paths, the length of the promenade route shortened by half, preserving the reduced urban corso in the part of the street nearest to the town's cultural institutions, such as the National Museum, the Historical Archives, the theatre and the cinema hall.

Since the mid 1990s, the dynamic aspect of the corso exists during the summer months. Interviewees explain that due to the economic crisis it is possible to go out only during the weekend, so that the corso hardly exists on workdays. The cafés have become the primary places for socializing, substituting the corso completely in the winter and partially in the summer. The corso has become a mere thoroughfare between cafés, so that the repetitive circulation, the main characteristic of the classic corso, is reduced to a minimum – a few circles in the summer, and possibly half a circle in the winter.

Static features of the corso

The static features of a corso include the *standing places* of the participants, which are characterized by their specific position along the corso path, the differential right to occupy them as well as their relative importance, i. e., social ranking. The standing places appeared in the 1930s and existed until the mid-1990s. Since then, their function for the summer period has been transferred to the café and pastry shop gardens and the newly placed street benches.

The standing places were and are located in front of objects with commercial, crafts or entertainment use. Before and during WW II these places were positioned along the southwestern pavement. When the youth corso moved to the northeastern pavement, the standing places moved along with it (see figures 1 and 2).

In all following periods, the standing places were more numerous in the half of the corso that, after its reduction in the 1980s, remained its central part. Also, the northern end of the corso (towards Karadjordjeva Street and the National Museum), has become the standing/gathering place of marginal(ized) groups who, hidden in the small park, experiment with drugs and alcohol.

The right to occupy a standing place reflects, in the first place, gender differences in spatial behaviour at the corso. Until the 1980s, only the male corso participants are entitled to standing places. Girls walk and boys make eyes at them *(šacuju)*, and some chat *(dobacuju)*. From the 1980s on, girls could also be seen standing there, but only in male company. Female groups still do not have the right to occupy separate standing places, they only join the male groups.

The observation of the use of standing places also reveals an age differentiation at the corso. From the 1930s to the late 1960s, young men who have graduated from secondary school or older occupy the standing places. In the 1970s, the standing places were taken by male youth half way through secondary school and older, while in the 1980s this age limit moved to the freshman year. This change towards an earlier right to occupy standing places is paralleled by the gradual shift to a younger age of the overall corso participants.

The standing places possess different relative importance. The ranking of a place is correlated with its permeability, i. e., the measure of frequency with which the corso participants pass by. Places most frequently passed during the corso are of highest value. All the "best" standing places in all periods were in that part of the street that remained the corso after its reduction in the 1990s, and can thus be considered the core of the corso.

In the period before and during WW II, the standing places were located primarily along the southwestern pavement. The interviewees do not remember a great number of such places, and they do not point to the most popular ones, but they do talk about the popularity of *kafanas* that had small front gardens in the summer and could thus be treated as sitting or standing places at the corso. It is well known that *Kafana Central* was an elite place, frequented by men of high social standing, that *Kafana Kruna* was the middle class place, and that the working class went to *Kafana Terzibašić* (see figure 1).

Interviewees who participated in the corso of the post-war period, tell that this was the time of solidarity and equity, and they do not recollect any divisions among the youth. However, when mentioning concrete people they went out with, the closeness of the communist youth groups on one hand, and those who were not involved becomes apparent. The most popular standing place of that time was in front of the *Dom Studenata* [Students Hall],[12] which was known for organizing most of the cultural and entertainment activities in town. Young men who had graduated from high school were often seen standing in front of this building.

During the 1960s, the right to the "best" standing places was again with the young men who had graduated from secondary school, and among them, the priority was with the high school graduates who were considered the elite. The most popular standing places of that time were in front of *Kafana Lovac* [Hunter], situated in the central part of the corso. This period is the only one characterized by a differentiation based on residential location. The rivalry between the town youth and the youth from *Kolonija* [Colony], the working-class residential district built in the late 1940s and early 1950s on the outskirts of Smederevska Palanka, is clearly visible at the corso, and thus in the appropriation of standing places. The standing place of the youth from *Kolonija* was in front of the *Nolit* bookstore, next to popular town youth places. This explicit territorial and implicit class differentiation is remembered very distinctly.

In the 1970s, the same pattern of the older male youth occupying the best standing places continued. The best places were now in front of *Pošta* [Post office]. From this time on, the corso sees the appearance of groups perceived as marginal. It is the *hippies* who are a novelty, and whose behaviour and appearance is strongly disapproved by the *čaršija,* i.e., the local community. Their standing

---

[12] From 1949 to 1958 the town had a Students Hall, building no. 21. After 1958, similar activities were organized in the Dom Omladine (Youth Hall), situated in the old building where Kafana Terzibašić used to be. The building was torn down in 1971 with no replacement for its previous use.

places are at the edge of the promenade, in the small parks across the street from *Narodni Muzej* [National Museum], away from the mainstream corso activities.

In the 1980s, the right to best places was with the young men who graduated from one of the town secondary schools and the older high school pupils. They stood in front of the pastry shops *Korzo* and *Pelivan* or café *Bravo*. The marginal groups now included the *punks*, *head bangers* (heavy metal sympathizers) and *rockabillies,* whose dress style and behaviour was in stark contrast to that of the other youths. Their places were either outside the corso or in its vicinity. Generally, this was the period in which everyone stood in front of cafés on the corso or close to it. The choice of café was in accordance with the preferred music style. Youths who liked alternative music frequented *K. M.*, while *Time* and *Bravo* were the favourite places of those who preferred commercial music.

In the 1990s, the same male groups reserve the high-ranking places at the corso – the secondary school graduates, older high school pupils and youths from well-to-do families. They stand in front of café *Bravo* (later called café *Six*) and the pastry shops *Korzo* and *Pelivan*.

The mid-1990s are characterized by the disappearance of standing places. Their function was taken over by the gardens of cafés and pastry shops, which are open only in the summer period. The benches placed along the pavement since 2000 are used by younger youths, mainly girls who finish elementary school or begin secondary school, and who do not yet go to cafés. Popularity, and thus greater or lesser concentration of youths in particular cafés changes from one season to another. Older secondary school pupils and graduates are the main visitors there. The subcultural affiliation is no longer visible in the choice of cafés at the corso, but in the choice of cafés outside it: the so-called alternative social scene is to be found in the cafés *Butterfly* and *Mec Koy,* both outside the corso.

Finally, it can be concluded that the logic of transversal segmentation of the corso remained the same throughout the entire period studied, preserving the simple principle of exhibiting the social status of the youth by means of the relative ranking of the standing places. The implicit function of this kind of segmentation is the differentiation between the "in-crowd" *(gradske face)* and the "outsiders" *(gradski marginalci)* in town.

Dress codes at the corso

The dress codes at the corsos of different periods also signified social differentiations. In the period preceding the 1950s, dress reflected the difference between the younger youth, who still attended secondary school, and older youth, who had already left. After the 1970s, dress primarily reflects subcultural affiliation.

From the 1930s to the mid-1950s, the youths who attended secondary school were obliged to wear uniforms at school and other public places. Throughout this whole period, the girls wore a black overdress with a white collar and a barrette with the class number on it, while the boys wore formal attire and a cap with the class number as a mandatory part of the uniform. The introduction of the eight-grade elementary and four-grade secondary school system also meant departure from the practice of wearing the uniform outside school, so that the difference between secondary school pupils and graduates disappeared from public life, and from the corso as well.

The dressing style of both older and younger youths was influenced by the dominant fashion tendencies, particularly after the 1960s. Between 1930 and 1946 boys wore suits and girls wore midi skirts. From 1945 to 1950 boys still wore suits while girls wore white tennis shoes and knee length skirts. In the 1950s girls wore knee-length dresses with ruffled petticoats and pumps, while boys still wore suits. In the 1960s the length of girls' skirts became shorter and the mini was the hit; young men began to wear blue jeans. The 1970s are characterized by blue jeans (worn by both boys and girls), crushed nylon macs, and Terylene skirts. Men began wearing longer hair. From this period onwards, the subcultural affiliation became visible in the style of dress. In the 1970s, it is the hippie style, in the 1980s the youths wear mostly jeans, while the subcultural style is specific for each group. The punks wear short, oddly clipped hair, bomber jackets, tee shirts with subculture signs (mostly punk rock bands), leather pants and Doc Martins. Head bangers have long hair, leather jackets, tee shirts with subculture signs (heavy metal bands) and black pants. Rockabillies wear biker jackets (called *rokerke*) and a specific hairstyle accentuating longer hair in the front. The 1990s are characterized by a widespread jeans culture. Altogether, it can be noted that the youths appreciating alternative music dress in a distinct, avant-garde manner, while those enjoying commercial music dress more trendily and conventionally.

Corso as a total social phenomenon

As argued in the Introduction, the corso is here understood as a complex phenomenon, which simultaneously reflects different religious, political, economic, legal, moral, and social institutions, producing specific aesthetic and morphological effects. Some of these institutions influence the socio-spatial behaviour at the corso directly, others indirectly, while some have no influence at all.

We will start with *religion,* with respect to the Church, the only institution that is not reflected at the corso of Smederevska Palanka. The reasons are that, even though the corso is a highly ritualized phenomenon, it has a solely secular character, and that the residents of Smederevska Palanka belong dominantly to the

Serbian Orthodox faith and thus have a homogeneous religious background, which makes this corso resistant to religious differentiations. In towns that are characterized by religiously and ethnically heterogeneous populations, however, the position of the various groups at the corso becomes visible, especially in their standing places.[13]

The seventy-year period under consideration was characterized by deep structural political changes in Serbia. The corso was traced from the Kingdom of Yugoslavia, throughout WW II, the period of the Socialist Federal Republic of Yugoslavia, to the Federal Republic of Yugoslavia. The above description of the corso tells that larger political shifts, such as the changes from monarchy, wartime occupation and socialism to post-socialism, seemed to have been mostly expressed in the political/ideological definition of a stratified, then a class-less, and again a reemerging class society. This changing definition of "society" was obviously reflected in the social practices of the respective periods, especially visible in the change of the after-corso entertainment places, which went from class-distinct kafanas to the less socially distinguished gatherings in the socialist youth associations, and finally again to increasingly stratified cafés. At the same time, it can be said that in this town the first larger political shift (to socialism) did not disturb the structure of the primary corso activities, while the second shift (to post-socialism) eroded its fullness of time, space and sociability. The influence of *politics* could also be recognized through the changes introduced in the economic and legal system and thus in the policies put into practice on the local level.

Coupled with politics, the *economy* influenced the life of the corso in different ways. Firstly, the space of the corso changed its external and internal morphology in a few waves of partial urban reconstruction: in the late 1950s, the local municipality, or the firms run by it, invested in the cultural institutions and restaurants on the central street, while the Yugoslav army invested in a large apartment building for its officers. In the 1970s, the liberalisation of economic politics brought about the flourishing of large state-run Serbian firms, mostly dealing with international trade, especially with metal, textile, leather, and food products. Thus, this period saw the restructuring of central town areas, where many of the old one-storey *čarsija* objects were torn down and replaced with new, socialist-style multi-storey buildings built by powerful investors such as large national firms (*Ateks* dealing with textiles, *Robna kuća Beograd,* a department store chain, *Dragoslav Djordjević – Goša,* a large company that repaired trains for the Yugoslav Railroads Co., and *Lovac,* a restaurant chain). In the 1980s, private cafés substituted most of the remaining privately owned crafts and state-owned commercial establishments. Thus, changes in the ownership and use of objects along the corso route

[13] This fact has been noted, for example, since the 1950s in the corso of Pljevlja, Montenegro, a town with mixed Serbian Orthodox and Muslim populations.

produced aesthetic and morphological changes at the corso. The transformations in the urban and architectural features of the corso space, in turn, strongly influenced the choice of paths and the most popular standing places.

The second influence of economy is tied to *leisure time institutions*. The corso in Smederevska Palanka reflects an overall change in places for socializing and entertainment, starting from kafanas and voluntary association clubrooms in the pre-socialist period, the cultural centres organized by socialist youth or workers' organizations in the early socialist period, all the way to cafés in the late socialist period. Until the early 1950s, kafanas were the main party places where dances were regularly organized, and they have remained the principal socializing places for adults until the present. The clubs are also enduring institutions, reflecting the changes in ideological shifts and segmentation of the society according to different criteria. Appearing in the 1980s as a novel institution for socializing, the café has in time appropriated the essential functions of the corso, and thus strongly influenced its degradation. It may also be said that by substituting the standing places in their classic form, the cafés have become an integral part of the corso.

The third major economic influence is the *general standard of living*. The frequency of going out on the corso, especially since the period when the frequenting of cafés became an obligatory part of this, has been correlated with the pocket money of the corso participants. This is why, for example, in the 1990s, with the economic crises created by civil war in former Yugoslavia and complete isolation of Serbia and Montenegro, the promenade experienced a temporal reduction to weekends only. Of course, there is a visible expenditure paradox here, but also a definite change of socializing patterns – from utilizing the dynamic (and economic) form of the corso on a daily basis (which does not necessarily involve spending money for a drink), the Palanka youths switched to utilizing the static (and non-economic) form of "corso-ing" in cafés on weekends.

Finally, internal economic aspects of the corso, understood both as a spatiality and as a practice, are also recognized in what can be labelled a *"prestige economy"*. Social negotiations described as part of the corso reflect the presentation of power to impress or influence because of wealth, success, achievement or character.[14] Prestige of the Palanka inhabitants, distinguished by age, gender, educational level and profile, material and social status, is visible in the longitudinal and transversal segmentation of the corso space, i. e., in their positioning along and across the corso space.

The corso in Palanka also reflects *legal institutions,* i. e., how legal decisions at the national level are scaled down to the local level. In the domain of the educa-

[14] This is the definition of the term "prestige", with an interesting etymology: French orig. illusion, trick, < Latin *praestigium*, deception: Webster's New World College Dictionary on CD. Zane Publishing 1995.

tional system, public order and time schedules, the following changes become visible: the change from a “four plus eight” to an “eight plus four” educational system, the change from the six- to a five-day workweek, the ban on the high school youth from open public spaces after 8 p. m., the school uniform as mandatory dress outside school (in public), and school teachers as controllers of students’ public behaviour.

One of the most visible processes at the corso was that the authority over the public youth domain gradually shifted from the school to the family. In the earlier periods, the school, as a representative state institution, controlled the public behaviour of pupils – proper behaviour and punctual leaving from the corso were expected to be strictly observed. If a high school teacher saw a student on the street after 8 p. m. sanctions were employed. In the 1930s, for example, the name of such a student was read out with condemnation in all classrooms, and punishment or even suspension from school would follow. Since the early 1960s, the authority of the school as the dominant controller of the students’ public conduct was transfered to the domain of the family. Now, the parents determined the time of going out and coming home from the corso. At the same time, the adult corso became temporally detached from the youth corso, so that the presence of both authorities – teachers and parents – was avoided.

In the course of time, patriarchal *morality* weakened, and this process is visible in the gradual but steady shift of the time spent at the corso towards later hours, in the continuing penetration of female corso participants into the (earlier strictly male) groups gathering at the standing places along the corso, and more frequent visits to pubs and cafés in solely female company, in more freedom for physical expression of romantic relationships for young couples (holding hands, walking with his arm around her shoulder), as well as in a more leisurely dress code at the corso. Despite liberalization of institutional and informal attitudes about how youths should behave, one feature of the corso in the domain of gender relations remained unchanged – the right to occupy a standing place along the corso was never taken by (or given to) exclusively female groups.

The corso is, most of all, a socio-cultural phenomenon, reflecting different *social phenomena* (i. e., institutions) and their dynamics. In other words, the corso is a mirror image of local society. Its space is segmented according to the social structure of the town, reflecting the size, status and power of every social group. The youth groups participating in the corso of Smederevska Palanka are distinct by age, gender, educational level and profile, social status, territorial (residential) status and subculture.

Differentiation by *age* has been visible in both the dynamic and static aspects of the corso. Specific age groups used different walking paths – adults and youths used different longitudinal parts of the street while they shared the corso (1930–1945), and a similar situation appeared with the younger and older youths in the 1960s. Standing places in all periods were appropriated by the older youths, i.e., young men graduated from secondary school and considered as having passed the test of maturity. The changes in corso dynamics tell of the separation of the youths' and adults' corso as well as the gradual incorporation of the younger youths into this informal social institution. *Gender* differentiation is reflected, as already noted, in the gradual change in the character of the standing places at the corso, which from solely male became mixed (from the 1960s on), but with a definite absence of female-only standing places until present.

The youths participating in the corso are also differentiated by their *school and grade*, which strongly determined their overall social status. Attendance of high school *(gimnazija)* as opposed to vocational school *(srednja škola)* was definitely a sign of higher social ranking. This is why senior high school students were ranked equally with vocational school graduates (visible in the right to occupy the best standing places from the early 1960s on), as if their school's primacy pushed them into maturity a year ahead of the others. In the 1960s, the geographical/residential area in which a school was located was also a measure for the social status of the youths attending elementary school. This is why pupils attending "prestigious" town schools competed for standing places at the corso with the pupils attending school in the Colony, the working-class outskirts of Smederevska Palanka.

Since the late 1960s, *subcultural groups* became visible in the corso of Smederevska Palanka. Starting with hippies in the 1970s and continuing with punks, heavy metal fans, and rockabillies in the 1980s and 1990s, the far end of the corso became the gathering space for these marginal groups. They found seclusion in the parks across the street from the present National Museum, or on the steps next to the same building, thus appropriating the far periphery of the corso. Condemned by the local community for their oddness, drinking habits and experimenting with drugs, they kept their out-of-the-way segment of the corso all along, and found cafés that accommodated their music taste elsewhere. It can thus be noted that paradoxically, the institution of the corso simultaneously marginalises (excludes) but also incorporates (includes) the subcultural groups into its structure by granting them an adequate gathering space.

In the whole post-WW II period, the corso participants marked one longitudinal segment of the corso, the southwest pavement, as the "peasants' side". This relation with the *"rural"* must, as the research shows, be understood in two ways. First, this pavement was used by those who did not participate in the corso activities. It was actually a transversal for those adults and children who were passing by in a hurry. Apart from this, the countryside residents did not have any real connection to the corso. They were visible in the town during the day selling their produce or passing along the main streets on private business. It seems that an imaginary "rural" segment was added to the corso space, thus moulding an image of the "peasant" as "the boring and insignificant" people who did not follow the "promenade of the townsfolk" during the corso and the real rural folks who upon entering the town from the bus or train station walked along the same, negatively loaded side of the street.

The corso is, we can conclude, a complex socio-cultural phenomenon, reflecting different political, ideological, economic, legal, moral and social institutions and their dynamics. Influenced by these global institutions, the corso is, at the same time, a mirror image of local society. Its space is segmented according to the social structure of the town, reflecting the size, status and power of every social group. It can thus be noted that the youth groups participating in the corso of Smederevska Palanka are distinct by age, gender, educational level and profile, social status, residential location and subculture.

Literature

Çelik, Zeynep 1986: The Remaking of Istanbul: Portrait of an Ottoman City in the Nineteenth Century. Seattle: University of Washington Press.

Debie, Franck 1993: Une Forme Urbaine du Premier Age Touristique: Les Promenades Littorales. In: Mappemonde 93, 1: 32–37.

Del Negro, Giovanna P., Harris M. Berger 2001: Character Divination and Kinetic Sculpture in the Central Italian Passeggiata (Ritual Promenade): Interpretive Frameworks and Expressive Practices from a Body-centered Perspective. In: Journal of American Folklore 114: 5–15.

Gavrilova, Rayna 2003: Historische Anthropologie der Stadt. In: Karl Kaser, S. Gruber, R. Pichler: Historische Anthropologie im südöstlichen Europa. Eine Einführung. Wien, Köln: Böhlau, 269–289.

Gavrilović, Ljiljana 1984: Korzo – iskazivanje generacijske polarizacije u strukturi grada [Corso – the expression of generational polarization in the urban social structure]. In: Etnološke sveske 5 (Belgrade) 33–37.

Gyaeni, Gaebor 2004: Identity and Urban Experience – Fin-de-siècle Budapest. Boulder, CO: Social Science Monograph; Wayne, NJ: Center for Hungarian Studies and Publications.

Jerman, Katja 2003: Promenada v Ljubljani [Promenade in Ljubljana]. Ljubljana: Viharnik.

Lawrence, Henry W. 1988: Origins of the Tree-Lined Boulevard. In: The Geographical Review 78, 4: 355–374.

Mišetić, Anka 1997: Socijalne značajke Rive u životu grada – primjer Splita [The social characteristics of the coastal promenade in the life of a town. The case of Split]. In: Društvena istraživanja 6, 1 (27): 71–87.

Mos [Mauss], Marsel 1982: Ogled o daru: oblik i smisao razmene u arhaičnim društvima [Marcel Mauss 1950: The Gift]. In: Sociologija i antropologija 2. Belgrade: Prosveta.

Novaković, Voja 1970: Palanka kroz vekove [Palanka through the centuries]. Smederevska Palanka: Centar za kulturu biro "Hermes".

Perunišić, Branko 1980: Palanka i njena okolina [Palanka and its surroundings]. Belgrade: Privredni pregled.

Ristić, Nenad 1993: Goša - zapisi o jednom trajanju [Goša - Notes about one duration]. Smederevska Palanka: Goša Holding Korporacija.

Rotenberg, Robert 1992: Time and Order in Metropolitan Vienna: A Seizure of Schedules. Washington, London: Smithsonian Institution Press.

Scobey, David 1992: Anatomy of the Promenade: The Politics of Bourgeois Sociability in Nineteenth-Century New York. In: Social History 17, 2: 203–227.

Stevanović, Mihailo, Ljudevit Joke et al. (ed.) 1967: Rečnik srpskohrvatskoga književnog jezika 2 [Dictionary of Serbocroatian literary language 2]. Novi Sad, Zagreb: Matica Srpska, Matica Hrvatska.

Telste, Kari 2002: Karl Johan's Gate around 1900. Gender, Space and Moral Boundaries. In: Tidsskrift for samfunnsforskning 43, 3: 361–380.

Vučinić, Vesna 1994: Dubrovački Stradun kao korzo i njegova socijalna segmentacija [Stradun as the Corso and its social segmentation]. In: Zbornik Filozofskog fakulteta, Serija A: Istorijske nauke 18, Spomenica Radovnu Samardžiću. Belgrade, 423–441.

Vučinić, Vesna, Smiljana Antonijević 1998: Društvena funkcija i simbolika beogradskog korzoa u vreme Kraljevine Jugoslavije (1931–1941) [Social function and symbolism of the Belgrade corso during the Kingdom of Yugoslavia (1931–1941)]. In: Glasnik Etnografskog instituta Srpske akademije nauka i umetnosti 47: 85–101.

Vučinić, Vesna 1999: Prostorno ponašanje u Dubrovniku: antropološka studija grada sa ortogonalnom strukturom [Spatial behaviour in Dubrovnik: An anthropological study of a city with orthogonal stucture]. Belgrade: Filozofski fakultet Univerziteta u Beogradu.

Vujaklija, Milan 1972: Leksikon stranih reči i izraza [Lexicon of foreign words and idioms]. Belgrade: Prosveta.

Cremation as an Urban Phenomenon of the New Age
From Ecology to Ideology: the Serbian Case[1]

Aleksandra Pavićević, Belgrade

Madame Sofia was one of the rare persons whose life lasted almost a century. She was an agile and vital old lady who died at age 95, after a short illness. Madame Sofia left a daughter in Belgrade and a son in Chicago, where she spent most of her working years, and many grandchildren and great-grandchildren scattered around the globe. She did not have any special wishes concerning her funeral and remains. Still, she was a member of a posthumous fund association named *"Oganj"*, so in accordance with her own personal beliefs, her daughter decided to cremate her mother and to place her urn in the family vault at the old and prestigious New Cemetery in the centre of Belgrade. Thanks to the unusual efficiency of a local funeral undertaker, all preparations were done promptly and surprisingly swiftly, since the system is known for its ineffectiveness. An order for cremation was promptly attached to Sofia's coffin, so that, according to the procedure, it could be transferred on a "funeral" day to the special hall at the *Novo groblje* [New Cemetery], which serves for cremations only. Nevertheless, it seems that it was not Madame Sofia's destiny to rest in peace: her son, unable to attend the funeral due to illness, plainly ruled out the idea of his mother's cremation. He explained the decision by saying that the family owned a vault so economically that there was no pressure or burden as in classical funeral procedure. Furthermore, he argued that a cremation itself was an uncivilized act, violence against the deceased. His sister, hurt by her brother's ingratitude and lack of comprehension of her own position, decided to return the mother's body from the cremation room to the cemetery's morgue, where it would wait for "someone" to bury it "prop-

---

[1] The main source of this work particularly the part which deals with history of Modern Cremation Movement, was the journal of the Association of cremation supporters *Oganj,* the reports from annual conferences of the Association, as well as different texts and supplements from the documents of the Association. It is necessary to mention that most of the materials which belonged to a personal archive of Vojislav Kujundzic, MD, the leader and elected President of the Association for life, were destroyed in fire during the bombing of Belgrade in 1941. I would like to take this opportunity to thank all the *Oganj* employees, especially its current President, Miss Dušica Vučković, for her selfless support, information and materials. I would also like to thank employees of Public communal firm *"Pogrebne usluge",* especially Mrs. Miljana Selaković, and art historian Katarina Obrenović, who also provided valuable information. A part of this paper dealing with the contemporary funeral and ritual practice among the population of Belgrade is based on a questionnaire given during 2004 and 2005 to 30 members of the association *Oganj,* as well as to 40 randomly chosen informants whose attitudes toward the burial type was unknown.

erly". The waiting lasted around thirty days, until the deceased's daughter-in-law showed up with an authorization from Chicago, and buried Sofia in a coffin, in the family vault, without any special rituals.

Although this unusual life story took place in the last month of 2004, at a time when Serbia, that is, Belgrade, had already accepted cremation as an appropriate way of dealing with the dead, it still testifies to a 100 year old antagonism which still continues. Namely, there are two opposed practices, two orientations, two convictions or ideologies: one which favours burials in the ground and the other preferring cremation. In order to understand this antagonism we must look into its history and try to grasp its meaning under the conditions of contemporary life.

Rites and procedures connected with the deceased in a given community stand as both a reflection of the intra-group social relationships and stratifications, and as an expression of the group beliefs about afterlife, the deceased's journey to the otherworld, and the possible influence and relationship between two worlds: the world of the living and world of the dead. A number of studies from the first half of the 20th century discuss burial/funeral rites, incineration and its occurrence among the natives of the Balkans and among the later Slavic colonists. Some of them mention the thesis that incineration was the older and more widespread type of burial among all Indo-Europeans. This argument does not seem to be supported by archeological evidence which implies that ground burials are in fact older, but at the same time strongly supports the assumption that ground burials and incineration existed side by side not only in different cultures but also within communities.[2] The available data show that incineration, since its first occurrence, had the same cultural contents as ground burial. The rite of incineration was connected with particular religious beliefs and accompanied by specific ritual behaviours and was part of social patterns

Since the beginnings of Christianity and within the borders of Christian civilization, ground burials began to replace cremations which came to be labelled as a heathen practice; in 785, Charlemagne issued a ban on cremations for the whole empire, threatening perpetrators with the death penalty. However, the custom of cremating vampires and such creatures was observed for a long time, so that a Code of Emperor Dušan (1331–1354) prohibited both the exhumation of the dead, their additional cremation, and their stitching with a hawthorn stick. In spite of this, the last "suspicious" dead was cremated in Bosnia in 1923 (Čajkanović 1994: 221). It is possible that the rulings of the Church and customary law made the persistence of cremations possible: according to the Church, suiciders and unbaptized individuals could not be buried in the church cemeteries, as was also the case with children born out of wedlock and all individuals who had not died of

---

[2] Erdeljanović 1922: 228; Vasić 1901: 1040; Vasić 1948: 188; Filipović 1959: 120; Ćorović 1956: 127; Trojanović 1901: 52.

a natural cause. Their burial was also prohibited in village cemeteries. But actually there is no firm evidence that these categories of deceased were cremated.

Although the Enlightenment and secularization changed the perception of death, death and burial nevertheless kept their religious character longer than other rites of the life cycle. Thus, for example, the number of people baptized, and especially the number of couples who married in the Serbian Orthodox Church in the second half of the 20th century steadily declined, while the number of dead buried with the participation of the Church has not changed (Shematism 1999: 253).

However, the idea of, and the movement for modern cremation, which dates back to the mid-19th century, can be called the beginning of the process of desacralisation of death. It appears that the first official initiative for modern cremation was launched at the international medical congress in Florence in 1869, although certain intellectuals, especially in Germany, had supported this idea even before this date (Oganj 1974, no. 1: 5). The first international congress on cremation, which took place in Dresden in 1876, gathered the ardent supporters of cremation from several European countries. Most participants came from various fields of medicine, but there were also representatives of other sciences and arts. The movement – which later became the International Cremation Federation (ICF) founded in London in 1937 – stood for the legalization of cremation. It justified its goal firstly with environmental needs and issues of modern humankind. The long process of decomposition of the body after a classic funeral and the survival of deadly bacteria were pointed out as serious sources of infection and potential dangers for the living. Apart from this, it was believed that cemeteries took up too much valuable living space and increased its price. These first reasons for accepting cremation were supplemented by others with the increased practice of cremation in more and more countries and at international conferences held in Düsseldorf (1926), Prague (1936) and London (1937) (Kujundžić 1936: 63; 1937: 69).

The greatest opponent of cremation was the Catholic Church which continued to call it a pagan practice and forbade its priests to take part in funerals of those whose body was to be cremated. Cremation supporters interpreted this prohibition with the fact that cemeteries were mostly the property of the Church and that burials gave the priests a certain income which they would otherwise lose. The first crematorium in Europe was built in Walking, England, in 1873, while the first cremation using special equipment was performed in Dresden in 1874. It appears, though, that the first official approval for optional cremation was obtained in Milano, where the first modern crematorium in Europe was built in 1876.

Unfortunately, 19th century statistics of the number of cremations are not available, except for the USA. The extant sources contain records on the number of cremations in the first decades of the 20th century.[3]

Although the idea of cremation appeared in Serbia as early as in the 19th century in the works and activities of the poet and doctor Jovan Jovanović Zmaj, local cremation supporters saw their dream come true only in 1964, when the first, and until 2004 only crematorium in the region opened in Belgrade. After Zmaj's death his friend and successor Vojislav Kujundžić, MD continued to fight for the "fiery idea", becoming one of its most ardent supporters in Serbia. In 1904, Kujundžić founded the Association of Cremation Supporters *Oganj* in Belgrade. The work of the association was supported by members of the Belgrade intellectual elite and by distinguished individuals from Serbian towns. Activists, members and supporters of the association were mainly doctors, artists, merchants, active and retired politicians and lawyers. The aim of the association was to have a crematorium built in Serbia so that some day the custom of burying the dead in the ground would be entirely replaced by cremation. These ideas and intentions were first propagated through published records of the regular meetings of the association, and, since 1934, the journal *Oganj* as an organ of the association. Cremation was propagated as a "more modern", "more humane", "more civilized", and "more hygienic" way of treating the mortal remains: as common practice in other European countries, as an ancient practice (for which the names of famous persons who were cremated were given), and as a benefit for the environment and the economy (Rad 1921: 5, 6, 7). Apart from this, numerous texts stressed the aesthetic side of the issue, some of them giving detailed descriptions of the process of decomposition of the corpse and pointing out the cleanliness and speed of modern cremation.

Apart from informing the public about the advantages of cremation, the association, that is, Dr. Vojislav Kujundžić (who was nick-named *Oganj*) persistently kept contact with the municipal institutions and state authorities for many years, requesting the legalization of cremation and construction of a crematorium in Belgrade. These activities were long conducted without any tangible results, due to, as stated in some places, the conservative environment and deep-rooted customs among the people. The main obstacle to the legalization of cremation, however, was the fact that the Serbian Orthodox Church, which had a significant social role and which has never, to the present day, changed its attitude towards cremation, strongly opposed it. According to lay interpretations, this intolerance was connected to the central Christian dogma on resurrection, but the real reasons why the (Serbian) Orthodox Church never approved of cremation are of a very different nature (Glasnik 1983: 127). Unlike the cremation supporters, however,

[3] Internet Cremation Society site: http://www.cremation.org; Rad 1921: 18, 23.

the church was never interested in informing the public about its position. This may have been unnecessary at a time when loyalty and obedience to Church discipline was taken for granted, but one can say that the failure to act at that time had a strong impact on the attitudes of generations to come.[4]

On the other hand, in public debates with the Church, representatives of the cremation supporters emphasized that their movement had nothing to do with faith and religion (Kujundžić 1934: 2). Some pre-war issues of *Oganj* emphasized: "The fiery movement is out of politics and religion." The members of the association even declared themselves as Christians, so in accordance with their Christian identity they did not deny belief in resurrection which they themselves hoped for, but rejoiced that they would be resurrected "from a clean urn", not from "rotting graves" (Rad 1933: 14).

Vojislav Kujundžić, who died in 1946 in Belgrade, did not live to see his dreams come true. He was buried in *Novo groblje,* and there are no data on whether a priest attended the funeral. However, his story did not end with this last "earthly" act. According to some data, the remains of his body were exhumed 18 or 22 years later by members of the association, cremated in Belgrade crematorium and placed in an urn in the Rosary No. 1 in *Novo groblje*. Describing this event, the last successor of Kujundžić and great champion of the idea, the famous doctor Aleksandar Kostić stated in the first post-war issue of *Oganj* in 1974: "We exhumed his *holy relics*,[5] burned them and placed them in an urn on 15 June 1968" (Milenković 1974a: 12).

Although placed in an honorary rosary, a vessel with Kujundžić's remains was not the first to find its eternal resting place in one of Belgrade's cemeteries. According to evidence from the municipal firm "Funeral Services", between 1914–1963 (the period before the Belgrade Crematorium was built), 24 urns were deposited in Belgrade's cemeteries. The deceased were mostly respected citizens of Belgrade whose remains had been cremated abroad in various Western European cities; in accordance with their own wishes, their urns were placed in existing family vaults in Belgrade.

As time passed, and cremation supporters were getting no closer to achieving their goal of legalization of cremation and construction of a crematorium, *Oganj* began to publish texts with more or less explicit anti-Church contents. Priests and the national-Christian funeral tradition were ridiculed through folklore motifs and

---

[4] Although in the second half of the 20th century only the Serbian Orthodox Church remained true to its position, records on the number of members of pro-cremation associations in the Yugoslav republics show that the majority of members were registered in Serbia (Oganj 1976, no. 5: 9).

[5] The expression "holy relics" (italics by A. P.) usually denotes non-decomposable bodies of Christian saints.

heavy criticism was directed against the teaching and practice of the Church. The last pre-war issue of *Oganj* was published in 1941. An attempt to revive the journal resulted in the publication of one double issue in 1946. The next issue was not published before 1974, and until 1994 the journal was issued only occasionally. During this 20 year break, the supreme and most important goal of the cremation movement was achieved: cremation was legalized by Yugoslav state laws, and a crematorium with a special funeral hall was erected on *Novo groblje* in Belgrade in 1964. Two years later, in 1966, the Catholic Church allowed its priests to perform funeral services for the deceased who were to be cremated, with only one restriction: the funeral service could not be performed in the cremation hall (Oganj 1974, no. 1: 11). The Orthodox Church did not change its attitude, but established a rule, i.e., a kind of selective permission for performing a funeral service before cremation: the right to a Christian funeral was granted to those deceased who were cremated not at their own wish, but at the wish of their heirs. If the deceased expressed his/her wish to be cremated, the funeral would have to be performed without a priest.[6]

As can be expected, in the early socialist period cremation became a part of the atheist philosophy of life. In addition to physicians, artists and intellectuals, declared opponents of Church and religion, military officers, former partisans and members of the Communist Party were most frequently among those who were cremated. Most of the slabs in rosaries and columbaria posted during the 1970s are not marked with a cross sign; when they are marked at all, it is usually the five-pointed star or, more rarely, the symbol of the profession of the deceased.

Oganj headings no longer had the anti-religious and apolitical features of the cremation movement, whereas newspapers often published texts which were openly against the Church and "Christian superstitions" (Milenković 1974b: 5). A text in the first issue of the new series of *Oganj* titled "Atheists, come together!" invites those who have "made a break with illusions" about life after death to decide for this type of funeral, and appeals to those who "fear the flame ..." because of resurrection to "come to their senses" (Nešović 1974: 9).

A new column titled "Why we opted for cremation" appeared in the newspapers, giving the answers of supporters of cremation. Their statements allow for conclusions as to the dominant reasons for cremation in the socialist period: aesthetic, environmental and hygienic arguments certainly account for the majority of answers, but there was often fear of decomposition and of the underground fauna living on corpses. In addition, and in contradiction to this fear, cremation was justified by the belief that religious superstitions about life after death were a matter of the past. The idea of immortality (of the souls of righteous persons) was

6 Since the 1990s, most Belgrade priests do not observe this restriction.

transferred to "deeds, pleasant memories and results of labour" (Oganj 1975, no. 3: 6, 7).

The last decades of the 20th century, especially the 1990s, brought new developments whose main feature was the disappearance of almost all rules concerning the social status, religious belief, professional or age group of the cremated. In the previous period, only the elderly were cremated, as well as confirmed atheists, people without family tombs, middle and upper class people, and those whose families by all means wanted to put them to rest in a prestigious cemetery. In recent years, cremation is performed for children and adults, the rich and the poor, believers and non-believers, those who have family tombs and those who do not.[7] In addition, members of the "neo-paganism" movement also prefer cremation because of their belief in the constant circulation of energy and substance in nature and in ideas of the ancient Slavic pantheon (Tucić 2005).[8]

The fact that urns containing ashes of the dead are increasingly placed in family vaults suggests the need of families to pay respect to their dead in one place. The survey among members of the *Oganj* association shows, however, that there are relatively few members who opted to cremate their loved ones for that reason; only 25% responded positively. Obviously, the reasons for cremation are not only practical but also ideological ones, which is confirmed by the new phenomenon of transporting the deceased from provincial towns to Belgrade for cremation and of taking the urn back and placing it in the family tomb. Such cases are indicative of the acceptance of cremation not only in provincial towns[9] but also in villages, particularly because such transport of the deceased significantly increases the costs of funerals.

In order to answer the question of whether the development of the idea of cremation indicates changing attitudes toward death in the Serbian population, one has to place the problem in its wider context of funeral rites and behaviours of those who cremate their dead as compared to traditional funeral rites.

The cremation funeral hall in Belgrade's *Novo groblje* is several times larger and more spacious than the chapels which are used for traditional funerals. Even though it does not display any religious items or symbols, its architecture is

---

7 Number of cremated according to the records of the Belgrade municipal firm "Funeral services": 1965: 11 (percentage not calculable), 1975: 228 (=4.1%), 1985: 469 (percentage not calculable), 1995: 1002 (=10.2%), 2004: 2258 (=21.12%).

8 In 2004, the Belgrade public was "shaken" by an event seen as a rebirth of pagan thought: the body of the well known Belgrade painter and publicist Dragos Kalajić was cremated without the knowledge and attendance of his family. This was done, as the press argued, by director and writer Dragoslav Bokan who, according to Kalajić's daughter, violated "the death taboo" (Jovanović 2005: 13). Unofficial sources argue that Bokan was familiar with the deceased latent Christian orientation and organized a Christian service, and then cremated the body.

9 Until the 1990s, only inhabitants of Belgrade were cremated.

reminiscent of a Byzantine style Orthodox church. The funeral rites do not differ profoundly from those at ground burials.

Parting with the deceased is performed in a procession around the coffin which is placed on a pedestal in the back of the hall, which, by its architecture, can be viewed as a kind of altar. According to employees, since the 1990s, priests have increasingly attended the ceremony and a cross has become more frequent.[10] As a rule, the cross is taken together with the coffin to the crematorium and is burned or kept, depending on the family's choice; in most cases it is burned which is probably related to the fact that the families without a family vault choose cremation more often, as they have no place to put the large wooden cross. The burning of the cross has, in any case, several meanings and shows a certain ambiguity toward religion.

In the ceremonies without a priest the family can choose or bring its own music to be played; at classical funerals in chapels there is no such option. The music played ranges from religious chants, classical and military music, to (not infrequently) pieces which the deceased especially loved. In the hall one can therefore hear popular rock and pop music.[11]

The behaviours of the mourners and those offering condolences do not depend on the type of funeral, but on the attitudes toward religion. Some people light candles, others do not, some kiss the cross and the coffin, while others only walk by or put flowers on it. At cremations there were no requests to have an open coffin during the ceremony, while this custom persists to some extent at classical funerals.[12]

A custom common to both types of funeral is the offering of specially cooked wheat, brandy and beverages. It is followed by a meal at the deceased's home or in a restaurant which marks the end of the funeral rites and the beginning of the post-funeral ritual practices. Here we find some significant differences between the two funeral types: after a classical funeral it is customary to offer a meal to all attendees at the deceased's home or in a restaurant, while after a cremation it is usually only a symbolic gathering of the closest relatives and friends at the deceased's home which may include some food and drinks, while sometimes this custom is omitted altogether.

After a classical funeral a first commemoration is held on the 40th day after death, attended by a priest and accompanied by the offer of grain and brandy; after a cremation, the families sometimes decide to place the urn on the 40th day after

[10] Mostly a large wooden cross placed in front of the coffin during the ceremony.

[11] At two ceremonies we attended the deceased were bidden farewell with the songs *Yesterday* by the Beatles and *Chiquitita* by ABBA.

[12] The employees said that there were only two or three such requests in the past years, all at classical funerals.

death. This kind of request is still rare, according to the cemetery employees, and the ceremony is not attended by a priest. There are, however, two significant elements which can be seen as rituals. The first is related to the act of placing the urn and the other involves traditional food offerings (Žečević 1982: 80). The procedure requires that one of the cemetery employees places the urn, but this can also be done by a relative of the deceased, usually one of the closest relatives or a close friend, who usually kisses the urn or honours the deceased by a minute of silence. The second element, the offering of food and drinks, is less frequent than at classical funerals and commemorations, but it is still observed. The same goes for the meal after the ceremony. The most striking answers of the informants concern their need to de-formalize the customs and not to observe the fixed and established days and dates. This is particularly emphasized by their behaviours and thoughts during traditional commemoration days such as half-annual and annual commemorations and All Souls Day. Most informants said that they visited cemeteries and their ancestors' and friends' graves only "sometimes", "when they feel like it", or "not that often". Only a small portion of the informants stated that they visit cemeteries on specific days, mostly on the birthdays or the anniversary of the death of the deceased, while no one even mentioned All Souls Day. However, all fifteen informants who had recently lost their loved ones and had cremated them, had observed, in one way or another, the half-annual or annual commemoration. Twelve of them also performed a religious ritual with a priest, but none visited the sites on All Souls Day. If the commemorations were attended by a priest, food and brandy were served, a fact that contradicts the attitude of cremation supporters who usually argue against food offerings in cemeteries.

Regardless of the differences in the observance and practice of funeral and post-funeral rites, the fact is that they depend less on the individual's resolve than on religious conviction. The only stable variable among the informants who chose cremation is their declared atheism or unclear religious belief.[13] The latter can explain the differences between their behaviours and their attitudes (expressed in the survey) which become explicit in their combination of heterogeneous patterns of ritual behaviour.

As for the motives for choosing cremation, financial reasons can be disregarded as both kinds of funeral cost about the same price. The environmental argument (which was prominent among the initiators of the cremation movement) was mentioned only by four supporters of cremation, while fear of decomposition of the body dominated in all responses.

---

[13] Although they say they are Orthodox Serbs (or even "Orthodox atheists"), their answers show a variety of "objects" of their faith: *I believe in "something", "in existence of some supernatural power", "a higher principle that rules the world", "in the harmony of natural elements"*, etc.

It appears that, from the very beginning, the environmental dimension of the cremation movement had a meaning that remained latent for a long time and became explicit only in the new historical and cultural context. It concerns a new attitude towards death which emerged over the last two centuries, linking different periods, developments and motives in the history of modern cremation of the dead: the need of modern individuals to (verbally, mentally and physically) eliminate death from their environment as soon and as imperceptibly as possible.[14] This need is expressed in the institutionalization of death and the specialization of activities connected with it in the contemporary, especially urban environment (Dušanić 2004: 586). Cremation, rather than classic funeral, is an efficient and quick way to eliminate traces of death from the world of the living. The reduction in funeral rites, which is especially evident in cities, finds its expression in parting before cremation which practically implies a shortened funeral ritual. As crematorium employees said, ever since the crematorium was built there have been only a few requests of relatives to attend the process of cremation.[15] There is also fascinating data that in the same period there were as many as 700 urns which no one claimed (Mirić 2004: 18). It is obvious that for the relatives of these deceased the "funeral" ended in the parting hall before cremation.

The wish of the initial cremation supporters that cremation should be made compulsory must be reconsidered from this viewpoint (Kostić 1974: 1). The same holds true for their belief that a time will come when cemeteries will disappear and the ashes of the deceased will be scattered in gardens of remembrance, or in places the deceased were especially fond of. This is why a "Garden of Remembrance" was established in Belgrade's *Novo groblje* in 1970, and until 1975 the ashes of 153 urns were scattered in it (Oganj 1974, no. 2: 7). Aleksandar Kostić openly argued for "sublimation", i.e., total destruction of all mortal remains (Kostić 1974: 1). As for the present period, it is indicative that the Garden of Remembrance is the least attended area of *Novo Groblje*; there are only very occasional vases with fresh flowers, even on All Souls Day when the rest of the cemetery is "flooded" with visitors.

What are the implications of removing traces of death from the world of the living? The perceptions of death among members of a community equally depend on their beliefs regarding the "afterlife" and on the values which are dominant in their lives on Earth. Being reminded of death may have a destructive impact on the

---

[14] In the words of an informant: *"Having watched funeral rites, I understood that every family wants to take the deceased out of their home as soon as possible, regardless of their sorrow and loss, as there is awkwardness and fear and some indescribable atmosphere at home, even at the cemetery and in the church until the deceased is either buried or cremated"*. Another one said: *"One should avoid ceremonies, as they trigger painful memories of the deceased"* (Milenković 1975: 7).

[15] These requests were often based on the suspicion that coffins are not burned, but resold.

community and the individual, but it may also represent a good reason to preserve certain ethical principles. The balance between chaos and order, sense and non-sense, is mainly achieved through various institutional mechanisms which place the reality of death in a particular position in society. Cemeteries have a significant role, being places of intensive remembrance of death. A society without cemeteries and other reminders of the finiteness of life may become a society without a constructive awareness of death, a society that, for fear of environmental disaster, will be in danger of spiritual disaster, even though the latter will, logically, result in the former.

References

Broj članova po republikama [Membership evidence by republics]. In: Oganj, no. 5 (1976) 9.

Ćorović, Vladimir 1956: Prilog proučavanju načina sahranjivanja i podizanja nadgrobnih spomenika u našim krajevima u srednjem vijeku [Contribution to the study of burial forms and tombs in our countries in the Middle Ages]. In: Naše starine III (Sarajevo) 127–147.

Čajkanović, Veselin 1994: Ubijanje vampira [Killing vampires]. In: Studije iz srpske religije i folkora 1910–1924 (Belgrade) 221–239.

Dušanić, Marjanović, Smilja 2004: Smrt i svetost [Death and sacredness]. In: Privatni život u srpskim zemljama srednjeg veka. Belgrade: Clio, 586–608.

Erdeljanović, Jovan 1922: Niderleovo delo o starim Slovenima [Niederle's work on the old Slavs]. In: Glasnik Geografskog društva 7–8 (Belgrade) 218–239.

Filipović, Milenko 1959: Spaljivanje mrtvih kod Južnih Slovena [Burning of the dead among the South Slavs]. In: Rad Vojvodjanskih muzeja 8 (Novi Sad) 119–131.

Jovanović, S. 2005: Porodica optužuje [The family accuses]. In: Kurir, 3 August (Belgrade) 13.

Jovanović, Zmaj, Jovan 1993: Pesme [Poems]. Novi Sad: Matica srpska.

Kostić, Aleksandar 1974: Posle 28 godina [After 28 years]. In: Oganj, no. 1: 1.

Kujundžić, Vojislav 1934: Religija u beogradskoj opštini [Religion in the Belgrade municipality]. In: Oganj, no. 5: 2.

Kujundžić, Vojislav 1936: Svetski ognjeni kongres [The world fiery congress]. In: Oganj, no. 9: 61–63.

Kujundžić, Vojislav 1937: Londonski kongres [The London congress]. In: Oganj, no. 9–10: 69.

Milenković, Milivoje 1974a: In memorian, dr Vojislav Kujundžić. In: Oganj, no. 1: 12.

Milenković, Milivoje 1974b: Sećanje na dr Jovana Jovanovića Zmaja i dr Vojislava Kujundžića [In memoriam Jovan Jovanović Zmaj PhD and Vojislav Kujundžić PhD]. In: Oganj, no. 2: 5.

Milenković, Milivoje 1975: Odlučio estetski momenat [Aesthetic reasons in first place]. In: Oganj, no. 3: 7.

Mirić, M. 2004: Ne ostanu ni dugmići [Nothing left after cremation]. In: Kurir, 23 December.

Nešović, Mila 1974: Ateisti na okup! [Atheists come together!]. In: Oganj, no. 1: 3.

Opredelili smo se za kremaciju [We opted for cremation]. In: Oganj, no. 3 (1975) 6–7.

Rad I godišnje skupštine društva "Oganj", održane u Beogradu 12 decembra 1921. godine [Paper from the 1st regular annual meeting of the "Oganj" association, held in Belgrade on 12 December 1921]. Belgrade 1922.

Rad XIV godišnje skupštine društva "Oganj", održane u Beogradu 30. aprila, 1933.god [Paper from the 14th regular annual meeting of the "Oganj" association, held in Belgrade on 30 April, 1933]. Belgrade 1933.

Razvoj krematističkog pokreta u svetu [Development of the world cremation movement]. In: Oganj, no. 1 (1974) 4–5.

Šematizam Eparhije šumadijske [The schematism of the Šumadija eparchy]. Kragujevac 1999.

Skinuta zabrana kremiranja [Abolishing the cremation ban]. In: Oganj, no. 1 (1974) 11.

Stav Srpske pravoslavne crkve prema kremiranju njenih vernika [The attitude of the Serbian Orthodox Church towards its believers]. In: Glasnik Srpske pravoslavne crkve (Belgrade 1983) 127–136.

Trojanović, Sima 1901: Stari slovenski pogreb [The old Slav funeral]. In: Srpski književni glasnik III (Belgrade) 50–60, 125–137.

Tusić, Živica 2005: Hrišćansko spaljivanje [Christian incineration]. In: Nin no. 2850 (Belgrade).

Vasić, Miloje 1901: Stari slovenski pogreb [The old Slav funeral]. In: Brankovo kolo 33 (Sremski Karlovci) 1040–1054.

Vasić, Miloje 1948: Jonska kolonija Vinča [The Ionian colony Vinča]. In: Zbornik Filosofskog fakulteta I (Belgrade) 85–237.

Zečević, Slobodan 1982: Kult mrtvih kod Srba [The cult of the dead among Serbs]. Belgrade.

Želja postaje stvarnost [The wish becomes reality]. In: Oganj, no. 2 (1974) 7.

New Urban Trends in Serbia, 1990–2004: From Urban Life to Popular Culture and Vice Versa

Ivana Kronja, Belgrade

Introduction

The aim of this paper is to explore representations of urban life in contemporary Serbia in the field of mass-media and cinema, and how popular culture in turn has influenced the ways, habits, and "rituals" of modern urban life in Serbia. For this purpose I will examine two significant examples: the phenomenon of "Silicone Valley", the popular café district in downtown Belgrade, and representations of the lifestyle of urban youth in the cinematic trilogy by director Radivoje Raša Andrić.

The question of the mutual influence between lifestyles and urban pop culture on the one hand, and the content of mass-media, on the other, is one of the most challenging of all the attempts to theoretically define the impact and significance of the media in the contemporary world. One does not need to be a scholar to recognize that mass-media play a tremendous role in individual, family and even professional time structuring and in the shaping of our political and cultural realities. As Croteau and Hoynes argue, "it is easy to see that near-constant exposure to media is a fundamental part of contemporary life ... Indeed, some argue that the media have become the dominant social institution in contemporary society, supplanting the influence of older institutions such as the educational system and religion" (Croteau, Hoynes 1997: 5). Cultural theorists predominantly perceive the contemporary world as a world of "media culture". Mass media, particularly television, prove to be interrelated with all other aspects of life. In her book "The Production of Culture", Diana Crane stresses that "television functions as a vast cultural arena in which certain types of information are available to all members of the audience. [I]n today's postmodern society, the cultural arena, rather than high culture, sets standards for culture and shapes popular taste" (Crane 1992: 50).

Post-communist European transitional countries, including Serbia and Montenegro, have also experienced the expansion of mass media, particularly television, which has become the key factor of family and social life. It exerts an enormous influence on political choices and the lifestyle of ordinary people. The breakthrough of the media through all forms of popular culture – popular music, fashion, entertainment – additionally reflects the growing orientation towards capitalism and consumerism in these societies.

In this light, I argue that the reality of urban life and culture in contemporary Serbia (and elsewhere) strongly depends on the continuous parley between media representations and role models, which create dominant paradigms in society, and the individuals' self-understanding within the social and political processes that define their status and lifestyles. Media contents play a crucial role in this development, shaping the reality of urban life and culture today to an unprecedented degree. During this process, Serbia is rapidly becoming part of the global media culture.

"Silicone Valley" and Belgrade contemporary nightlife: A subculture within the mainstream

The phenomenon of the so-called "Silicone Valley" dates back to the late 1990s in Serbia, and has continued up to the present, even after the fall of the Milošević regime. This phenomenon, being a recent one, has not yet been theoretically studied. My aim here is to present the case of the "Silicone Valley" as a specific youth subculture practice that has been, to my deepest conviction, initiated by mass-media representations of and, more precisely, instructions for modern youth urban lifestyle and gender roles. A deeper understanding and a possible proof of the direct influence of mass media contents on everyday urban youth culture cannot be achieved without serious scientific research. My report, though, is based solely on informal observation of Belgrade nightlife and dominant mass media contents, and some informal interviews. In this paper I can therefore only raise questions and trace some of the possible directions for future research.

I want to argue that "Silicone Valley", the popular café district in downtown Belgrade, together with some other popular clubs and discotheques represent the scene for a new urban subculture in post-Milošević Serbia, which could be called the "Silicone Valley" subculture. This subculture practice is a successor of youth subcultures associated with turbo-folk and pop-dance music formed in the early 1990s: these were the *"Warrior Chic"* subcultures (Marić 1996: 236–238), including *"Dieselmen",*[1] criminal youth, young war veterans, thugs, drug dealers, sponsored girls, and also intermingled with the new Serbian war-profiteering elite of the 1990s. The elite consisted of the Milošević family, politicians, military commanders, paramilitary warlords, nouveau riche businessmen and underground bosses, and turbo-folk singers, the erotic queens of folk. The "Silicone Valley" subculture maintains some of the values admired in *"Warrior Chic"* subcultures, while it also develops some new and authentic values and styles.

As was the case of youth subcultures of the early 1990s, which entered the mass media scene from a marginal position and became the widely practised mainstream of the 1990s, the "Silicone Valley" subculture also developed under

---

[1] Young, dangerous-looking men, wearing *"Diesel"* jeans.

the strong influence of mass media. This subculture is directly related to the effects of the so-called *"Pink culture"*, created by the namesake popular entertainment television station, on nightlife in Belgrade and other Serbian cities and on urban youth subcultures since the end of the 1990s. In this case we can speak of a certain boomerang effect, i. e., of a complex process where the gender role models for youth, created by a dominant mass culture embodied in *TV Pink*, had such a strong influence on Serbian society that they initiated a whole youth subculture practised in the "Silicone Valley" district in Belgrade and in similar café areas and clubs in other Serbian cities. The values of the subculture then returned as a content of mass media in fashion TV shows and entertainment programmes on *TV Pink* and similar television channels. They were shaped during the 1990s and include machismo, commodification of women, anti-civic behaviour, and the criminal values of the new Serbian war-profiteering elite, together with body culture, glamorisation of everyday life and Western-like capitalist-consumer cultural patterns.

Where is the "Silicone Valley" subculture practised? It occurs in the café area on Strahinjića Bana Street, in the old part of Belgrade rich in cultural heritage; at the discotheques *F-16* and *XL*, now known as *Drama*, also in the city centre; at night clubs on the barges on the Danube River, focussed around hotel *Yugoslavia* in New Belgrade; in cafés and discotheques in other Serbian cities, where folk-pop music is played or performed live; at many teenage and youth parties and partially at wedding celebrations, where it mixes with other (sub)cultural models, such as new folk culture, usually a "parent culture".

Why do I claim that we have a subculture here? First, there is the style – sport-macho or yuppie-nouveau riche for men, sexy for women. The female style and role are central to this subculture. We see the over-exaggerated details that stress female sexuality: long, mostly dyed hair, cut in the latest fashion, evening makeup, provocative clothing: tight dresses, short skirts, low décolletage, high heels, all the possible glamorous accessories and jewellery. The style resembles *R'n'B* and hip-hop music video styles, photographs in fashion magazines that have become accessible with globalisation, the latest designer collections and the appearances of TV presenters on *Pink* and sometimes other TV stations. The style perfectly corresponds to the female role of a sex object that all the female participants interject; the very title of "Silicone Valley" is a misogynist qualification referring to silicone implants in female breasts[2] (although breast shape is stressed, very few women here really have implants). Style uniformity also indicates that it belongs to a specific subculture.

---

[2] Of course, *Silicon(e) Valley* originally signifies the centre of the US computer industry, but in this context the title ironically mocks the presupposed low intelligence of the girls, who, like all "dumb blondes", have no brain but only breasts.

"Silicone Valley" subculture is the dominant teenage culture in Serbia. In the discotheques we find striptease dancers, young males with macho attitudes who "come to watch" both dancers and girl visitors, and young women self-designed in a porno-glamorous way, resembling the dancers, who are familiar with their own role as objects and hope to "catch" a guy. Promiscuous behaviour, typical of many teenage cultures, is understood here as a sort of "selling" and "buying" – borderlines between simple dating and more or less sophisticated prostitution are blurred, at least in the way the participants see their relationships. This brutal and unnecessary combination of rigid patriarchal subordination of women and post-modern hedonism without moral scruples seems to suit a society without a stable economy or civil role models for its youth. It seems that the youth understood too literally the confusing message of symbols of nationalism plus patriarchy plus glamour plus consumerism, which the entertainment programmes are full of.

Popular culture in Serbia during the Milošević era was largely defined by its political function. It provided the regime with both escapism for the masses and promotion of the above mentioned values, which could help keep the regime in power. These values were presented through specialized music and entertainment TV channels, such as *TV Palma* and *TV Pink*, established in 1991 and 1994 respectively. Turbo-folk and pop-dance music developed at the time as a fascinating musical hyper-productive industry, whose main advertisement was music videos and, later, television talk-show programmes. Ideological messages were delivered to the audience through the style, lyrics and statements of turbo-folk singers and television presenters.

The cult and culture of street criminals and the paramilitary warrior culture (pronounced "national-patriotism" by the local media propaganda), the pornographic glamour of *TV Pink*, criminal businessmen and "sponsored girls", and turbo-folk and dance music and style (as "porno-pop" music), which used to shape erotic imagination and the understanding of gender roles during the 1990s, also continue after 2000. Their influence is maintained by way of the tabloid press, folk-pop music culture, television entertainment programmes, and in the culture of buying and consuming foreign trademark fashion products and cosmetics, which have become accessible since the end of the 1990s and particularly after October 5, 2000 (when Milošecić was toppled). They also continued their life within the manifestations of the "Silicone Valley" subculture. The prevailing cultural practices of young people in Serbia show striking similarities with the visual and social models offered by domestic media.

"Minimal-action strategies" of ordinary urban youth in the film trilogy by director Radivoje Raša Andrić

At the opposite pole – or maybe it only seems that way – of this glamorous picture of urban youth culture stands the representation of the Belgrade urban youth lifestyle in the cinematic trilogy by director Radivoje Raša Andrić. This trilogy includes the following films: "Three Palm Trees for Two Punks and a Chick/Goldfish"[3] (1998), "Lightning!" (2001) and "When I Grow up I'll Be Kangaroo" (2004). Serbian film scholar Nevena Daković labels these and several other films coming from Serbian directors of the younger generation as the "Belgrade film school" (Dakovic 2004: 38–41). Daković considers the urban cult comedy *Mi nismo anđeli* ("We Are Not Angels", 1992)[4] by Srđan Dragojević, now a middle-aged film director, as the founding film of this school. According to Daković, this school "does not have a firm generational nucleus, but is rather a group of individuals belonging to successive generations, whose most significant films create a wave of various 'guerrilla' stories about urban losers" (Dakovic 2004: 38). Daković claims that in addition to the fact that all of these directors graduated from the Faculty of Dramatic Arts in Belgrade (FDU), or are close to completing their studies, what unites the work of them into a distinct school are their similar thematic interests and formal sensibility. This is embodied in the focus on the urban milieu of 1990s Belgrade, represented by a combination of popular Hollywood genre idioms and local cultural traditions, including the spirit of their own generation.

One of the school's predecessors is certainly the well-known 1974 nostalgic film *Grlom u jagode* ("Straight with Throat into the Strawberries") by Srđan Karanović[5] about the growing pains of his own generation (Dakovic 2004: 38). Other young directors who can be considered part of the "Belgrade Cinema Wave" are Dejan Zečević, Boban Skerlić, Srdan Golubović,[6] Mladen Matičević, Dušan Milić, and Miloš Petričić. Describing these works and authors as being formative for a film "school" or "style" may be a bit exaggerated in terms of film criticism, but they certainly have a lot in common regarding production conditions and style.

---

[3] In the original Serbian title, *"ribica"* has a double meaning: it refers both to a goldfish and to an attractive girl.

[4] The sequel *Mi nismo anđeli 2* ("We Are Not Angels 2") was released in 2005.

[5] Member of the famous "Prague school" of ex-Yugoslav directors, who had graduated from the celebrated Prague Film Academy, FAMU.

[6] Srđan Golubović also explored the topic of youth violence in a convincing social youth drama showing the disorder of post-war society, in his first fiction film *Apsolutnih sto* ("Absolute Hundred", 2001).

What makes Andrić's three films the most adequate for our analysis? Firstly, it is the continual historical perspective in his oeuvre which treats the development of youth over almost a decade: the first film shows a group of youngsters involved in a melodramatic gangster plot during the worst period of recent Serbian history, i. e., the height of Milošević's rule in the early 1990s; the second film describes Belgrade close to Milošević's fall on October 5, 2000, while the third depicts the continuing reality of post-Milošević times.

Furthermore, it is the continuity of style and topics within the trilogy that makes it noteworthy. Finally, I believe that the last film in the trilogy brings a valuable conclusion to the director's exploration of strategies for the emotional, cultural and even physical survival of the young urban protagonists and/or, as Daković says, "losers", within the troubled historical and political circumstances of civil war, poverty and the break-up of their country, but also within the social dislocation and cultural isolation of their world(s). Due to their exploration of the social and cultural survival strategies of young people in 1990s Serbia, the three films remain key films of the "Belgrade film school" for our analysis.

In terms of their aesthetic value, these films do not represent any substantial achievement, but still they are good films and among the best examples of this trend. The trilogy by Andrić has some elements of *auteur cinema,* understood in a Hollywood rather than a European sense. The auteur theory, which originated in the 1960s first in the US and then in Europe, provides legitimacy for "investigation of popular films that had previously been dismissed as 'trash'. Auteurs are directors who put a strong personal stamp on their films ... [I]nsights can be gained by comparing films of the same director" (Lacey 2000: 12). Today's understanding of auteur cinema in Europe stresses the artistically independent and elitist position of the film's author (as in the so-called "festival films"), while for American films it is fully accepted by critics that working within commercial genre idioms can also be a creative auctorial contribution. Working in the field of commercial cinema, Andrić uses the patterns of genre cinema in "Lightning!" as an author procedure: a great undertaking – bank robbery, teenage and youth comedy and even musical film.

In Andrić's trilogy we can distinguish certain recurring elements of personal style in the author's work. First of all is the prominence he gives the characters in the film plot, and his directing of the actors towards a realistic, relaxed and spontaneous action. Andrić also gives great significance to the elements of subcultural style in his young heroes' clothing, hairstyle, makeup etc. He uses these style signifiers as signs of the character's social and even ideological position within the youth micro-group, but also within society as a whole. Since they determine the hero's position, these signs play a key role in the narrative development. The young people's roles within the youth space, such as unemployed salesmen, musicians, DJs, music producers, or fashion models, also plays an important function in this context. Regarding his mise-en-scène, Andrić provides a realistic treatment of space and action in his films and a balanced rhythm. One of the main specificities of his directing style certainly is a recurring presence of vibrant, vigorous scenes of parties and rock concerts that represent pillars in his films' structure, contrasting with long, flat scenes of inaction that account for large portions of the films. These slow, almost contemplative scenes, in which characters carry on some general, abstract and even nonsense dialogues, are very typical of this director. The scenes have a deeper meaning than it might appear at first glance: they actually express the underlying fears, depression and unclear social position of his heroes.

It is also important to situate Andrić's oeuvre in the wider context of the cinema of ex-Yugoslavia and Serbia in the 1990s. Most members of the so-called Belgrade film school, and Andrić in particular, avoid the prevailing horrific atmosphere of the majority of Serbian cinema, which is preoccupied with topics and graphic depiction of social decay and violence. Some of the most distinct achievements of Serbian cinema of the period 1990–2000 are *Underground* (1995) by Emir Kusturica and *Bure baruta* ("The Powder Keg", 1998) by Goran Paskaljević. Kusturica's *Underground* "is a historical film which offers a framework for interpreting the current violent state of affairs in the Balkans" (Iordanova 2001: 112). Its usage of "magic realistic" style (Gocic 2001: 171–173) in combining war, violence and poetic images further underlines the complexity of the Yugoslav political and cultural heritage. Similarly, Paskaljević's "The Powder Keg" depicts "one night of Balkan madness as a small group of characters entangle in a series of violent vignettes. ... Paskaljević's aim in *Bure baruta* was to show how the war in Bosnia affected ordinary people who were not in the frontline" (Horton 1999: 3).

In her introduction to a programme of Serbian cinema of the past decade, curator Milana Vujkov states that the contemporary domestic cinema "serves as an appropriate metaphor for a nation's inner battle. It was devised as homage to ordinary people fighting valiantly to preserve the last shreds of decency in a society over-powered by fear. Held hostage by their home grown war-lords they were, ironically, often media-stereotyped along with them. These widely acclaimed films, scheduled in chronological order (1995–2000), are not about war, but the effects of war – on the young, the powerless and the civilized. In their distinctly different styles, they depict a universally human vulnerability, the irreversible imprint of choices individuals are forced to make in the face of collective historical circumstance" (Vujkov 2005: 1 f.).

The programme included works by Gorčin Stojanović (his film "Premeditated Murder", based on a novel by Serbian novelist Slobodan Selenić), Ljubiša Samardžić, Srđan Dragojević, and documentaries produced by B92-ANEM. Of these films, "The Wounds" by Dragojević is most obviously devoted to the exploration of youth cultures, showing a lot of violence and a tragic ending to its adolescent anti-heroes, who chose the path of crime and violence due to society's corruption, breakdown of civic values, and lack of any hope for a normal life.

But unlike Kusturica or Paskaljević, who created catastrophic narratives of "Balkan madness", or Dragojević, who gives a bitter critique of both the civil war in *Lepa sela lepo gore* ("Pretty Village, Pretty Flame", 1995), and of the criminalisation of society, which catches the young urban population in his "The Wounds", Andrić opts to remain within the boundaries of teenage comedies. This is due both to his escapism and his desire to explore the youth culture of the epoch with humour and an ironic distance. His trilogy, indeed, provides strong escapism from the difficult circumstances of the 1990s and beyond, but we would be making a mistake if we were to see it as some superficial, light content. Like the other films of the decade, as explained above by Vujkov, Andrić's films provide an analysis of the effects of war, this time on the youth, and of the choices individuals are forced to make due to the complicated and often hopeless historical circumstances.

The films

In the first film of the trilogy, "Three Palm Trees for Two Punks and a Chick/Goldfish" (1998), the heroes of the film face the gravest circumstances: civil war in the region, international sanctions, poverty and hyperinflation, and social decay. In a humorous manner, the film shows how these conditions forced people to abandon civil values and "decent" professions in order to survive. Namely, our heroes resort to some basic strategies of survival: the girl, Nadica, works for a phone sex agency, Lane's brother paints kitsch and pornographic canvases, and finally, Lane (the main character) and his best friend rob a bank – with Nadica's help. The dark reality of Serbia in 1993 (the time of the film's plot), when the criminalisation of society and hyperinflation, consciously produced by the regime, were at their height, would have produced such desperate attempts to make a living. But the film takes a step beyond reality into the genre of gangster-comedy, in which the main heroes, ordinary people who are losers in real life, decide to become gangsters. As one of the protagonists explains: "In order to remain sane, one must get out of here, and for that you need some cash." Still, the film realistically shows young people's sense of despair.

The film is particularly successful in depicting the atmosphere in a pyramidal bank scheme and its lascivious lady chief, in a brilliant interpretation by one of our best 'character role' actresses, Mirjana Karanović. The female director of the pyramid wears a glamorous but kitschy, erotically provocative outfit, hair and make-up in the best tradition of the notorious "Warrior Chic" of 1990s iconography. It is a bank where crowds of people invest money to live from the absurdly high monthly interest. The female director and corrupted guards only serve the invisible "Boss" (which is an allusion to Milošević himself, who was referred to as "Chief" or "Boss" by his closest collaborators). The secret plan goes that the main "Boss" would one day flee abroad with all the money previously collected from the clients, while that last day's entire deposits (about a million German Marks) would go to the bank director. A similar situation happened in reality with at least two pyramid schemes in Serbia, owned by so-called Boss Jezda and Dafina Milanović. These two people also escaped abroad, while according to their later confessions their banks' funds went to the Milošević family.

The bank director tries to run away with one of the main characters (Lane's best mate who works as a security guard in her bank), whom she tried to seduce earlier. She tells him about the secret plan: "It was all planned from the beginning, as you probably guessed." The most comical, and at the same time most tragic moment for our heroes comes when the night they had planned for the robbery, turns out to be the very night when the director would run away with the last money delivery. All the money is already gone from the bank's safe. But, of course, with the help of a little luck, which follows the desperate nature of the moment, and because of their naivety and good spirit, the heroes turn the situation into a victory, and safely run away with the money across a roof.

They are saved by an old woman, a hospitable neighbour, who lets them in through her window. This detail is very important: the scriptwriter and director explicitly favour old informal networks of friendship and the hospitality of ordinary people against the new, hostile surroundings in the urban environment, where corruption and money run the game and "humans are a wolf to their fellow citizens". The very real, albeit minimal strategies of youngsters to survive within the regime, i.e., to participate in the society's corruption by gaining only a little money, are therefore humorously overcome by a poetic happy ending: they end up on an exotic beach with three palm trees and a fish in the sea – which is what the main character Lane has always dreamed of.

The second film "Lightning!" (2001) is a teenage music comedy which follows the "girl and a gun" recipe.[7] It depicts Belgrade in the second half of the 1990s. Like all other Serbian films using elements of this genre, this one is also immersed in its social context. For example, Skerlić's film debut *Do koske* ("Rage", 1997), which was advertised as the "first domestic action film" and was directly inspired by new representations of violence in American movies (Slocum 2001: 1), "still has a recognizable social background atypical for average stylised violence mainstream cinema" (Kronja 2004: 2).

---

7 According to French sociologist Edgar Morin, "the gun", or "girl & a gun" are one of the constant motifs of the "universal mass culture", spreading from the US all over the globe (Morin 1962).

In "Lightning!" Andrić is preoccupied with music-related youth subcultures more than in any of his other films. The film is visually well designed, with superb styling of its protagonists, two main heroes and two heroines, of which three (two boys and one girl) actively produce music. Our main heroes are Serbian hip-hoppers, creating the first Serbian drum'n'bass project, whose clothes and total styling are completely "hip" and expensive. These stylish outfits are contrasted by the heroes' problems with cash – they are unemployed and broke. At one point in the film the two boys decide to secretly sell their father's and brother's substantial possessions – a Black & Decker machine and a collection of records – in order to collect money for the release of their CD. The girls, unfortunately secondary in the story narrative, which is typical of Serbian cinema, are two best friends; one of them plays hard-core music, desperately trying to organize the first performance of her band in the rock-club *Dno* ("Underdog").

As was the case with the first film, here again we see the contrast between the lives of youths and "normal" life: we find two main heroes at home, still sleeping in the late morning, while their mothers complain that they are doing nothing – neither studying nor making anything for a living – and curse them. They escape to a cellar adapted to an improvised recording studio, to make music.

The owner of the rock-club and main music producer in the city represents the "new debutants" (Maric 1996: 250), the criminal *turbo-diesel* urban youth subcultures of the 1990s: he is the one who has the cash and guns, and who is in the (new) position to threaten representatives of the "alternative" music subculture, such as our heroes, and decide whether their album will be released and whether they will play concerts. In terms of the relation between media and youth music subcultures, we can say that our heroes are facing a constant obstacle which they are trying to overcome throughout the entire film: the problem of how to enter the next "stage" of their position within the hierarchy of youth community and music production, i.e., to release an album, step out of anonymousness and improve their status.

They cannot make this step because of the now-powerful intruder (whom they had harassed in primary school), Gojko, coming from the new, rough militant "Warrior Chic" subculture of the 1990s. One of the ways this new subculture proves its predominance is by controlling the "more urban" music. In the film we do not see Gojko actually enjoying turbo-folk or some similar music, but his looks and manners explicitly belong to the notoriously "criminal" iconography of the 1990s. Gojko is actually usurping the cultural capital of "authentically urban" music subcultures, appropriating the power to create and define who is going to be "hip" – i.e., to occupy the most prestigious position on the subcultural scene. British sociologist Sarah Thornton sees "hipness" as a main indicator of what she defines as subcultural capital – a form of cultural capital (as defined by Bourdieu) typical of youth subcultures (Thornton 1995). "While subcultural capital may not convert into economic capital with the same ease or financial reward as cultural capital, a variety of occupations and incomes can be gained as a result of 'hipness'. DJs, club organizers, clothes designers, music and style journalists and various record industry professionals all make a living from their subcultural capital" (Thornton 1995: 12). The tension between Gojko's power to usurp this specific form of capital and the real value of the alternative urban heritage greatly defines most of the film's plot.

In his study "The Culture of Power in Serbia" (1999), American sociologist Eric Gordy reveals the techniques of Milošević's regime to destroy political, informational, social, and finally musical alternatives. Gordy reports that the protagonists of youth subcultures in 1990s Serbia were involved in an ideological battle using music as a means: former leaders of the pro-Western musical youth subcultures of the 1980s found themselves totally pushed out by the new urban protagonists, by militant subcultures of criminal youth and the new, war-profiteering Serbian elite that praised nationalist and consumer-oriented neo-folk and turbo-folk music (Gordy 1999: 115–175). In my own study on turbo-folk music, "The Fatal Glow: Mass Psychology and Aesthetics of Turbo-Folk Subculture" (2001), in the analysis of the visual style of turbo-folk and pop-dance music videos, I showed how the iconography of popular urban subcultures – such as rock, hippy, or rave – had been appropriated by the initially marginal and later dominant "Warrior Chic" subcultures related to turbo-folk music and incorporated into their iconography and rhetoric of power (Kronja 2001).

The uncertainty and uneasiness of the position of the leading male heroes is also manifested by "low-budget" sexual economizing during the course of the film: although from the very beginning one of the main preoccupations in their conversations – the other one is, naturally, music – is the desperate desire to "get laid", this will not happen to them until the end of the film, and both guys will have to satisfy themselves only with a few shy kisses, as if their "masculine" power directly depends on their success and status within the music industry – which is not so unusual for youth music subcultures.

Symbolically, the narrative shows the co-existence of "normal", middle-class citizens with the new criminal elite. The middle class is not as humiliated as in the early 1990s, as depicted in "Three Palms ...". Now the heroes have good clothes, they have food, but they are still strongly dependent on the will and power of people who assume the highest positions in this new re-distribution of wealth, power and influence, and who can – in terms of cultural and subcultural capital – usurp and appropriate these capitals from people who previously had laid claim to them. There is also an interesting comparison with the 40-year-old "veterans" of the urban youth & music subculture scene, whom our heroes met at their "decadent" party in a dilapidated urban flat, while previously we watched youngsters having fun in a stylish, bourgeois and fully refurbished apartment.

A policeman and a drug and pill dealer, who will join our heroes for their night of adventure, also belong to this generation. Although these two generations of "normal" (i.e., non-turbo-folk, non-nouveau-riche) urban protagonists have different origins – the 1980s of Yugoslavia's peaceful experience and the 1990s with civil war and social decay – they come together in these post-war circumstances. The film ends with a middle-aged policeman and two young musicians brought together in an old car on the roof of a city public garage at dawn. This image offers a possible solution to the previous urbicide[8] of the 1990s. It suggests reconciliation and union of all urban protagonists who steer clear of the patterns of militant culture(s) and violence.

The third film in the trilogy, "When I Grow Up I'll Be Kangaroo" (2004), is Andrić's most mature work to date. Although this film is a teenage comedy, its story is in fact tragic. The film depicts sad characters: a young man who suffers a nervous breakdown overwhelmed by fear that he will lose the girl that he loves; the girl who is hurt and left without a boyfriend; a group of young men who sit on a roof all day and night, without job or verve, and desperately shout the names of girls they had secretly desired into the night without any answer; local young and middle-aged men living off betting and longing for a more fulfilling life, etc.

The film's narrative portrays a deep social crisis, perceived as a crisis of masculinity. This crisis affects men of all ages and consequently women of all generations. The fact that the problems of these people are illustrated through humorous situations makes the depth of their pain even more visible. Still, the film's focus is on the younger generation and its "minimal-action strategies" for emotional survival. Showing its characters' apathy, lack of perspective, and fitting into the lifestyle of not working and willingly "doing nothing", the film actually depicts the low aspirations, restricted dreams, and "post-Milošević" depression among the young as well as the adult population.

The film's plot unfolds during a single day. The main hero, Braca, has a date with a girl who works as a fashion model, and plans to take her out to the movies. But the objective circumstances – lack of audience in the movie theatre, cruelty of the theatre staff – and his insecurity connected to his own position – he is studying film editing, without money and a good status – is so deep that he does not succeed in establishing a normal relationship with this young woman. The girl is also uncertain whether she can give him any confidence, since she is aware that she is only perceived by society as "a stupid model with her stupid personality" (a line from her inner monologue). The date ends in a disaster, since Braca gives a

---

[8] In discussing narrative forms in 1990s Serbian prose and cinema, David Norris applies the term "urbicide", originally used in a book on Belgrade during the 1990s by Sreten Vujović (1997). Vujović uses the term to express the destruction of the capital city, and Norris sees this process as the main topic of the novels and films he analyses (Norris 1998).

speech of hatred towards models, mannequins, fashion and all people connected to the media, and there is nothing left for the girl, Iris, to do except to leave in order to salvage her dignity. Although she phones him on his mobile phone near the end of the film, it remains uncertain if they will ever see each other again. The long scene in an empty cinema hall, where Braca and Iris desperately await the beginning of the screening, signifies on a symbolic level the emptiness in the lives of ordinary young people, which cannot be fulfilled with any meaningful and rewarding activity due to the social crisis.

At the same time, Braca's friends are expecting an important football game, in which their former street friend, whose nickname is Kangaroo, plays for the English club Eastwich. Young and middle-aged men gather in the evening to watch the game at a local café, excited about their bets. The only women present are Kangaroo's mother and his ex-girlfriend, the waitress, who is now dating the local thug. The criminal (played by a Serbian sports star) stops by and harasses the group excited in anticipation of a victory by Kangaroo's team. The situation perfectly depicts Serbia in transition and globalisation: a single very successful man, Kangaroo, is seen only on the TV screen, seeming distant and unapproachable; the nation's destiny is to "play for the other team", i.e., to work for the more powerful countries such as the UK, both at home and abroad.

The group watching the game include a hysterical taxi driver, a gigolo telling stories of the "good old times" and selling stolen suits, a shrewd professional gambler, Cile, and two or three men without any indicated occupation. They are joined by two representatives of the young generation, who seem to live the same life: they have no jobs, money or girlfriends, and try to gain some cash by betting (they don't prove to be very successful even at that, since one of them secretly sells the winning ticket to the gambler and consequently loses most of their money). The scene is completed by the jailed criminal and a harmless fat imitator of a famous ex-Yugoslav sports commentator, who "doubles" as the television commentator.

The third thread within the plot gives an even graver example of young men in crisis: two guys sitting on the roof of an old skyscraper all day long, drinking beer, sharing a joint and discussing how one can get rich, for instance by making a fortune out of an insurance if he finds a dead bug or a piece of a mouse in a beer bottle(!). When their third mate, a fresh real estate agent who uses public transportation since he earns very little – and therefore his hard work seems pointless – asks them: "Why are you guys not doing anything?", one of them will reply in the spirit of the sad philosophy of the young generation, which feels deprived of its very existence: "Can't you see, bro, it's like this. I am the most economical: I have no income, but I also have no expenses."

While men are unemployed, young women, Iris and the TV presenter, are connected to the mass media oligarchy – such as *TV Pink* – being steadily employed by fashion industry and news production, although not at a higher, decision-making level. This polarisation of occupation reflects the consequences of globalisation and economic crisis in Serbian society for (young) men. Their position is inferior and their relationship to women is medialised: like Braca, they dream of attaining the women whose attractive image is projected by the media, but don't have the economic power to reach them. The new social rules make common men incapable of gaining money and women, and the media give them only an unattainable image of a glamorous, sexually fulfilling life embodied in the billboard commercials and fashion shows that Iris works for.

Only a miracle can move things in Serbia from a standstill, and this miracle will come from the heavens: one of the guys on the roof sees a flying saucer in the night sky (it is worth noting that at the beginning of the film the two young men with a betting ticket go to a church to ask God for help; their desire is fulfilled and Eastwich wins the game, but they still lose the big prize). A neighbour saw the flying saucer too, but he fails to confirm it for a radio station audience, offering vague conspiracy theories instead. The real estate agent tries to use this event for fame and fortune, and brings a TV crew with an overbearing reporter to the roof. But his mate refuses to speak as a witness, and the TV crew angrily leaves in search of further "sensations" – in fact, other people in the countryside also reported the strange incident. The last film sequence takes place on the roof at dawn, when the guys together with Braca open up their hearts and shout out loud the names of their frustrated loves. It seems that "the intelligent aliens", after all, brought a miracle: these "invisible friends" taught them that to start solving the problem you must speak out your frustration. The episode involving the "flying saucer" therefore stands as a powerful metaphor for the position of young people and adults in Serbia and brilliantly concludes the entire film.

Conclusion

Within the trilogy Andrić explores three of the possible responses of youth to the difficult circumstances of their existence in Milošević's and post-Milošević Serbia: active participation in the grey economy, symbolic rebellion within the field of popular music and culture, and a passive, "doing nothing" stance, practised by depressed young people after the great social turmoil. By this, Andrić offers a precise record of young people's behaviour in contemporary urban Serbia and depicts their responses to the major problems of society. Andrić's choice to use genre idioms of teenage comedy, crime and fiction is made deliberately. It stems from the desire to offer a comforting narrative to a devastated audience as well as from his strong affection for all aspects of the local, and general popular youth culture.

References

Crane, Dianna 1992: The Production of Culture. London: Sage.

Croteau, David, William Hoynes 1997: Media/Society: Industries, Images, and Audiences. London, Thousand Oaks: Pine Forge Press.

Daković, Nevena 2004: Beogradska filmska škola: gerilci i luzeri [The Belgrade film school: Guerrillas and Lucifer]. In: Vreme, No. 692, 8 April 2004: 38–41.

Gocić, Goran 2001: Notes from the Underground: the Cinema of Emir Kusturica. London, New York: Wallflower Press.

Gordy, Eric D. 1999: The Culture of Power in Serbia: Nationalism and the Destruction of Alternatives. Budapest: CEU.

Horton, Andrew J. 1999: Vignettes of Violence. Different Attitudes in Recent Yugoslav Cinema. In: Central Europe Review 1, 18, 25 October 1999. Internet: http://www.ce-review.org/99/18/kinoeye18_horton1.html.

Iordanova, Dina 2001: Cinema of Flames – Balkan Film, Culture and the Media. London: bfi Publishing.

Kronja, Ivana 2001: Smrtonosni sjaj: masovna psihologija i estetika turbo-folka [The fatal glow: Mass psychology and aesthetics of turbo-folk subculture]. Belgrade: Tehnokratia.

Kronja, Ivana 2004: Violence as a Cause and a Response to Frustration: Serbian Cinema and Violence Culture, 1990–2004. Paper presented to the conference "Cultures of Violence", University of Oxford, 2004. Internet: http://www.inter-disciplinary.net/ati/violence/v5/kronja%20paper.pdf.

Lacey, Nick 2000: Blade Runner. York Film Notes. London: Longman, York.

Marić, Ratka 1996: Značenja potkulturnih stilova – istraživanja omladinskih potkultura [The meanings of subcultural styles – Studies of youth subcultures]. PhD thesis, University of Belgrade.

Morin, Edgar 1962: L'esprit du temps. Paris: Editions Bernard Grasset.

Norris, David 1998: Narativne forme u prozi i filmu devedesetih godina: Priče o Beogradu [Narrative forms in prose and film of the 1990s. The story of Belgrade]. In: Književnost. Lettre Internationale/Međunarodno pismo, srpsko izdanje 11–12: 2024–2053.

Slocum, J. David 2001: Introduction – Violence and American Cinema: Notes for an Investigation. In: ibid. (ed.), Violence and American Cinema. New York, London: Routledge, 1–34.

Thornton, Sarah 1995: Club Cultures: Music, Media and Subcultural Capital. Cambridge: Polity Press.

Vujkov, Milana 2005: Introduction. In: [flyer for the exhibition:] No Exit at the Institute of Contemporary Arts, London, Essential Serbian Cinema, 1995–2000, 4– 6 November 2005.

Vujović, Sreten 1997: Grad u senci rata: Ogledi o gradu, siromaštvu i sukobima [The city under the shadow of war. Observations on the city, poverty and conflict]. Novi Sad, Belgrade: Prometej, Institut za sociologiju filozofskog fakulteta u Beogradu.

Abstract

While discussing the examples of the phenomenon of "Silicone Valley", the popular café area in downtown Belgrade, and of a cinematic trilogy by Radivoje Raša Andrić, the paper aims to explore representations of urban life in contemporary Serbia in the field of mass-media and cinema, and, conversely, how popular culture has influenced the ways, habits, and rituals of modern urban life in Serbia.

Belgrade Graffiti: Anthropological Insights into Anonymous Public Expressions of "Worldview"[1]

Dragana Antonijević and Ljubomir Hristić, Belgrade

Introduction

Graffiti refer to anything that is drawn, painted, scratched or scribbled on any surface visible to the public. They appear mainly in modern city streets, but they are also seen in passages, stairways, on buildings, and fences; nearly all are on white, clean walls that become "desecrated" by the act of graffiti writing. As a way of expressing one's "worldview", graffiti are part of something that could be characterised as "folk epigraphy",[2] a form of verbal and artistic expression. Although the writing of graffiti has a long history, according to some authors, they began to change drastically during the early 1960s as a result of the Civil Rights Movement, when they became more literate, self-conscious, and concerned with political and social issues (D'Angelo 1976: 102 f.).

In the post-modern city of the 20th century, as understood by Jean Baudrillard, graffiti become a legitimate part of the urban culture as a space for signs, media and codes. Urban messages in the form of graffiti operate as signs having a certain meaning. As for the expressional aspect, graffiti messages are mainly aggressive and active, their goal being to reach into the public. According to the contents of graffiti and their meaning, we can distinguish social, political, cultural, subcultural, and countercultural messages. Evidently, "graffiti deal with a wide range of significant contemporary topics; they throw light on usage, slang, idioms and dialects, and reflect contemporary customs and moral values. They give intimate details about everyday life" (D'Angelo 1976: 105).

The rationale for graffiti to be written and read is their basic expressive and communicative function within the complex semiology of a city. Whether by their content or location, graffiti are an "eyesore", calling one's attention to them. One never finds graffiti where they cannot be seen by others. Graffiti writing is both a concealed and public action bringing new elements of understanding and behaviour

---

[1] The research is the result of the ongoing scientific project "Anthropology in the 20th century: Theoretical and Methodological Perspectives", funded by the Ministry of Research and Science of the Republic of Serbia (project grant no. 147037).

[2] We think a distinction should be made between graffiti and wall painting, although they are often considered as one form. We distinguish graffiti found in streets and other public spaces also from *"latrinalia"*, i. e., inscriptions on restrooms and toilet graffiti. The folklorist Alan Dundes was the first to use the term "latrinalia" (Dundes 1966).

into existing urban cultures. It is an obscure act, for almost no one has ever seen anyone writing graffiti, and the majority of people swear they have never written one. At the same time, it is a public and profoundly social act that consciously intents to convey and publicly express certain personal notions, ideas or opinions. "In this sense, graffiti is a 'peephole' into minds of individuals who speak not only for themselves but also for others like them and thus reflect current social conditions and community concerns" (Klingman, Shalev 2001: 405).

Graffiti communication is specific, never oral, and never face-to-face (as is typical in folklore communication), it is a "silent conversation among anonymous partners" (Bruner, Kelso 1980: 240). The graffiti author is by definition anonymous, probably a younger person,[3] eager to state his/her opinion, approval, or more often disapproval of official values, ideas and ideologies of the community. On the other end of the communication chain is the recipient of the message – an accidental, anonymous passerby who is an unwilling reader of graffiti at the same time, and whose reaction, indifferent or not, remains unknown to us in most cases. And yet, there is another type of graffiti reader who finishes the message by editing, erasing or adding words to it, sometimes altering its basic meaning. In this way, graffiti become an open semantic ground, a wall paper, an invitation for adding new messages and meanings.

By their humorous, wise, obscene, vulgar, potentially subversive, (non-) tolerant and alternative ideas, graffiti as part of urban folklore and communication are symbols of a subculture. We consider the subcultural dimension of graffiti to be especially significant, given that the primary objective of these urban messages is to influence various social groups, preferably bringing about certain changes in the very field of culture. Many subcultural occurrences eventually become part of a given culture's mainstream. For example, this process is noticeable in mottos, messages, slogans and graffiti written during the political rallies in Serbia in the winter of 1996/7. Then that phenomenon was oppositional and subcultural, opposing mainstream culture, even countercultural at that time. Subsequent to the triumph of the democratic forces in 2000, many of these messages inconspicuously and almost imperceptibly became part of the contemporary official cultural, political, and social scene in Serbia.

Opinions on whether and to what extent the contents of graffiti actually reflect dominant cultural values, or confront them are divided. Stocker et al. suggested that graffiti "reveal patterns of customs and attitudes of a society, and are accurate indicators of the social attitudes of a community. Their thematic content will discriminate similar communities with different socio-political ideation" (Stocker

[3] Some authors even consider graffiti "as a gateway for accessing the *discoursive space of youth culture*" (Best 2003: 828).

et al. 1972: 358).[4] However, Gonos et al. disputed the idea according to which "collective conscience is only reflected, not refracted or inverted in this medium," suggesting that graffiti are mainly used to express values which oppose those dominant in the culture of a given time (Gonos et al. 1976: 40). They too had analysed graffiti on university campuses in the U.S. and, against their expectations, found out that the majority of graffiti on liberal universities were opposite to the official liberal trends concerning rights of homosexuals, feminism, or greater numbers of black students. Consequently, the more conservative universities proved to have far more pro-liberal graffiti. On that ground they concluded that "the relative frequencies of different thematic contents of graffiti will vary *inversely* with relevant dominant values of the social milieu in which the graffiti are found. What we call expressive graffiti may not be a direct reflection of a dominant community value-system at all, but a manifestation of that content which is proscribed, restricted or taboo in the graffitists' ordinary circle of social life" (Gonos et al. 1976: 41 f.).

Some other social scientists also stressed graffiti as a "symbolic form of resistance", as a counter-hegemonic response to hegemonic categories, while others attach greater importance to the authors' ties with local situations and a variety of social factors than with macro-political and ideological issues (cf. Best 2003: 830).

There are, of course, other theoretical approaches to graffiti which not necessarily come from socio-cultural studies. This is, for example, the position of the new literary criticism by which "graffiti represent text and thus can be explicated by close analysis of the words themselves, without emphasis on the social and historical factors" (Best 2003: 830). Today's interactive and technological age of the "secondary orality", which "generates a sense for groups immeasurably larger than those of primary oral cultures", facilitates alternative readings of graffiti (Best 2003: 830). Insofar, post-culturalist approaches ascribe to graffiti the potential to mean anything that their wide audience wants them to mean.

Mainstream culture looks down on this outburst of anonymous messages that "blemish" the city's appearance. Graffiti are usually negatively viewed as acts of vandalism, destruction, violence, inadequate responses, etc. Therefore, the everlasting conflict between anonymous graffiti sprayers and the city authorities, who constantly erase and remove graffiti, represents a special feature of the urban semiotic war. During this research, we witnessed graffiti erasing *in situ* enacted by the city government at the end of 2004. Unintentionally, we found ourselves in a

---

[4] Stocker et al., for example, state that "most homosexual graffiti are a result of societal condemnation of homosexual behavior, which permits this behavior to be used as an insulting device; and, with Gay Liberation as liberalizing influence, homosexual graffiti will decrease" (Stocker et al. 1972: 358).

race with the "graffiti cleaners" endeavouring to document what would be erased in a matter of minutes in front of our own eyes.

Street graffiti in Belgrade

We conducted our research with the assistance of several students of ethnology and anthropology[5] in Belgrade's broader city centre[6] during autumn and winter 2004/5. We were interested in documenting the existing graffiti inside this time segment and in detecting the type of messages they were conveying. The assumption was that this synchronised fragment would give us an idea of the current frame of mind of the graffiti authors, as well as their alternative view of the present of which we all are part. On the other hand, the research on Belgrade street graffiti had a diachronic dimension as well. We were interested in determining whether graffiti contents had changed compared to the period of 1996–2000, when the largest proliferation of graffiti in Belgrade was noticed.

Our research method was quite common for this kind of investigation. We took photographs and notes of graffiti and then proceeded with content analysis. We took a semiotic approach to thematic and communicative aspects of graffiti, assuming that there are many levels of meaning. Communication with others is possible, provided a certain amount of common codes and mental schemes are shared by the participants in the communicative act. The meaning directly depends on the relations between concepts, matters and signs and is constructed by a system of representation (Hall 1997). We tried to identify the surface text, which contains the manifest message, with often one and the same manifest meaning and, whenever possible, the underlying meaning of the graffiti message according to specific social, political or cultural factors. However, such an approach has its shortcomings, since it is sometimes difficult, or almost impossible to determine when, why and to what end a graffiti was created, unless its contents unambiguously reveal its position towards well-known events and persons. The texts were then divided into categories according to their content.

In 1996, civil unrest caused by the outright manipulation of the local elections of that year and the theft of the opposition's election victory by the ruling regime forced the population to the streets, commencing peaceful protests. The leadership

---

[5] The Belgrade streets graffiti research and analysis has been conducted within the course in Anthropology and Folklore of the Department of Ethnology and Anthropology at the Faculty of Philosophy in Belgrade. The participants were assistant professors Dragana Antonijević and Ljubomir Hristić, and the (postgraduate) students Dunja Njaradi, Deana Jovanović, Maja Ilić, Bojan Tepavčević and Damir Matas.

[6] This comprises the city municipalities Stari grad, Vračar, Savski venac, Zvezdara, Palilula, Novi Beograd and Zemun.

of the protest was soon assumed by the opposition parties, with participation from the student population of Belgrade University. This mass event went on until the results of the elections were acknowledged by the Milošević regime by a special law. The enormous, potentially subversive energy released during the protest, proved the existence of a community which showed a high degree of closeness, freedom, humour, creativity and democratic spirit, and which turned itself into a uniquely political carnival. At that time, the streets became a popular ground for political battles and clashes between the mainstream and marginal discourses.

Graffiti writing, especially that with a political content, was accepted as a legitimate means of rebellion and struggle against Slobodan Milošević's regime, with the obvious function of a socio-psychological vent, a form of distraction from economic tensions. Aside from graffiti, the popular means to express counterculture were badges, different signs, stickers, cups, tee shirts with subversive prints, etc. Such material formed a non-verbal utterance for the transmission of political messages. The opposition's lack of access to the media made walls a suitable place for expressing anti-regime attitudes. As a reminiscence of that period remain graffiti such as: "We have no media, we have walls" *(Nemamo novine – imamo zidove)*.

After Milošević lost the elections of 2000, a change in the government and ruling ideology took place in Serbia, as expressed by graffiti such as:

"Die Slobo" *(Umri Slobo)*

"Slobo you're done with" *(Slobo padaš 100%)*

"Hit the road Slobo" *(Slobo, odlazi!)*

"He's finished!" *(Gotov je!)*

"You blew it Slobo!" *(Slobo, popušio si ga!)*

The later political crises were also mirrored on the walls. We found graffiti that protested against DOS, the coalition of the Democratic Opposition parties, which had been in power in Serbia from 2001 till 2003. These slogans, which express opposition to the new government, are supposed to have been written by members of the ultra-nationalist Serbian Radical Party, glorifying also the party's president (Vojslav Šešelj):

"We save Serbia – DOS sucks" *(Spasimo Srbiju, DOS je najgori)*

"Democracy stinks!" *(Demokratija smrdi!)*

"Šešelj Serbian hero" *(Šešelj srpski junak)*

Similar to these are the graffiti that emerged as a response to the beginning of Slobodan Milošević's trial in The Hague, such as "Slobo Saviour" *(Slobo slobodo)*. However, the key feature of the graffiti we recorded is the proliferation of different themes drifting away from the direct, daily political events. There are graffiti that penetrate the socio-cultural, national, and ideological issues of the society in a more profound manner. Most often this group of graffiti transmit a violent message.

Guaranteeing anonymity, walls provide the liberty to insult and belittle those who are of a different sexual orientation, nationality, or political belief.

The number of graffiti with purely local, narrow significance took us by surprise. Obviously, they were "markers" of presence of certain social groups (school students, neighbours, and fans) in a given area. This group of graffiti authors communicates with a small group of recipients, primarily addressing those familiar with local meanings and peculiarities.

Among the non-violent graffiti with rather idiosyncratic contents are those expressing individual, philosophical and identitarian meditations, including those that could be described as "anti-discourse", i. e., graffiti with unintelligible messages. The latter can only be analysed from the standpoint of new literary criticism, which assumes that "the meaning is the message, and that graffiti mean what the graffiti say, without any attempt to interpret the text" (Bruner, Kelso 1980: 240).

Ethnic intolerances

The most aggressive, politically and nationally non-tolerant and potentially most dangerous graffiti are those with ethnic discriminatory messages. Although they had been emerging from time to time since the early 1990s (the time of the disintegration of former Yugoslavia and the beginning of the civil war), one gets the impression that their expansion coincides with the resurrection of democracy in Serbia. We assume that this phenomenon can be explained by seeing graffiti as a counter answer to official political positions that advocate political correctness and tolerance towards other national and ethnic groups. The reaction of the displeased, non-tolerant and nationally imbued individuals has as one of its expressions the writing of graffiti which, in this case, articulate officially unacceptable ideas. In other words, these graffiti fall into a category of anonymous, marginal and alternative messages in a phenomenological sense, which find their way to the public by means of city walls and streets. These graffiti have a particular significance because they give us an idea about which national and ethnic groups are objects of hatred and verbal assault:

"Serbia to the Serbs, axes for Albanians – SRS" [Serbian Radical Party] *(Srbija Srbima, Šiptarima sekira)*
"Serbia to Serbs" *(Srbija Srbima)*
"Serbia to Serbs, death to the others – SRS" *(Srbija Srbima, smrt drugima)*
"Serbia to Serbs, out with the Gipsies" *(Srbija Srbima, napolje sa Romima)*
"Out with the Chinese" *(Kinezi napolje!)*
"Kill, slay, till there are no Croats" *(Ubi, zakolji, da Hrvat ne postoji)*
"Serbs, we are disappearing" *(Sve nas je manje Srbi)*
"Serbia to Tokyo" *(Srbija do Tokija)*

Gender and Sexuality

Many graffiti have messages with clear references to homosexuals, broadly articulating two opposing viewpoints. On the one hand there are graffiti "sympathetic" to the homosexual population, and on the other there are graffiti with hostile messages. The first group is marked as "gay" graffiti, the second as "anti-gay".

The collected sample showed a struggle in the communication between these diametrically opposed groups: the "editing" of graffiti, crossing out and erasing of messages, or adding new elements, so as to change the pro- or anti-homosexual meaning of certain graffiti. First of all, such conflicts are detected in cases where graffiti with homosexual symbols are crossed out. Gay-affirmative graffiti are represented by graphic symbols of the same gender and the plea for the need to accept such relationships as actual, tolerable facts of life. Provoked by these graffiti, other authors frowning upon such a sexual orientation cross out these symbols using different colours. The expressed intolerance and scorn is purposely offensive:

"Death to faggots" (*Smrt pederima*)

"Faggots fuck up their shitty assholes" (*Pederi se jebu u čmarine govnave*)

These examples illustrate the unambiguous attitude of some groups' beliefs that non-heterosexual orientations should not be welcomed in the community. However, graffiti which explicitly show homosexual relationships as undesirable only insult relationships between men, but not between women. Graffiti which we denoted as "anti-gay" also mirror current political problems which Serbia has been facing in the past couple of years, such as the delivery of war criminals to the tribunal at The Hague, which is one of the principal challenges for today's Serbia. Homophobia can be connected with opposition to the international tribunal, such as expressed by the graffiti "Gays to Hague?" *(A pederi u Hag?)*.

Thus, heterosexuality is equivalent to patriotism, while non-heterosexuals, i.e., gays, are associated with being non-patriotic. This example illustrates how the construction of the individual (sexual) identity becomes a means of constructing national identity. It shows that the interpretation of sexual graffiti cannot be separated from the political context of Serbia. Marginalised groups are perceived as a "threat" to conventional, heterosexual orientation. Homosexuals are excommunicated as a group of people with different identities that "have to be dealt with".

Nevertheless, we also recorded other graffiti such as "Gay is OK" and "Faggots are humans too" *(I pederi su ljudi)*. These graffiti affirm homosexuality, so we call them "gay" graffiti. The self-acknowledgment and self-identification which these graffiti express, allow marginal groups' identities to augment. Seeking the acceptance of the community, they point to the marginals' lack of public space and illustrate the fight for a "liberated" ground that accepts their sexual orientation and personal identity.

Expressions of rebellion

Rebellion and the critical nature of these graffiti are often condensed to aggressive displays of a particular group's beliefs, of making their existence present in such a manner. Prevailing among the graffiti are the ones clearly declaring themselves as fan graffiti. Football fans are often connected to negative and undesirable behaviour which stems from the numerous conflicts they themselves initiate or are drawn into. And yet, at the time of mass protests against Slobodan Milošević's rule, fans played the role of unique 'resistance heroes', even showing the audacity to clash with Milošević's police. This ambiguous, volatile, and varying position of fans caused their additional rebellion against public condemnation and rejection:

"Whoever comes will have a hard time" *(Ko god došo, loše prošo)*

"A wave threatening to demolish everything !– B.B.R.S." *(Talas koji preti da poruši sve! B.B.R.S.)*

"There's great competition in being insane – heroes" *(Velika je konkurencija biti lud – Heroes)*

"Stop oppressing football fans – Delije" *(Stop represiji nad navijačima – Delije)*

Within the resistance discourse, graffiti of the ASI movement ("Anarcho-Syndicalist Initiative") have a distinct position. They are engaged in the struggle against corruption, the opposition to privatisation, and the administrative state apparatus, and are against modern neo-liberalism in general. This movement focuses on alter-globalisation and since it openly confronts the public order with aggressive messages, it can be recognised as anti-social. Their messages feature rebellion against the existing value system. However, what these graffiti lack is the very thing for which the anti-globalisation movement is criticised: "We must be able to articulate the kind of world we desire. Protest is not sufficient anymore, we need a vision!" (Roddick 2003: 20). Therefore, these graffiti are but a mere signal with no tangible ideas, they are but a negative attitude bearing no affirmative message. The typical graffiti of this movement are:

"Death to the state – ASI" *(Smrt državi – ASI)*

"Armed strike – ASI" *(Štrajk oružjem – ASI)*

"Capitalism is cannibalism – ASI" *(Kapitalizam je kanibalizam- ASI)*

"Death to the state and capitalism – ASI" *(Smrt državi i kapitalizmu – ASI)*

"Privatisation is pillage – ASI" *(Privatizacija je pljačka – ASI)*

"The law ends here" *(Ovde zakon prestaje)*

"Fuck the system"

"Fuck all the rest"

"Fuck the cops"

"Philosophical" graffiti

The graffiti whose content we tentatively denoted as "philosophical" articulate the effort to create individual ideology and express personal needs. They do not refer to daily political issues, though they can be thought of as a response to current circumstances faced by their authors. These are probably most often young people in various identity crises, trying to find soul mates by writing graffiti and thereby confirm their distinctiveness vis-à-vis the dominant social discourse. Thus, these graffiti can be read as acts of self-examination and self-presentation. They are almost always non-violent, although actively referring to the existing social surrounding. Their active role reflects "youth resistance" against normative identities, endeavouring to detach themselves from the official and dominant socio-cultural streams which adolescents feel to be imposing and repressive:

"Bye bye brain – IMT" *(Pozdrav s mozgom – IMT)*

"It's our world, you just live in it"

"You ignorant human"

"I like it when you are uncomfortable" *(Sviđa mi se da ti ne bude prijatno!)*

"Rest if you have something to rest from. Eat if you have something to eat. Think if you have something to think about!" *(Odmorite se ako imate od čega. Pojedite ako imate šta. Mislite ako imate o čemu!)*

"The goal of our path is to find the path to our goal" *(Cilj našeg puta je da nađemo put do našeg cilja!)*

"They are born stupid, live stupid, work stupid, will die stupid – They are YAS (young and stupid)" *(Rođeni glupi, žive glupi, rade glupi i umreće glupi... – oni su MIG , Mladi i Glupi)*

"I like Plato, but prefer sex" *(Volim Platona, ali sex još više!)*

"I like life – I'm dying for it" *(Volim život – umirem za njim)*

"Weed and beer make things clear – we agree" *(Od trave i piva gotiva – Slažemo se!)*

"A different world is possible" *(Drugačiji svet je moguć)*

"Anywhere beyond this world" *(Bilo gde izvan ovog sveta)*

"Non-expressive" graffiti

Graffiti which disturb the communication process, in our opinion, can be classified as so-called "non-expressive" graffiti, seemingly senseless wall scribbles, empty signs, slapping into the face of the firmly coded urban matrix. They defy any interpretation through their reduced contents, designating apparently no one and nothing; thus, as anti-discourse, they intrude the sphere of imbued city signs. Some of them are:

"I think the universe, I create the universe" *(Mislim svemir, stvaram svemir)*

"Do make say think"

"Dog, daddy, son, aunt, family" *(Kuče, tata, sin, tetka, family)*

It is not clear who the conveyer of these messages is, what is his/her aim, and who should be the recipient. These graffiti are hard to interpret and to fit in any organised discourse of Serbia from the past ten years. They symbolise a kind of "wall" philosophy, undefined and unintelligible in many ways. They might be a calling for something, but it remains unclear for what. Their presence on walls is confusing because they do not communicate or initiate a dialogue, neither as an authoritative nor as a marginal text.

Pastiche graffiti

Among the "pastiche" graffiti we reckon those playing with political contents in different ways, refusing to be explicit, with a touch of irony attached. Although pastiche graffiti are not without meaning, their messages are very complexly coded, and their political activism remains implicit:

"The plant is working again!" *(Fabrika ponovo radi!)*

"Down with oppression and injustice" *(Padaj silo i nepravdo)*

"Tito is not dead"

The first two graffiti simulate the meta-narratives of the former Yugoslavia (appeal for the workers to fight, achievement of full production power, reference to popular songs, etc.). In the political context of Serbia, which undergoes transition, they are meaningless, but by simulating an action call which is non-contextualised, they may want to state that the government cannot be undermined by political opposition. It can be weakened only if we refuse to enter into a dialogue with it. The third graffiti alludes to the famous slogan "Punk is not dead", replacing punk with Tito, once an almost mythical political figure, who was deprived of his political aura a long time ago, and became part of mass-culture.

Motivational basis of graffiti

From a psychological standpoint, R. Blume suggested a categorisation of the motives to write graffiti (Blume 1985). She believes that there are two major groups of motives: (1) mass communication and reflexive communication; (2) categorical and individual communication. Each group is further divided into additional subcategories. Comparing our material with this categorisation, we suggest the following conclusions:

1. Ethnic discriminatory graffiti fall into the group "categorical and individual communication", subcategory "expression of criticism and rejection".

2. Gender graffiti refer to motives serving “mass and reflexive communication in public” (as does the first category), subcategory “existence proof, need to express oneself and documentation of group membership”.
3. On the other hand, graffiti denoted as “anti-gay”, which are merely means of criticism, protest and refusal, belong to the category “categorical and individual communication - expression of criticism and rejection”.
4. Rebellion and resistance graffiti possess mixed motivational bases, all the more so as different groups of graffiti belong to them, stemming from different intentions. Therefore, at the same time they can be fitted in the first group as “existence proof, documentation of group membership”, but also in the second category as “expression of criticism, protest and rejection”.
5. Football fans’ graffiti belong to the group of rebellion and resistance, and can be characterised by the “existence proof and marking out of territories” motive because fans can be linked to the part of the city where their club or stadium is located, or where large groups of them live, therefore marking their belonging and devotion to certain sports institutions, and also their reign over a certain territory, clearly warning other fan groups that they are not welcome.
6. Philosophical and pastiche graffiti primarily articulate the need for self-expression, subcategory “need to express oneself”.

Conclusions

In the light of these theoretical considerations, we believe that the majority of the identified graffiti unambiguously oppose or invert the current socio-political and cultural discourses, thereby confirming the hypothesis of Gonos et al. This holds true especially for the rebellion and resistance graffiti, as well as for some philosophical and pastiche graffiti. On the other hand, there are many graffiti publicly manifesting conservative attitudes that, although hidden and unwanted within the official discourse, are still latently present and influential in the traditional value system (for example anti-homosexual and nationalistic graffiti). The emphasised presence of fan graffiti, which are very dominant in some parts of the city, leads us to the conclusion that war and national tensions, so characteristic for the 1990s, made place for ‘peaceful’ quarrels between football fans and the need to show their affection to their beloved clubs. Diversity in the topics of graffiti, including those with love, humour and poetic messages, which were not of our direct interest, brings us to conclude that the changes since 2000 have effected an easing of tensions, bringing various urban, group and individual contents and cravings to the attention of the graffiti authors.

References

Best, Curwen 2003: Reading Graffiti in the Caribbean Context. In: Journal of Popular Culture 36, 4: 828–852.

Blume, R. 1985: Graffiti. Discourse and Literature. Amsterdam, Philadelphia: John Benjamins Publ., 137–148.

Bruner, Edward M., Jane P. Kelso 1980: Gender Differences in Graffiti: a Semiotic Perspective. In: Women's Studies International Quarterly 3: 239–252.

D'Angelo, Frank. J. 1976: Fools' names and fools' faces are always seen in public places: a study of graffiti. In: Journal of Popular Culture 10, 1: 102–109.

Dundes, Alan 1966: Here I Sit – a Study of American Latrinalia. In: Kroeber Anthropological Society Papers 34: 91–105.

Gonos, George, Virginia Mulkern, Nicholas Poushinsky 1976: Anonymous Expression: a Structural View of Graffiti. In: Journal of American Folklore 89, 351: 40–48.

Hall, Stuart 1997: Representation: Cultural Representations and Signifying Practices. London: Sage.

Klingman, Avigdor, Ronit Shalev 2001: Graffiti: Voices of Israeli Youth Following the Assassination of the Prime Minister. In: Youth & Society 32, 4: 403–420.

Roddick, Anita 2003: Globalization – Take it Personally. London: Element.

Stocker, Terrance L., Linda W. Dutcher, Stephen M. Hargrove, Edwin A. Cook 1972: Social Analysis of Graffiti. In: Journal of American Folklore 85, 338: 356–366.

Alternative Voices in Public Urban Space: Serbia's *Women in Black*

Orli Fridman, Arlington

> *"'Srebrenica' is a bad word for modern Serbia, even worse than 'feminism', and Women in Black put the two together ..."* (Tešanović 2004: 35).

Introduction

On July 10, 2004 a group of activists led by *Women in Black*[1] in Serbia gathered at the *Republic Square* in Belgrade to hold their silent vigil in memory of the 1995 massacre of thousands of Bosnian Muslim men in Srebrenica. Approximately fifty women and a small number of men, all dressed in black, positioned themselves in silence at the heart of the city, holding banners in memory of the victims and reminding passersby of the massacre that took place in Srebrenica nine years ago. But that day at the square, there were others who thought that such a vigil in memory of the victims of Srebrenica should not be allowed to take place.

As the *Women in Black* protesters gathered, the square was already being used for a big summer event, colored by the light festive atmosphere of a warm summer evening in Belgrade's city center. A large stage occupied the middle of the square, over which stretched a banner announcing the Belgrade Peace Festival, with music and the sounds of an ice cream promotion blaring out of speakers on either side of the stage. The protesters could hardly find enough free space on the square to position themselves and begin their ritual of the silent vigil.

As the protesters were gathering, minutes before seven o'clock in the evening, they were approached and attacked by a few women who slapped some of the

---

[1] *Women in Black* is a feminist group formed in 1991 by a group of women from Belgrade. The Serbian *Women in Black* were inspired by the Israeli *Women in Black*, formed in 1988 in Jerusalem in resistance to the Israeli occupation of the Palestine territories. During the 1990s, they reacted to the policies of the Milošević regime and to the population's indifference, protesting against the aggression and wars in Croatia, Bosnia-Herzegovina and later Kosovo. During the war in Bosnia, they stood, every Wednesday, in silent vigil against the war. After the Dayton Agreement was signed, vigils were organized depending on the need and urgency of events. After the change of regime in October 2000, they still appear in the street as part of Serbia's civil society, demanding a more just and democratic society.

Women in Black activists on their faces and heads, shouting "Why are you here? Dressed in black? All of you should be hung and slaughtered ..." At that point, three policemen intervened and prevented the women from continuing their physical assault. Later, during the silent vigil, the same women now accompanied by a group of loud men, yelled and cursed at the demonstrators, mocking their presence in the city center and threatening them and their lives.

In this article, based on qualitative field work which I conducted in Serbia in 2004, I look at Belgrade's main square, *Republic Square*, and at the silent vigils of *Women in Black* taking place on it, as at a site of contested territory and space in which Serbia's collective memories of the wars of the 1990s are being created, and in which the boundaries of what will be left out of and what will be included in that memory are being debated. I argue that in order for parties in conflict to reconcile, aside from the necessity of any political dialogue, a process of negotiating the conflicting memories of the past wars and atrocities must first take place within each party. This process may include, among other things, the exploration of the narratives and collective memories of the wars (or conflicts) and of the various interpretations of what happened and of who is to bear responsibility. As of 2004, although this process has begun in Serbia, it has been kept marginalized. *Women in Black* as well as other groups and organizations of Serbia's civil society are trying to promote the process of dealing with the past in their discursive and social practice.[2]

Serbia's alternative scene in 2004

The struggle by Serbia's civil society to coalesce to resist the Milošević era wars was believed to be over with the victory of the opposition forces in October 2000. The result was contested by Milošević, but then the streets of Belgrade were taken over by hundreds of thousands of people who turned out to defend the opposition victory in front of the parliament building. These were days of euphoria, a euphoria that for many would soon evaporate. Rather than the end for Serbia's anti-war

---

[2] Here I am referring to Serbia's alternative scene, to what was called, during the 1990s, "druga Srbija" ("the other Serbia"). This scene, composed of NGOs, alternative media and cultural centers, later formed and created what was, in 2004, Serbia's civil society. Acting as Serbia's alternative civil opposition during the 1990s to the Milošević regime and his pro-war politics, groups such as *Women in Black*, The Helsinki Committee for Human Rights, The Humanitarian Law Fund, The Center for Cultural Decontamination, YUCOM and others, are still active in 2004. The alternative voices of the anti-war and human rights activists in Serbia were and still are marginalized, both in scholarly literature analyzing the conflicts in the former Yugoslavia and in their own society.

circles, October 5 and the formation of a new government in Belgrade marked the beginning of a new phase in their struggle for a democratic and more just society. As the country was emerging from a decade of brutal war, hopes for genuine change were raised with the belief among members of Serbia's alternative scene that their struggle was not in vain and that the time for the revitalization and democratization of the system had come. However, it soon became clear that what they considered to be essential for change was not what reality brought upon them. The "democratic revolution", as many outsiders characterized the ouster of Milošević in October 2000, did not bring an end to his legacy – a legacy entrenched in the institutions of the country and in the persons at the highest levels of those institutions. After a decade in which Serbia's political scene languished under the excessive power of politicized military and security apparatuses and in which organized criminal gangs flourished, the hope was that the new government headed by President Vojislav Koštunica would promptly complete its mission of removing these pillars of the former regime. But in reality, this did not occur at the pace nor to the extent expected. Criticizing this lack of systematic change, demanding a genuine transformation that would allow Serbia to deal with its past in order to be able to move towards the future, then became one of the main focuses of Serbia's civil society and human rights organizations in the post-Milošević days.

Those who were already documenting war crimes and asserting the importance of the questions of guilt and responsibility during the wars, now found themselves struggling for these questions to be included in the public sphere, resisting denial and obliteration of the past by their government and the public. In 2004, a year after the assassination of Prime Minister Zoran Đinđić, these issues were at the heart of the agenda of Serbia's alternative scene that was again feeling threatened and almost as marginalized as before.

Republic Square as a metaphor

On July 10, 2004, in Serbia (which was still officially denying the massacre in Srebrenica)[3], those who attended the *Women in Black* vigil had to fight not only for physical space on the square, but also for their message in memory of Srebrenica and of all victims of wars to be seen and heard. They did approach the

[3] The original conference paper was written and presented prior to the panel discussion held in May 2004 at the Belgrade faculty of Law, celebrating the "liberation of Srebrenica" and prior to the June 2004 release of the video showing the killing of six Muslim men by members of a Serbian paramilitary police unit, which was shown at the International Criminal Tribunal for the Former Yugoslavia in The Hague and broadcast on Serbian television, leaving no space for further official denial (Wood 2005).

police who were present, to remind them that they had registered at the police station and to warn them that a vigil in memory of Srebrenica would not go well side-by-side with the loud music and advertisements of the festival simultaneously taking place, but as some of the protesters said: "The police, along with many others in the square, could not care less about Srebrenica."

Eventually, those who had gathered managed to find the space to stand and form a circle, smaller than usual. As in all of their vigils marking the anniversaries of war crimes, they stood in silence, this time with banners that read: "Nine years in memory of Srebrenica," "In memory of all the victims of the wars," "Women from Srebrenica are searching for the truth" and others. Only meters away, about ten or fifteen people were standing, including some of the women who had earlier assaulted the *Women in Black* activists, and others – mainly young men – singing, cheering, threatening, insulting and shouting. From, *"ko to kaže ko to laže Srbija je mala"* ("Who is saying? Who is lying that Serbia is small?") to cheering *"živeli"* for Karadžić, Mladić and Milošević ("Long live Karadžić, Mladić and Milošević"). They also shouted repeatedly, "What sect do you belong to? We are Orthodox! Soros traitors! Traitors to the court! Bitches, who pays you to stand here?"

The group of men and women continued to chant for a long hour even after the vigil ended, with the *Women in Black* activists still on the square, sitting in a café terrified to leave, as the young men were threatening: "We know where you live, we will come after you." These threats were only too real, as a few months earlier several activists had been beaten after a vigil on the short walk back to the *Women in Black* office.[4] The atmosphere was harsh, the feelings were heavy. As one activist commented, "I haven't heard these songs in the main streets of the city since the days of the wars in the '90s."

The difficulty that the demonstrators had in finding the space to stand and convey their message on the square that evening serves as a metaphor for the similar effort to raise those same issues in the public sphere, and include them in Serbia's public discourse. The struggle to make the memory of Srebrenica present in the streets of Belgrade is a metaphor for the struggle over the memory of the wars, the atrocities, and the war crimes. This is a struggle over the creation of collective memory, as it addresses the question of how Serbian society will deal with and remember the events that took place during the wars in Croatia, in Bosnia and Herzegovina and later in Kosovo. Collective memory, according to Maurice Halbwachs, is not a given, nor static, but rather a socially constructed

---

4 This incident occurred after a silent vigil held on April 6, 2004, commemorating the beginning of the war in Bosnia-Herzegovina. After the vigil, two male activists of *Women in Black* were attacked and beaten as they walked back to the office to return the banners they had been holding on the square.

notion. There are as many collective memories as there are groups and institutions in a society. Through commemorative meetings, groups may reconstruct the past, which can otherwise slowly disappear (Halbwachs 1992: 22). Yael Zerubavel developed the concept of commemoration as it shapes the dynamics of the creation and alteration of memory. The commemoration of the past can thus become a contested territory in which groups engaging in political conflict promote competing views of the past in order to gain control over the political center (Zerubavel 1995: 10). By commemorating Srebrenica and its victims in the heart of Belgrade, Republic Square becomes a contested territory in which the boundaries of the Serbian collective memory are questioned and challenged, a contested territory over the question of how to remember, and how to forget.

The *Women in Black* message "Not in my name" implies that they will remain in the streets as a constant reminder of what actually happened – in their name. It implies the opposite of the general tendency to move on, to only look forward and not back, and to avoid addressing the problematic and loaded questions of responsibility and guilt. In holding their hour-long vigil on July 10, while the streets and the public strove for normalcy, the message of the anti-war activists was to remind those passing by that all was not normal. In doing so they threatened to ruin the "beauty" of a pleasant Sunday evening in Belgrade.

In fact, only a few people on the square actually reacted aggressively. Most passersby observed the demonstrators with little interest, apathetic towards the vigil and its message. This apathy may be seen as a response to the attempt to force people to face these difficult and unpleasant questions. Denying the past, not only in Serbia or in the Balkans, serves as an effective defense in the search for normalcy. But those who insist not only on remembering but also on reminding others, believe that only by breaking this state of denial will their society be able to truly move forward towards real normalcy and peace. The reactions of passersby that day on the square reflect the complexity of and the resistance to the attempt to open a public discussion about these questions. Those who choose to remember and to remind others are perceived by many as anti-Serbian and as traitors.

The question of moral responsibility

Those who insist on remembering and on reminding others, as many of them have asserted, feel that their choice to be publicly visible was, and still is, a matter of their personal moral position both during and since the wars, as these events and issues are being confronted. In Belgrade's city center, at the heart of this contested territory, morality has been questioned and debated, as one of the founders of *Women in Black* told me: "It is my moral responsibility and commitment. I was and still am standing in the streets of my city as a witness of the loss of moral dignity, but this is what people did not and still do not want to see, and this is why our presence makes them feel uncomfortable. I can understand the wish of people not to know, but I can not accept it!"

The spectrum of the debate over the question of blame and responsibility is wide. This debate is taking place on several levels: among scholars and journalists who wrote about the break up of Yugoslavia and the wars, within the societies of the former republics, and within Serbia proper among politicians and the main actors of civil society. In Serbia, the lines of debate are drawn between those who deny any responsibility, those who advocate for personal responsibility only, and others who argue for collective responsibility, or at least struggle with the concept and its implications for the Serbian case.

The question of responsibility became inherent to the project of "dealing with the past," which is at the heart of the issues addressed by civil society in their current activities.[5] The Serbian project of dealing with the past that originated as a concept from the German language[6] is a controversial and unpopular one in Serbia. The main goal of the project is to raise public awareness on the issues of war crimes, and to foster the discussion on crimes and responsibility in order to reject oblivion as the solution for dealing with these problems (Ilić, Matić 2000: xv). It also aims to approach the discrepancy between the image outside Serbia of the Serbs as the culprits, sinners who either perpetrated evil or stood idly by, and the image inside Serbia of the Serbs as innocent victims (Gojković 2000: 3–5). This endeavor raises the questions of collective responsibility, collective guilt, and the need for collective apologies.

While some have argued that it is impossible to talk about the moral responsibility of an entire nation, others have concluded the exact opposite. In defending both arguments, many have turned to Karl Jaspers and his famous work *The Question of German Guilt* to approach these questions.[7] Jaspers' discussion is relevant to Serbia today, as in this book he explicitly advocated the thesis of German collective guilt. "What is interesting about Jaspers' use of the term of collective guilt is not the condemnation of the German community, but the

---

5 In the report titled "From Multiplicity to Synergy? Organizational Perspectives of Dealing with the Past Process in Serbia and Montenegro" issued by the Quaker and Social Witness in 2003 (Milenković 2003), I found a helpful display of the different approaches to the project of dealing with the past. From art and culture, to documentation and research, education, advocacy and policy influencing, public events and debates, and media. The *Women in Black* street actions were mentioned under public events and debates.

6 In the content analysis of the above-mentioned report, Marina Blagojević points out the etymological problem of the concept of "Vergangenheitsbewältigung", as it translates into Serbian as "facing the past" and not "dealing with the past" (Blagojević 2003).

7 For examples see the edited volumes of Ilić and Matić (2000) and of Zaharijević, Zajović and Belenzada (2005). Jaspers' book was translated into Serbian by the B92 publishing house.

political-ethical appeal made by that term. What Jaspers primarily wants to do is encourage the raising of moral awareness, with direct political consequences" (Gojković 2000: 21). That is exactly what the *Women in Black* were aiming to do in standing silently on Republic Square evoking the memory of Srebrenica, though the reactions they received were far from what they had hoped for.

In limiting my investigation to the *Women in Black* message,[8] I ask how the question of responsibility came into play for the anti-war activists in Belgrade and for the *Women in Black* in particular, as they became politically engaged. During the 1990s, the *Women in Black* devoted hours of discussions and workshops to this matter. Their message regarding this issue was among the clearest ones recognizing war crimes as a matter to be dealt with by the entire population, as a subject of collective responsibility.

In 2004 as one activist reflected: "When the war in Bosnia began, especially with all the stories and reports from Sarajevo, people from there were already referring to me as 'You Serb guys who are killing.' But why would 'You Serb guys' be me? I had to accept it even though I didn't identify. I realized that the issue of responsibility for me meant that even though I don't identify myself as a Serb, I have to accept that Serbs from this place, from the same address as mine, were going to kill there... therefore it had something to do with my responsibility ... behaving as though it had nothing to do with me was not an option."

The generational gap and the question of responsibility

There is a significant difference in the way that activists of different generations approach the issue of responsibility. As one university professor who was active in the student demonstrations of the early 1990s told me: "I feel guilty or responsible that we were not able to prevent it [all that happened] and I think that whoever seriously wants to think, and who comes from my generation, should feel responsible. We were obliged to prevent it ... I have a feeling that as a generation we simply failed."

One of the founders of *Women in Black* voiced similar concerns: "I have to stand for Srebrenica, this is part of my life now, this is my commitment, and not only for us here, but also for the women there ... but for my daughter and her friends it is different, they wouldn't go there, they wouldn't stand here ... they don't feel they did anything wrong and they are not willing to take any collective guilt ... they were young when it happened, I can understand their need to protect

8 In my dissertation, where this is discussed in length, I also analyze reactions to the *Women in Black* and to other actors of Serbia's civil society.

themselves. They think it is the problem of my generation because we were grown-ups when it all happened. Some of them don't want to have anything to do with it."

Nevertheless, among the *Women in Black* activists there are some younger activists, the younger generation. Not in significant numbers, not as many as the group would like to have, but still some younger voices of those who joined later, who were still young kids when Yugoslavia fell apart. As one young female activist recalled, "The first vigil I joined was for Srebrenica in 1997. That was the first time when I exposed myself in the street, which is a great difference from only knowing and recognizing that something happened ... going out in the street and trying to send a message to others felt courageous at that time ... standing in the street meant sending a message so that other people can recognize and admit that something happened in Srebrenica, not to deny and claim that it never happened ... standing in the street at that time felt relatively secure because there were [the students] demonstrations every day, but there was a huge difference between us. Those who were anti-Milošević, it didn't mean that they were politically aware ... they were politically active, but not aware ... *Women in Black* for me had the meaning of anti-war, anti-militarization, trying to send a message to people, informing people that a crime happened somewhere and that it was committed by Serbs."

Activism and its motivation

People voice a variety of motives for action, for standing in the streets. While for some it was mainly a moral imperative, especially during the war years, for others it was a way of keeping their sanity: "That is how we survived," as some activists told me. Joining *Women in Black* meant and still means joining street activism. As one of the young female activists I interviewed told me:

> "For me it was important to go out and be seen in the streets. I began to realize that street actions mean that you publicly say what you think, what you are [standing] for and against ... after the fall of the Milošević regime we had more space, suddenly even the media became more interested in the *Women in Black* ... this was a very creative period of time for me. Now [2004] I feel more threatened, especially after two of us were beaten. I have moments when I have a sense of a crisis, is this at all useful to anyone? Are those passing by realizing anything? After all, they are used to us standing in the square. It is useful to me. I feel like I am doing something. I am not sitting at home and only talking, I am seen in the street, in public places. The square is a traditional place where people say or shout what they want. When I am in the square I am doing something, I am not just part of the quiet majority."

Indeed, the questions of efficiency and influence were and still are a source of disagreement and self criticism that goes along the lines of saying, "it was not enough what we did, it only served for our own good feelings, but we did not have enough impact." Or that, "offering a moral critique only had and has no influence on the society mainly because it implied that you, as the moral authority, have the absolute truth and all the others are stupid. It does not leave much space for discussion, the results then are limited and people reject the message: they say, do not attack me, I am already confused."

Breaking *States of Denial*

Indeed, such confusion has contributed to the atmosphere of resignation in the public sphere, to the tendency of the general public to make the choice not to know, to the creation of cultures of denial (Cohen 2001). This choice later becomes translated into the will not to remember; and therefore those who remind are an obstacle on the road to normalcy.

In his book *States of Denial*, Cohen refers to groups such as the *Women in Black* in Israel, or the *Mothers of Plaza de Mayo* in Argentina as "anti-denial movements", as groups of "consciousness raising" who combat the numbing effects of the culture of denial. In many conflict areas in the world, such anti-denial groups are led by women. This was and still is the case in Serbia. Women's involvement in Serbia's alternative scene was significant not only as participants, but even more so as founders and leaders of the most prominent NGOs. Such anti-denial groups, when functioning in their own societies as internal bystanders, pay a price for standing against the consensus, very often being isolated and even stigmatized as traitors (Cohen 2001: 95). In his books *The Roots of Evil* and *The Psychology of Good and Evil*, Staub refers to realities in which feelings of responsibility for others' welfare and inhibitions against killing are gradually lost when morality is missing. Opposing the perpetrators in such a reality requires moral courage that is essential for becoming an active bystander (Staub 1989, 2003). For Hannah Arendt, the freedom to choose not to collaborate, the refusal to obey, both among perpetrators and victims, was the essence of humanity. She extensively referred to those who were able to exclude themselves from the masses and maintain their ability for independent thinking; that was for her, above all, a moral and political act (see Zertal 2002: 212–215). It is therefore little wonder that Arendt's picture appears in most of the offices of Serbia's alternative scene, and that she is often quoted and her work used by so many of them.

During the wars, and especially during the years of the hyper-inflation, when many people in Serbia were engaged in a daily struggle to attain basic necessities, the line between knowing and not knowing about the atrocities being committed far away was a thin one, a twilight zone. Many people I spoke to, referred to the process of "coming to know". "Coming to know" what happened in Srebrenica, in Sarajevo, in Vukovar and other places, repeated itself as a theme in interviews with anti-war and human rights activists. Many spoke about the fear of going to Sarajevo after the war, the shame of revisiting such places. As one interviewee expressed, "I didn't know what was really going on there [in Sarajevo] ... in 1996 I went to Bosnia, nothing around me was whole, I saw houses that were completely looted ... I didn't realize how terrible it was. I thought to myself, 'if only we [in Serbia] were to organize buses with people to go to Bosnia and see what happened there, everything would change.'"

On the road to Srebrenica

On July 11, 2004, the day after the vigil in Belgrade, a group of activists organized a bus that took them to Potočari near Srebrenica, to participate in the official memorial and burial ceremony. Members of the *Youth Initiative for Human Rights*[9] were on the bus with some of the *Woman in Black*. Some said: "We are only fifty here today, we should have had many more people with us." But on the very same day, at noon, Belgrade celebrated the inauguration of its new president – Boris Tadić. As in the words of Jasmina Tešanović, a *Women in Black* activist and writer, "... it became more significant to stand for Srebrenica on 11 July, rather than to assist the first democratic president we supported with all our might to be elected, while he was inaugurated the very same day in Belgrade: why did we have to choose, and given the choice, how come only a few of us were in Srebrenica? Why is it that eight thousand missing people from Srebrenica, some of whom were found buried in Serbia proper, never ever became a reality in Belgrade?" (Tešanović 2004: 35).

In Potočari that day, around 20000 people gathered at what will become, if it is not already, what Pierre Nora referred to as a "site of memory" (Nora 2001). As the bus with the Belgrade license plates arrived in the Potočari valley, silence

[9] The Youth Initiative is a group of young activists committed to the participation of young people in Serbia in the process of *dealing with the past*. They were formed as an NGO in 2003 and have activists in Serbia-Montenegro and Kosovo. As the participation of Serbia's young generation in this process is rare, this group, formed by young people, is unique in its dedication and pledge of dealing with these issues.

overtook the passengers, as everyone retreated into their own private thoughts.[10] The bus slowly made its way to the place where passengers could get off and blend in among the thousands of other men and women attending the commemoration. But the group of *Women in Black* activists did not only blend in. After they were warmly welcomed by some of the local women who were waiting for them, they stood again, in silence, at the entrance to the memorial site, where everyone could see them. They held a big black banner with pink letters that read *"Žene u crnom protiv rata Beograd"* ("Women in Black from Belgrade Against War"). In Belgrade's city center they stand in order to remind, in Potočari they came to remember. In the city center of Belgrade they get no recognition, only disdain; in Srebrenica they came to acknowledge and recognize, they came to say we remember, we did not agree. At the heart of Serbia's urban center they have to struggle for their voices to be heard and seen, in rural Bosnia they receive some recognition for their efforts to be present.

Later during the ceremony, as the young female voices of the Zenica (a town in Bosnia) Youth Choir were singing, "Father, mother, I am searching for you ... you are gone ... Mother Bosnia, Sister Srebrenica ...," one of the activists who stood near me whispered, "imagine this choir singing this song on Republic Square in Belgrade ..."

Conclusions

If Republic Square is the public urban space in which the boundaries of what can be accepted in Serbia in 2004 are being defined, then the trip to Srebrenica symbolizes the crossing not only of the national border to Bosnia but also of the boundaries of Serbia's dominant discourse. Hence, this journey outside the city is significant in that it stretches the boundaries of Serbia's collective memory and public discourse. But at the end of the day, the participants in this journey must still return to the familiar streets of their city, to where they must continue to struggle in order to create space for the memory of Srebrenica.

Commemorative rituals are being created not only in Potočari, but also on Republic Square. Belgrade's city center is yet another space where the process of creating the future collective memory is occurring. The *Women in Black* vigil and the public reaction to it mirror the tensions in present-day Serbia, as well as what

---

[10] One cannot ignore the panoramic beauty of the nature along the way to Srebrenica. As Jasmina Tešanović wrote, "I wonder why nature becomes so beautiful wherever war crimes are committed ... I never pay attention to nature unless I am obliged to, but the Srebrenica valley demands attention: the intense green colors, the soothing sounds of the wind and birds, the blazing sun which heats without hurting, the shapes of the clouds, the neat borderline of the place of the crime" (Tešanović 2004: 36).

Serbian society will still have to face. By commemorating Srebrenica in the heart of Belgrade, the *Women in Black* are determined to keep the discussion about the wars and responsibility alive. By reminding in Belgrade and remembering in Potočari, their acts serve as a tribute to the memory of Srebrenica.

By silently commemorating the horrors of the past, the *Women in Black* are contributing to and enlarging the space for debating the questions of dealing with the past. *Women in Black* are one of the only groups in Serbia today still committed to street activism. In remaining so, they are maintaining their unique and important role as that part of Serbia's civil society that is still facing and struggling with questions of the past, of responsibility, and of war crimes, while striving for the democratization of society and its institutions.

References

Blagojević, Marina 2003: Dealing with the Past: Perspectives from Serbia and Montenegro. A Report Issued by the Quaker Peace and Social Witness. Belgrade.

Cohen, Stanley 2001: States of Denial: Knowing about Atrocities and Suffering. Cambridge: Polity Press and Blackwell Publishers.

Gojković, Drinka 2000: What Do We Do Now? In: Dejan Ilić, Veran Matić (eds.), Truths, Responsibilities, Reconciliations: The Example of Serbia. Belgrade: Samizdat Free B92, 1–12.

Gordy, Eric D 1999: The Culture of Power in Serbia: Nationalism and the Destruction of Alternatives. University Park: Pennsylvania State UP.

Halbwachs, Maurice 1992: On Collective Memory. Chicago: University of Chicago Press.

Ilić, Dejan, Veran Matić (eds.) 2000: Truths, Responsibilities, Reconciliations. The Example of Serbia. Belgrade: Samizdat Free B92.

Milenković, Nataša 2003: From Multiplicity to Synergy? Organizational Perspectives of Dealing with the Past Process in Serbia and Montenegro. A Report Issued by the Quaker Peace and Social Witness. Belgrade.

Nora, Pierre 2001: Rethinking France. Les lieux de mémoire. Chicago: University of Chicago Press.

Staub, Ervin 1989: The Roots of Evil. The Origins of Genocide and Other Group Violence. Cambridge: Cambridge University Press.

Staub, Ervin 2003: The Psychology of Good and Evil: Why Children, Adults, and Groups Help and Harm Others. Cambridge: Cambridge University Press.

Tešanović, Jasmina 2005: The Square and Victims. In: Staša Zajović (ed.), Women for Peace. Belgrade: Women in Black, 34–36.

Wood, Nicholas 2005: Video of Serbs in Srebrenica Massacre Leads to Arrests. In: New York Times, 3 June 2005.

Zaharijević, Adrijana, Staša Zajović, Tamara Belenzada (eds.) 2005: Suočavanje sa Prošlošću – Feministički Pristup [Dealing with the past – a feminist approach]. Belgrade: Women in Black.

Zertal, Idith 2002: Ha-Umah v.eha-mav.et: hist.oryah, zikaron, polit.ikah [Death and the nation. History, memory, politics]. Or Yehuda: Devir.

Zerubavel, Yael 1995: Recovered Roots: Collective Memory and the Making of Israeli National Tradition. Chicago: University of Chicago Press.

Roma Musicians as Tradesmen in Urban Cultural Environments

Ana Hofman and Iva Tarabić, Belgrade

In October and November 2003, the Centre for Balkan Music Research (CIMB) in Belgrade initiated a research project on the music and culture of Roma in the vicinity of the town of Obrenovac in Serbia and in suburban communities of Belgrade. This research was part of the project "Respecting Diversity" aimed at studying the music of minorities on the territory of Serbia and Montenegro. The *modus operandi* was inter-regional student collaboration under the sponsorship of the Higher Education Support Program (HESP) of the Open Society Institute in Budapest. The team consisted of students (both under- and post-graduate) of Ethnomusicology (Faculty of Music, Belgrade) and Ethnology (Ethnology Department, Faculty of Philosophy, Zagreb).

Two groups of Roma were interviewed: *Gurbeti*[1] (both indigenous and refugees from Kosovo), who speak Romani, and *Banjaši,* whose mother-tongue is Romanian.[2] The so-called Music Colony, a former suburb of Obrenovac, was of special interest for ethno-musicological explorations, for the main trade in this community is – and has always been – music. The inhabitants of the Music Colony are a suburban population who live within the area of the town, but, on the other hand, the Colony is spatially completely isolated from the rest of the town, with minimal possibilities of mingling with other ethnic groups.[3]

In this paper we will focus on the processes of continuity and change in the musical practices and styles of performance of the investigated Roma groups. This approach complicates the existing ethno-musicological literature on Roma which rarely differentiates Roma music by ethnic and other parameters, but rather considers it an entity beyond such internal differentiation.[4]

---

1 These terms come from the vocabulary of the particular groups.

2 The members of this community also use the term *Romanian Gypsies* to distinguish themselves from other groups. In the literature, many different terms are in usage: *Vlah Cigani* (Tihomir Đorđević), or *Cigani Rumuni, Romanian Cigani, Karavlasi Cigani* (Biljana Sikimić).

3 Discussing the origins of prejudices against Roma in this part of the world, and their social segregation, Aleksandra Mitrović points to the fact that they were the "newcomers" who arrived together with the "occupiers" (the Ottomans). See Mitrović, Zajić 1998: 51.

4 The problem of sub-ethnic differentiation among Roma in neighbouring countries was covered by many authors, e. g. by Kertesz-Wilkinson 1994, 1999 and Kovalcsik 1999; for the former Yugoslavia see Vidić 1989.

1.1 The "Gypsy" music canon

According to testimonies by representatives from both of the groups interviewed, *Banjaši* were once (certainly before World War Two) the most famous pub musicians in the wider surroundings of the Serbian towns of Obrenovac and Ub, in part Valjevo and Šabac, and including the vicinity of Lazarevac. The main instrument of their craft was the violin. Therefore, the Obrenovac settlement "Music Colony" emerged as a valuable subject for studies of long-lasting performing practice within one and the same surrounding. This could certainly enhance the understanding of the *Banjaši* and *Gurbeti* music performance in the specific social context.

By looking at the basic characteristics of *Banjaši* and *Gurbeti* music practice, at their former and present instrumental and dancing repertoire, at the specific features of their vocal and instrumental performance, and especially at the aspect of Roma as professional musicians, it was inevitable to first face the methodological issues, and then to discuss the very position of Roma music in general.

Although Roma music is often treated with certain reservations[5] in the dominant ethno-musicological discourse, there is also a general trend either to discover "original" and "authentic" Roma music, or to completely deny its very existence.[6] As Irén Kertész Wilkinson points out, Roma musicians simply do not fit the ideas about "authenticity" and a "pure" cultural and musical matrix. This fact causes confusion among dominant paradigms, for the music in question is subject to numerous influences:

> "A proper understanding of Roma cultures and musical practices, however, has long been obstructed by 'national-culture' mind-sets – approaches which cover a preoccupation with a unitary origin of the given ethnic group; myths about its homogeneous use of a common language, a communally shared set of ideas and values, and a uniform repertoire of music and dance; and its association with a geographically fixed territory or ethnicity. These elements are perceived as omnipresent and traceable back to an imagined prehistoric time, and any group failing to meet these criteria is

---

[5] Ana Matović mentions two reasons for the refusal to write down "violin Gypsy music": first, because of its complex ornaments and fast tempo in the past, it was very difficult to pick up by ear; second, Gypsy music was seen as second rate music compared to traditional Serbian music, less important than that performed by the local Serbian population, especially the rural one (Matović 1993: 115).

[6] In Serbian textbooks on ethnomusicology, besides other problems, there is also the opinion that Roma do not have their own authentic music, but reinterpret the indigenous people's music wherever they settle, even if only temporarily. This means that there is no Roma music, but only Roma style. In this view, the Roma first make a trade out of the art of music, and then this trade is presented as their own tradition, both by themselves and by others (see Đorđević 1984: 32–40, Gojković 1994: 87–94).

> considered to 'lack' a culture of its own. Such approaches, which are increasingly challenged even in relation to nation-state societies, are certainly not applicable to peoples who have lived and are still living in a transnational society" (Wilkinson 1999).

Thus, the use of the terms Roma or Gypsy music does not only deny the differences of specific categories among Roma ethnic groups (such as Banjaši), of their different status, place of residence or of generational aspects, but it also imposes an "ethnic" label on music, which may lead to further connotations. On the other hand, the term "ethnic" is used by the "others" – consumers or "more competent" groups, not by the performers themselves. In this sense, a definition which implicates that any music performed by Roma musicians, because of its specific style, should be considered as "Roma music" contradicts the emic point of view. According to Speranta Radulesku, who discussed the question of Roma's self-identification with different musical genres, "... for their ethnic fellows, the Gypsy musicians often perform pieces borrowed from other ethnic groups – certainly, with the required stylistic adjustment" (Radulesku 2003: 81).

Furthermore, considering the insider view of Roma music in the sense of self-identification of the members of the community, it should be stressed that this music is not performed on the level of the community as a whole. This music, being mostly local and temporary, cannot be used as a permanent characteristic, but should rather be considered in relation to the place, generation, status, and other aspects of the performers.

1.2 Professional Roma musicians

The historical record on the Balkan Roma confirms that already in Ottoman times, they were registered within "city garrisons" not only as ironmongers, but also as musicians *(mehter)*. "By the way of *mehterluk*, they became Muslims in the Vranje fortress and settled in the Džemat. First they numbered eight, and later 16 (plus two unmarried), and maybe even more houses" (Mitrović, Zajić 1998: 73). Tihomir Đorđević, in his dissertation on "Gypsies in Serbia"(1902), concluded that the Roma differed from the rest of the population by their trade. They were predominantly ironmongers, potters, horse sellers, bear tamers – and musicians (quoted in Gojković 1994: 87, Zirojević 1976: 73). Music was one way in which Roma eventually acquired respectful social positions. This is reflected in the esteem of the social position of the *Banjaši* and *Gurbeti* in Obrenovac and Belgrade, whose reputation within their own community is significant. The special status of the professional musicians among them is confirmed by the informants themselves:

> "Here, in Obrenovac, we ... don't find ourselves insulted, Serbs have never been good players; since 1990 – from the Dimić school, 100 accordion-players came from Obrenovac alone. For further regions I can only count up. I, myself, was a winner of former Yugoslavia. Then, Australia, France, America and Europe; in Austria all of those children from Obrenovac came from this Dimić school" (Bora Dimić, informant, born 1965).

Accordingly, Roma musicians can be perceived as a special social group, on the basis of their trade and both its internal and external reception. Considering the social respect for an individual or a group within a society to be an important indicator of social position, it could be stated – with some reservations – that the *Banjaši* and *Gurbeti* musicians represent a specific layer of, first, their highly specialized local community, and then of the Roma community in general.

2.1 "Local" musical style

The ethno-musicological discourses about Roma music often use various oppositions, dualities and dichotomies, such as Roma – non-Roma music, professional – non-professional, popular – traditional (cf. Gojković 1989: 401–5, Vidić 1989), folklore – professional (cf. Acković 1999: 10), local – popular (Vidić 1989: 35), ascribing to them different meanings and interpretations. In contrast to this, we look at the local musical style, by which we understand the internal, but not necessarily unique musical style and repertoire, which endures, develops, and changes among the professional musicians, who are active inside one specific space (in our case, the Music Colony). This style is shaped by different "master schools", from one generation to another. The usual repertoire of *Banjaši* and *Gurbeti* musicians includes many different genres, such as newly composed folk music, turbo-folk, hip-hop, rap, pub music, along with the "internal style" especially for local use (cf. Gojković 1993: 108–112). As much as the local Banjaši and Gurbeti population might like both the local and other genres, the local is far less intended for broader commercialization. Therefore, both the music and the players we are going to focus on represent a totally local trade with local pretensions.

The most influential factor for the conservation of the "local" musical style is its nourishment as an old trade, and the consciousness about the necessity of this attitude towards the profession. This distinct style survives thanks to the specific "master schools" that consider it their trademark. Each of the musicians of any fame has his own pupils, the way he himself once was a pupil with his own raw models. As in the past, the learning of the music trade is a matter of having the time and means for both the pupil and the teacher. Today, as the informants testify, the schooling of Roma musicians involves serious investments. Nowadays, talented children often attend music schools besides having their "local teacher".

As the number of Colony musicians abroad is great and still growing, the Colony children often go for "master studies" to Austria, Switzerland, or Germany. They belong to a younger generation of musicians in the Colony, who have been educated abroad.

From about 1900 up to 1985, the violin was the dominant instrument, played by violin orchestras or, later, violin orchestras in combination with other instruments, as the informants point out. In the mid-1980s, the first accordion players became famous in Music Colony (such as Zoran Dimić and Momir Jovanović) and the accordion took over the violin's prestige. Of course, there is no such thing as a fixed orchestra setting, but different kinds of instruments are combined. Later, they also included electric ones, such as electric organs and drums, synthesizers, and e-guitars. The frequency of an instrument depends directly on the popularity of the musician who plays it, and the same goes for the musical style. Thus, when Aca Šišić was famous, the violin was the most common instrument, but when the accordion schools became active and commercialized, the focus was transferred from the former to the latter instrument.

From the present perspective, to highlight the problem of sub-ethnic differentiation and put it into the context of musical practices seems worthy of a theoretical essay, if not for any other reason than because it was permanently overlooked in the ethno-musicological literature. Our attempt, though, to find differences between the music of the *Banjaši* (as the oldest commercial musicians in the Colony) and the *Gurbeti* (who established themselves later as professional musicians) had somewhat dubious results. While *Gurbeti* musicians do not see any particular differences in repertoire and interpretation other than those imposed by historical circumstances (use of Romanian vs. Romani), the *Banjaši* believe that differences did once exist, even with respect to the repertoire. The fieldwork revealed that today there are no apparent differences in style, interpretation, and other parameters between the musical practices of these and other Roma groups in their surroundings, except for those related to the internal traditions of the "master schools", which are mostly the results of developing and nourishing one particular "master's" individual style of performance, and the choice of the main repertoire. This means that *Banjaši* and *Gurbeti* mainly play the repertoire to which their audience is most willing to listen (depending on whether the listeners are local or Serbian).

A specific feature of *Banjaši* and *Gurbeti* musicians from Obrenovac is that they increasingly accept ethnic Serb musicians in their orchestras, which also has an influence on the repertoire. Informants of various age groups (the oldest had already made music before WW II, the youngest started to play during the 1980s) point out that the older generations played much more for an urban audience than the younger ones, and that this certainly affected their repertoire and style, and also their "taste", i. e., aesthetic criteria, and understanding of their own musical tradition.

Any further exploration of the relation between music and internal (sub-ethnic) differences would require far more detailed research and a more adequate analytical and methodological approach. Indirect testimony points to such differences, when *Banjaši* orchestras started to include first *Gurbeti* musicians and then also Serbs. The music practices of these groups affected the changes of repertoire and style of playing.

2.2 Music for the others

As professionals, Roma musicians have an exquisite feeling for the taste of the audience. Music being their only source of income, they had to be sensitive to how their audience was feeling, i. e., they had to know their audience very well. Furthermore, musicians used to travel quite a lot and play in different towns and places, which made their repertoire very wide and adaptable to different audiences:

> "So many cities I passed through. All, except Slovenia. Montenegro, Bosnia, Croatia ... all the way to Skopje. Forty-four stamps I have in my work-booklet. Thirty-two years is my length of service, from *kafanski* (pub) to this kind of work ... I can play whatever you like: Hungarian, Rumanian, I did it all, from Novi Sad to Sarajevo ... but that's how it is" (Vasić Mikajlo, from the village of Gomilice).

After the Second World War, the promotion of so-called popular music by production houses such as PGP RTB, Jugoton, and Diskoton had opened opportunities for bands and individual performers of various forms of *narodna muzika* (folk music), including some famous "pub-musicians". This period, during which *Banjaši* and *Gurbeti* performers from Music Colony travelled all over former Yugoslavia, and in which some of them released records at the most important production houses, modelled and technically oriented the further development of their music:

> "I used to work in Obrenovac, Ribica for nine years, me and Đurica Šarbanac, and then I started to work for Radio-Television Belgrade (RTB). My first LP was in the Romani language, the second one was in Serbian: *'Znaš li kume, znaš li šta me brine?'* or: *'Tražim te, možda te sakrila tama'*. So, I kept on working for them ... as well as I do the pubs *(kafana)*. Uh, but now, I do weddings mostly. The season is almost over right now, so there remains the pub. And so on ..." (Dragoljub Đorđević-Šarbanac, born 1945, from the village of Stubline).

During the Yugoslav period the Music Colony produced some of its most celebrated performers, which made the Colony popular. Apart from Bora Dimić (winner of the prize "First Accordion of Yugoslavia"), there were artists such as Snežana Šikica, Stevica Jovanović and, later, Vida Jovanović, etc. It seems that, thanks to its short-lived glory as "pub-music", *Banjaši* and *Gurbeti* music succeeded to develop further as a genre (which means to keep in touch with contemporary trends, preferably in the field of technology). At the same time, it remained a petrified form of musical expression characteristic for the performers from one specific area (in the sense of a professional, "guild" tradition which still lives and develops thanks to its many "schools"). Although they tried to adopt each and every "outstanding" and "current" product of the "dominant" culture, one part of the local music repertoire still existed by itself. It is not a copy of anything that already exists, but it develops and enriches itself by the adaptation of contemporary concepts. In fact, it presents a "matrix" for variations and creative alternatives, such as Silverman has observed with respect to cultural change among Roma:

> "Although many innovations have occurred in Rom culture, they do not point to loss of ethnic identity; rather, change is a strategy of adaptation to new environments – both a strategy of manipulation of new situations and a creative response to them" (Silverman 1988: 261–262).

Nevertheless, a dual attitude towards the culture of the majority population is frequently observed, not only when it comes to music: on the one side, there is a constant tendency towards mimicry, and on the other the urge to create a "parallel culture" (what Jasna Mijailović calls a "natural alternative" to the cultural patterns of the majority population, Mijailović 2000: 288):

> "This colony never used to play Romani music, you know. Musical Colony is populated by people who are called Roma, but they are not Roma and no one in this settlement speaks Romani [the Roma vernacular]. Everyone here speaks Romanian. No, Romanians spoke 30 percent Romanian and 70 percent Serbian ... We are so cultivated, we are so 'Serbianised'. We feel like Serbs, but others call us Roma, but when someone asks us something in the Romani language, we cannot answer, my kid couldn't say anything not even in Romanian ... And what happens now: Roma music is now really good, and we are performers of Roma music. We are engaged in any kind of music. But, since the 1990s the music has progressed a lot. It's very rich now" (Bora Dimić, informant, born in 1965).

As was mentioned in the previous paragraph, commercial opportunities were very important for the choice of repertoire. As the informants stress, what is played is what is listened to, what makes money. For that reason, those who study Roma musicians often observe that they are dominant in the musicians' guild, and they, without any doubt, more readily accept new musical styles than others (see Radulesku 2003: 80). As a consequence, these musicians are open to the innovation of both their repertoire and their choice of instruments. Their musical logic is commercial with a high degree of openness to anything new and with an eye on new trends. On the one hand, the influence of new trends on their music becomes visible in the usage of new instruments and, on the other hand, in the adoption of new genres. The examples gathered during our fieldwork illustrate these changes: acoustic bands, first of all string orchestras, are replaced by bands with electric instruments, lately enriched with synthesizers and rhythm machines. In that sense, the influence of urban culture is also expressed by the acceptance of new genres (pop, rock, hip-hop, rap) and, maybe, constitutes a specific departure from the attribution of being "Roma". As a result of these, musicians strive to keep in contact with current trends, including the repertoires of radio and TV stations. Electronic media had a great influence on the repertoire, as we could observe on the spot. The informants insist that they learned many songs by listening to Radio Beograd. Lately, the main supplier of new repertoire is television, where Roma broadcasting stations are the most recent source of influence in Roma communities, both those on the local level, which cover the area of Obrenovac and its surroundings, and those on the national level. The music programme of these stations consists mainly of Roma music productions, ranging from older, and more popular songs to the "most recent" ones, and coming from all meridians thanks especially to the intense emigration of Roma. Thus the repertoire of *Banjaši* and *Gurbeti* musicians from Obrenovac is regularly updated, both for the needs of the Serbian and the local Roma population.

During the 1980s and 1990s, as Colony musicians stress, the genres of "popular music" became globally mixed, which was initiated by the activities of the producing house *Južni vetar* ("South Wind"). In contrast to performers, which they call the classical models and bearers of the "pure" style (such as P. Jašarović, Lepa Lukić, Aleksandar Šišić, Ljubiša Pantelić, and Branimir Đokić), the new productions bring, according to our informants, a totally new style, both with respect to music and performance (such as the so-called Turkish thrillers in the songs from the Šumadija region, etc.). The already mentioned foreign training of musicians also has a substantial impact on the combination of genres and on the changes in the use of instruments (such as the new popularity of the synthesizer, while the violin and accordion are completely discarded). The hybrid which results from the combination of different musical styles includes the fusion of pop, folk, disco, and jazz, combined with elements of the local style. The informants attribute special importance to the so-called "Viennese" productions, which are extremely popular and highly rated among younger generations in the Colony. However, there are some differences in the music for the "others" and the "own" audience. While the music which *Banjaši* and *Gurbeti* musicians, who have a more or less unified repertoire, perform for others – mainly Serbs – is determined by their demand, they play other songs within their own community, mainly of the following types:

1. Widely popular Roma ballads, with binary rhythm and characteristically "stretched" melodies, with slow tempo and descending movements, but with the characteristic initial leaps on beginnings of melostrophes. These songs are popular among all Roma in the region and sung in Romani[7].
2. The so-called *"Ciganska dvojka"* ("Gypsy Two"); slightly faster songs, usually with binary rhythm, close to the dancing repertoire; some of them are actually variants of *čarlama-dance* (a type of *kolo* dance). The local origin of these songs is difficult to establish. They have recently become well known to an international audience through films (such as Emir Kusturica's "Black Cat, White Cat") and their inclusion in the domestic "world music" production. They are sung in Romani, Romanian, or in combination with Serbian[8].
3. Original songs by locally famous musicians, songs with authors; with heterogeneous musical features and obvious influences of newly composed popular music; usually they are slower versions of *"ciganska dvojka";* their melodies, cadences and formal structure are more similar to the so-called *"šumadijska dvojka"*[9] but with the accent on the first beat.[10] Other songs have different influences, but mostly take the current "slower" folk music as a model.[11]
4. Songs by renowned Roma performers and "showbiz" songs, which include a wide, often individual choice, mostly from so-called "raw models" but also from contemporary "Roma show business". They are of various styles.[12]

Conclusion

Music Colony represents an especially interesting environment for many reasons, including the ethnic profile of its population, and its historical role in the creation of musical styles. The fact is that in the Music Colony, as a specific place for training professional musicians, a particular repertoire survived vividly and is still being performed within it and its vicinity. Thus, as much as the musicians might

---

[7] Examples of songs would include "Čerdah Mile Bariškoda", "Piravelo Mile plišano šeširi", "Saeroma pene", and "Amala" (the latter is also sung in Serbian).

[8] Examples: "Ko Kamel", "Ladala", "Sandala", "Mndra mja", "Lidi lidi", all with Romani words.

[9] Unlike the "ciganska dvojka", *"šumadijska dvojka"* has the accent only on the second beat, and it is slower.

[10] Examples: "Na proplanku iznad sela" (author unknown, but from Colony); "Zvoni zvonce zatvorsko" (D. Đorđević-Šarbanac).

[11] Examples: "Plakala sam sinoć" (M. Petrović), "Gledam druga svoga" (M. Pantelić-Pumpi).

[12] Some of these songs are less known among the majority of the population but popular among the Roma, such as "Nataša", which is sung in Romani and Serbian.

try to find a Roma response to each and every one of the conspicuous and current products of the dominant culture, this local music, the style which originates from the 1960s and 1980s, stands for itself, developing and enriching itself through new, contemporary contents. On the other hand, what the musicians actively perform to "others" depends exclusively on commercial demands, which means that the profile and the taste of the "audience who pays" makes the repertoire, in mutual influence with the preferences of the performers themselves. In this sense, the specific heterogeneity of their music and its intercultural mix, which is characteristic for the performances of *Banjaši* and *Gurbeti* musicians, directly depends on the audience and current trends.

The current situation on the domestic music market is largely illustrated by the transfer, or take-over, of the *Banjaši* repertoire by *Gurbeti* and later also Serb musicians. This is illustrated by one of the most popular bands (even well known beyond the borders of the country), the brass orchestra of Boban Marković, who comes from southern Serbia. His music, along the path of its commercial success, has grown out of its original ethnic connotations. Even within the community it is no longer considered as Roma, and by the majority of Serbs easily recognized as "Serbian". In the same way, the style of the Music Colony once had some pretensions to become equally popular within the wider area of the former Yugoslavia, but – for better or for worse – did not enjoy the same success.

References

Đorđević, Tihomir 1984: Cigani i muzika u Srbiji [Gypsies and music in Serbia]. In: Naš narodni život (Belgrade) 3: 33–40.

Đurović, Bogdan 2000: Društvena segregacija i getoizirana svest Roma [Social segregation and the ghettoised consciousness of Roma]. In: Cigani/Romi u prošlosti i danas [Gypsies/Roma in the past and today]. Belgrade: Odeljenje društvenih nauka SANU (= Naučni skupovi, vol. 93; Komisija za proučavanje života i običaja Roma, vol. 3), 89–96.

Gojković, Andrijana 1989: Romska muzika u Jugoslaviji [Roma music in Yugoslavia]. In: Međunarodni naučni skup "Jezik i kultura Roma" [International scientific conference "Language and Culture of the Roma"] (Sarajevo, 9.–11.6.1986.). Sarajevo: Institut za proučavanje nacionalnih odnosa (= Posebna izdanja, vol. II), 401–405.

Gojković, Andrijana 1993: Prilagođavanje Roma današnjem muzičkom životu Srbiji [Adoption of Roma to Serbia's musical life today]. In: Odeljenje društvenih nauka, vol. 2; Naučni skupovi, vol. 70. Belgrade: SANU, 108–112.

Gojković, Andrijana 1994: Cigani u proučavanjima Tihomira Đorđevića sa posebnim osvrtom na cigansku muziku [Gypsies in Tihomir Djordjević's explorations with special respect to music]. In: Balkanika (Godišnjak Balkanološkog instituta SANU) 25, 2 (Appendix): 87–94.

Kovalcsik, Katalin 1999: Folklore Musicians, Revivalist and Electronic Gypsies. Classification of Stage Performers and Musics in Southwest Hungarian Boyash Gypsy Communities. Abstract from the XV European Seminar in Ethnomusicology, 12–15 November, 1999. London: SOAS.

Matović, Ana 1993: Rukopisna zbirka Živojina Kitića: Narodne igre i pesme u izvođenju Cigana violinista iz Srbije [The Živojin Kitić's manuscript collection: Folk dances and songs performed by Gypsy violinists from Serbia]. In: Zbornik Matice srpske za scenske umetnosti i muziku [Matica Srpska review of stage art and music] 12–13. Novi Sad: Matica srpska, 115–130.

Mijalović, Jasna 2000: Cigani – usamljena ili paralelna kultura [The Gypsies – a separated or parallel culture]. In: Cigani/Romi u prošlosti i danas [Gypsies/Roma in the past and today]. Belgrade: Odeljenje društvenih nauka SANU (= Naučni skupovi, vol. 93; Komisija za proučavanje života i običaja Roma, vol. 3), 283–290.

Mitrović, Aleksandra, Gradimir Zajić 1998: Društveni položaj Roma u Srbiji [The social situation of Roma in Serbia]. In: Aleksandra Mitrović et al. (eds.), Romi u Srbiji [Roma in Serbia]. Belgrade: Centar za antiratnu akciju i Institut za Kriminološka i sociološka istraživanja, 9–64.

Mitrović, Aleksandra 2000: Društveni status Roma [The social status of Roma]. In: Cigani/Romi u prošlosti i danas [Gypsies/Roma in the past and today]. Belgrade: Odeljenje društvenih nauka SANU (= Naučni skupovi, vol. 93; Komisija za proučavanje života i običaja Roma, vol. 3), 71–78.

Nešić, Vladimir 2000: Socijalna funkcija etničkog stereotipa Roma [The social function of the ethnic stereotype of Roma]. In: Cigani/Romi u prošlosti i danas [Gypsies/Roma in the past and today]. Belgrade: Odeljenje društvenih nauka SANU (= Naučni skupovi, vol. 93; Komisija za proučavanje života i običaja Roma, vol. 3), 79–88.

Promicer, Kristijan [Promitzer, Christian] 2004: (Ne-)vidljivost skrivenih manjima na Balkanu. Neka teorijska zapažanja [The (in-)visibility of hidden minorities in the Balkans. Some theoretical remarks]. In: Tanja Petrović, Christian Promitzer, Biljana Sikimić (eds.), Skrivene manjine na Balkanu [Hidden minorities in the Balkans]. Belgrade: Balkanološki institut SANU (= Posebna izdanja, vol. 82), 11–24.

Pettan, Svanibor: Gypsy Musicians and Folk Music Research in the Territories of Former Yugoslavia. Internet: http://www.journeyswithgypsies.com/articles/Svanibor_Pettan2.pdf.

Radulesku, Speranta 2003: What Is Gypsy Music? On Belonging, Identification, Attribution, the Assumption of Attributio. In: Romani Music at the Turn of the Millennium, Proceedings of the Ethnomusicological Conference, Prague, 26 May 2003, 79–84.

Sikimić, Biljana 2003: Banyash Culture in North Serbia: Bear. In: Yugoslav Society for the Scientific Study of Religion (ed.), Roma Religious Culture. Niš: Yuroma Centre, Punta, 76–83.

Silverman, Carol 1988: Negotiating Gypsiness. Strategy in Context. In: Journal of American Folklore 101, 401: 261–275.

Vidić, Ljerka 1989: O muzici Roma u BiH i tradiciji novog [About Roma musicians in Bosnia-Herzegovina and the tradition of the new]. In: Zvuk (Sarajevo) 4: 33–41.

Wilkinson, Irén Kertész 1994: "Xatjares?" Do You Feel/Understand It? Mind, Body and Feeling in Hungarian Vlach Gypsy Song Performance. Paper Presented to the European Seminar in Ethnomusicology, Oxford, 1994. Internet: http://www.music.ed.ac.uk/colloquia/conferences/esem/wilk.html.

Wilkinson, Irén Kertész 1999: Study of Roma (Gypsy/Sinti/Traveller) Music and Ethnomusicological Theories. (To be published on the Internet by Archivi di etnomusicologia of the Accademia Nazionale di S.Cecilia (http://www.santa cecilia.it).

Zirojević, Olga 1976: Cigani u Srbiji od dolaska Turaka do kraja XVI veka [The Gypsies in Serbia since the arrival of the Turks until the end of the 16th century]. In: Jugoslovenski istorijski časopis 1–2: 67–78.

Consuming Electronic Music in Bucharest: "Low-profile" Locations and Their Public

Raluca Nagy and Cristina Plecadite, Cluj-Napoca

In order to understand the specificity of clubbing life in Bucharest as compared to that in the West, we will firstly provide a brief overview of the electronic phenomenon in the West and in Romania. Secondly, we will define our goal and theoretical framework as well as argue the utility of seeing this phenomenon as a musical subculture, describe the locations and analyse their public. We will cover issues such as the initiatives that underline the existence of these locations and events, the characteristics and motivation of people who attend them and, eventually, their social interactions and life-style.

We tried to understand the general phenomenon of clubbing and we found resemblances between clubbers and subcultures originating in Britain, such as *skinheads*, *teds*, *mods* or *punks*. The first real clubs, equipped with more than a jukebox or a record player, were founded by *teds* and *mods*. The increased popularity of rock and pop music during the 1960s led to a boom in clubs. The period can be characterized by the split between clubs playing recorded music and those where a music band was hired to perform live for the public. This division led to the differentiation between dance music and rock music. But the predecessors of today's type of clubs are found in the 1970s: the discotheques, where not only the music was important, but also the design of the venue. The DJ slowly became a central figure for the public, using new technologies and mixing records. This was the dominant type of club until the end of the 1980s, but did not remain the only one because rock and punk music also had their own establishments.

The beginnings of techno-rave-electro should be placed in Detroit, USA, and more specifically with a trio of pioneers, namely Derrick May, Kevin Saunderson, and Juan Atkins. The latter seems to be *the* pioneer of electronic music under the stage name *Cybotron* with the first ever techno release, *Enter*. Kraftwerk, a German band, is also credited as being the first real electro-band, coming out with this new type of music between 1975 and 1981.

In the UK, *house* music appeared in 1987 and gave birth to the contemporary *club culture*. Shortly after that, the old discos became unfashionable for the public and promoters of house music. They started to look for alternative places such as open-air spaces, warehouses or industrial buildings. This was practically the birth of rave parties.[1] Thousands of people came to these parties to dance and take Ecstasy, considered the most appropriate drug. These parties took place in the major cities of the US, Canada and Europe. Electronic and rave music started to entail mass movements but, shortly after their debut, these kind of parties were forbidden. The main reason was drug consumption, but the noise and disturbance they produced also played an important role, so house culture moved back indoors. The number of outdoor parties has decreased drastically, but they still exist informally: the participants are usually announced by word-of-mouth, mailing lists, etc; changes have also occurred in the labelling of this phenomenon. By the early 2000s, the terms *rave* and *raver*[2] had fallen out of fashion, particularly in Europe. Many Europeans went back to identifying themselves as clubbers rather than ravers. It fell out of fashion with many electronic music aficionados to describe a party as a rave, perhaps because the term was bastardised. Some groups preferred the term festival, while others simply called the events parties.

Clubs started to become more specialised and to be classified according to the subtype of electronic music they offered, e. g. drum and bass, jungle, chill out, etc. The role of the DJ became more and more important for directly attracting the public.

As far as we have noticed since we started this research, Bucharest follows the Western countries' model regarding the existence of electro clubs where the main importance is given to the DJ. There is no distinction between clubs according to a particular subtype of electronic music, so the scene is not specialised. The reason could be the fact that this music was only recently popularised and spread in Romania and generally in Eastern Europe.

During our research (September 2004 – February 2006), we witnessed an extraordinary boom in the Romanian electro scene. We have browsed a large number of clubs, some of them with a very short existence, that promote this kind of music. Moreover, in the second part of our research we noticed that pop-rock and punk clubs started to promote one or two special electro nights per week. Most of the DJs from the International Top 100 came to mix in Romania, some of them several times. In Mamaia, a Black Sea resort, there are several clubs that host only electro events throughout the whole summer; Timişoara, one of the main cities in Romania, hosts two festivals. Two other festivals take place in the Danube Delta every summer. In the framework of these events, Romanian clubbers find a context in which they can associate their subculture to the Western one. Two foreign electro festivals mainly caught the attention of Romanian clubbers, the "Sziget" Festival in Budapest and "Exit" in Novi Sad, Serbia. Compared to

---

1 Rave is "an all night dance event where DJs and other performers play electronic dance music and rave music" (source: Wikipedia).

2 Consumer of rave music.

other similar events (e. g. Ibiza, Amsterdam, Berlin), the success of these two festivals is also due to their geographical proximity. Many clubbers start considering them one year in advance and save money throughout the whole year to go there. This can also be seen as some kind of initiation or ritual because a real clubber should go at least once to Sziget, the Mecca of regional electro scenes. Many people meet there and start hanging out with each other and continue their clubbing life in Bucharest. There is also the question of meeting foreign clubbers and identifying with them. *"Clubbers in Bucharest definitely see themselves as part of a global phenomenon. That's precisely why it's so popular. People think that they're doing something Western and modern and new"* (m, 25, DJ).

The results of the Barometer of Cultural Consumption[3] 2005 place the percentage of electronic music listeners over 15 years of age somewhere between 1.7 % and 2.7 %, according to the first or second preference. Although we find these percentages rather small given the boom of this phenomenon during the last couple of years, we underline that this is still a very small scale phenomenon.

From the same research the profile of the average electronic music fan is the following: young male, speaks English, French and possibly other foreign languages, does not live alone, rarely watches the news or political shows, but watches documentaries very often, earned a lot of money the previous month, and has a high personal income, tends not to think of himself as religious and lives in a large town or city.

Besides all the mainstream events, publications and web sites, there are several low-profile[4] events that take place in party-houses, former factories or even in official clubs. The aim of our research is to study the public of these low-profile events in the broader context of the clubbing scene.

From its beginnings in the West, club culture was considered a subculture. This view persisted even when clubbing was no longer an underground activity. Therefore, there is no contradiction between being able to talk about club culture and, at the same time, viewing it as a subculture.

---

[3] A study undertaken by the Center for Research on Culture, the cultural policies subdivision of the Ministry of Culture and Religious Affairs.

[4] We have chosen to use the label *low-profile* and not *underground* because the latter, antonym of mainstream, implies the unknown in the sense of not famous; we avoid *underground* also because it references directly the *subculture* concept, especially in the case of music and youth subcultures: Researcher: *So you are organizing these events because you want to support the underground?* Event organizer: *but ... this is not underground; well, I don't know ... what underground? These DJs haven't been underground for a long time now, none of them is. Underground would have been – as a concept – if they were completely unknown. And if they called their friends, I just provided the equipment for them, they paid the entrance fee, and the rest would be their problem. This is organized ... to me it doesn't look underground at all ...*

The literature on subculture emphasises that "subculture is a compromise solution between two contradictory needs: the need to create and express autonomy and difference with the (main) culture and the need to maintain the identifications with this same culture" (Cohen 1980 in Hebdige 1999). Subculture can also be seen as "an imaginary set of relations – the raw material out of which they are constructed is both real and ideological; it is mediated to the individual members of a subculture through a variety of channels: school, family, work, media, etc. Moreover, this material is subject to historical change" (Hebdige 1999).

Culture and subculture are bound together as much through difference as through similarity and they constitute different levels of the same social formation. Individual subcultures can be more or less conservative or progressive, integrated into the community, continuous with the values of that community or extrapolated from it, or defined against the parent culture. It is through the distinctive rituals of consumption, through style, that the subculture reveals its secret identity and communicates its forbidden meanings. It is basically the way in which commodities are used in subculture which sets the subculture apart from more orthodox cultural formations (Hebdige 1991: 103).

Much of what finds itself encoded in subculture has already been subjected to a certain amount of prior handling by the media. The relationship between the spectacular subculture and the various industries which service and exploit it is ambiguous. After all, such a subculture is concerned first and foremost with consumption; we should thus avoid making a clear distinction between the ideological and commercial manipulation of subculture. The subcultural stylistic ensembles – those emphatic combinations of dress, dance, argot, music, etc. – bear approximately the same relation to the more conventional formulae ("normal" suits and ties, casual wear, twin-sets, etc.) that the advertising image bears to the less consciously constructed news photograph.

The communication of a significant difference (and the parallel communication of a group identity), then, is the point behind the style of all spectacular subcultures. Subcultures are expressive forms, but what they express is, in the last instance, a fundamental tension between those in power and those confined to subordinate positions and second-class lives. This tension is figuratively expressed in the form of subcultural style (Hebdige 1991: 132).

Recent approaches to club culture criticize the subculture paradigm, traditionally coined by the Centre for Contemporary Cultural Studies (CCCS) at the University of Birmingham in the early 1970s. "Sub-cultural theory cannot be applied carte blanche to youth today, it is invariably the case that the perspective has been too easily dismissed and stereotyped" (Hollands 2002: 155); Hollands disapproves of subculture's potential to explain youth cultures in their integrity. Hall (1995: 16) also admits that nowadays subcultures "may be less significant than what most young people do, most of the time".

The concept of lifestyle[5] seems more appropriate; it is broader than subculture and potentially takes into account the notions of consumption and consumer culture. It also allows, more than a mainstream club culture, a diversified scheme of styles and cultures countered by social divisions and transitions.

It is interesting to see how these characteristics and critiques of the music subculture fit the phenomenon we have studied in Bucharest.

Bucharest clubbing life is characterized by clubbers with different motivations, a relatively large number of events, though modest compared to Western capitals, drug use and high prices. The reasons why people go to such events are either linked to their musical taste, their lifestyle or to fashion in general. All this does not differentiate the Bucharest scene from the Western world. But there is one

---

[5] "Active expression of 'a way of life' (Miles 2000: 16) and 'the outward expression of an identity'" (Miles 2000: 26).

variable that seems to make a large difference: *affording to be a clubber,* and its implications.

In the West, clubbing is and has been widely accessible; it is a way for middle and lower class people to escape their ordinary lives during the weekend. The currently very small Romanian middle class cannot afford to pay expensive drinks and entrance fees or buy designer clothes:

> "Clubbing imposed itself in a tragic way as a vibrating and happy answer to that selfishness created by the '80s, the period of excess. By the time house music started to be heard, in 1988, with its *Summer of love,* this music meant love, communion, breaking all the social barriers. Instead of going to dance in the discos of businessmen, people were conquering empty storehouses or running to the countryside to do it – illegally, for free, and, most important, together. (...) The Romanian clubs (...) are, due to the unfair Romanian class system, full of businessmen that look like actors from the *Godfather*, young girls that take maximum advantages from their charms, and expats[6] (...) So I have to be thankful for the end of the clubbing era" (Wilson 2004: 42).

Angela McRobbie (2002) provides a more appropriate theoretical framework or at least a softer approach for our research. Her main argument is that across several sectors of the life of today's youth in the creative sector, there is a *network sociality* which is influenced by the persistent impact of dance and club culture. This way of behaving in the club is translated even into work life where it becomes the happy or unhappy intersection between the transformations of the liberal-capitalist economy and the work market mixed with the access of youth to club culture and the importance of it in their lives. This network sociality is also marked by de-specialization, by the intersection with the Internet, by the use of creative capacities provided by new media, by the rapid growth of multi-skilling, etc.

The dance or rave culture that came into being in the late 1980s as a mass phenomenon has strongly influenced the shaping and contouring, the energizing and entrepreneurial character of the new working scene. The level of self-generated economic activity that dance-party-rave organizations entailed served as a model for many of the activities and fields of life after the 1990s. The intoxicating pleasures of leisure culture have now, for a certain sector of the under 35 year olds, provided the model for managing an identity in the world of work, a whole symbolic panoply of jargon, clothes, music and identity.

We think that clubbing, especially for our target *core* of people in Bucharest, has more to do with a certain life-style as Hollands puts it or the way of living and

---

[6] I. e., foreigners working in Romania.

working that McRobbie calls network sociality than a subculture. Interesting features of some studied subcultures can nevertheless be applied to this case, especially the element that differentiates the punk subculture: the idea that beautiful people are not foreign or exotic stars, but the young audience itself. This somehow post-modern or hedonistic characteristic of punk can apply to clubbers and particularly to the core on which we focussed.

The clubbing scene in Bucharest[7]

The places and events

The reasons for choosing most of the locations are simple: our pilot research revealed them as key locations because most informants mentioned them, and conducting participant observation in them was easier. First we tried to focus on one club, *The Web Club* and two unconventional party-houses, *Tra la la House* and *La Ota;* later on we included in our research a museum and a former factory. There are more such places in Bucharest. In the second half of our research period we noticed a veritable boom of such locations, and added them to our initial map. We began our research in *The Web Club*, one of the most famous and probably the oldest electro club in Bucharest. Its importance is confirmed by the interviews and the data provided by all our informants. *"I went to Web for the first time, in '96, and I was fascinated because I had no idea there was such a club in Romania where people listened to that kind of music"* (event-organiser, 40).

Since its opening, *The Web Club* organized mostly parties with Romanian DJs or electro bands. The club has a very interesting strategy of promoting unknown DJs: anyone can go to the bartender with their music and if he likes it one can be a DJ for the night. Thus Web is a very important launching pad for a lot of beginners and very important, talented DJs. This also follows the punk philosophy we rediscovered with clubbing: anyone can be or become a star; someone from the audience can make the music.

In the interviews or conversations with clubbers it came up very often, however, that *"The Web Club is not what it used to be any more: it changed for the*

---

[7] Short methodology note: we used mostly participant and non-participant observation and interviews with different actors of the clubbing scene: clubbers, DJs and event organizers. We used participant observation only for a long period of time, doubled by Internet research and analysis; there are many web sites where we could analyze the forums' content, comments upon the parties or DJs, etc. We added interviews only in the later months. The research team also included three students from the National School of Political Science and Administration in Bucharest: Cristina Colotelo, Viorela Popa and Valeriu Antonovici. The research was developed within the framework of a 3-year project financed by the Open Society Institute – Higher Education Support Program called "Teaching Anthropology – Means and Meanings".

worse" (f, 28, clubber); it has changed from an initial remote, underground, cosy atmosphere to a more public and glamorous one. The location that used to be the pivot of the whole electro-underground scene has gradually lost its importance and is less and less frequented. The explanation is the boom and diversified types of new locations. *"At some point it became clear that there was a migration in the sense that when I organised a party elsewhere, The Web was empty"* (event-organiser, 40).

Two other early unconventional places, the party houses *La Ota* and *Tra la la* host irregular informal events with a selected public which are announced on existing mailing lists, exclusively in the case of *La Ota* and mostly in the beginning in the case of *Tra la la House* which also advertises in a local magazine and on the Romanian MTV channel. The reduced publicity does not mean that entrance is barred to people not on the mailing lists, although there are events for which members must register.

At *La Ota* the owner of the house is also the event organizer. The location is registered as a regular club, but this information is held back in order to give the place a low-profile flavour and to keep a certain control of the public. Most events are irregular and some are based on a particular concept, the so-called theme-parties; these two characteristics set *La Ota* apart from other locations. Normally, there is no entrance fee and apparently no control at the door. But when asked if there are bodyguards, the owner replied: *"It is denigrating to call them that; they are a couple of friends who do this for money. Fortunately, people who come here do not engage in conflicts."*

The parties organized at *La Ota* look more low-profile. The only thing that makes them different from private parties is the paying bar. The atmosphere makes the parties calmer and cosier. The decoration of the basement gives the impression of a normal house inhabited by a family; there is even a nice kitchen where soup is cooked for everyone now and then. The soup even turned into the theme or pretext for a very interesting event. Every Thursday evening there is a crowd of some 70–80 people, Ota's friends and friends of friends, which is also part of *the core*. The owner chose to put this event on Thursdays because it is a week-day, but sufficiently close to the weekend and people already start thinking about partying and switching to the weekend mood, so having a drink and a soup is a good introduction. The idea worked very well and people transformed it into a habit very soon.

The public of *La Ota* is invited through the DJs' mailing lists. Ota keeps this location low-profile also for space reasons: *"It is a small space where I cannot bring more than 200 people ... the DJs have over 300 persons in their databases, so it's fine. At one party in April with 500 people I got scared by the dimensions of this story and stopped the parties till autumn."*

Tra la la is the second party-house on our map. In the beginning it had an ambiguous legal status; it is a rented house which will be renovated or torn down because of its high risk of collapsing during an earthquake. Being an uninhabited house, *Tra la la* is not as cosy as *La Ota;* apart from the graffiti on the walls, one can even notice "no drug consumption" warnings, the toilets are of questionable standards, etc.

In the beginning, *Tra la la* parties were not very successful and not very well organised. After a few parties, the management started a partnership with another association that introduced the concept of *Substil* for parties and was also responsible for the music and the guests, while *Tra la la* only provided the infrastructure. The place began to be more and more popular; besides the DJs' mailing lists, advertising through flyers, posters in the streets, commercials in local magazines and on Romanian MTV was part of the strategy. A database with party attendants was created: *"I made a database. With a dictaphone. I went to the people that came to the first party and I asked for their e-mail addresses. I asked them if they liked it here and they said yes, we would like to come again. Plus the DJs that automatically draw their public wherever they go"* (m, 26, event organiser).

After several parties the two associations split up, but *Tra la la* kept the *Substil* concept: two stages where several DJs mix during the party, a projection room and a chill-out room in the attic. The same party continues on Fridays and Saturdays. The entrance fee is quite high and there are bodyguards at the door, mainly for "face control" than to ensure security. The face control is more important than we expected and we will return to it later.

MNAC, the National Museum of Contemporary Art, was opened in October 2004 inside the famous *Casa Popolului* (former dictator Ceauşescu's Palace). Various events are organised there, from art exhibitions or magazine launchings to concerts and festivals; at all these events we met the same people as in *The Web, Tra la la* or *La Ota*.

There are grounds for including the MNAC in our research. Art specialists maintain that MNAC failed being a contemporary art museum: *"It is way too elitist and clientelistic, it has no public policy, there is a network of people who are managing it and who think they are very hip and know what they are doing, but they are wrong; this has nothing to do with a museum of contemporary art in Europe, Tokyo or New York. This place is a club"* (f, 30, curator).

TEST Point is a former socks factory that hosted its first party in the last weeks of our research. It has a very different concept and is the most "underground" location. The former factory has the atmosphere of a pioneer rave party location, and discovering it was a sign of our integration into the clubbing scene: the first party was popularised exclusively through word-of-mouth and mailing lists. There is a single stage where several DJs mix during the night, the bar is placed together with the chill-out room; the entrance fee is quite expensive. The organisers rented the place for three years which is an indicator for regular activities.

In trying to categorise the places and events under the larger umbrella of mainstream versus underground/low-profile we use the following criteria: (a) status: formal vs. informal, (b) frequency of use: continuously vs. only for special events, (c) prices and targeted public, (d) promotion of events or locations: public (flyers, magazines, MTV) vs. low-profile (word-of-mouth, mailing lists, SMS), (e) organiser: club vs. party-house owner, vs. event organiser vs. DJ or an association created for this purpose.

Obviously, these categories can overlap: one of the informal places is promoted in magazines and has media partners *(Tra la la)*. *The Web Club*, although a formal club, is perceived as a friends' place and hardly a public space: *"not the kind of place that gets noticed when passing by ... it is not like people see it and think: I wonder what it is like in there"* (m, 25, DJ). So all the locations we described have both underground/low-profile and mainstream characteristics but they are all linked by their public, the *core* that constitutes the subject of our research. The public is mostly the same in all locations and sometimes one can find other people according to the specificity of the event. The choice of location was eventually dictated by this *core*. There are different degrees of participation of outsiders according to this mainstream-underground mix of characteristics. But our main interest is in the practices, motivations and characteristics of the *core*.

The people

Our main interest is to determine the position of the *core* in the mass of people who go out and spend time in various kinds of clubs. In order to understand them we observed their practices both inside and outside the club. Their practices also reveal their motivations and their specific character.

People who attend mainstream clubs generally differentiate between real and fake clubbers. Musical knowledge and taste remain the most important markers: *"A real clubber is one who comes for music and not because he heard that Tiesto*[8] *was coming and was famous. A real clubber must know how to distinguish between subtypes of this music. He has to know: that is drum and base, this is dub. This is a real clubber. And he has to have a history; I have been listening to electronic music for years. I go to Bulgaria if there is some DJ I appreciate"* (m, 26, clubber).

8 A famous Dutch DJ who used to be the world's Number One for a long time.

The general belief is that the majority of people do not have this knowledge: *"If I go to Martin tonight and ask half of the club if they know at least one song mixed by the DJ, I bet they don't"* (m, 30, event organiser).

Next to musical knowledge there come appearance and behaviour. Lifestyle and looks are closely associated with a clubber: *"I think sunglasses, fairly cheap looking distressed jeans – jeans with tears, patches – tight tee-shirt"* (m, 25, DJ). Describing their dress is a challenge for the ethnographer: how to describe *trendy, hip* or *funky*? One's first impression in an electro club is that people live in a different world; they are not the people you see out in the streets of Bucharest. Clubbers may combine clothes in very original ways or may wear jeans and t-shirts. Usually they have special accessories and hair styles. *"A funny example: the boy who works at the shop in my girlfriend's block of flats saw me with my hair in a mullet ... and he immediately said to me: 'House!'. For him, having a mullet was a sign of being a clubber"* (m, 25, clubber). The importance attached to looks is obvious, as in any classical case of a music subculture. But the trendy clothing rule does not always apply: some clubbers prefer to spend their money on the entrance fee and drinks rather than clothes.

Clothes can also have an inclusive function: sometimes DJs give details about the dress code for a certain event: "Wear punk / wear funky / wear '80s / wear black and white". Persons who are not on the mailing list but show up at the event are not familiar with these requirements.

The clubbers' behaviour is very connected to the real/fake issue; persons who think of themselves as real clubbers told us that the fakes, those who come for reasons other than music, do not dance near the DJ but stand and watch them from a distance.

The DJ is a very important figure. By attracting his audience he acts as a marketing instrument. When an event organiser chooses a certain DJ he automatically selects the public. The music and the DJ are the ultimate criteria for attending an event. Every DJ has his loyal public and the relationship is not unilateral: some DJs have mailing lists and send invitations to their public.

Apart from this issue of identity, a special interest in low-profile events and locations is typical for the *core,* mostly as a result of social networking. A mainstreamer does not have access to the low-profile, mailing list events and goes to well-known places and events, e. g. big parties with well-known DJs and media promotion. Unlike these mainstream clubbers, the *core* has access to low-profile locations. *Tra la la* parties are a case in point: during our research this venue was publicised more and more, mainstream clubbers and a lot of outsiders began to frequent it and the party house lost its low-profile features. As a consequence the *core* stopped attending the events at *Tra la la*, regardless of the quality of the music or the DJs. For some party organizers and actors of the electro-scene, quitting *Tra la la* was a statement against its association with the Bucharest electro phenomenon which brought a lot of negative media coverage: *"I saw it on the news: at some point all this underground electro movement was associated with Tra la la where people were pissing on the walls ... I got pissed off that all the underground scene equalled Tra la la; not true"* (m, 30, event organiser).

We can thus surmise that the actual driving force of the whole phenomenon is what the *core* does outside the club. Mainstreamers go with the music and the DJ but for the *core* the location goes hand in hand with the social aspect, which is their main motivation and transforms the subculture into a lifestyle. Recent studies have shown that "more exclusive places act to separate this group from the more traditional mainstream, providing an atmosphere for networking, socializing and meeting" (Hollands 2002: 165).

The *core* is homogeneous and limited in number: only a few hundred people are on the DJs' and organisers' mailing lists. Its homogeneity is granted by their similar social status (occupation, income, background, age). Musical knowledge and clubbing lifestyle are of no use for outsiders who want to become part of the *core*. Not even knowing the locations is helpful. Information on the irregular events is spread by e-mail or face-to-face among friends or colleagues of the same social background. The *core* has a tight social network.

As stated earlier, low-profile is not restricted to private locations but also organised in public locations such as Web or MNAC and advertised in magazines, flyers and websites. From this follows that the line between audience and event organisers is hard to define as they all belong to the same network. The same persons switch roles from audience to owners and event organisers, e.g. the organisers of most MNAC events are part of the loyal public of *La Ota*.

Most of the event organisers do these things primarily for themselves, for their own pleasure, beside commercial gain: *"It all started here, I wasn't desperate to organise and make money, but I thought it would be better to make my own events. If I could convince some more people to join, even better!"* (m, 30, event organiser). Some event organisers express their desire to be simple consumers, but then the offers for the kind of events they want would be very limited.

The examples of low-profile locations where the distinction between organiser-producer and public is shallow have a Western equivalent: *"Examples of more underground alternative provision include warehouses, house parties or squats, where the link between production and consumption is literally indistinguishable"* (Hollands 2002: 167, Chatterton 2002).

As for the social status, occupations, and wealth of the *core*, the following interview is very indicative: *"We come from approximately the same world. We work in similar fields, so I can identify with the others and they* [the fields] *are not indifferent to me: the media, as in press, film-industry, music, then advertising. There is a group of people who have to do with art, more or less veritable, generally creative people; some architects, but not many. That's about it"* (f, 24, clubber); *"There are many from advertising, actors, musicians, dancers, journalists"* (m, 40, organiser); *"Web is a place (...) for junkies, freaks, snobs, arrogant, blasé and talented creative persons"* (f, 26, clubber).

Work and training in stylish occupations and the new cultural economies help produce very different youth identities than traditional service employment like retail and office-work. Those employed in similar occupational strata may differ in their leisure choices from the mainstream or just try to achieve social status through consumption of a more premium lifestyle. This environment and the lifestyle constitute the main motivation for the *core*, while there is no strong intrinsic motivation or ideology concerning the musical paradigm. Most of them do not feel like a community: *"There is no value here, everything is reaction. This subculture swallows everything that is not mainstream. I mean ... if you run away from other clubs, you bump into Web, I think ... because you have nowhere else to go. What I know is that there is no value-system. But still, getting into this network is based on more than superficial criteria"* (m, 27, clubber).

The average age of the *core* appears to be over 25 years, higher than the age of the mainstream clubbers.[9] They often mention their similar backgrounds, e. g. the schools they attended. The *core* may be a group of classmates from three or four major high schools in Bucharest, so that their socialisation goes back to the teenage period, which also explains the similar age of this public. One can speak of a generation, the first one that turned from rock to electro.

Listening to electronic music changed the relationships within the old groups of friends. Most clubbers we interviewed told us that before going to these kinds of clubs they listened to other styles of music, especially rock, and went to rock clubs: *"I listened to Depeche Mode and rock music. A friend told me to come to a DJ party and I laughed at him. But it caught me, you know? I realised how cool it was and I stopped going to the rock clubs"* (m, 26, clubber). However, not all of them left the old locations, some of them still go to the clubs for old time's sake or for a different kind of fun, to dance or to socialise.

We can state that the change in social status and friends determined a change in music and club taste: *"I changed my options concerning the clubs because of my daily friends; with my old friends I still go from time to time, randomly, to the old clubs but just for a drink, not particularly to have fun"* (m, 28, clubber). They meet their old friends more infrequently and spend most of their leisure time with new friends. The average share of friends whom clubbers keep from their rock period is a quarter. But what we find very interesting and somehow contradictory is the fact that nobody spoke of making new friends at these electro events. They usually go to a club with a group of friends and stick to them. Clubbers meet new

[9] As an organiser put it: *"Today we can speak about a Romanian club culture because the young generation is already growing up with this music."*

people, change phone numbers in many situations and socialise because, after all, this is one of the main purposes of being there; but they almost never make new friends: *"We tried to maintain a relationship, we went out with these people outside the club but it didn't work. We meet in the clubs, say hi to each other, dance together but that's all. I don't know why. If I went alone I would find for sure somebody to stay with in the club; because we are not so many we have begun to know each other. I know I will see them at the next event, why should I call them? I call and go out with my best friends"* (f, 25, clubber). As leisure time is limited because most of the clubbers have a job, this passion for clubbing enforced some relationships and broke others.

We have focussed on the *core* as the subject of our study, but, probably with the exception of *La Ota,* there is an "auxiliary" audience that attends these low-profile events which is more heterogeneous and not always financially independent: *"Some of them still live with their parents; some of them steal from home to buy K*[10]*; some sell drugs. I don't think you can put all these in the same drawer"* (m, 27, clubber).

The *core* is not totally segregated from the mainstream clubbers or the auxiliary audience. Their exclusivist consumption and social networking are not the only motives of their nightlife; many low-profile clubbers also frequent mainstream clubs because they are the only ones who have the means to engage famous foreign DJs. This does not mean that low-profile locations do not take into account the importance of the DJ, as music is very important. In order to gain the desired audience, the organisers try to invite their favourite DJs who, in turn, have their own mailing lists.

Uncontrolled diversity has an impact not only on the structure of the audience but also on the organisation process. This is where a very important character must be introduced, the bodyguard. We were surprised to meet them even in exclusive places such as *La Ota*, even though the owner characterised them as *"buddies who are doing this for money"*. They indicate the presence of the "auxiliary" audience. Even though the clientele is selected via mailing list, there is a second filter, the face control performed by the bodyguards who are the most trained persons to recognise a clubber of the network. Asked why the bodyguard carefully measures everybody, the event organiser said: *"He knows, that's what he has been doing for so many years now, changing so many clubs. – He knows the whole public? – He knows ... – I was afraid he wouldn't let me in, I am dressed inappropriately. – Oh, no, he doesn't have such problems; you can come undressed, he knows who goes in and who doesn't."*

[10] I. e., Ketamine Hydrochloride.

A whole commercial mechanism was revealed to us by the bodyguard. When there is no audience in a club, the bodyguards find out from one another if there is some event in another place. For a mainstream club a low-profile event can ruin the profit for the evening. It would be naive to leave aside the economic factor. It is obvious that apart from being in the audience, the low-profile event organisers still have a clear purpose: profit. All locations are profit-oriented which is best reflected in their price policy. Prices are invariably high, and sometimes too are the entrance fees, which leads to the selection of the public. Combining this selection through mailing list and high prices appears to work very well. Describing his audience, one of the organisers said: *"These are generally people who have money. They either come from wealthy families or they earn enough money in order to be very open. More or less."*

The audience of the clubs has financial clout but is small in number. The event organisers and owners thus compete in attracting the same small group but try to hide their dispute. In spite of the fact that the electro scene has been growing over the last years, they do not cease their competition and focus on programmes that are better and more sophisticated than those of their competitors.

Finally, with regard to drug use as a common practice accompanying clubbing, we tried to find a possible link between the legal restrictions of drug consumption and the low-profile clubs. This issue is inherent to any study concerning club culture and our initial difficulties in accessing the *core* were due to the possible drug use in these locations. Hiding drug-related issues could be a way of strengthening the in-group through self-protection by maintaining relationships only with persons one can trust. At this point in our research it was very difficult to get adequate insights because people are generally reluctant to speak about drugs. They mentioned drugs mostly when discussing after-hours parties; apparently one of the reasons why such parties disappeared or failed was indeed drug use. Occasionally the subject came up in connection with other issues: *"Club culture? It starts growing, I think it already exists. Yes, it is developing together with drug use. I mean quality drugs started to appear, I don't know, I mean from quality grass to ... everything excluding heroin. Heroin addicts do not go to clubs to dance because they are not really able to ... And if they go, they sleep in the toilet, so they don't really know what is going on. Ecstasy professionally made. LSD is still rare and very expensive. Anyway, for people with a certain social level and a lot of money there is something going on. They have their own language, codes, they have everything they need"* (m, 26, clubber).

Conclusions

Our initial goal was to give an overview of the electronic music scene in Bucharest, taking *The Web Club* as our entry point and drawing a map of this phenomenon. Our research developed parallel to the boom in clubbing and we were slowly driven from the mainstream to the low-profile places and automatically to what we called the *core*, a group of people whom we met in all low-profile locations. This change turned out to be a lucky one as it offered an interesting and new perspective not covered by the rich Western literature on subculture.

The term *subculture* proved inadequate for Romanian clubbing whose patterns differ from those of Western clubbing. The "pioneers" of Romanian clubbing, the *core,* do not consider themselves a subculture. Contrary to the sometimes romantic wishful thinking in (Western) subculture research, the economic aspect proved to be a main driving force behind clubbing, while for the clubbers it is part of their lifestyle. For a sector of those between 25 and 35, clubbing provides a model for managing one's identity in the world of work, a whole symbolic panoply of jargon, clothes, music and identity. Clubbing, especially in Bucharest, is a way of living and working which McRobbie called *network sociality* rather than a subculture. This approach relates cultural consumption to the economic reality of post-socialist Romania. Part of this reality is that clubbing and the electronic music scene are quite expensive – with the consequence that Romanian audiences must be wealthier than Western ones.

In Romania, electronic music is played in separate mainstream and low-profile locations, while in the West mainstream and rave coexist since the 1980s and specialised locations have only recently appeared. There are otherwise many common elements with the Western scene, among them the strong link between professional status and cultural identities in the night time economy. Hollands' argument that there are "special divisions and socially segmented consumption patterns among different youth groupings" (Hollands 2002: 153) fully applies to the Romanian case. We also noticed clear examples of the importance of youth identities in the night time economy which "exploits the existing cleavages in the population and segregates young adults into particular spaces and places" (ibid.). The existence of our *core*, a sophisticated and elitist public with a relative wealth combined with the existence of economic actors smart enough to provide low-profile spaces to attract this clientele. Moreover, these economic actors are themselves part of this lifestyle and there is no clear distinction between provider and consumer. The members of this group are not passive ones that can be easily manipulated because they are often economic actors themselves. The low-profile locations and events also provide the proper environment for the social networking of the group, people with the same educational and professional backgrounds and social status – a group that is very different from its Western counterparts.[11]

Literature

Borthwick, Stuart 1998: Dance, Culture and Television: an Analysis of the Politics of Contemporary Dance Culture and its Televisual Representations. Liverpool, John Moores University PhD thesis.

Chatterton, P., R. Hollands 2003: Urban Nightscapes. Youth Cultures, Pleasure Spaces and Corporate Power. London: Routledge

Chatterton, P. 2002: Squatting is Still Legal, Necessary and Free. A Brief Intervention into the Corporate City. In: Antipode 34, 11:1–7.

Hall, Stuart (ed.) 1995: Resistance through Rituals: Youth Subcultures in Post-war Britain. London: Routledge.

Hebdige, Dick (ed.) 1991: Subculture – The Meaning of Style. London: Routledge.

Hebdige, Dick 1999: The Function of Subculture. In: Simon During (ed.), The Cultural Studies Reader. 2nd ed.. New York: Routledge, 441-450. Internet: http://web.syr.edu/~tjconnel/145/Hebdige-Subculture.html.

Hollands, Robert 2002: Divisions in the Dark: Youth Cultures, Transitions and Segmented Consumption Spaces in the Night-time Economy. In: Journal of Youth Studies 5, 2: 153–171.

Jecu, Marta 2004: Imaginea nomada. Turism visual si spatiu identitar. Bucharest: SNSPA, MA Anthropology and Social Development.

McRobbie, Angela 2002: Clubs to Companies: Notes on the Decline of Political Culture in Speeded-up Creative Worlds. In: Cultural Studies Review 16, 4: 516–531.

---

[11] *"Bucharest's perverted class system means that ordinary people cannot actually buy into the clubbing lifestyle like they could in the UK. In the UK and in the West a lot of working class youths lived to dance and take ecstasy. In fact clubbing began as a very working class thing: the biggest clubs are in ex-industrial centres where the rates of poverty and unemployment are very high. I'm thinking of Cream (Liverpool), Gatecrasher (Newcastle) – very very deprived areas. Clubbing was a kind of escapism from a fairly mundane, horrible existence. In Bucharest it is the opposite ... the House scene is dominated by very middle class kids who can afford to pay 10 Euros to see an act, to buy drugs, to drink Red Bull. It's a very divisive scene. If you look at the club owners who are behind the scene, they're often deeply unpleasant people with very dubious business connections. So yes, there has been a big evolution ... five years ago these people were listening to rock or latino. Now they're listening to house; however, I don't think that Bucharest is 'behind' the West. It's more that it is following an entirely different course of development. And the class system is what is driving this development"* (m, 25, DJ).

Miles, Steven 2000: Youth Lifestyles in a Changing World. Buckingham: Open University Press.

Salasuo, Mikko 2004: Drug Use within the Finnish Club Culture as Marks of Distinction. In: Contemporary Drug Problems 31: 213–229.

Thornton, Sarah 1996: Club Cultures, Music, Media, and Subcultural Capital. Middletown, CT: Wesleyan UP.

Torsello, Davide, M. Pappová 2003: Social Networks in Movement. Networking and Informal Exchange in Changing, Settling and Migrating Societies. Samorin: Forum Minority Research Institute.

Wilson, Tom 2004: Stay at Home. In: Romanian "Elle" Magazine, November, 42 f.

Sources

"Taxi-dancers" – The sub-cultures reader of the Max Planck Institute
Various Romanian magazines and newspapers
Various clubbing websites
Wikipedia

The Reconfiguration of Leisure in Transition: Pubs and Friendship in Constanţa

Raluca Petre, Bucharest

Introduction

The topic of this paper is leisure in Constanţa,[1] both in the past and in the present. The research[2] was undertaken between 2003 and 2005; its first part focuses on the present patterns of leisure, with a special emphasis on *pub culture* as a social practice of spending leisure time. The second part deals with leisure activities in Constanţa from the 1930s onward, memories of them and their significance for the interviewed people. The two perspectives help understand the changes from socialism to capitalism, from one generation to another. The limited space of this paper only allows for a sketch of the findings and their relevance for urban culture in general and for Constanţa in particular. I will focus on the transformation of social relations, especially in the form of friendship in the context of post-socialism. To this end, the emergence of the *pub* in Constanţa in the late 1990s is used as an indicator of a glocalised[3] version of the Anglo-Saxon public house. Social relations are the main indicator of the hybridization of the pub in post-socialist Constanţa. The recollections of past leisure activities are used to explain some of the findings on the pubs in Constanţa. I chose to deal with pubs rather than with clubs, discos or bars because this type of setting is an innovation in the region and a clear manifestation of the global influences penetrating the city on the Black Sea. This new type of entertainment was the appropriate place to explore hybridization, its glocal manifestations and the present as it stands against the past.

The underlying idea and premise of this paper is that leisure is a modern urban activity that can shed light on the overall setting and more of a city in a given

---

[1] Constanţa is one of the largest cities in Romania. In 1996 it had approximately 330 000 inhabitants. The city has a large harbour, which is its main source of income. It is also a tourist site in the summer months for those who visit the Romanian part of the Black Sea. The industry is underdeveloped because of the city's marginal position. The population decreased during the transition period.

[2] The umbrella of the research was the ReSET project on Anthropology. I have to thank the students who enthusiastically participated in this project: Monica Gogoneata, Daniel Marculescu, Oana Musat, Stefan Petrisor, Cristina Petrov, Raluca Selea, and Raluca Vlagea from the Journalism Department at "Ovidius" State University in Constanţa.

[3] The term as used by Zygmund Bauman, indicating a global phenomenon, object or institution as it manifests itself in a local context.

period of time, ultimately linking the particular to the general, the local to the global in the context of shared social knowledge and common sense (cf. Berger/ Luckmann 1991). I consider leisure to be an especially fruitful topic because it has been not as widely used[4] to explain the changes taking place in Eastern Europe after the fall of socialism which are mostly studied from a political or economic perspective. The understanding of this rapidly changing region can be enlarged by introducing the issue of leisure. From the anthropological point of view, one of the main reasons is the possibility to use direct observation and interviews on a topic that is pleasant to approach. Together with the students I came to realize that people enjoy talking about their leisure time, and frequently interesting views of the socialist or present system came up in the interviews.

Background

I will proceed by briefly outlining how Romanians habitually spent their spare time in the 1990s. The prominent feature was that of being rather private, with activities taking place mostly at home in front of the TV, partly because of the hardships of transition, but more specifically due to lack of money because a greater number of products were available on the market.[5] Going out was a privilege. A characteristic feature of the entertainment market in Constanţa is that there were many clubs in the 1990s which no longer exist, being active for only a few months or years. The same is true for the pubs, the first of which were opened in 1999; therefore I consider the pub to be a new phenomenon.

The situation before 1989 was very different. Leisure had various forms; it was a commodity that was strictly controlled by the system: lights were turned off in restaurants after 10 p. m.; from the mid-1970s on, locals were forbidden to have contact with foreigners; access to discos was indirectly forbidden because the entrance fees were charged in dollars and Romanians were not allowed to own foreign currency. Therefore, the privatization of leisure began in the 1980s, also due to economic shortages, the lack of products in restaurants, the spread of VCRs and the practice of paying to watch movies at home in large groups. The interviews allowed us to define the area where most entertainment sites were once located: the old town of Constanţa and the peninsular area that overlaps with the old promenade road.

The city has been transformed substantially in the sphere of leisure as the reflection of an overall transformation. Thus, in the 1990s, state control vanished

---

4 Although the topic of leisure is becoming increasingly popular.

5 This statement is based on statistics published in the media about the leisure time habits of Romanians.

and going out was still a privilege rather than a commodity, but the traditional leisure areas expanded from the peninsula area up to lower Mircea Street. In this street alone there are more than ten entertainment sites, among them two of the most active pubs in town, but their existence was always in jeopardy, some restaurants or clubs existing only for short periods of time. Not only the geography of leisure changed, but also the nature of social relations as a result of the transformation of friendships from a common pattern of social behaviour in leisure activities before 1989 to an exceptional behaviour in the transformation period, as reflected in the pub culture. The most striking element is the difference between friendship as remembered from the period before 1989 and friendship witnessed in the pubs today. This difference has to be explored, but I am aware of the limitations of this approach: the frail memories of the past cannot be compared so easily to the findings of direct observation.

Conceptual basis

Leisure is here understood as going out activities, or activities taking place out of school or working hours. It is a phenomenon of modernity, of the wage era, when subsistence is produced by means of paid labour in a set calendar, rather than by the household with its blurred separation between work and leisure.

The theoretical framework for interpreting leisure, especially pubs, is taken from phenomenology (Schütz 1962), the theory of interactions and roles in everyday life (Goffman 1974), and ethnomethodology (which made us aware of our limits and our position in the inquiry). Garfinkel's works helped us see familiar things with fresh eyes, shaking the "naturalness" of the settings. Bourdieu's (1979, 1980) concept of "habitus" offered the lenses through which to look at human characters and the tastes and arrangements of the pubs. The exploration of the urban environment was facilitated by the works of Robert Park (1915). The most important concept, however, is that of "hybridization" (Bhabha 2003), which helped grasp the variety of pubs in town and overcome the panic of not having anything to write about as we could not find a "genuine" *pub* in Constanţa. The concept was developed around the identity of migrants, but it was equally useful to describe the local variations of the "pub". The value of this concept is the acceptance of in-betweenness as a valid form of identity, and of combined, hybridized forms. Thus, the local forms of pubs could be grasped and explained, mainly against the ideal type of the Anglo-Saxon pub, considering them not as inferior but as different.

For the exploration of the past, the literature on the biographical method was helpful for conducting interviews and for being aware of the limitations of recalling the past "as it was", i.e., of the function of recall as individual story-telling rather than telling the "truth". The value of the biographical method lies in its "adequacy, aesthetic finality, accessibility, authenticity, credibility, explanatory power, persuasiveness, coherence, plausibility, trustworthiness, epistemological validity and verisimilitude" (Roberts 2002: 6) – a soft approach that helped us continue our work.

Methodology

In the first stage of research, the main tools were participant and non-participant observation as well as interviews. The best informants turned out to be experienced bartenders, but we also interviewed clients and owners. The locations were identified by their designation as "pub", with the help of Constanţa tourist maps and the website of the local administration (http://www.ccina.ro), and by walking around in the city, trying to determine whether the locations fit the criteria of the original concept of the pub. One of our first findings was that there are not many pubs in Constanţa. We tried to find out the way the pub had been started, why it was considered a pub by the informants, which were its characteristics, who were its clients and what they did, and how they perceived their pub in relation to the other pubs in town.

For the second part of our research, which began in October 2004, we used documents and conducted biographical interviews with 38 persons, 18 of them aged 30–45, 14 of them 45–60 years old, and 5 of them over 60. The last group was included in order to see how people who experienced the pre-socialist and socialist order remember and reconfigure the past, and how important socialism was in their accounts.

The hybrid Constanţa pubs

Our guiding question was how the concept of "pub" has been changed and hybridized in relation to the social structure and realities of post-socialist Constanţa. The point of departure was the characteristics that define the "pub" in its Anglo-Saxon form, namely a drinking area where people socialize and where there are many regular clients. Besides the social aspects there are also material ones, namely decoration.[6] Being casual is another element considered to be specific. The criteria were established on the basis of characterisations in the Internet.[7] This approach

6 Wooden furniture and a long wooden bar, decorations above the entrance door and inside the pub, pictures or illustrations, smoky windows, a public room, games (pool etc., lately also electronic games in British pubs).

7 http://www.irishabroad, http://www.irishpub.ro, http://www.wikipedia.

can be called the horizontal means of exploring hybridity. The vertical means is considering the past and the comparison of past and present leisure.

Fifteen "pubs"[8] were identified in Constanţa (see table). Some of them exist no longer, some were open only in the summer, others were discos or restaurants. Thus, the name "pub" does not necessarily mean it really is a pub. Therefore we concentrated on those locations that fulfilled more than half the criteria of a pub. The variety of locations that operate under the name "pub" was a clear indication of its hybridized nature in Constanţa, from which derives the question for the reasons and the main deviations from the original.

Characteristics	15 locations
name has "pub" in it	Adry's Pub, Asterix Pub, Captain Mondy's Irish Pub, Casa Mures S.R.L. Pub, Club F Pub, Megalos Pub,
decoration	Adry's Pub, Asterix Pub, Captain Mondy's Irish Pub – Pub, Epava, Irish Pub, Seamen's Pub
socializing	Adry's Pub, Asterix Pub (close to high schools where students know each other), Bourbon House (many thematic parties organized), Seamen's Pub (sailors), Epava, Irish Pub (the regulars)
casualness	Bourbon House, Seamen's Pub
live music, singing	Irish Pub, Oxford Pub, Bourbon House
regulars	Epava, Irish Pub, Seamen's Pub (for lunch) (+
beer/alcohol drinking	all
eating	Epava, Irish Pub, Captain Mondy's Irish Pub, Asterix,
games (pool, darts etc.)	no games
watching football	Epava, Irish Pub,

Thus, the first hybridization concerns the name, which in more than half the cases was just a name without the idea or characteristics of a pub. Some interviewees did not know why the place had that name and what it meant, others said that it was trendy to have the word "pub" in the name. The only cases where the name had something to do with the original idea of a pub were those where the owners had been abroad and had been in direct contact with "genuine" pubs.

Another element hybridizing the initial concept of the pub is dance. Some informants said that going to pubs used to be quite fashionable in 2000 when this type of location was new, but meanwhile people for whom dancing is important

[8] In alphabetical order: Adry's Pub, Asterix Pub, Bourbon House, Captain Mondy's Irish Pub, Casa Mures S.R.L. Pub, City Club Café, Club F – Pub, Epava, Megalos Pub, Deep Pub, Irish Pub, Oxford Pub, Seamen's Pub, Student Pub.

prefer to go to clubs or discos. One informant explained that a few years ago people used to dance in the pubs at and on the tables and on the bar. In some of these pubs it is customary to organize special or thematic events as there is a need for them. The owner of Bourbon House pub said that his place is a "pub in the day time and a club at night". Some pubs are also dancing sites, especially on days when it gets crowded or when special events are organized. When people get excited they would dance rather then sing, as became clear from informants' stories and from participant observation. Only high flexibility guarantees success in the entertainment business.

Vicinity is another important factor for the spirit of a certain pub. Pubs close to high schools are frequented by pupils at least during the day time,[9] while by night they have a very different public. For the "Seamen's Pub" in the harbour, vicinity is decisive, as its guests are exclusively sailors coming in from the sea and harbour labourers taking their lunch.

Two pubs located on the same street have quite different characteristics: "Epava" is a small place on Mircea Street qualifying as a "pub" in seven of the ten criteria we included, opening only in the non-summer months, while the "Irish Pub" is considered the fanciest place in town, both by its clients, by owners and employees of other pubs and by all informants who said it was "the" pub. The place has adequate furnishings,[10] live music, regulars and socializing among them, but scores very low on casualness. An informant said that some Irishmen visiting this pub were disappointed by its formal atmosphere, but it nevertheless belongs to a larger network of Irish Pubs and is the only one in Constanţa with its own website. Actually it is the place where rich locals, foreign tourists or expatriates go out. The pub has a terrace facing the sea.

High prices are another element of hybridization of the original concept. Pubs are not places for the working class, but for the *nouveaux riches*, maybe due to the foreignness of the concept which is associated with the values of capitalism. The types of drinks that are consumed are indicative: beer is indeed consumed, not the cheap local brews but expensive international beers; the guests also drink costly cocktails or strong drinks.

Asked about their motivation to open a pub, three of the interviewed owners pointed out that they had seen pubs abroad, liked the concept and wanted to import it to Constanţa. They consider it a business, and even if the regulars are usually their friends, they are affluent people working in the private sector who do not

---

9 Asterix Pub lies close to the important humanistic high school "George Calinescu", while "Adry's Pub" is close to "Energetic" High School; "Student Pub" is very close to an important dormitory area for university students.

10 The wooden decorations and the long wooden bar are genuine, while the tables and chairs are of the restaurant type.

mind spending a lot of money in order to feel good, be with friends and maybe watch football games. All the owners are men, a fact that could trigger further research on gender roles in the entertainment business.

Socializing and casualness

The most striking hybridization of the pub is socializing and casualness. I will treat this aspect in more detail and link it to the narratives about leisure in the past in Constanţa. One of the commonalities that we encountered and that was confirmed by the interviews was the almost complete lack of socializing and casualness in the pubs. People would not go there to begin spontaneous conversations. Having fun in the pub had little to do with friendship or being casual, but with spending money in a fancy environment. The people we asked would not consider making friends or meeting colleagues in the pub. For many people, the stiff atmosphere, the formal dress code, and the pressure to spend money were intimidating.

The arrangement of tables enhances a centrifugal character of the social space; the largest number of seats at a table is six. The room at the bar is an area for socializing, but it functions as that only in the few places where there are regulars. There are some other kinds of socializing such as flirting, but this is not the kind of socializing typical of pubs. These facts may be due to the specific character of Constanţa as a large city with basically atomized people and its lack of industry and workers who would know each other and have a beer together. The high prices also explain a lot, but these reasons seemed insufficient, so I turned to the past to find more consistent explanations.

The look into the past produced a very different picture, even considering the deviations that memory can bring. One element that came out was stability in almost all spheres of society. Some interesting conclusions emerged from the biographical interviews on leisure. Apart from the oldest informants and those who remembered their rural youth, very few informants mentioned their family as companions: most of them referred to their peers, their band, their workmates, classmates or other students as company. Leisure activities were mainly associated with people of the same age and the same environment. Gender was not mentioned as important, except by those who were over sixty who remembered control from parents, especially when it came to girls; in the socialist period, this control was exerted by the militia. Going out was an activity whose goal was not showing off, as there were strict laws concerning ownership of more than one apartment, car, etc. Friendship seemed to be confined to school or workmates, mostly due to the fact that changing one's work place or residence was a rare exception. Today, changing a job or place of residence has become common practice.

Constanţa pubs are hybridized in several ways, the most interesting aspect being socializing and casualness. The pubs are not places for ordinary people, rather (in 11 out of 15 cases) locations where prices are high and where people do not talk much to each other, but very carefully observe and comment on each other instead. The present picture is very different from that of the past, from stable patterns of representation to flexible social conditions which produce a sense of insecurity and lack of trust.

Conclusions

The "pub" in Constanţa is mostly a hybrid type of location. It has the outward features of a pub, but things take place according to rules that are very different from those of the classical pub. In Constanţa, pubs are quite formal places where the social distance is reinforced by the social setting of space. The high prices make them places for the *nouveaux riches*, not for ordinary people. As the owners and the regulars are exclusively men, pubs are basically male spaces, a fact that also concerns consumption, as it is customary for men to pay for their female companions. Asked about the reasons why people go to pubs in Constanţa, some informants pointed out that it was not for getting to know people or making friends, but for meeting old acquaintances, spending money in a nice place and, last but not least, for showing off. The institution of the regulars, a precondition for intimate social interaction and friendship, was observed in only two of the sites. It was also said that the pubs' clientele were mostly active persons, i. e., people who have a (good) job.

It was difficult to draw a common picture of the pubs as each one is defined by aspects that differ from the "original" pub. The locality and prices highly influence the composition of guests and the spirit of the place. As the pub is not traditional for Romania but an imported institution taking on local forms, it tells a lot about the people and more about the place in the process of social transformation. An analogy with non-canonical religious paintings of popular artists in Orthodox countries can help understand the concept. The peasant artists brought their local environments into their paintings, thus allowing the beholder to understand the culture of that time and place.

It is interesting to note that in Constanţa one of the main features of a "pub", socializing and casualness, is hybridized and deviates from the classical definition. It was this fact that made us look into the past in order to explore the issue of friendship. In the socialist period, stable patterns of friendship were common mostly due to lack of choice, while under the present conditions of transformation social distance replaces the old alliances. Thus, it is not that the people in Constanţa are not friendly and casual, but that they are no longer friendly and casual in places like the pub.

Bibliography

Berger, Peter, Thomas Luckmann 1991: The Social Construction of Reality. London: Penguin.

Bhabha, Homi K. 2003: The Location of Culture. London, New York: Routledge.

Bourdieu, Pierre 1979: La distinction. Critique sociale du jugement. Paris: Éditions Minuit.

Bourdieu, Pierre 1980: Questions de sociologie. Paris: Éditions Minuit.

Cook, Ian, Mike Crang 1995: Doing Ethnographies. London: Institute of British Geographers.

Garfinkel, Harold 1984: Studies in Ethnomethodology. Cambridge: Polity Press.

Giddens, Anthony 1999: Sociologia (Sociology). Bucharest: All.

Goffman, Erving 1974: Les rites d'interaction. Paris: Éditions Minuit.

Halbwachs, Maurice 1997: La mémoire collective. Paris: Albin Michel.

Lowenthal, David 1985: The Past is a Foreign Country. Cambridge: Cambridge UP.

Malinowski, Bronislaw 1944: A Scientific Theory of Culture. Chapel Hill: University of North Carolina Press.

McLaughlin, Paul 1992: How to Interview. The Art of Media Interview. Vancouver: Self Counsel Press.

Metzler, Ken 1986: Newsgathering. Englewood Cliffs, NJ: Prentice Hall.

Park, Robert E. 1915: The City: Suggestions for the Investigation of Human Behavior in the Urban Environment. In: The American Journal of Sociology 20, 5: 577-612.

Peretz, Henri 2002: Metode în sociologie. Observaţia [Methods in sociology. Observation]. Iaşi: Institutul European.

Radley, Alan 2001: Artefacts, Memory and a Sense of the Past. In: David Middleton, Derek Edwards (eds.), Collective Remembering. London: Sage.

Roberts, Brian (ed.) 2002: Biographical research. Buckingham: Open University Press.

Schütz, Alfred 1962: Common-Sense and Scientific Interpretation of Human Action. The Hagueye.

Silverman, David 2001: Interpreting Qualitative Data. Methods for Analysing Talk, Text and Interaction. Thousand Oaks: Sage.

Spradley, P. James 1980: Participant Observation. New York: Holt, Rinehart.

Weiss, Robert 1994: Learning from Strangers. The Art and Method of Qualitative Interview Studies. New York: Free Press.

Football and Political Symbolism in Bulgaria in the 1980s and 1990s

Iva Filipova-Kyurkchieva, Sofia

Introduction

Sports (including football) and their political dimensions are not a new subject for ethnologists and anthropologists, but the example of Bulgaria from the 1980s and 1990s adds new directions to the interpretation of this problem. Developments from the first years of the 21st century should not be underestimated either. They allow to follow, and comment on the changes in the political messages associated with football and to shed light on the contemporary situation. This span of time is not randomly selected: it includes the end of the socialist period when political activity was restricted by the state and democratic political parties were missing. During those years, the state also controlled and organised football according to its own principles, which led to the identification of typical social antagonisms with different football teams. The period under consideration also covers the 1990s, a time of intense political confrontation, which again extended to the football realm. It is an established fact that football is often used for political purposes and people related to football often actively participate in the political arena. The first years of the new century mark some new tendencies in the political connotation of football in Bulgaria.

The methods applied in this article include analysis of oral accounts (interviews with representatives of different age and gender groups) and of documented data, predominantly newspaper accounts from the 1980s until today. For the purposes of greater coverage and representativity, the major party daily newspapers have been reviewed: for the socialist period, *Rabotničesko delo* ("Workers' Affairs"), the organ of the then ruling Bulgarian Communist party, and *Otečestven front* ("Fatherland Front"), the organ of the "Fatherland Front", the largest mass organisation in socialist Bulgaria. For the early 1990s, I used the newspapers of the major political parties at that time: *Demokracija* ("Democracy"), the party organ of the new, anti-communist political party SDS ("Union of Democratic Forces") and *Duma* ("Word"), the newspaper of the Bulgarian Socialist Party (BSP, successor of the former Communist Party). I also analysed specialised sports publications, such as *Naroden sport* ("Popular Sport") and *Start*, which date from the socialist period, and *Meridian Match* and *Planeta Sport* from the 1990s. These selected newspapers provide a basis for comparative analysis. Additional important information sources are Internet websites, such as fan sites for the most popular Bulgarian football clubs *(http://www.levskihools.hit.bg; http://www.forzacska.hit.bg)* and graffiti by organised fan groups and extremist football fans.

The relation between sports and politics has been the object of abundant research. Among anthropological interpretations of sport, authors such as A. Cheska (1979), E. Wagner (1989) and R. Lipsky (1983) should be noted, who examine sports as an instrument for achieving political objectives and discuss the symbols of sport and its ability to distract from mundane problems and to reinforce the cultural codes of authority. J. Hargreaves places, in his discussion of the relation between sports and politics, an emphasis on the use of sports as a means of social control and of subjection to political order and authority (Hargreaves 1982; 1986: 3–5). In his study of "invented" political traditions, E. Hobsbawm alludes to innovations brought forward by mass movements perceiving sports, and football in particular, as part of these processes as well as a "mass cult" (Hobsbawm 1992: 289). Football not only reveals a lot about society and culture, but it is part of the more general process of social and political development. In the most recent research, emphasis is placed upon the interpretation of cultures of sport, and hence the social and political power of the language of sport and its ability to attribute certain meanings to social life: to create communities, to define political struggles, to include and exclude individuals and groups, to construct gender relations, to promote ideologies and to construct national identities (see Booth 2004: 103 f.).

Among the recent research by Bulgarian ethnologists on sport, the works of B. Georgieva and P. Petrov must be mentioned, who analyse various problems related to sport: its entertaining and social functions and its use for political purposes, including the construction of national identity at the end of the 19th and the beginning of the 20th centuries (Georgieva 2002; 2003: 69–118). Petăr Petrov discussed the use of sports as a source for acquiring local, regional, ethnic and political identities from the pre-socialist to the post-socialist periods (Petrov 2002). The work of M. Ilijčeva, which is dedicated to the relation between nationalism and the actions of sports fans, is also important for my discussion (Ilijčeva 2004).

Football in Bulgaria

At the end of the 19th century, sport in Bulgaria entered a new stage of development with the establishment of clubs, societies, and federations; in other words, sport was becoming institutionalised. The first steps in the transformation of sports from an amateur pastime into a professional activity can be dated to these years. In this period, the state also directly participated in the process of stimulating sports across the nation and provided the financial support necessary to do so (Georgieva 2003: 70, 110). The founders of sports associations and clubs were mainly Bulgarians who had studied abroad, or foreign nationals living and working in Bulgaria (Bardareva 1991: 9, 35, 47 f.). The names of the first Bulgarian football clubs from the beginning of the 20th century were not chosen randomly; most of them referred to famous personalities from the so-called Bulgarian Revival Period: Levski, Botev, Rakovski, Benkovski. These names enabled the state to use sports for political purposes, especially for the consolidation of the nation, the "rise of the national", or the "revival of the nation" (Georgieva 2003: 110).

Football was introduced in Bulgaria at the end of the 19th century by Swiss physical education teachers and became popular among university and high school students. The rules of the game were first published in the magazine *Učilišten pregled* ("School Review"), and the Ministry of People's Education recommended football as a sports activity in schools (Popdimitrov 1985: 232–235). This proves that the state took an energetic part in activities related to sports and used sports for political manipulation. The social groupings and organisations carrying out sports activities, including football, became part of the mobilisation of the nation. Not surprisingly, E. Hobsbawm devotes special attention to education, which was used for the "making-up" of traditions related to the construction of new political identities in West European countries at the end of the 19th and the beginning of the 20th century, and examines it as the secular equivalent of the activities of the church (Hobsbawm 1992: 271). The strong connection between sports and politics in Bulgaria would survive, and indeed flourish, during the entire 20th century, especially in the socialist period, but also thereafter.

"Red" vs. "Blue" – CSKA and Levski

In this article, I focus on the confrontation between two major football clubs from the Bulgarian capital Sofia – *Levski Sofia* and *CSKA Sofia* ("Central Sports Club of the Army") – as examples of the politicisation of football. I limit myself to this case because it can, on the one hand, most precisely serve as an analogy for the political confrontation between the anti-communist SDS party and the post-communist BSP in the 1990s and, on the other hand, is most indicative of the interconnectedness between politics and football in the 1980s. In order to track the development of the political agenda around football, I also include some instances from the period after the year 2000.

In the 1990s, *Levski* became a symbol of the process of democratisation or, more generally, of democracy. As a club established in 1914, i.e., before the 1944 communist coup, it symbolised change in Bulgarian political life. Bearing the colour of the new political formation SDS – blue – *Levski* gradually started to be equated with democracy and the political values of the SDS. It was the old, traditional and, most importantly, the blue, i.e., the anti-communist, club. These analogies were mostly superficial but with a categorically symbolic message. The clear and undoubted football duel between *Levski* and *CSKA* was projected onto the political scene. The number of supporters of both teams during the socialist period was comparable, but after the political changes in 1989, the number of *CSKA* supporters was visibly reduced, while those of Levski increased. This is probably logical considering the fact that *CSKA* was created in 1948 as the football club of the Ministry of Defence. It enjoyed the special support of the regime, especially in the 1950s and 1960s, and was generally known as the "red team". The continuing existence and eventual rise of *CSKA* in the 1990s was probably due to the fact that, at the time of its establishment, it had been able to fill an underdeveloped niche and to build a solid support base. This was similar to the development of army clubs in Romania and Yugoslavia, as opposed to countries like Hungary and the Czech Republic, which had a longer and broader pre-socialist football tradition, and whose army clubs were dissolved in the 1990s.

In the 1990s the confrontation between *Levski* (SDS) and *CSKA* (BSP) dominated the public space. The colour symbolism was not a new phenomenon in sports, and linked sports to national and party identifications (cf. Hobsbawm 1992: 293). For example, outfits with red shirts were worn by the members and supporters of the gymnastic society *Borec* ("Wrestler"), which was founded in 1902 in Jukbunar, a quarter of Sofia. The idea behind the society was to attract youth to the leftist movement and to expose them to ideological propaganda by left-wing leaders (Georgiev 1985: 40 f., 97). Thus, sports was used for political recruitment.

In retrospect, political symbolism in the football antagonism between *Levski* and *CSKA* had existed in the socialist period as well, but was naturally confined within the political framework of that time. There were, of course, no outspoken political elements in the antagonism, but *CSKA* was patronised by leaders of the Communist Party, such as M. Balev, who was described by a sports journalist as "an ardent supporter and number one fan among the Party elite" (interview with P. P., aged 32), and D. Djurov (*Meridian Match* 2004, No. 251: 4). *CSKA* even became national champion in the year of its establishment. *Levski* also had its patrons among the party elite, but they were less powerful, such as A. Solakov and B. Velčev. The latter even fell from grace due to disagreements with the family of party leader Todor Živkov. During the socialist period, there was a tendency of neglecting and gradually undermining *Levski*. In 1944, it had been turned into the sports club of workers in the postal services, the textile industry, the food industry and the printing industry; generally people with low and irregularly paid wages. From 1949 until 1957, the club was called *Dinamo* to copy the Soviet model. Popular opinion sometimes associated *Levski* with the Bulgarian National Legions extreme right-wing forces before 1944, and some people accused it of "fascist" tendencies before 1944. One male interviewee, aged 72, was categorical: "Not every *Levski* fan is a fascist, but all fascists are *Levski* fans." In 1957, the club was reinstated as "Levski Physical Culture Society", and in 1969 it merged with *Spartak* to form *Levski-Spartak DFS* – "Association for Physical Culture and Sports at the Ministry of Interior and Ministry of Communications" (Djundjulova 1986: 3 f.). The public jokingly commented that it was not "Levski-Spartak", but "Levski with a pistol", which in Bulgarian sounds similar – *"Levski s patlak"* (female interviewee, aged 67). Clearly, state and party leadership wanted to equalise the status of both clubs, to unify, model and control them according to their own objectives.

In the socialist period, due to the lack of political alternatives and competition, antagonisms inherent to any society were associated with, and expressed by the support for different football teams. The state, therefore, tried to control and organise football. The ruling elite was well aware of the importance of the irrational element in keeping groups together and preserving the social order (cf. Hobsbawm 1992: 268 f.). Although it was not explicitly political, the symbolism regarding the two football clubs was extremely strong. Party leaders also sensed the tendency of football to fill the niche of possible confrontational expressions. This is partially evident in the change of name imposed on the *Levski* and *CSKA* clubs in 1985. The formal reason for this decision, dictated by the party leadership, was a brawl between supporters of both sides during a game for the National Cup Finals. The Politburo of the Bulgarian Communist Party, "trying to reverse the development in Bulgarian football", dissolved both clubs, revoked the licences of players, coaches and managers, abolished football clubs attached to administrative institutions, established new clubs according to the territorial principle, and removed *Levski* and *CSKA* from the first football league in the country (*Naroden Sport*, No. 74, 22 June 1985: 1). The newspaper *Naroden Sport* fully supported the decisions of the central party leadership, which were confirmed at the respective plenums of the Bulgarian Union for Physical Culture and Sports and the Bulgarian Football Federation. In a series of consecutive issues, the paper's headlines read: "Uncompromising to the End", "Full and Total Approval", "Spontaneous and Unconditional Support". The two clubs were renamed *Vitoša* (Levski-Spartak) and *Sredec* (CSKA). The desire was to relieve the tension between the two clubs,[1] which although not political, was nevertheless unacceptable for the regime. Thus, the "societal contract" was renewed under the administrative control of the party. The symbolism, expressed by the supporters of these two

[1] Božidar Iskrenov, an emblematic Levski player, explains that the decision taken by the Central Committee of the Bulgarian Communist Party was due to the fact that, in 1984, *Levski-Spartak* won both the national cup and the championship (*Demokracija,* No. 207, 1994: 15). According to the opinion of sports journalist P. Pindrakov, this measure was a premeditated campaign provoked by M. Balev and his clique with the objective of stopping the rise of *Levski-Spartak*. Naturally, by taking the matter to the highest party level, reciprocal measures would be taken against both teams (*Planeta Sport,* 16 December 2000: 8).

clubs, had to be ignored because it went beyond the framework devised by the socialist system, within which there was no place for political debate.

The supporters of both clubs did not accept this change of names despite the authorities' attempts to forcefully impose it. They did not approve of the new names of their clubs and during games used the old names despite the presence of police detachments in the stadium and their attempts to intimidate the fans. The new names were formally kept until 1989 (even though *Sredec* had become *CFKA Sredec* in 1987), but the authorities unofficially gave up the idea to enforce them, which demonstrated their inability to destroy the symbolism that was vested in the names of the football clubs.

Political attitudes towards football were also reflected in the press coverage by the tightly controlled socialist newspapers. The articles in the sports newspaper *Naroden Sport* in the mid-1980s, for example, are dominated by technical commentaries emphasising results, sportsmen's skilfulness and sportsmanship, illustrated in headlines such as "Shower of Red Cards – Sound the Alarm", and "Good Results – Average of Four Goals per Game". The style of writing and wording fully corresponded to the spirit of the 1980s and emulated the two obliging official newspapers *Rabotničesko delo* and *Otečestven front*. The paper featured discussions about the instructional functions of disciplinary penalties, self-criticism, typical slogans and campaign initiatives. After 1987, the newspapers *Rabotničesko delo* and *Start* published critical articles against football hooliganism. The latter newspaper was an example of more attractive journalism by the Perestroika generation. However, there was no real change. Special attention was paid to football players with "deviant" behaviours – unkempt appearance, not observing a regimen (sleep, recuperation), use of alcohol; in other words, disregard for the code of professional athletes. The comments, although scarce, generally repeated the main postulates of the authorities. Sport was purposefully harnessed and used for conveying the political line of the socialist period.

After the changes of 1989, the two main party daily newspapers *Duma* and *Demokracija* were valuable sources for the political symbolism attributed to football in the 1990s. During the entire period reviewed, *Demokracija* notably favoured the team of *Levski*. Throughout the 1994 parliament election run-up, for example, soon after the start of the campaign the headline "I will vote for SDS again" featuring the picture of Levski player Plamen Getov appeared. Ten days later, the photo of another *Levski* star, Božidar Iskrenov, underlined the same statement in *Demokracija* ("I will vote for SDS again"; see Picture 1 in the appendix). This player, in an interview with the newspaper made his political attachment to SDS and more generally to "the blue idea" explicit (*Demokracija*, No. 207, 10 November 1994: 15). *Demokracija* returned these favours and made Iskrenov its most favourite face from the *Levski* team in the mid-1990s, nicknaming him "The Joy of the People", similar to the Brasilian football legend of the 1960s, Garinca. While the sports page of the socialist party newspaper *Duma* did not deal with Bulgarian football in detail and often did not comment on it, *Demokracija* did not conceal its bias. The positive hero on its sports pages, Nasko Sirakov (then the most renowned *Levski* player), was coloured in blue, (*Demokracija*, No. 202, 1994: 15; No. 247: 7; No. 248: 7). The negative hero was the forward Hristo Stoičkov, the star of *CSKA*, who was portrayed as the red "communist" footballer. Stoičkov himself, though, always denied any connection with the Bulgarian Socialist Party.

The intensity of the political messages associated with football changed during the 1990s. Towards the beginning of the period they were greatly emphasised, but as the bipolarity in political life gradually watered down after the middle of the 1990s, politicians and journalists lost interest in associating the "blue" club with the "blue" party, and the "red" one with the "red" party. Nowadays, association of *Levski* with the SDS party is no longer popular among the club supporters. In the early 1990s, SDS had symbolised the change in Bulgarian political life, while during recent years the party has substantially lost its significance and prestige.[2] The association of *CSKA* with communism is, however, still upheld until the present day by the opponents of the "red" club, as the following examples illustrate. The *CSKA* football club itself, and also the socialist party, have taken a passive stand on the issue and are not claiming any proximity.

The football club of the army rather aimed at distinguishing itself from the former regime, which had contributed to the negative perception of the club in the new political situation after 1989. Neither the supporters nor the fan club of *CSKA* identified themselves with the BSP after 1989 and did not seek any connections with the party. From the early 1990s until 1999 even the five-pointed red star was removed from the emblem of *CSKA*, the "Central Sports Club of the Army". The dispute about the star was finally settled in favour of its restoration, which was demanded by the fan club and the mass of unorganised supporters. The new management of the club, headed by Ljuben Penev, was elected exactly because this was one of their promises to the fans. There were also debates on whether to keep the acronym *CSKA* but to change the full name since it was deemed discrediting by some. For *CSKA* as well as for some other clubs, the upholding of the symbols, signs and names from the socialist period was the only way to stand out and demonstrate their distinct identities.

For their opponents' supporters, this only proved their "communist" sympathies. In the early 1990s, fans therefore stressed that *Levski* was the only counterpoint to *CSKA*, the club once favoured by the party elite during the socialist period, and therefore *Levski* was the club to be supported by the majority of the population. The supporters of *Levski* often defined their club as "the team of the

---

2 The visible sign of the crisis in SDS today is its splitting into a number of smaller political formations.

people", which was "alone against all", and in particular against the "communist conspirators". These perceptions are still firmly present today, as for example a look at Internet chat rooms reveals: "Only Levski is champion of the people, not the broth made of communists [a derogatory term for CSKA because, according to popular beliefs, the main food served in the army is broth]" (*http://www.big brother.bg*, 2 December 2004). A *Demokracija* feuilleton of 1994 attributed specific characteristics to the supporters of both clubs: the *Levski* fans waved posters and flags, while the *CSKA* fans were well-to-dos "and occasionally some generals" (*Demokracija,* No. 90, 1994: 12). The two-way influence between football and politics is also evident in the insulting slogan "Red thrash!", which was adopted by the *Levski* fan club from the rallies of SDS. During the first half of the 1990s this was the main chant against *CSKA*, which aimed to portray the team and its supporters as communist. The derogative slogan: "Red thrash!" was revitalised in Bulgarian political life in the beginning of 1997 during the mass protests against the BSP government headed by Žan Videnov. Since the end of the 1990s the use of this slogan in stadiums has been gradually disappearing, most likely as a result of the attenuation of political confrontation. Another significant factor for the relaxation of political overtones in the football arena is the generational change that can be observed among ordinary supporters as well as organised fan groups and their prominent members during the second half of the 1990s. This age group, born in the late 1970s and early 1980s, during the latter part of the socialist period, was thus not fully socialised in the system and displayed little passion for politics.

Football was not only used to express political sympathies, but also to gain political support. Some leaders of the "blue" political space often used football for shaping their image. Prominent figures of the SDS, such as Stefan Sofijanski (ex-mayor of Sofia) or Georgi Markov (ex-leader of SDS),[3] were regularly present at team activities. The latter was also a member of the Management Board of *Levski* and coined the famous political slogan: "The communists are up for a good kick from the SDS". Generally, the connection between politics and sports language can be easily traced in statements by politicians, who use language from various sports in order to convey their ideas (Billig 1995: 123). In the spring of 1991, Maria Louisa, sister of the last Bulgarian king (and prime minister 2001–2005) Simeon Sakskoburgotski, appeared at a *Levski* game as representative of SDS circles close to the former monarch.

The opposite process also occurred, as individuals who had become famous in football sought political office. This desire was not coincidental, as prominence in

[3] In the early 1990s he was one of the leaders of SDS; later he became judge in the constitutional court and currently he is one of the leaders of the rather obscure political formation *Red, Zakonnost i Spravedlivost* (Order, Lawfulness and Justice).

football brought essential political assets: popularity, contacts with people of authority and career opportunities. A telling example is the case of Hristo Protočanov, President of *FC Neftohimik*, a club based in the city of Burgas and associated with the big oil refinery there. Protočanov became (in-)famous in the 1990s for his offhand behaviour in football circles, maltreatment of referees, and rigged games. Through football, he accumulated popularity which he exploited for his personal political ambitions. At the end of 2000, he created the "Green Party" and ran for parliament as leader of this party. As V. Mihov, president of the Bulgarian Football Union between 1992 and 1994, stated, some members of parliament "realised that politics can be successfully entered through football" (*Demokracija*, No. 217, 1994: 8). This interrelationship between party politics and football is clear during the whole period. The relation between state policy and football also became evident during the 1994 World Cup Finals, in which Bulgaria participated. The popular sports daily *Meridian Match* then commented that participation in the finals would speed up the adoption of a new state emblem, an issue also raised by president Želju Želev in the National Assembly. After the remarkable performance of the national team at the World Cup (they reached fourth place), the national manager and most players received one of the highest state merits – the First Degree of the *Stara Planina* Medal for "exceptionally great service to Bulgaria" (Petrov 2002a: 208).[4] This high mark of honour had been created in 1966 in order to distinguish foreign nationals; coach Dimităr Penev and his players were the first Bulgarian nationals to receive this honour.

Due to its mass appeal and popularity, football is therefore used by the state for the advancement of its policies. It can create a feeling of community and has influence on the local as well as national level. Football also allows the Bulgarian communities abroad to assert their identity and extract political dividends from their "kin nation-state". For example in December 2000, the veterans of *Levski* came to the town of Bosilgrad in Serbia, which hosts a Bulgarian minority, for a game against the local club *Mladost* and were greeted by over 500 people. After the game, a *Levski* fan club was established at the Bulgarian Cultural and Information Centre in Bosilgrad, and its members received membership cards from the National Fan Club of *Levski* in Bulgaria (*Planeta Sport*, 6 December 2000: 2).

Football and nationalism

Another political element in Bulgarian football is evident in expressions of nationalism. Nationalist elements in the symbolism of football in the 1990s were copied from Western European, and predominantly English football supporter groups, but

---

[4] Promulgated in *Dăržaven vestnik* (State Gazette), No. 60, 26 July 1994: 1–2.

the specific characteristics of nationalistic prejudice in Bulgaria provided local flavour. The terms "Turks", "Turkish" and "Gypsy" were and are often used in the chants of fan groups during football games and often "adorn" graffiti dedicated to football issues.

But already in the 1980s, sports events, as key collective rituals, had been used for a moderate boost to the national consciousness amidst the monotonous everyday life of socialism. Curiously though, the process of the forced renaming and assimilation of the Bulgarian Turks – the so-called "Revival Process" of 1984–1985 – did not influence the confrontations between *Levski* and *CSKA* until 1989, "due to lack of interest" according to one of my respondents (male, aged 33). Anti-Turkish feelings were also not present in the stadium probably because the minorities were not a problem for society but only for the Bulgarian Communist Party and the state, which played the nationalistic card to demonstrate and affirm administrative control. This issue was not commented upon in the public space and therefore did not influence the behaviour in the stadiums.

Aside from that, room for fans' activities was limited before 1989. Official fan clubs only appeared in the 1990s; the only attempt during the socialist period dated from the end of the 1960s and was initiated by a school teacher from Sofia, supporter of *Levski*, whose brother was a famous football player. But the "Levski Supporters Club" only existed for a few years. In the 1980s, supporters gathered for game or practice sessions at their team's stadium. Flags and banners were not used. Scarves were the only attribute allowed at the games. The only fan actions not banned by the Peoples' Militia (the police force at the time) involved the so-called "punished" scarves. After a game between *Levski* and *CSKA,* the fan groups of both teams had favourite meeting places, and the goal was to wrestle a scarf from a supporter of the opposing team. Usually the words directed to the opponent were, "Get out of the scarf!" and, after their forceful acquisition, scarves were burnt, thrown away or most often hung from trees around the fan groups' meeting places. Red scarves decorated trees around the so-called "Dead man" garden,[5] while blue scarves were hung around the Orlov Bridge. These places were not randomly selected: they were located along the routes leading to the respective National Stadium sectors designated for each of the fan groups, and Orlov Bridge is near the Bulgarian Army Stadium.

It is interesting to note that in the 1980s, the militia was exceptionally tolerant to the lighting of torches made from newspapers brought to the stadiums, in order to cover the seats in case of rain. According to my research, this represented the

[5] There are different popular etymologies of this name: some say that it comes from the particular architecture of the club-restaurant of the Bulgarian Army, which is located in this park and resembles the funeral house at the central cemetery of Sofia. Another version refers to a bomb that fell on that spot and killed an elderly person during World War II.

only symbolic gesture allowed at the stadium during that period. Generally the symbolism in the 1980s was poor and limited as opposed to the 1990s, when the forms of communicating one's message become more various. However, football hooliganism and its typical manifestations were already rampant in the 1980s. "Hooligans" struggled for territory and control and joined in street fights, where they publicly displayed aggression.

In the 1990s, open nationalism entered the activities and rhetoric of football fans. According to Ivan Čolović, nationalism as a behavioural pattern can go beyond the symbolic realm of games and, in certain political and social conditions, can be transformed into real participation of organised fan groups in military conflicts, as was the case during the break-up of Yugoslavia (Čolović 2000: 383–385). Vrcan and Lalic come to the conclusion that the confrontation between football fans can serve as a catalyst of political violence at the mass level. Attempts at symbolic domination of the public space can grow into real participation in ethnic conflicts, such as witnessed in the former Yugoslavia in the 1990s (Vrcan, Lalic 1999: 177–179). This did not happen in Bulgaria, but certain changes in fan behaviour were nevertheless apparent.

In the 1990s, the organised supporters of *Levski* began to represent the "C" in the *CSKA* acronym as a crescent, thus portraying the *CSKA* as Turks, because they had killed Vasil Levski – the national hero of the Bulgarian Revival also known as the Apostle of Freedom, and name patron of the *Levski* football club. The "logic" was as follows: *CSKA* were against us and therefore against Levski "the Apostle". And, since the Turks had been against Vasil Levski, then the CSKA were "Turks". In this case, the football club identified with the national hero and projected conflicts of the past upon the relations between various football supporter groups. This identification had also been typical for the period until 1944. The first anthem of *Levski* from 1921, for example, goes: "With zeal we defeated everyone – all because Levski is in our blood!" (Noikov 1994: 28). The association of the *CSKA* with Turks appeared at the very beginning of the 1990s, when the issue of the Turkish minority attracted much interest in the Bulgarian public, especially after the establishment of the "Turkish" party DPS (Movement for Rights and Freedoms), which won seats in the first democratic parliament in 1990. The increasing assertiveness of the Turkish minority influenced certain social groups and their respective reaction found its expression also in the stadiums.

The link between the *CSKA* and Turks is part of football supporter rhetoric even today, which is evident from graffiti messages and from electronic discussion forums, such as the "Big Brother Show". There one can read slogans such as "Kick out Alidžan [a participant in the show who is of ethnic Turkish origin] – he is a broth eater [the offensive term for CSKA supporters]. I appeal to all Levski fans to rout out the pig [another derogatory term for CSKA supporters]! ... All the broth eaters to Turkey!" (*http://www.bigbrother.bg*, 2 December 2004). Hristo

Stoičkov, an emblematic figure for *CSKA*, was often called "Turk" and "Kurd" by *Levski* fans during matches. Thus supporters use contradictory terms, which in reality exclude each other and demonstrate political incompetence, such as the combination of "Turk" and "Kurd". For comparison, in the Republic of Turkey, a common insult used by most fan groups is to label their opponents as supporters of the extremist Kurdish Workers Party PKK (Kozanoglu 1999: 124). Another example of anti-Turkish fan behaviour was related by one of my informants (male, aged 21) who told of a man who boasted to have urinated on a Turkish flag pole at the border checkpoint when entering Turkey for a fixing between *Levski* and the Turkish side *Galatasaray* in Istanbul, August 2001.

To describe the negative characteristics of Hristo Stoičkov (according to popular opinion he was the best *CSKA* player), fans also used other ethnic qualifications with contemptuous hue, which even entered newspaper discourse. *Demokracija* wrote" ... it has been proven that God is Bulgarian and his name is Stoičkov. In recent days it became apparent that the great football player is also a Gypsy god" (*Demokracija*, No. 228, 1994: 8). This reference alluded to the album "With the Name of God" by the Roma singer Ivo Barev, which Stoičkov particularly liked. The journalist's language thus reinforced the negative image of Stoičkov.

In response to these insults the fan club and extreme supporters of *CSKA* claimed that *Levski* were Turks and represented the letter "S" in *Levski* as a crescent ("S" is written "C" in the Cyrillic alphabet). Devoted fans categorically stated, "For me *CSKA* is a religion. For me *CSKA* is the team of the Bulgarians" (*CSKA*, No. 2, 2003: 42). Part of the organised supporter group explains the reasons for street fights with supporters of *Levski* in a clearly nationalistic context: "... in *Levski* 40 percent are Gypsies, 40 percent are Pomaks and 20 percent are Bulgarians. But with an unknown origin ..." (ibid.). In view of these comments, another important aspect should be discussed: the body of extreme supporters, so-called "ultras", from the fan group of *CSKA* is more homogenous and monolithic than that of *Levski*, which facilitates the easier adoption of slogans with nationalistic character. The supporters and fan-club members of *Levski* represent a larger and more diverse group with regard to age and social background. *Levski*'s organised fans are divided into two formations: one is the official fan group, which is more moderate and directly connected with the football club, from which it also receives money. The other, called *Sofija-Zapad* (Sofia-West), has a younger membership and displays some nationalistic tendencies akin to the *CSKA* fan group, which is lacking among the official *Levski* group.

Hence, the messages carried by the slogans of ordinary supporters and organised fan groups in the middle of the 1990s increasingly changed from an ideological to a nationalistic spirit. Obviously the generational change discussed earlier predetermined this process. With the opening of the country to the rest of the world after 1989 it became much easier for the younger generations to copy and adopt trends in European football, especially the nationalistic ones. These processes in football reflected certain tendencies in Bulgarian society and preceded their manifestation in the political scene. The increased popularity of nationalistic forces in society became finally evident during the last parliamentary elections in 2005, as the extreme right-wing formation *Ataka* (Attack) won seats in Parliament. Political commentators in Bulgaria explained this as a social reaction against the growing participation of DPS in the government of the country.

Slogans with fascist and national-socialist content were also often observed at football matches in the 1990s. Many of them carried the main ideas of such movements, such as "My honour is my loyalty", "One love, one struggle, one team". These were mostly used by the organised fan group of *CSKA*, mainly by its extremist representatives – the so-called "ultras" –, who used the latter slogan on one of their largest banners. In the 1990s *CSKA* fans started to write the acronym with Latin letters and represent the letter "S" similarly to the SS acronym of the German Nazi elite military unit (see picture 2 in the appendix). The official president of the fan club, who used to be a member of the extremist fan group, was known by the nickname *"il Duce"*, a suggestive analogy. On the website of "Blood and Honour", a neo-Nazi organisation in England related to football, the leaders of this movement recognise as their followers in Bulgaria part of the "ultras" of *CSKA* (*http://www.bloodandhonour.com*). Some of the extremist fans of *CSKA*, and also *Levski,* included swastikas in their graffiti, which clearly reflected their fascist, anti-Semitic and racist disposition. Often supporters of both teams used the same refrains, chants and slogans but simply substituted the name of their opponents (cf. Dal Lago 1994: 86 f.). It appears that in the 1990s, right-extremist, national-socialist, pro-fascist slogans and symbols were characteristic for the most ardent fans of both teams.

In comparison, in the 1980s, when there were no banners in the stadium, the chanting and songs at organised fan group fixings were full of sexual allusions: "Stoičkov's wife has spread her legs – let us all oblige her", "Ico [nickname for Stoičkov] fucked you on the stadium" or "The referee – *pederast* (a fag)", which was quickly changed to "The referee – pedagogue" when policemen were seen nearby. Banal patriotic spirit also abounded: "Bulgaria has natural resources, Bulgaria has unbeatable people, Bulgaria has a little of all, but only one Levski football team" or just neutral: "Red and white champions!". Following the typical socialist positivist spirit, the organised fan groups also emphasised the qualities of their own team. The supporters of *Levski* sang: "7:2 the greatest result in the world". Graffiti with football content were almost absent in the 1980s, but inscriptions could be seen, such as: "Only *CSKA*" or "Only *Levski*". These examples support Billig's theory about "banal nationalism", which rests upon the selective interpretation of history in order to confirm the collective identity among supporters, and which operates with prosaic, common words, reminding about homeland

and making national identity unforgettable (Billig 1995: 92). Political confrontation in the real sense of the word was absent in the 1980s. At that time the confrontation between fans of *Levski* and *CSKA* was mostly at the domestic level, with sexual innuendos and comments regarding the football qualities of the respective team. During the socialist period, clashes between supporters of both teams happened mostly in informal settings, especially in casual conversations, arguments at home or in school and, foremost, among colleagues at work.

Conclusion

The changes of 1989 led to two new tendencies among the football supporters of Sofia's two biggest clubs, *Levski* and *CSKA*. The first is related to the introduction of Western influences and, as a consequence, right-extremist ideas among organised fan groups. Along with the symbolism of the extreme right, copied from other European fan groups, the "ultras" also demonstrate a specific Bulgarian nationalism characterised by a negative attitude towards local minorities, which are projected upon the adversary in the game (it is fair to note that similar examples can be observed in Serbia and Turkey as well). Both of the studied fan groups accuse each other of being Turks or Gypsies. This is how they probably denote "the otherness", "the difference" and "the opponent" in the most general sense. Their chanting and songs reflect the self-perception of the fans and clearly demonstrate the dominant ethnic and social stereotypes. By emulating fascist ideology and symbols, fans also partially use anti-Semitic slogans. On the whole, right-extremism is more typical for the "ultras" of *CSKA*, but is not uncommon among the fans of *Levski* either. Organised fan groups and general supporters, though, are not precise in their use of terms and concepts but rather recreate sustainable stereotypes characteristic of Bulgarian mass culture.

Another tendency derived from the new political setting after 1989 is a multiparty system and freedom of expression, which led to the projection of the major political confrontation between SDS and BSP on all levels of society. The turbulent political processes in the 1990s and the emotions and confrontations related to the change of the political system constituted an important part of the lives of individuals and of society. Moreover, they interfered in areas such as football, which was a world with its own rules and symbols that became coloured by the rhetoric and unrest of the political encounters of the 1990s. Ultimately, the world of football in Bulgaria became aware of its power, responded to the flirtation with politics and introduced its own representatives and ideas, which diversified the local political landscape. The language and symbols of football, thus, were used as one of the instruments for constructing the political space.

Acknowledgment

Thanks to Teodora Dragostinova for her editorial support.

References

Bardareva, R. 1991: Sportăt v Bălgarija - pojava i razvitie 1878–1944 [Sports in Bulgaria - Appearance and development 1878-1944]. Sofia.

Billig, M. 1995: Banal Nationalism. London: Sage.

Booth, D. 2004: Escaping the Past? The Cultural Turn and Language in Sport History. In: Rethinking History 8, 1: 103–125.

Cheska, A. 1979: Sport Spectacular. A Ritual Model of Power. In: International Review of Sport Sociology 14: 51–72.

Čolović, I. 2000: Football, Hooligans and War. In: N. Popov (ed.), The Road to War in Serbia, Trauma and Catharsis. Budapest: CEU.

Dal Lago, A., R. de Biasi 1994: Italian Football Fans, Culture and Organization. In: R. Giulianotti, N. Bonney, M. Hepworth (eds.), Football, Violence and Social Identity. London: Routledge.

Damjanov, M. 1981: Za načaloto na bălgarskija futbol [On the beginning of Bulgarian football]. Sofia.

Djundjulova, I. 1986: Letopis na sportnata slava na družestvo za fizkultura i sport "Levski-Spartak" 1914–1986 [Chronicle of sport glory of the association for physical culture and sports "Levski-Spartak" 1914–1986]. Sofia.

Duke, V., L. Crolley 1996: Football, Nationality and the State. New York: Longman.

Georgiev, A. 1985: Metežnijat kvartal. Starijat Jukbunar [Rebellious quarter. The old Jukbunar]. Sofia.

Georgieva, B. 2002: Razvlečenijata v bălgarskija grad 20-te i 30-te godini na XX vek [Entertainment in the Bulgarian town, 1920s and 1930s]. PhD thesis, Sofia University "St. Kliment Ohridski".

Georgieva, B. 2003: Sportăt v bălgarskija grad (kraja na XIX - sredata na XX vek) [Sport in the Bulgarian town, end of the 19th - middle of the 20th c.]. In: Godišnik na Sofiskija Universitet 93–95: 69–118.

Hargreaves, J. 1982: Sport and Hegemony. Some Theoretical Problems. In: H. Cantelon, R. Gruneau (eds.), Sport, Culture and the Modern State. Toronto, Buffalo: University of Toronto Press, 103–140.

Hargreaves, J. 1986: Sport, Power and Culture. A Social and Historical Analysis of Popular Sports in Britain. New York: St. Martin's Press.

Hobsbawm, E. 1992: Mass-producing Traditions: Europe 1870–1914. In: E. Hobsbawm, R. Ranger (eds.), The Invention of Tradition. Cambridge, New York: Cambridge UP, 263–307.

Iliycheva, M. 2004: "Faithful until Death": Sports Fans and Nationalist Discourse in Bulgarian Internet Forums. Budapest: CEU.

Kozanoglu, C. 1999: Beyond Edirne: Football and the National Identity Crisis in Turkey. In: G. Armstrong, R. Giulianotti (eds.), Football Cultures and Identities. London: Macmillan Press.

Lipsky, R. 1983: Toward a Political Theory of American Sports Symbolism. In: J. Harris, R. Park (eds.), Play, Games and Sports in Cultural Contexts. Champaign, Ill.: Human Kinetics Publishers, 79–91.

Noikov, S. 1994: S *Levski* po dălgija păt prez vremeto [With Levski on the long road of time]. Sofia.

Petrov, P. 2002: Praznični tradicii i političeski praktiki [Festive traditions and political practices]. Dissertation, Institute of Folklore at the Bulgarian Academy of Sciences, Sofia.

Petrov, T. 2002: Bălgarskite ordeni i medali [Bulgarian decorations and medals]. Sofia.

Popdimitrov, D. 1984: Istorija na futbola [The history of football]. Sofia.

Vrcan, S., D. Lalic 1999: From Ends to Trenches and Back: Football in the former Yugoslavia. In: G. Armstrong, R. Giulianotti (eds.), Football Cultures and Identities. London: Macmillan Press.

Wagner, E. 1989: An Overview of Sport in Asia and Africa. In: E. Wagner (ed.), Sport in Asia and Africa. A Comparative Handbook. New York: Greenwood Press, 3–11.

Newspapers and magazines

CSKA
Dăržaven vestnik
Demokracija
Duma
Meridian Match
Naroden Sport
Otečestven front
Planeta Sport
Rabotničesko delo

Appendix: Pictures

Picture 1: Footballer Božidar Iskrenov in favour of SDS (1994)

Picture 2: Graffiti by CSKA fans with Nazi-symbols

Addresses of authors and editors

Prof. Milena *Benovska-Săbkova* (Sofia), milena@multicom.bg
Prof. Keith *Brown* (Rhode Island), Keith_Brown@brown.edu
Dr. Ulf *Brunnbauer* (Berlin), ulf@zedat.fu-berlin.de
Dr. Jasna *Čapo-Žmegač* (Zagreb), capo@ief.hr
Prof. Nicolae *Constantinescu* (Bucharest), nicolacon@from.ro
Albert *Doja* (France), albert.doja@ul.ie
Prof. Christian *Giordano* (Fribourg), christian.giordano@unifr.ch
Prof. Robert *Hayden* (Pittsburgh), rhayden@ucis.pitt.edu
Dr. Deema *Kaneff* (Halle/S.), kaneff@eth.mpg.de
Prof. Karl *Kaser* (Graz), karl.kaser@uni-graz.at
Dr. Jutta *Lauth Bacas* (Athens), bacas@academyofathens.gr
Damiana *Otoiu* MA (Bucharest), damiana.otoiu@icp.ro
Prof. Klaus *Roth* (Munich), K.Roth@lrz.uni-muenchen.de
Dr. François *Ruegg* (Fribourg), francois.ruegg@unifr.ch
Stephanie *Schwandner-Sievers* MA (London), Sschwand@aol.com
Dr. Vesna *Vučinić-Nešković* (Belgrade), vvucinic@f.bg.ac.yu

Dragana *Antonijević* (Belgrade), daa457361@EUnet.yu
Konstantina *Bada* (Ioannina), kbada@cc.uoi.gr
Iva *Filipova-Kyurkchieva* (Sofia), ivaphilipova@yahoo.com
Orli *Fridman* (Arlington), ofridman@gmu.edu
Siegfried *Gruber* (Graz), gruber@gewi.kfunigraz.ac.at
Maximilian *Hartmuth* (Istanbul), melange@gmx.at
Ana *Hofman* (Belgrade), anchica@EUnet.yu
Ljubomir *Hristić* (Belgrade), ljubahristic@yahoo.com
Ivana *Kronja* (Belgrade), i.kronja@yubc.net
Ermis *Lafazanovski* (Skopje), ermisl@ukim.edu.mk
Ana *Luleva,* Cvetana *Benčeva* (Sofia), analuleva@yahoo.com
Marija *Maksin-Mićić* (Belgrade), marija@yubc.net
Aleksandar R. *Miletić* (Belgrade), H05MIA01@student.ceu.hu
Raluca *Nagy,* Cristina *Plecadite* (Cluj-Napoca), ralukkia@yahoo.com
Aleksandra *Pavićević* (Belgrade), Aleksandra.Pavicevic@sanu.ac.yu
Mirjana *Pavlović* (Belgrade), Mirjana.Pavlovic@sanu.ac.yu
Raluca *Petre* (Bucharest), rpetre@univ-ovidius.ro
Ivanka *Petrova* (Sofia), ivpetrova@yahoo.com
Cristofer *Scarboro* (Urbana), cscarbor@uiuc.edu
Ivana *Spasić* (Belgrade), spasic@instifdt.bg.ac.yu
Iva *Tarabić* (Belgrade), patujko@verat.net
Katarina *Višnar* (Ljubljana), kvisnar@gmail.com
Vesna *Vučinić-Nešković,* Jelena *Miloradović* (Belgrade)
Rory *Yeoman* (Peckham), Rory.Yeomans@southwark.gov.uk

Instructions to Authors

Ethnologia Balkanica is a refereed journal. We welcome submissions by ethnologists, folklorists, ethnographers, cultural and social anthropologists as well as scholars from related disciplines working on the ethnology of Southeast Europe. Submissions should meet the criteria below. The decision about acceptance or rejection rests with the editorial board. When a manuscript has been accepted the full text incl. notes, references, and summaries must be forwarded as a printout and as a data file on diskette or by e-mail. Data files should contain no styles and a minimum of formatting. Authors should send their full postal and e-mail addresses as well as their affiliation together with their paper to the editors.

Length: Articles should have a minimum of 4500 and a maximum of 9000 words.

Languages: Manuscripts can be submitted in English, French or German. Authors who are not writing in their mother-tongue must have their text checked by a native speaker of the language of the text. Titles of publications in southeast European languages must be followed by a translation in the language of the text in brackets [ ].

Abstracts: All manuscripts must be supplied with an English summary of 150 words that summarises the main arguments and findings of the article.

Spelling: Though we prefer British spelling for texts in English, American spelling is also acceptable. In any case the spelling must be consistent.

Transcription from Cyrillic alphabets should follow the scientific style (ISO standard). Do not use ch, zh, sh, iya but č, ž, š, and ija (see transcription list on next page). If your programme does not know these letters, use the popular form of transcription but mark all letters that require diacritical marks with a "*". Romanian names must be written in the original, i. e., with all diacritical characters.

Citations and References: Citations should be in Harvard style, author, date and page as follows (Verdery 1983: 27); if there are two or more authors, separate authors with commas. This applies also to footnotes. No comma after the author's name. Don't use p. or pp. Always cite page numbers where you are quoting or paraphrasing from a specific part of a text, and avoid too much citation where a work in its entirety is referred to. Avoid the use of ibid. and op.cit, but if you do so, make sure you use them correctly. Note that "cf." means "compare to", not "see also"; if you mean the latter, say so. If a cited scholarly work is not (yet) published, use for example (Smith forthcoming) if the work will be published with certainty. References to archival sources should be given in footnotes, particularly when they are lengthy. Make sure that you use dashes between numbers and dates, for example April – May, 22–30, and not hyphens (-). All references cited, and only these, should be listed under the heading "References" or "Literature", according to the style indicated below. Always give page numbers for papers in edited volumes or journals. Do not forget to mention the publisher.

For all questions of style, format, headings, quotation, notes, and references please take earlier volumes of this journal as a model. Other styles are not accepted.

Pictures and diagrams: Please always send photographs, graphics, and diagrams separately, never imported into the text. Photographs should be saved in the TIF format; please avoid all compressed formats such as JPEG. Resolution should be from 300 dpi (photographs) up to 600–800 dpi (drawings, caricatures). If you send pictures taken with a digital camera please adjust to maximum resolution and minimal compression.

The author will get one free copy of the journal and a free supply of 10 offprints.

Table: Transliteration of south slavic cyrillic characters (ISO standard):

а	a	к	k	ф	f	ю	ju
б	b	л	l	х	h	я	ja
в	v	м	m	ц	c	ђ	đ, (dj)
г	g	н	n	ч	č	ѕ	dz
д	d	о	o	ш	š	љ	lj
е	e	п	p	щ	št	њ	nj
ж	ž	р	r	ъ	ă	ћ	ć
з	z	с	s	ы	y	џ	dž
и	i	т	t	ь	j	ѣ	ě
й	j	у	u				

Journal of the Department of Ethnology and Anthropology
Faculty of Philosophy, University of Belgrade

ISSUES IN ETHNOLOGY AND ANTHROPOLOGY

Vol. 1, No. 1 (n.s.), 2006

Translation to English: Ljubomir Hristić; Translation to French: Jelena Dobričić; Technical support: Miroslav Niškanović; Lector: Slobodanka Marković. Accepted for publication by Editorial board of IEA on May 22nd 2006. ISSN 0353–1589.

Address: Faculty of Philosophy, University of Belgrade, Čika Ljubina 18–20, 11000 Belgrade. eap@f.bg.ac.yu, http://www.f.bg.ac.yu/index.php?sid=132.

Vol. 1 contains the following contributions: